THE LETTERS OF MARGARET FULLER

Fuller's letter to Mary Howitt, 8 October 1846. By permission of the Pennsylvania State University Libraries.

THE LETTERS OF
Margaret Fuller

Edited by

ROBERT N. HUDSPETH

VOLUME IV · 1845–47

Cornell University Press

ITHACA AND LONDON

PUBLICATION OF THIS BOOK WAS ASSISTED BY A GRANT
FROM THE PUBLICATIONS PROGRAM OF THE NATIONAL ENDOWMENT
FOR THE HUMANITIES, AN INDEPENDENT FEDERAL AGENCY.

First published 1987 by Cornell University Press.

International Standard Book Number 0-8014-1972-7
Library of Congress Catalog Card Number 82-22098
Printed in the United States of America
*Librarians: Library of Congress cataloging information appears
on the last page of the book.*

*The paper in this book is acid-free and meets the guidelines for
permanence and durability of the Committee on Production Guidelines
for Book Longevity of the Council on Library Resources.*

PREFACE

Inevitably the reader of this volume of Margaret Fuller's letters will sense the quickening tempo of her world. Publicly she moved from the United States to Europe; privately she fell in love and was rejected, then fell in love again and this time was loved in return. In part this sense of acceleration is created by our knowledge that Fuller lived only thirty months beyond the period spanned by this volume. Yet in important ways the compression and density of her life from 1845 to 1847 were quite real. She was thirty-four years old when she immersed herself in New York City; at thirty-six she moved outward, to the cultural centers of London, Paris, and Rome, and into the gathering Italian Resorgimento.

The New York of Fuller's day was rowdy as the Hunkers and Barn Burners fought for control of the state while the new president, Democrat James Polk, tried to put together an administration in Washington. Upstate New York was racked by antirent wars, and Horace Greeley pursued his reforming schemes with vigor in the *Tribune*. Nationally, the annexation of Texas in 1845 intensified the conflict between abolitionists and slave owners. In May 1846 the United States declared war on Mexico, having barely escaped one with England over Oregon.

Fuller watched as Washington sank further into imperialism, but this daughter of a Massachusetts politician kept herself aloof from such issues. While Greeley regularly damned the administration, especially after the outbreak of the war, Fuller concentrated on New York City. She reviewed its concerts, plays, and operas; she surveyed the charitable institutions, and reminded her readers that the poor deserved their attention. She reviewed New York authors—J. T. Headley, Edgar Allan Poe, and Cornelius Mathews—and she went to Anne Lynch's literary

5

salon, which she found tiring even though she apparently was the center of attention there. She fell in love with James Nathan, who for four months occupied her as much as her writing did. The pace, as it ever was for Fuller, was hectic but rewarding. Never had she written so much, and never, apparently, had she been so physically strong.

At first Fuller lived with the Greeleys and took pleasure in their small son, who returned her love with an adoration that she evoked from many children. After several months, however, she found Mary Greeley's emotional outbursts hard to bear. After a vacation in New England in October 1845, she took an apartment in the city.

Fuller's accomplishment in New York is remarkable: she published two books and wrote 250 essays for the *Tribune*. Readers who regularly followed her columns received a cosmopolitan education. Although she had an acute and growing interest in social reform, her *Tribune* forum was literary: she ranged among French, German, English, and American authors. She scrutinized the great (Alexandre Dumas *père*, George Sand, Thomas Carlyle), the not yet great (Poe and Herman Melville), and those who were thought to be great but whose appeal has faded (Longfellow and Headley), and she tried to bring her audience to an appreciation of poets whom she valued (Philip James Bailey, Walter Savage Landor, and Richard Monckton Milnes). Fuller made the most of the forum provided by the *Tribune*.

New York inevitably drew Fuller, for by 1845 it was the energizing center of American intellectual life. During her stay the New York literary world was changing inexorably, if not yet dramatically. The dominance of William Cullen Bryant, Washington Irving, and James Fenimore Cooper was coming to an end. Bryant was wholly devoted to his Democratic paper, the *Evening Post*; Irving was abroad in Spain and England. Only Cooper was very much his old self; his *Littlepage Manuscripts* trilogy appeared while Fuller was in the city. Earlier critics would not have ignored his books as Fuller did. The writers we now think their betters were in and around New York, but their fame was far in the future. Poe published *The Raven* and his *Tales*, and Melville brought out *Typee* (all of which Fuller reviewed), but in 1845 Walt Whitman had not yet found his voice.

It was not Poe, Whitman, or Melville who interested Fuller but rather Evert A. Duyckinck, Cornelius Mathews, and William Gilmore Simms, the writers known as Young America.[1] While never a part of

---

1. Young America is discussed in John Stafford, *The Literary Criticism of "Young America"* (Berkeley: University of California Press, 1952), and Perry Miller, *The Raven and the Whale* (New York: Harcourt, Brace, 1956).

the group, Fuller had cordial relations with them all and vigorously supported Mathews, first by praising him in her essays and then by publishing part of his drama *Witchcraft* as an appendix to her *Papers on Literature and Art*. Simms wrote her for copies of the *Dial* to complete his set, and Duyckinck became her editor at Wiley and Putnam. They often wrote for John Louis O'Sullivan's *Democratic Review,* a magazine that also published works of her friend Nathaniel Hawthorne; Fuller herself considered sending articles to O'Sullivan in the late 1830s. Fuller was attractive to the younger writers because she was something of a radical, known as a champion of George Sand, Emerson, and Goethe and thus of everything the literary conservatives considered Germanic. More often than not, Fuller praised Young America and they praised her.

Even with this mutual appreciation, Margaret Fuller's easy relations with these writers were not without paradoxes. They were staunch Democrats; she worked for the most influential Whig newspaper in the city. Duyckinck's friends had scant interest in Emerson, Fuller's closest intellectual associate in the earlier part of the decade, and Duyckinck was as fearful of Germany as was the *Knickerbocker* set. Fuller's enthusiasm for Goethe was waning, however, and she was moving away from Emerson. Greeley himself was full of contradictions (he opposed, for example, the anti-Irish nativism of New York City's Whigs). No one, least of all Margaret Fuller, bothered with such anomalies. She had never had any use for coteries.

These years are dominated by the love Fuller felt for James Nathan, a German businessman. The fifty-odd letters she wrote to him in 1845 and 1846 stand out not only for their number (they represent almost half of the surviving letters Fuller wrote while she was in New York), but more important, for their intensity. To Nathan she poured out her longing for emotional acceptance. The reader is startled by her willingness to be subservient. As Bell Gale Chevigny says, "it would be difficult to say which of the effects Nathan had on Fuller was stronger: the awakening of her sensuality or the putting to sleep of her mind."[2] From February to June 1845, when Fuller was intensely involved in her work at the *Tribune,* she was writing to Nathan or seeing him almost every day. Even after he left for Europe, she wrote long letters to him up to the time she herself went to England.

Granting the perils of drawing inferences from scant evidence, we can see that during the first half of April 1845 Fuller had an emotional

2. Bell Gale Chevigny, *The Woman and the Myth: Margaret Fuller's Life and Writings* (Old Westbury, N.Y.: Feminist Press, 1976), p. 137.

crisis with Nathan that was as painful as the one she had had with Emerson in 1840. Her letters show that Nathan represented himself as being responsible for an "English maiden" whom he was trying to "rehabilitate." In fact, the "maiden" was certainly his mistress. Shortly after Fuller learned of his involvement with the young woman and trustingly accepted his self-serving explanations, she was rocked by an apparent sexual proposition brought on by his misunderstanding of her language in her letters. She was a passionate woman whose words could appear sexual when she was deeply moved. Nathan probably had no experience with a woman of her sophistication or complexity, one to whom passion did not automatically mean sexual activity. At the end of the relationship with Fuller, he bitterly recalled his own attempt at plain speaking and acknowledged his inability to understand her.[3]

Soon after this storm passed, Nathan and the young woman left for Europe. He apparently had assured Fuller that he was going to return to New York, but then he began to temporize. After using her to get letters of recommendation from George Bancroft, Polk's secretary of the navy, and to get his essays published in the *Tribune*, Nathan drew away from her. Despite her fervent pleas for letters, he seldom wrote.

While she waited to hear from him, she busied herself with her work and her friends. At Anne Lynch's Valentine party in 1845, she met Marcus and Rebecca Spring, reform-minded New Englanders who, like her, had found their way to New York. Marcus was a wealthy businessman; Rebecca was the daughter of a Quaker abolitionist from Rhode Island. At length, having grown close to Fuller, the Springs invited her to accompany them to Europe in 1846. They would pay her travel expenses if she would tutor their son during the trip.[4]

Though she was successful at the *Tribune*, Fuller was irritated by the reluctance of Thomas McElrath, Greeley's business partner, to issue a second edition of *Woman in the Nineteenth Century*. Moreover, she was eager to see the culture that she knew so well from books. Though she mistakenly had little expectation of personal growth in Europe, it did offer her a new audience for her writing. Finally, she still nursed a fond hope for a reunion with Nathan, who was now in Germany. By the spring of 1846 the pieces fell into place: the Springs completed their travel plans, Greeley offered to pay her for travel essays, and her

---

3. Three letters from Nathan to Fuller survive in the Fuller papers at the Houghton Library, Harvard University: those of 5 June, 6 November, and 24 November 1846. Fuller destroyed the one he wrote her on 1 September; her replies to that letter and the two in November have not survived.

4. Rebecca Buffum Spring, "Journal Abroad," Raritan Bay Union Collection, New Jersey Historical Society.

family promised the support their slender means would allow. On 1 August Fuller sailed from Boston for England on the *Cambria*.

England was troubled that summer. Its worst problems came from bad harvests at home and famine in Ireland. Robert Peel's government moved toward reform of the Corn Laws but could not survive the Irish distress. His government fell on 29 June and was replaced by the Whig government of John Russell. England thus avoided revolution, but much still remained to be done by the reformers whom Fuller was to meet.[5]

Upon her arrival at Liverpool after a record-setting trip, Fuller embarked on an eighteen-month journey that seldom gave her a chance to rest and reflect, though she continued to write thoughtful and intelligent essays for Greeley's paper. She was no mere tourist, for she was equipped to understand what she saw. She knew the implications of the political situation; she knew her political and literary history; she knew that she wanted to see the most promising younger writers as well as the literary icons. She had no faith in the political or literary status quo.

From Liverpool, Fuller and the Springs made the conventional journey to Westmorland and Scotland. She visited the literary landmarks that recalled her enthusiasm for Scott and Burns; she met the aging Wordsworth, and she renewed her acquaintance with Harriet Martineau. Fuller visited workers and toured a mine; she saw the lochs and kirks, and she heard the preaching of James Martineau and W. J. Fox (neither of whom, she thought, measured up to Theodore Parker or William Channing in eloquence).

On 1 October, Fuller arrived in London. There she failed to find Tennyson, who was out of town, and Elizabeth Barrett, who had just married Robert Browning and left for Italy. She did get to see Philip Bailey, whom she considered the most important of the younger poets. Finally, she met Thomas Carlyle. Her visits with the great Scotsman were intriguing if wearying experiences for Fuller. At first she was delighted by him, but the second time they met, he tyrannized Giuseppe Mazzini, who had come to visit her, and he never let Jane Carlyle get in a word. Fuller wrote a lighthearted account of the evening to Emerson, but clearly she was deeply offended. Once an intellectual force for her, Carlyle in person was disappointing.

Mazzini influenced her more than anyone else she met in London. A political exile since 1837, he wrote for several British journals, including John Saunders' *People's Journal*. He was the first significant writer in

5. A. W. Ward et al., eds., *Cambridge Modern History* (New York: Macmillan, 1909), 11:9–19.

England to see the importance of Lamennais in France, thus bridging the reforming interests of two societies.[6] Fuller got to see a bit of Mazzini's humanitarianism when she visited the school he had opened in 1841 for impoverished Italian boys in London.[7] Fuller attended an award ceremony at the school, made a speech, and came away with "deep pleasure, though tinged with sadness."[8]

Before she left London with letters of introduction to Mazzini's friends in Paris, she and the Springs apparently developed a scheme to take him to Europe on a forged American passport. Mazzini, however, came to see the extreme danger of the idea, for he had been sentenced to die if he should be caught.[9] They parted, but Fuller was convinced that he had "an understanding of what *must* be the designs of Heaven with regard to man, since God is Love, is Justice."[10] The next time they met, Mazzini was leading a free Roman republic.

On her arrival in England she had written to Thomas Delf, an English bookman who served as go-between for her and Nathan, asking him to urge Nathan to join her in Scotland for a tour, or, if Nathan would not come, to forward to her any letters he sent her in Delf's care. Instead of Nathan himself, she got a letter from him dated 1 September announcing his coming marriage to another woman.[11]

In what appears to be at first fury and then depression, Fuller destroyed Nathan's letter before she set out with the Springs for Scotland. Rebecca Spring, who knew of Fuller's love for Nathan and of his rejection of her, later remembered that, to their surprise, the deeply despondent Fuller stayed outside on the top of the coach in a driving rain as they headed for Loch Katrine and Ben Lomond.[12] What followed is open to interpretation. On a walk on the mountain by herself, Fuller lost her way and had to spend the night in a cold mist without food, shelter, or warm clothing. She passed off the episode easily in her letter to the *Tribune,* but the context of the depression described by Rebecca Spring raises the possibility of a suicidal gesture, whether it was a conscious one or not. At the least, the night on the mountain is bound up with her sense of loss and betrayal.

6. W. G. Roe, *Lamennais and England* (London: Oxford University Press, 1966), pp. 43, 172–73, 180.

7. Bolton King, *Life of Mazzini* (London: J. M. Dent, 1911), pp. 73, 97–98.

8. *New-York Daily Tribune,* 19 February 1847.

9. Joseph Rossi, *The Image of America in Mazzini's Writings* (Madison: University of Wisconsin Press, 1954), p. 52.

10. *New-York Daily Tribune,* 19 February 1847.

11. Nathan describes the letter in his to Fuller of 27 November 1846.

12. Beatrice Borchardt, "Lady of Utopia: The Story of Rebecca Buffum Spring," p. 59, Huntington Library.

On 25 October, Fuller wrote what must have been a blistering letter to Nathan, if we can judge from his response to it of 6 November. Nathan defended himself by reminding her that he had promised nothing, and then he took her to task for a lack of faith in *him*! He coyly refused her demand that he return her letters and proffered his continued devotion. To this casuistry Fuller heatedly responded on 11 November from Paris, renewing her demand for her letters and accusing Nathan of deception. The correspondence ended with Nathan's letter of 27 November, in which he denied deceit and even went so far as to say that the letter announcing his engagement might have been Delf's forgery and that her haste in destroying it showed poor judgment on her part. Whatever his attitude earlier, Nathan at the end hid behind a screen of insult, falsehood, and evasion.

The Nathan affair was well known to Fuller's family and friends. He visited her at the Greeleys' and the Cranches'; he knew the Springs and probably the Mannings. Mrs. Fuller knew of Nathan and so did brother Richard. Both William Henry Channing and Thomas Wentworth Higginson, her biographer, knew of Nathan and of her letters to him, but they omitted any mention of him in the works they produced on Fuller.[13] Apparently her friends attempted to get her letters from Nathan, but it was not until the turn of the century that they became public knowledge with the publication of *Love-Letters of Margaret Fuller, 1845–1846*, and their purchase by the Boston Public Library for $110. Apparently Fuller returned all of his, probably before he left for Europe.[14]

Fuller left London for Paris in mid-November. France was an unhappy nation. The previous July (almost immediately after Peel's defeat in England) the French Chamber of Deputies had been dissolved. The middle class was disenchanted with the Citizen King, and the workers were increasingly attracted to the several socialist movements that were thriving in 1846. A typically European crisis occurred in October when, under pressure from Louis-Philippe, the queen of Spain and the

13. This much is certain: In a letter to Margaret of 21 February 1848 (in the Houghton Library, like the others cited below), Mrs. Fuller discusses Nathan's marriage and Mary Greeley's reaction to it. Borchardt says in "Lady of Utopia" that Rebecca Spring knew about Nathan and urged Fuller to retrieve her letters from him. On 14 July 1851 Richard and Eugene Fuller empowered William Henry Channing to deal with Nathan for the return of Margaret Fuller's papers; a note in Channing's hand dated 1851 says he failed to get them; a note in Edith Fuller's hand says Channing knew of the letters when he wrote his portion of the *Memoirs of Margaret Fuller Ossoli*. I infer from this record that when Higginson wrote his *Margaret Fuller Ossoli*, he must have known what Channing knew.

14. Richard F. Fuller to James Nathan, 14 February 1863 (MB: Ms. Am. 1451 [74]).

infanta were wed on the same day, the former to a man old enough to make it unlikely that he would father an heir. The infanta married the duc de Montpensier, thus all but ensuring the succession of Louis-Philippe's son to the Spanish throne. Minor in itself, the affair outraged England and drove France into an unlikely alliance with Austria. These events, coinciding with the liberal and revolutionary stirrings in Switzerland and Germany, were ominous to the French.[15] Indeed, Fuller herself saw the pressure that was building under a regime that allowed little suffrage and seemed incapable of inspiring confidence in any of its constituencies: "While Louis Philippe lives," she wrote, "the gases, compressed by his strong grasp, may not burst up to light; but the need of some radical measures of reform is not less strongly felt in France than elsewhere, and the time will come before long when such will be imperatively demanded."[16]

In Paris Fuller was nonplussed to find that her spoken French was so inadequate that she had to hire a teacher. There were, of course, galleries and buildings to see, but Fuller was most taken with Rachel, the premier actress of her lifetime. In Paris Fuller met an illustrious group of writers: Lamennais and Sand (to whom Mazzini sent letters of introduction), Pierre-Jean de Béranger, Victor Considérant, and Pierre Leroux. She heard the astronomer François Arago lecture, but she was unable to gain entrance to the court where Dumas was defending himself against a suit for breach of contract. France welcomed her by publishing in *La Revue indépendante* a translation of her essay on American writers. She was pleased by the attention, even if the *Revue* did identify her as "Elizabeth Fuller."

Then, as she had done in London, she met a powerful European revolutionary in exile. Just as Mazzini had dominated her stay in London, Adam Mickiewicz shaped her response to Paris.[17] The differences between the Pole and the Italian were as significant as their shared ideals. While both wanted a political revolution, Mickiewicz was a champion of women's rights and urged Fuller to be more emotionally expressive. Unlike the ascetic Mazzini, Mickiewicz stirred Fuller emotionally, so much so that she was bitter about having to leave Paris.[18] Mazzini had a vision of a free Italy; Mickiewicz envisioned a free self for Fuller. "The relationships which suit you," he wrote her, "are those which develop and free your spirit, responding to the legitimate needs of your

15. Ward et al., eds., *Cambridge Modern History*, 11:23–39, 555.
16. *New-York Daily Tribune*, 19 May 1847.
17. Their friendship is treated in Leopold Wellisz, *The Friendship of Margaret Fuller D'Ossoli and Adam Mickiewicz* (New York: Polish Book Importing Co., 1947).
18. See Fuller's letter to the Springs, 10 April 1847.

organism and leaving you free at all times. You are the sole judge of these needs."[19]

On 25 February 1847 Fuller and the Springs began to make their way toward Italy, the land that was to become her adopted home. Italy's brightest hope that year lay in the new pope, Pius IX, elected the previous summer. Pius electrified the radicals and infuriated the Austrians. Barely six weeks after his accession, on 16 July, he declared an amnesty that freed a thousand political prisoners. Other European nations might see change coming; the Italian states saw it at hand. They varied in their condition: some were relatively independent, some were under strict Austrian control. Some had despots for rulers; some benefited from more enlightened sovereigns. For some time the revolutionary unification preached by Mazzini had had to compete with the moderate program of Vincenzo Gioberti, the priest who called for a federated Italy. Pius quickly showed that he was Gioberti's follower by assuming the role of the liberal pope described in the priest's writings.[20]

Events hurried on throughout 1847, when Fuller was traveling in Italy. The pope permitted the creation of civic guards, and he seemed receptive to constituent assemblies. When the Austrians made a show of power in Ferrara during July and August, they found that, while they had more military power than the pope, they had only intensified Italian nationalism and increased Pius's popularity.[21] It took less imagination in Italy than in France to see that a revolution was at hand. Fuller's timing could hardly have been better.

Her visit had a rough beginning, however: the weather was seasonably bad; the ship on which they sailed for Leghorn was struck by another and forced to turn back. After such a beginning, Fuller was relieved to have a warm three-day visit with Mazzini's mother in Genoa.[22] She arrived in Naples in mid-March and then embarked on a six-month tour of Italy. She and the Springs went from Naples to Rome, where she met a young man named Giovanni Ossoli. They stayed in Rome from April to late June. From there they traveled to Florence for a two-week visit, then moved to Venice the first week of July.

During the six months following the blow of Nathan's rejection,

19. Wellisz, *Friendship*, p. 24.

20. Ward et al., eds., *Cambridge Modern History*, 11:67–74.

21. G. F. H. Berkeley and J. Berkeley, *Italy in the Making, June 1846 to 1 January 1848* (Cambridge: Cambridge University Press, 1936 [1968]), pp. 190–213, 216–24.

22. E. F. Richards, ed., *Mazzini's Letters to an English Family, 1844–1854* (London: John Lane, 1920), p. 53.

Fuller had met three men who gripped her imagination: Guiseppe Mazzini, Adam Mickiewicz, and now Giovanni Ossoli. Mazzini may not have evoked a romantic response from her, but Mickiewicz certainly did, and Ossoli was even more attractive to her. Like Nathan, Ossoli was a man of little formal education, but he shared the ideals of Mazzini and Mickiewicz. In him Fuller found a man who was capable of responding to her, of being a genuine part of her life, and of keeping her faith rather than betraying it. From the men of public affairs Fuller drew intellectual and moral sustenance; from Ossoli she drew emotional security. Fuller had unwillingly left Mickiewicz in Paris in order to fulfill her commitment to the Springs' travel plans, but she was not willing to deny herself a second time. When they suddenly announced their intention to leave for home by way of Germany, Fuller decided to return to Rome without them, despite the uncertainties of travel in a foreign land.

From Venice she crossed northern Italy to Lake Garda and on to Milan, where she arrived on 9 August. She met the poet Alessandro Manzoni and several Milanese patriots, the most important of whom to her was Costanza Arconati Visconti, who had recently returned to Milan with her husband after two decades of political exile. In Milan she continued the political education begun in London with Mazzini and furthered in Paris by Mickiewicz.

Fuller took a side trip to Bellagio and Lake Como, remembering with pleasure her enthusiasm for Henry Taylor's description of it in *Philip van Artevelde*. After a brief return to Milan, she set off for Rome, only to fall deathly ill on the trip. She stopped in Florence, short of her destination, where she was nursed by Joseph Mozier and his wife, friends who in later years slandered her to Hawthorne. By mid-October, however, Fuller was back in Rome with Giovanni Ossoli, who had become her true love.

Only now, when we can read Fuller's letters in the context of all the details of her life from 1845 to 1847, can we begin to assess what was happening to her, to understand Nathan's impact on her, and to evaluate her subsequent reaction to Mazzini, Mickiewicz, and Ossoli. In the same way, we can now begin to see more clearly the contours of her growing radicalism as she moved from New England to New York, from there to London, Paris, and Rome. In December 1847 "Italy" was a collection of separate states, a land divided and oppressed but impatient and ready to burst out into the war that led in a few years to modern Italy, free and united. The American best equipped to understand what was happening took up residence on Rome's Corso.

From her arrival in New York in December 1844 to her immersion in prerevolutionary Rome in 1847, Fuller was a growing socialist, though not a social theorist. From the perspective that time now affords, we can trace a unity that is complex and occasionally contradictory. From at least 1841 to her death, Fuller was interested in social and communitarian experiments, though she joined none. She was a close personal friend of George and Sophia Ripley; she even had her own room at Brook Farm, but she refused to join the community. She sympathized with Charles Lane, who left Fruitlands for the Shakers. As New York's poor and degraded citizens became a familiar sight, she became vocal in her critiques of a society that was creating an ever larger class of outcasts. Rebecca Spring said that Fuller even considered a life devoted to rehabilitating New York's prostitutes.[23] She warmly supported the Prison Reform Society, and she was committed to William Henry Channing's vision of reform based on Christian charity.

It is this union of socialism and religion that is at the center of Fuller's last six years. In the United States and in Europe she found friends among the reformers, many of whom were notably radical, people whose vision of society in some way brought together religion and social change, even if the religion was sentimental and the change was timid. Fuller had always been close to men who had left the church (Ripley and Emerson) or who were radical reformers within it (Channing and Parker); in France she moved toward a near heretic (Lamennais).

In New York, Fuller was intimate not only with Horace Greeley and Channing but with the abolitionist Quaker Isaac Hopper and his daughter Abigail; Lydia Child, who was editing an abolitionist newspaper; and R. H. Manning and Marcus Spring, reform-minded businessmen who were in the mold of Frank Shaw in Boston, who retired from business to pursue Fourierite socialism. In England she met Alexander Ireland, William Ballantyne Hodgson, William J. Fox, Garth Wilkinson, William James Linton, John Saunders, and William and Mary Howitt. Of course it was Mazzini above all who fired Fuller's social conscience in London. Even when one takes into account the inherent randomness of acquaintances made during a short stay at the worst "season," the pattern is clear: the people she met, those she claimed as genuine friends, were the Victorian social reformers with a religious enthusiasm.

Paris was even more congenial to her than New York or London, for here were Mickiewicz; Pierre Leroux, the Saint-Simonian editor and writer; Lamennais, the most influential Christian reformer of the time; and, most important of all, George Sand, the woman who brought all

23. Rebecca Buffum Spring, "Journal and Notes for Auld Acquaintances," Huntington Library.

the threads together: religion, social reform, and literary brilliance.[24] Slowly but inevitably, France supplanted Germany as Fuller's intellectual touchstone. In New England she had read Fourier and Leroux; she was moved by the spirituality of Lamennais's *Parole d'un croyant*; and the unabashed feminism of Sand's novels—especially those that were full of religious mysticism, such as *Les Sept Cordes* and *Consuelo* —spoke to Fuller's condition in the 1840s. For a few weeks in 1846 and 1847 she could be a part of a world she had before then known only in books.

It is appropriate that Fuller did not meet several of the writers she most sought: Tennyson, Robert and Elizabeth Browning, and Dumas. Both her changing interests and the events around her were moving her away from literature to social reform. Indeed, many of the writers she did meet were also reformers: Harriet Martineau, William Thom, the Howitts, Lamennais, Sand, and Manzoni. By chance, Fuller missed the brilliant display of English literary genius from 1846 to 1850 when she was in Italy (the novels of the Brontës, Dickens' *Dombey and Son,* Thackeray's *Vanity Fair* and *Pendennis,* and Mrs. Gaskell's *Mary Barton*), but she had an immediate view of a drama that surpassed even these triumphs—she witnessed the birth of modern Italy.

Too many facts elude us to allow us to draw absolute conclusions about Fuller's life at the end of 1847. She may or she may not have been married. Her personality gives us no warrant for choosing one possibility over the other. While she was conventional in her attitude toward sexuality within marriage, she was also bold enough to follow her own emotions. Almost certainly Fuller was pregnant by the end of December 1847, though she may not yet have known it. On the surface Fuller was close to uniting all the forces that were working on her during the period spanned by this volume of letters. She was in love with Ossoli, and he was faithful to her. Rome was electric with political change. The pope seemed to go from triumph to triumph. Austria was on the defensive. Fuller could clearly see that Italy was on the brink of major changes. Margaret Fuller's private and public worlds were rich. She could love without restraint, and she embraced a revolution. Each act would bring pain, but each was fulfilling in ways that Fuller had never before experienced.

ROBERT N. HUDSPETH

State College, Pennsylvania

24. George Douglas Howard Cole, *Socialist Thought: The Forerunners, 1789–1850* (London: Macmillan, 1953), pp. 190, 199. I follow Cole's lead in associating Lamennais with the socialist movement although he was not himself a socialist.

CONTENTS

Contents

Contents

1846

Contents

Contents

1847

Contents

Illustrations

Acknowledgments

I am grateful to John C. Fuller, Willard P. Fuller, Elizabeth Channing Fuller, Richard E. Fuller, and Willard P. Fuller, Jr., for permission to publish Margaret Fuller's letters. I also thank the following institutions and individuals for permission to publish the Fuller letters in their possession that appear in this volume: the Trustees of the Boston Public Library; the Bancroft Library of the University of California at Berkeley; the Chicago Historical Society; the Butler Library of Columbia University; the Sarah Margaret Fuller Papers, 1840–46, Essex Institute; the Fruitlands Museums, Harvard, Massachusetts; Mrs. Mary Lillian Haight; the Trustees of the Ralph Waldo Emerson Memorial Association, the Harvard College Library, and the Houghton Library, Harvard University; the Autograph Letters Collection of the Haverford College Library; the Huntington Library, San Marino, California; the Library of the University of Illinois at Urbana-Champaign; the Iowa Historical Library, Department of History and Archives; the Charles G. Slack Collection of Autographs, Marietta College Library; the Massachusetts Historical Society; the New Jersey Historical Society; the Library of the New-York Historical Society; the Duyckinck Collection, Manuscripts and Archives Division, and the Henry W. and Albert A. Berg Collection of the New York Public Library, Astor, Lenox, and Tilden Foundations; the Historical Society of Pennsylvania; the Libraries of the Pennsylvania State University; the Princeton University Library; the Arthur and Elizabeth Schlesinger Library, Radcliffe College; the Humanities Research Center, University of Texas; the Department of Manuscripts, Universiteits-Bibliotheek, Amsterdam, Holland; the Sarah Margaret Fuller Collection, Barrett Library, University of Virginia Library; the Special Collections, Wellesley College Library.

Acknowledgments

The following librarians have generously aided this volume: John Alden of the Boston Public Library; Eloise Beil of the Staten Island Institute of Arts and Sciences; Barbara Bennett of the Georgia Historical Society; Edmund Berkeley, Jr., and Barbara Bettcher of the University of Virginia Library; William H. Bond of the Houghton Library, Harvard University; Mary Ceibert of the University of Illinois Library; Leslie Clarke of the Bancroft Library of the University of California at Berkeley; John Cushing of the Massachusetts Historical Society; Susan Davis of the Essex Institute; Rodney G. Dennis of the Houghton Library, Harvard University; Ellen S. Dunlap of the Humanities Research Center, University of Texas; Rudolph Ellenbogen of the Columbia University Library; Carla M. Faas of the Universiteits—Bibliotheek of Amsterdam, Holland; Mrs. Aloys Gilman of the Iowa State Department of History; Hazel C. Godfrey of the Wellesley College Library; Lida Lisle Greene of the Iowa State Department of History; Jules Hardwick of the Highgate Cemetery Operating Company; William Henry Harrison of the Fruitlands Museums; James J. Heslin of the New-York Historical Society; Maude L. Jones of the Marietta College Library; John D. Kilbourne of the Historical Society of Pennsylvania; Patricia King of the Schlesinger Library, Radcliffe College; Carl Lane of the New Jersey Historical Society; James Lawton of the Boston Public Library; Kenneth A. Lohf of the Columbia University Library; Richard M. Ludwig of the Princeton University Library; Jean R. McNiece of the New York Public Library; Charles Mann of the Pennsylvania State University Library; Ellen B. Mark of the Essex Institute; Marian Marx of the Schlesinger Library, Radcliffe College; June Moll of the Humanities Research Center, University of Texas; Irene Moran of the Bancroft Library of the University of California at Berkeley; Archie Motley of the Chicago Historical Society; Eleanor L. Nicholes of the Wellesley College Library; Jean F. Preston and Wanda M. Randall of the Princeton University Library; Richard S. Reed of the Fruitlands Museums; Stephen T. Riley of the Massachusetts Historical Society; Elizabeth Ryall of the University of Virginia Library; Elizabeth Shenton of the Schlesinger Library, Radcliffe College; Faye Simkin and John D. Stinson of the Manuscripts Division, New York Public Library; Sandra Stelts of the Pennsylvania State University Library; Lola L. Szladits, of the Berg Collection, New York Public Library; Louis L. Tucker, of the Massachusetts Historical Society; Daniel H. Woodward, of the Huntington Library; Sophie Zdziechowski of the Société Historique et Littéraire Polonaise, Paris.

I am grateful to the following individuals for help in securing illustrations for this volume: Elaine Evans Dee of the Cooper-Hewitt

Museum, Smithsonian Institution; Suzanne Embree of the National Portrait Gallery, Smithsonian Institution; Patricia C. Geeson of the National Museum of American Art, Smithsonian Institution; Guénola Groud of the Musée Carnavalet, Paris; Kristine K. Hogan of the Staten Island Institute of Arts and Sciences; Anastasio Teodoro of the New York Public Library; Ross Urquhart of the Massachusetts Historical Society; Theresa Witt of the National Portrait Gallery, Smithsonian Institution; Daniel H. Woodward of the Huntington Library; Helena Wright of the National Museum of American History.

Among the scholars who have answered my many queries are Patricia Barber, Charles Blackburn, Paula Blanchard, Arthur W. Brown, Lynn Cadwallader, Joseph Jay Deiss, Russell E. Durning, Alfred R. Ferguson, Elizabeth Maxfield-Miller, Howard N. Meyer, Margaret Nussendorfer, Bruce A. Ronda, Carl F. Strauch, and Richard P. Wunder. I am particularly grateful for the generous advice of Eleanor M. Tilton and Madeleine B. Stern. Kathy Fuller of the Division of Research Programs at the National Endowment for the Humanities was generous with her help. Karen Szymanski and Donald Yannella called my attention to previously undiscovered manuscripts, and Robert Burkholder provided a copy of a previously published letter. Mary Lillian Haight extended me many kindnesses in making available to me the Fuller letters in her possession. I am glad to be able to acknowledge the patient support extended me by my departmental chairmen: Robert B. Heilman and Robert D. Stevick of the University of Washington, and David Stewart, Arthur O. Lewis, Robert Worth Frank, Jr., Wendell V. Harris, and Christopher Clausen of the Pennsylvania State University. The two deans of the College of the Liberal Arts at Penn State under whom I have served, Stanley Paulson and Hart Nelsen, have supported my work in several ways; Irene Johnston Petrick has efficiently overseen the details of my grants. My colleagues Wilma R. Ebbitt, James Rambeau, and Philip Young have given freely of their advice and expertise. Charles Mann, the Rare Books and Manuscripts Librarian of the Pennsylvania State University, has helped me gather manuscripts and illustrations for this edition. I want to emphasize my gratitude for the repeated assistance I have received from Joel Myerson of the University of South Carolina. His work as Fuller's bibliographer has been of special use to me in the preparation of this volume of her letters.

I am again pleased to be able to acknowledge the expert help given me by several skilled research assistants: Iris Malveau worked on my calendar of Fuller letters; Carolyn Kephart read manuscripts to me; Charles Hackenberry not only read manuscripts but hunted down elusive quotations. Larry Carlson undertook responsibility for obscure annotations, and Lewis Ulman checked the draft of the completed body of annotations. Robert DiNicola made typescripts of Fuller's essays. As he did in previous volumes, Robert D. Habich not only worked on the notes but gave freely of his excellent advice. Barbara Salazar of Cornell University Press lent expert guidance. My wife, Kay Hudspeth, has taken time from her career to give me unfailingly cheerful help with this edition.

I thank the Houghton Library, Harvard University, for permission to quote letters written to Fuller; the New Jersey Historical Society for permission to quote from Rebecca Spring's travel journal; and the Huntington Library, San Marino, California, for permission to quote from Rebecca Spring's autobiography.

This volume of Fuller letters has received financial assistance from the University of Washington Graduate School Research Fund, the Pennsylvania State University College of Liberal Arts Research Fund, and the Pennsylvania State University Institute for the Arts and Humanistic Studies. I am grateful for this support. The preparation of this volume was made possible in part by grants from the Program for Editions of the National Endowment for the Humanities, an independent federal agency.

R. N. H.

Editorial Method

This edition brings together for the first time all of the known extant letters written by Margaret Fuller. The texts are presented in their entirety in chronological order. Only conservative emendations, as outlined below under "Text," have been incorporated in the text; all others are recorded in textual notes. The text has been prepared from holographs whenever possible. When a holograph is lacking, the text is based on a manuscript copy of the lost holograph. When two manuscript copies of the same letter survive in the absence of a holograph, the more nearly complete version has been chosen. If both are of the same length, I have chosen the copy prepared by the Fuller family, because a spot comparison of other family copies with their surviving holographs shows them to be more nearly accurate than copies by other hands, if not exact. Only those letters with no manuscript authority have been taken from printed sources. Those letters dated by year only appear at the head of the year; those dated only by month, at the head of the month; undated letters come at the end of the edition, arranged alphabetically by recipient when known.

To establish the text, I first gathered microfilm or photocopies of all the manuscript letters and then made typed copies of these photoreproductions. I also typed all of the letters that now exist only in printed versions. I then corrected the typescript twice: first an assistant read aloud to me all of the photoreproductions and the printed versions of the letters; later, two other assistants (working with me at different times) accompanied me to the libraries that hold the original manuscripts and read those manuscripts aloud to me as I again corrected the typescript. (Seven letters did not receive this second check, as I was unable to visit five libraries.)

The final text derived from the corrected typescript, and proof was read aloud.

Format

The letters are numbered chronologically and the recipients identified in uniform headings. All dates, locations, salutations, and signatures are regularized in the following manner: dates and locations are set flush against the right margin, salutations flush against the left margin; signatures are set in large and small capitals and indented from the right margin at the bottom of the letter; when two or more initials are used in a signature, they are regularized with a space between each pair.

Text

The text is presented as faithfully as possible with conservative emendations. Fuller's spelling, capitalization, and punctuation are retained, as are her occasional slips of the pen (e.g., *and and*). Punctuation of canceled words and interlined insertions follows Fuller's final intention with the original versions reported in the textual notes. Her end punctuation is often ambiguous, for her period resembles a comma. In all instances this mark is preserved as a period. Punctuation is supplied in brackets only when its absence leads to confusion. A paragraph is often indicated in the holographs only by a space at the end of the preceding line. In all such instances the following paragraph is silently indented. Fuller used the dash as an all-purpose mark of punctuation; her dashes are consistently retained. Abbreviations are not expanded save in those instances where ambiguities might otherwise result. When expanded, the additions are enclosed in square brackets. Cancellations are omitted from the text, and interlined additions are lowered; all such emendations are reported in the textual notes. Cross-hatching (Fuller occasionally turned the sheet and wrote at a right angle across her letter) and all symbols, notes, and marks added by later hands are emended and unreported. The German ß is set as "ss"; "&" becomes "and." Unless otherwise noted, the matter canceled by a later hand in the collections at the Boston Public Library has been recovered. All the letters and fragments taken from Emerson's "Ossoli" journal (MH: bMS Am 1280 [111]) are in his hand.

Annotation and Index

The text of each letter is followed by a provenance note that indicates the source of the text, any surviving manuscript copies, and any previous publishing history; the name and address of the recipient as written by Fuller; the postmark; and the recipient's endorsement, if any. A brief biography of the recipient follows the provenance note to the first surviving letter to him or her, unless the recipient has already been identified. Then come textual notes listing editorial emendations, Fuller's cancellations, and her interlined insertions. Fuller's words here are set in roman type; editorial interpolations are set in italics.

The numbered annotations that follow the textual notes identify all people mentioned in the letter except those well known to readers (e.g., Dante, Shakespeare, Milton) and those previously identified, and all books, literary and historical allusions, and quotations that can be established. Brief biographies of well-known individuals who are not identified in the notes can be found in *Webster's Biographical Dictionary*.

Citations to the Massachusetts vital records office take two forms. Citations to nineteenth-century records refer only to volume and page numbers. Thus "MVR 119:345" cites page 345 of volume 119 of the death record. Beginning in this century, the reference has a preceding date. Thus "MVR 1924 11:167" cites the death record for 1924, volume 11, page 167. Unless otherwise noted, all citations are to death records.

Publication data come from the *National Union Catalog* of the Library of Congress or, when necessary, from the *British Museum General Catalogue of Printed Books*. Occasional notes explain ambiguities in the text, summarize events in Fuller's life, or refer the reader to other letters. The surviving letters written to Fuller have provided explanatory material for many of the annotations. Unidentified items are silently passed over.

An appendix in the final volume lists chronologically the letters Fuller is known to have written but which have not survived.

Each volume of the letters has a separate index. A comprehensive index appears in the final volume.

Editorial Apparatus

Textual Devices

The following devices are used in the text:

[Square brackets] enclose editorial additions.
[*Italics*] indicate editorial comments.
[I] [II] [III] indicate sections of a letter recovered from various sources.
[   ] marks matter missing from the text.
Superscript^n refers the reader to a textual note.
Superscript^1 refers the reader to an explanatory note.

The following devices are used in the textual notes:

⟨Angle brackets⟩ identify recovered cancellations.
⟨?⟩ identifies unrecovered cancellations.
↑ Opposed arrows ↓ indicate interlined insertions.
Italics indicate editorial comments.

Descriptive Symbols

AL	Autograph letter, unsigned
ALfr	Autograph letter fragment, unsigned
ALfrS	Autograph letter fragment, signed with name or initial(s)
ALS	Autograph letter, signed with name or initial(s)
EL	Edited letter, as previously published; holograph now lost
ELfr	Edited letter fragment, as previously published; holograph now lost
MsC	Manuscript copy of a Fuller letter in a hand other than Fuller's; unless otherwise indicated, the holograph has not been recovered
MsCfr	Manuscript copy of a fragment of a Fuller letter in a hand other than Fuller's; unless otherwise indicated, the holograph has not been recovered
TCfr	Typed copy fragment; holograph now lost

Location Symbols

CSmH	Huntington Library
CU-B	University of California at Berkeley, Bancroft Library
IaHa	Iowa State Historical Department, Division of Historical Museum and Archives
ICHi	Chicago Historical Society
IU	University of Illinois, Urbana
MB	Boston Public Library, Department of Rare Books and Manuscripts
MCR-S	Radcliffe College, Schlesinger Library
MH	Harvard University, Houghton Library
MHarF	Fruitlands Museums, Harvard, Massachusetts
MHi	Massachusetts Historical Society
MSaE	Essex Institute
MWelC	Wellesley College Library
NBu	Buffalo and Erie County Library
NjHi	New Jersey Historical Society
NjP	Princeton University Library
NN-B	New York Public Library, Henry W. and Albert A. Berg Collection
NN-M	New York Public Library, Manuscripts and Archives Division
NNC	Columbia University Library
NNHi	New-York Historical Society
OMC	Marietta College Library
PHC	Haverford College Library
PHi	Historical Society of Pennsylvania
PSt	Pennsylvania State University Library
TxU	University of Texas, Humanities Research Center
ViU	University of Virginia Library

Short Titles and Abbreviations

Annals of Opera: Alfred Loewenberg, *Annals of Opera, 1597–1940*, 3d ed. (Totowa, N.J.: Rowman & Littlefield, 1978).

Banks, *Genealogical Notes*: James Lenox Banks, *Genealogical Notes Concerning the Banks and Allied Families* (New York: Privately published, 1938).

Borchardt, "Lady of Utopia": Beatrice E. Borchardt, "Lady of Utopia: The Story of Rebecca Buffum Spring," in Huntington Library (HM 46724). Another copy may be found in Raritan Bay Union Collection, New Jersey Historical Society (MG 285 [Add. 1, item 15]).

Chevigny: Bell Gale Chevigny, *The Woman and the Myth: Margaret Fuller's Life and Writings* (Old Westbury, N.Y.: Feminist Press, 1976).

Child, *Selected Letters*: Lydia Maria Child, *Selected Letters, 1817–1880*, ed. Milton Meltzer and Patricia G. Holland (Amherst: University of Massachusetts Press, 1982).

DAB: Dictionary of American Biography, ed. Allen Johnson and Dumas Malone, 20 vols. (New York: Scribner, 1928–36).

Derby, *Fifty Years among Authors:* James C. Derby, *Fifty Years among Authors, Books, and Publishers* (New York: G. W. Carleton, 1884).

Dictionnaire de biographie française: Dictionnaire de biographie française, ed. J. Balteau et al., 15 vols. to date (Paris: Librairie Letouzey & Ane, 1933–).

DNB: Dictionary of National Biography, ed. Leslie Stephen and Sidney Lee, 22 vols. (London: Oxford University Press, 1937–38).

Emerson–Carlyle Correspondence: The Correspondence of Emerson and Carlyle, ed. Joseph Slater (New York: Columbia University Press, 1964).

Enciclopedia italiana: Enciclopedia italiana di scienze, lettere ed arti, 36 vols. (Rome: Istituto della Enciclopedia Italiana, 1949).

Festus: Philip James Bailey, *Festus: A Poem* (New York: James Miller, [1862]).

Frothingham, *Memoir of William Henry Channing:* Octavius Brooks Frothingham, *Memoir of William Henry Channing* (Boston: Houghton Mifflin, 1886).

Fuller, *Recollections:* Richard Frederick Fuller, *Recollections of Richard F. Fuller* (Boston: Privately published, 1936).

Greeley, *Greely-Greeley:* George Hiram Greeley, *Genealogy of the Greely-Greeley Family* (Boston: F. Wood, 1905).

Haight, *George Eliot Letters: The George Eliot Letters*, ed. Gordon S. Haight, 9 vols. (New Haven: Yale University Press, 1954–78).

Higginson, *MFO:* Thomas Wentworth Higginson, *Margaret Fuller Ossoli* (Boston: Houghton Mifflin, 1884).

Hudspeth, *Ellery Channing:* Robert N. Hudspeth, *Ellery Channing* (New York: Twayne, 1973).

Ireland, *Records of the New York Stage:* Joseph N. Ireland, *Records of the New York Stage, from 1750 to 1860*, 2 vols. (New York: T. H. Morrell, 1866–67).

JMN: The Journals and Miscellaneous Notebooks of Ralph Waldo Emerson, ed. William H. Gilman et al., 16 vols. (Cambridge: Belknap Press of Harvard University Press, 1960–82).

Kirby, *Years of Experience:* Georgiana Bruce Kirby, *Years of Experience* (New York: Putnam, 1887).

Love-Letters: Love-Letters of Margaret Fuller, 1845–1846 (New York : D. Appleton, 1903).

Memoirs: Memoirs of Margaret Fuller Ossoli, ed. R. W. Emerson, W. H. Channing, and J. F. Clarke, 2 vols. (Boston: Phillips, Sampson, 1852).

Miller: *Margaret Fuller: American Romantic*, ed. Perry Miller (Garden City, N.Y.: Doubleday, 1963).

Milne, *George William Curtis:* Gordon Milne, *George William Curtis and the Genteel Tradition* (Bloomington: Indiana University Press, 1956).

MVR: Massachusetts vital records, Boston.

NAW: Notable American Women, 1607–1950, ed. Edmund T. James, 3 vols. (Cambridge: Belknap Press of Harvard University Press, 1971).

OCA: The Oxford Companion to Art, ed. Harold Osborne (Oxford: Clarendon Press, 1970).

OCFL: Paul Harvey and J. E. Heseltine, *The Oxford Companion to French Literature* (Oxford: Clarendon Press, 1959).

Odell, *Annals of the New York Stage:* George Clinton Densmore Odell, *Annals of the New York Stage*, 15 vols. (New York: Columbia University Press, 1927–49).

Rusk, *Letters of RWE: The Letters of Ralph Waldo Emerson*, ed. Ralph L. Rusk, 6 vols. (New York: Columbia University Press, 1939).

Sand, *Correspondance: Correspondance de George Sand*, ed. Georges Lubin, 13 vols. to date (Paris: Garnier, 1964–).

Spring, "Journal Abroad": Rebecca Buffum Spring, "Journal Abroad," in Raritan Bay Union Collection, New Jersey Historical Society (MG 285 [Add. 1, item 12]). Another version, titled "Auld Acquaintance," is in Huntington Library (HM 46944).

Sturgis of Yarmouth: Edward Sturgis of Yarmouth, Massachusetts, ed. Roger Faxton Sturgis (Boston: Privately published by Stanhope Press, 1914).

Van Doren: *The Lost Art: Letters of Seven Famous Women*, ed. Dorothy Van Doren (New York: Coward-McCann, 1929).

VR: vital records.

Wade: *The Writings of Margaret Fuller*, ed. Mason Wade (New York: Viking Press, 1941).

WNC: Margaret Fuller Ossoli, *Woman in the Nineteenth Century, and Kindred Papers*, ed. Arthur B. Fuller (Boston: John P. Jewett, 1855).

Woman in the Nineteenth Century: S. Margaret Fuller, *Woman in the Nineteenth Century*, ed. Joel Myerson (Columbia: University of South Carolina Press, 1980).

Works: Manuscript copybooks, Fuller family papers, 3 vols., in Houghton Library, Harvard University.

THE LETTERS OF MARGARET FULLER

507. To [?]

[1845]

I am pleased with your sympathy about the Tribune, for I do not find much among my old friends. They think I ought to produce something excellent, while I am satisfied to aid in the great work of popular education.[1] I never regarded literature merely as a collection of exquisite products, but rather as a means of mutual interpretation. Feeling that many are reached and in some degree helped, the thoughts of every day seem worth noting, though in a form that does not inspire me.

ELfr, from *Memoirs*, 2:164.

1. When Greeley founded the *New-York Daily Tribune* in 1841, he was determined that it would set a high intellectual standard. First he had Albert Brisbane write; then he hired Fuller, and finally he brought George Ripley to the paper to review books. As a result of these efforts, Greeley's paper was both a literary and a financial success.

508. To [?]

[1845]

Body and mind, I have long required rest and mere amusement, and now obey Nature as much as I can. If she pleases to restore me to an energetic state, she will by-and-by; if not, I can only hope this world will not turn me out of doors too abruptly. I value my present position very much, as enabling me to speak effectually some right words to a large circle; and while I can do so, am content.

ELfr, from *Memoirs,* 2:163–64.

509.   To [?]

[1845]

Mr. Greeley is in many ways very interesting for me to know. He teaches me things, which my own influence on those, who have hitherto approached me, has prevented me from learning. In our business and friendly relations, we are on terms of solid good-will and mutual respect. With the exception of my own mother, I think him the most disinterestedly generous person I have ever known.[1]

ELfr, from *Memoirs,* 2:151.

1. Horace Greeley was an energetic social reformer. A staunch but eccentric Whig, he supported Henry Clay but often rejected Thurlow Weed's leadership in New York. He had exhausted himself on behalf of Henry Clay in the presidential campaign of 1844, only to see Clay lose both New York State and the election itself (*DAB*).

510.   To [?]

[1845]

It is not well to keep entirely apart from the stream of common life; so, though I never go out when busy, nor keep late hours, I find it pleasanter and better to enter somewhat into society. I thus meet with many entertaining acquaintance, and some friends. I can never, indeed, expect, in America, or in this world, to form relations with nobler persons than I have already known; nor can I put my heart into these new ties as into the old ones, though probably it would still respond to commanding excellence. But my present circle satisfies my wants. As to what is called "good society," I am wholly indifferent. I know several women, whom I like very much, and yet more men. I hear good music, which answers my social desires better than any other intercourse can;

and I love four or five interesting children, in whom I always find more genuine sympathy than in their elders.

ELfr, from *Memoirs*, 2:165.

511. To Richard F. Fuller

N. Y. 9th Jany 1845.

I thought, dear Richard, that you so clearly understood that it would very seldom be in my power to write to you that it would never give you pain or be a cause of disappointment. Never let it, in future, I cannot conceive of your supposing that I would be *offended* by some trifle and omit answering a letter on that account.

I am very busy, and I receive, now I am separated from all my friends, letters in great number, which I do not attempt to answer, except in urgent cases. Nor do they expect it, but write to me again and again. They know that, if I had the time and strength which I have not, I must not fritter away my attention on incessant letter writing. I must bend it on what is before me, if I wish to learn or to do.

I am truly disappointed to hear from you so seldom, and more so that the two letters I have received are so meagre. During the two years we lived at Cambridge I made you a first object, and supposed that, when it was no longer possible for me to do so, your desire to acquaint me with the progress of your mind and life would continue. However, if it does not, there is no use in forcing such things. I dare say you will wish to talk to me fully when we meet.

What you say of being fickle and easily impressed by circumstances gives me pain, the rather that I have the impression that those you are in, now, are not in all respects of an ennobling character. Perhaps I need feel none.

Lloyd writes me, in answer to a letter which I wrote him at great inconvenience, for the sake of giving him pleasure, that he wishes, next time, I would write *at leisure*.[1] He seems in better spirits. Ellen much the reverse. She takes, however, great pleasure in the baby.[2] We hear nothing from Eugene.[3] William H. you probably know has a son.[4] Dear Mother is in Boston. It seems to me that, if Arthur is not to return in Spring, it would be better for her not to keep house till autumn.[5] It will be expensive for her, and liberty through the summer wd do her good. She could then visit me, for I do not expect to go to Mass till July or August. I know you are pretty "set" as well as pretty "fickle," but I think, if for the best, under all considerations; ie if best fo[r] Mother and she can keep the house let till she wants it, you wd not dislike this.

This is a most lovely place where we live, completely country. I wish you could see it. It is so bold and free, yet so soft a scene. I have been[n] in N. Y a good deal, only now, have been unwell some days and confined[n] with Influenza. I make pleasant acquaintance, quite as fast, as I have time for them[n] I have a good deal to do to get acquainted with the ground I am to occupy. Am now about to visit all the public institutions here, of a remedial or benevolent kind. This will occupy my time for several weeks. I am getting out my book, but slowly, if Cousin George can tell any way to send from here, I will send you a copy.[6] I have such a bargain for this that if it succeeds in a sale my profits will be considerable. Near 700 of "Summer" &c were sold, when I heard last; this is better than I expected.[7] As matters look to me I lay my plans to stay here a year and a half, if not longer, and have told Mr G. so. I like him much. He is a man of strong mind and most generous heart. Ellery works industriously but is discontented. I should be the same if I thought of all I have given up and many discomforts, but I put all that out of the way. I feel when unwell that I am not at home, and when well have to spend too much time on my personal service now I have no one to help me, in any way, but *then* I do not have to feel anxious whether the bread and beef can possibly be paid for.

A letter from Arthur tonight not very well in health, but well every other way. Always affecy yr sister

M.

Upon looking at your letter again I see that, though brief, it contains a good many facts. I am truly pleased to hear of the Lyceum and of improvement in the outward man.[8]

Dont pay your letters and I will not mine. It is not convenient for me to now.

ALS (MH: fMS Am 1086 [9:110]); MsC (MH: fMS Am 1086 [Works, 2:749–57]). Published in part in Higginson, *MFO,* p. 209. *Addressed:* To / Richard F. Fuller / Greenfield / Mass.— *Postmark:* New York Jan 11.

After his graduation from Harvard in 1844, Richard Frederick Fuller, Margaret's favorite brother, went to Greenfield, Massachusetts, to study law with George Davis, a distant cousin whom Margaret had loved in the 1830s.

have been] have ⟨only⟩ ↑ been ↓
days and confined] days ↑ and confined ↓
for them] for ↑ them ↓

1. Lloyd, the youngest of the Fuller children, was emotionally troubled.

2. Ellen Kilshaw Fuller, Margaret's only surviving sister, married the poet Ellery Channing, nephew of Dr. William Ellery Channing, in 1841. Lonely and unhappy, Channing was working for the *Tribune*. Ellen, however, was living in Concord, where her first child, Margaret Fuller Channing (Greta), had been born on her aunt's birthday in 1844.

3. Eugene Fuller, next oldest of the Fuller children after Margaret, was a business-man in New Orleans.

4. William Henry Fuller, another brother and businessman, lived in Cincinnati with his wife, Frances Hastings Fuller, and their three children, the youngest of whom was William Henry, Jr. Born 12 December 1844, he died 6 August 1845 (William Hyslop Fuller, *Genealogy of Some Descendants of Thomas Fuller of Woburn* [Palmer, Mass., 1919], p. 145).

5. Margarett Crane Fuller, Margaret's widowed mother, was living in the family home on Ellery Street in Cambridge. Arthur Buckminster Fuller, Margaret's brother, graduated from Harvard in 1843 and moved to Illinois, where he became the owner of the Belvidere Academy. In 1845 he returned to New England to prepare for the Unitar-ian ministry.

6. Fuller's *Woman in the Nineteenth Century* was published in February.

7. *Summer on the Lakes, in 1843* was a travel book based on Fuller's trip to the West.

8. Richard answered his sister on 4 February (MH), saying that his performances at the Greenfield lyceum had "raised me in the market." He was, however, unhappy with what he inferred would be her response to his letter: "I feel too conscious of being unable to retrieve the dullness of my letters which you justly find fault with. Perhaps I might tim-idly & in a whisper be allowed to insinuate that yours too have contained fewer thoughts than facts, & have not been such as to stimulate me to a thoughtful reply."

512. To Margarett C. Fuller

N. Y. 12th Jany 1845.

Dearest Mother,

I hear with much satisfaction that you are now in town. Be sure and stay there some time, and see everything that may fill your mind with new and pleasant images You are one of the few people that are apt to push ideas of duty to an extreme, and, though I am glad you can do so much for *your* Mother's happiness, you must not, in health and spirits, injure yourself; for it is a vital point with us, your children, that you should not.

You have reason to believe that the world, whether I be sick or whether I be well, can never be the same to me without your tender care, and without the oppory of talking with you and trying to minister to your peace and comfort. But you know my view of these things; when the plough is once set in any direction, to look back as little as may be, till that furrow is turned. I find much good in my present posi-tion, with prospect of more, if I show patience and energy, so I must think as little as may be of the privations it brings with it. One of the greatest of these to me is not seeing little Greta at this stage of her little life. That is an irreparable loss. Tell Ellen, with much love, that I have not time to write to her tonight, but will so, whenever I can. Tell her that both[n] Mr Greeley and Mr Johnson have spoken of Ellery as doing well in the office, and that persons who see him speak of him as being amusing and lively, but I have not, myself, seen him now for some time.[1]

I have had Influenza for near a fortnight now, which, though much better, still hangs on, and gives me pain in the eyes as it did last winter, so that I write as little as possible just now. The weather having changed from damp to a brighter cold,[n] I hope to get better fast.[n] I have *not* heard from Eugene and want to know if you have yet. Have heard[n] this week from A. R. and L.; all well.

It seems to me that, if Arthur is not to return and you can continue[n] let the house, it might be better not to keep house till autumn. I want you to visit me in Spring and the Gs are very desirous you should.[2] They would be glad to see you now, but I dont think you would be comfortable, and in May, their place will be beautiful. I do not now expect to see Mass before July.

Should you like to lend me thirty dollars? If you have it on hand, I will put it to your acct on interest the same as the rest. If you have not it, feel no regret. I am not in immediate want of it, but thought it would be a safe oppory to send by William.[3] I can send again by and by, when you have it, or if you want all *your* money, send to Uncle.[4] If E. Cumming is going back, will she not pass through N. Y.[5] If so, charge her to come and see me. Let her take the Haarlem omnibus and come to 49th St. There inquire and any one will show her the way to Mr Greeley's . I wish B. could come on with her. Love to them both and to Anna.[6]

William will tell you all about me, so I will end now with your affecy.

M.

If you have the thirty dollars and there is any thing especially needed by Ellen or the baby to the amount of *two* dollars, I wish you would buy and give it from me, and send me the remainder. If you had any towels out of the store room that could be sent me, it would add to my comfort. Much love to Aunt Kuhn [an]d family[7] Am *very* glad to hear Anna is so much better.

Love to Mrs Farrar.[8] Perhaps she will write. I am covetous of hearing from my friends, though I cannot make much reply.

I want you to go to Chelsea and see Jane.[9]

ALS (MH: fMS Am 1086 [9:112]). *Addressed:* Mrs Margaret Fuller / Boston / Mass. / By W. H. Channing.

that both] that ⟨t⟩ both
brighter cold,] bright⟨?⟩er cold,
better fast.] better ⟨?⟩ fast.
Have heard] Have ↑ heard ↓
can continue] can ↑ continue ↓

1. Oliver Johnson (1809–89) became Greeley's assistant in 1844 after serving as the Boston correspondent for the *Tribune* from 1842 to 1844. A Vermont native, Johnson was "'a wheel horse in every humanitarian movement for almost half a century,'" most notably in the service of abolition. He was one of the founders of the New England Anti-Slavery Society (*DAB*).

2. Fuller was staying with Horace and Mary Greeley at their home in Turtle Bay, then at the upper edge of New York City.

3. William Henry Channing, Fuller's close friend, was preaching Fourierite socialism in New York City at this time. A Unitarian minister, Channing was searching for a focus in his vocation.

4. Her uncle Abraham Williams Fuller, a wealthy Boston businessman-lawyer, was the executor of her father's estate.

5. Elizabeth Randall Cumming was a friend from Fuller's youth.

6. Belinda and Hannah (called Anna) Randall of Boston, sisters of Elizabeth Randall Cumming.

7. Nancy Weiser, Mrs. Fuller's half sister, married George Kuhn, a Boston business-man.

8. Eliza Rotch Farrar, wife of Professor John Farrar of Harvard, had befriended Fuller in the early 1830s and remained a lifelong friend.

9. Jane Tuckerman King, a friend and former pupil. In 1843 she married John Gallison King, son of John Glen King of Salem.

513. To Mary Rotch

N. Y. 15th Jany, 1845.

Always dear Aunt Mary,

Your letter, with its commission, which shows so much affectionate care for me, comes sweetly. I have not time to think much about being alone here; still, there is enough feeling of it to make such remembrance from my friends doubly grateful.

I do not, at present, take wine, as I can have excellent milk and my head bears it, but in the spring, I may need wine. I shall fulfil your design by keeping your gift, as a little treasure, to which I shall go for indulgences which might be good for me, but which I should otherwise go without. Many things to which I have been accustomed, both for food and medicine, do not come in my way, now; as my hosts are Grahamites and Hydropaths.[1] However, I get along very well; my health has been most unusually good, only, this last fortnight, I have had influenza, but, now, it is almost gone.

This stopped me just as I had begun to visit the Institutions here of a remedial and benevolent kind. So soon as I am quite well, shall resume the survey. Mr G. is desirous I should make it and make what use of it I

45

think best in the paper. I go with William C. it is a great pleasure to us to cooperate in these ways. I do not expect to do much, practically, for the suffering; but having such an organ of expression, any suggestions that are well-grounded may be of use. I have always felt great interest in those women, who are trampled in the mud to gratify the brute appetites of men, and wished I might be brought, naturally, into contact with them. Now I am so; and think I shall have much that is interesting to tell you when we meet.[2]

I go on very moderately, for my strength is not great, and I am now connected with a person who is anxious I should not overtask it. Yet I shall do rather more for the paper by and by. At present, beside the time I spend in looking round and examining my new field, I am publishing a volume of which you will receive a copy, called "Woman in the 19th Century" and part of my available time is spent in attending to it as it goes through the press. For, really, the work seems but half done when your book is *written*. I like being here; the streams of life flow free; and I learn much. I feel so far satisfied as to have laid my plans to stay a year and a half, if not longer, and to have told Mr G. that I probably shall. That is long enough for a mortal to look forward, and not too long, as I must look forward in order to get what I want from Europe.

Mr. Greeley is a man of genuine excellence, honorable, benevolent, of an uncorrupted disposition, and, in his way, of even great abilities. In modes of life and manners he is the man of the people and of the *Amern* people, but I find my way to get along with all that. I have some privations as to comfort and elegance, and am separated from all the friends of my past life, except my friend William, but I do not dwell on the shadow side. Some pleasant acquaintances I have formed and, no doubt, shall more, quite as fast as I have time to attend to them.

I rejoice to hear that your situation is improved. I hope to pass a day or two with you next summer, if you can receive me when I can come. Meanwhile, I want to hear from you, now and then, if it be only a line to let me know the state of your health. Love to Miss G.[3] tell her I have her cologne bottle on my mantle-piece now. I sent for the little things I had from my friends that my room might look more like home.

My window commands[n] a most beautiful view, for we are quite out of town in a lovely place on the East River. I like this, as I can be in town[n] when I will, and *here*, have much retirement. Ever affecy, dear Aunt Mary, yours

MARGARET

How can I send you my book when it comes out? You are right in supposing my signature is the Star.

ALS (MH: fMS Am 1086 [9:114]); MsC (MH: fMS Am 1086 [Works, 1:41–47]. Published in part in *WNC*, pp. 371–72; *Memoirs*, 2:150, 151, 163; and Higginson, *MFO*, pp. 212–13. *Addressed:* Miss Mary Rotch / New Bedford / Mass. *Postmark:* New York Jan 20.

Mary Rotch, Eliza Farrar's aunt, was a member of a wealthy and powerful Quaker family in New Bedford, where Fuller often visited her.

window commands] window ⟨at⟩ commands
be in town] be ⟨there⟩ ↑ in town ↓

1. Both of the Greeleys were enthusiastic health fadists. They had met at a boarding-house devoted to the regimen of Sylvester Graham, whose sensible reforms were often mocked.

2. Fuller wrote about her visit to the city's charitable and penal institutions in "Our City Charities" (*New-York Daily Tribune*, 19 March 1845). As she had done earlier at Sing Sing prison, she recognized the hypocrisy of a society that jailed the women and let the men remain free: "Here are the twelve hundred, who receive the punishment due to the vices of so large a portion of the rest."

3. Mary Gifford was Mary Rotch's companion.

514. To James Nathan

[ca. 7 February 1845]

Dear Mr Nathan,

My mind dwells often on what you are to tell me. I have long had a presentiment that I should meet, nearly, one of your race, who would show me how the sun of to-day shines upon the ancient Temple,—but I did not expect so gentle and civilized an apparition and with blue eyes!

It was one of those little incidents that have in them somewhat fate-full, that, last Monday morning, a friend, with whom I was walking, asked me to go in and see the Jerusalem,[1] and I, at first, said yes, and then, I did not know why, changed my mind. But, in the evening, you asked me and told me of yourself.

Some day when you are not bound to buying and selling, and I, too, am free, and when the sun shines as gloriously as it has some days of late, and the birds are again in full song! you will perhaps take me from Dr Leger's in the morning,[2] and show me some one[n] of those beautiful places which I do not yet[n] know, and, while I look, I will listen, too, and, as we return, you will show me the holy city.

On my side, I have a poem I wish to read to you; it is so correspondent with the story you told me. Is this little plan a dream? if so, it will only fade like other buds of this premature Spring. Tomorrow will be the first day of Spring.

AL (MB: Ms. Am. 1451 [1]). Published in *Love-Letters,* pp. 9–10.

James Nathan (1811–88), a shadowy, important man in Fuller's life in New York, was a Jewish businessman from Germany. Fuller immediately fell in love with him, apparently misunderstanding his feelings for her. Nathan (who changed his name to Grotendorf in 1855), emigrated to the United States in 1830. At various times he was a commission merchant and a banker. In 1862 he retired to Hamburg (*Love-Letters,* p. 190).

some one] some ↑one↓
not yet] not ↑yet↓

1. The *New-York Daily Tribune* for 3 February advertised "Mr. Catherwood's New Panorama," which was described as "a most magnificent view of JERUSALEM and its vicinity."

2. Theodore Leger, a New York hypnotist, published *Animal Magnetism; or, Psycodunamy* (New York, 1846) and *The Magnetoscope* (London, 1852). Fuller reviewed the first book in the *Tribune,* 30 May 1846.

515. To [?]

[ca. 9 February 1845]

You have heard that the Tribune Office was burned to the ground.[1] For a day I thought it must make a difference, but it has served only to increase my admiration for Mr. Greeley's smiling courage. He has really a strong character.

ELfr, from *Memoirs,* 2:151–52.
Dated from the reference to the Tribune *fire.*

1. About 4:30 in the morning of Wednesday, 5 February, a fire broke out in the Tribune building. It destroyed the entire office, the stock of paper, and all the manuscripts in Greeley's possession. The loss was estimated at $18,000. A raging storm had been blowing for twenty-four hours, so almost no fire equipment reached the scene. Only the mail books, which were in a fireproof safe, survived. Despite the extent of the loss, Greeley did not miss an issue of the paper. Several of his competitors put their offices at his disposal, so the *Tribune* appeared every morning. Fortunately for Fuller, *Woman in the Nineteenth Century* was in press in another building and thus escaped destruction (*New-York Daily Tribune,* 6 and 7 February 1845).

516. To Anna Loring

[16? February 1845]

My dear Anna,

I was very glad to get your letter and your beautiful present. I like the purse better than any ever given me, except one Jane made for me once, that was like a water lily, and *like that,* too easily tarnished to be carried in the open street. Richard will value one from you highly; it was a great disappointment to him that you and your Mother did not come to Greenfield last autumn. I value something from your hand more than I could any book or picture, because I hope thoughts you had about your distant friend, while at work, are woven into it.

I am staying now with the friends of Jane and John, Mr and Mrs Spring.[1] They are people of whom any one would say "To know them is to love them" Their children are very interesting. Eddy is of a singular firm and refined character at once.[2] I have seen no child at all like him in character. The little Jeanie is the most arch, graceful, intelligent little thing imaginable.[3]

I have heard Pico [of]ten but you can have n[o] idea of the pleasure she can give from hearing her at a concert.[4] The opera has given me great" pleasure and her part in Semiramide the best opera I have heard" is one of the finest. I heard that opera three times.

You will receive from me my book on Woman when it comes out and you must read such parts as interest you and persuade Father and Mother to read it. Give them much love and say that I shall go to hear Mr Hudson and he is invited here for tomorrow eveg[5] I have not seen him yet he did not find me, when he left the letters Always dear Anna's friend

MARGARET.

ALS (MWelC). *Addressed:* Miss Anna Loring / Winter St / Boston.

Anna Loring, the daughter of Ellis and Louisa Loring of Boston, was the woman whom Richard Fuller loved at this time.

Dated by the reference to Hudson, who lectured first in New York on Monday, 17 February (New-York Daily Tribune, *18 February 1845*).

me great] me ⟨in⟩ great

Semiramide the best opera I have heard] Semiramide ↑ the best opera I have heard ↓

1. Marcus Spring (1810–74), son of Adolphus and Lydia Taft Spring of Northbridge, Massachusetts, was a drygoods merchant who became a prominent reformer. It was on Eagleswood, Spring's New Jersey estate, that the Raritan Bay Community was founded. In 1836, Spring married Rebecca Buffum (1811–1911), daughter of Arnold Buffum of Providence, who was a founder of the New England Anti-Slavery Society. A determined abolitionist, Rebecca visited John Brown in jail, in an attempt to free him (Northbridge VR; Maud Honeyman Greene, "Raritan Bay Union, Eagleswood, New Jersey," *Proceedings of the New Jersey Historical Society* 68 [1950]:1–20). After she met them at Anne Lynch's Valentine party in 1845, Fuller became a close friend of the Springs, who invited her to accompany them to Europe in 1846.

2. Edward Adolphus Spring (1837–1907), the Springs' oldest child, became a sculptor and a teacher. In 1898 he married Anna Voelcker (Borchardt, "Lady of Utopia").

3. Jeannie Spring (1843–1921) was the second of the three Spring children. She was

married three times: to James Steele MacKaye, T. L. Johns, and Dr. Gilead Peet (Borchardt, "Lady of Utopia").

4. Rosina Pico first appeared in New York in November 1844. On 3 January 1845 she performed in the New York premier of Rossini's *Semiramide* (first staged in Venice in 1823). Fuller wrote that she was an "unfinished singer. Still, if she should never go beyond her present marks, she is a singer able to give great pleasure to the ear and some satisfaction to the heart" (*New-York Daily Tribune,* 14 May 1846; *Annals of Opera,* col. 686). Another critic remembered her as a "swarthy, sweet-lipped woman . . . and her voice, a rich, creamy contralto, in no way very remarkable." Nevertheless, she was "the favorite contralto of New York for some three or four years" (Richard G. White, "Opera in New York," *Century* 23 [1881–82]:876).

5. Henry Norman Hudson (1814–86) began his lecture career in 1844 with a series on Shakespeare, which he published as *Lectures on Shakespeare* (New York, 1848). Later ordained in the Episcopal priesthood, Hudson served as a chaplain in the Civil War, when he became embroiled in a controversy with Benjamin Butler over the general's tactics (*DAB*).

517. To James Nathan

Saturday, Feby 22d [1845]

My dear friend, for the memory of the frank words of yesterday makes it impossible for me to address you more distantly.—I feared, when you went away, that you believed I, too, did not sympathize with you, or I could not have said I was so happy when you had just been telling me of your deep wants. You seemed repelled by this; but, indeed, it was not because I did not feel. It is difficult for me to put into words what was in my mind, but you will undersand it when you know me more. Yet let me say to you that I think it is great sin even to dream of wishing for less thought, less feeling than one has. Let us be steadfast in prizing these precious gifts under all circumstances. The violet cannot wish to be again imprisoned in the sod, because she may be trampled on by some rude foot. Indeed our lives are sad, but it will not always be so. Heaven is bound to find for every noble and natural feeling its response and its home at last. But I cannot say much, only I would have you remember yesterday with pleasure as does

*[1]

The birds this morning were in full song, like April.

Should you like to go with me on *Monday eveg* to hear the Messiah? If so, will you come to tea to Mr Cranch's at 6 or a little later and take me.[2] You may be engaged, or you may not love Handel's music, in either case, let me know by note and I can find another guardian without difficulty. They will send a note from the Tribune office, if you wish, but, if it be your desire to go, that is not necessary.

AL (MB: Ms. Am. 1451 [3]). Published in *Love-Letters*, pp. 12–13.

1. Her *Tribune* signature was an asterisk.

2. The New-York Sacred Music Society performed *Messiah* on 24 February. Christopher Pearse Cranch graduated from the Divinity School in Cambridge but never became a minister. He turned instead to literature and painting, wrote for the *Western Messenger* and the *Dial*, and later moved to New York, where Fuller often saw him and his wife, Elizabeth (1821?–98), daughter of John Peter and Caroline Smith DeWindt of Fishkill, New York. Elizabeth Cranch was a great granddaughter of John and Abigail Adams (MVR 482:145; *New Letters of Abigail Adams, 1788–1801*, ed. Stewart Mitchell [Boston, 1947], n.p.).

518. To Sarah Shaw

N.Y. 25th Feby 45

My dear Sarah,

I do regret never getting time to write letters, but I cannot yet. Do not forget to think of me sometimes. I wish I could have letters to tell me of all your news. I sent my book on Woman &c to my three female friends, in your house, as, indeed, I know no better women.[1] Write me, if any thoughts come to you about it. Also of your own private news. Anna, too, I want to hear from. Next August I expect to see you all. I shall then be in Mass for several weeks. Meantime I hear much of Frank in Fourierite association.[2] Sarah seems more quiescent in the grand measures of social renovation.

I like living here. All flows freely; and I find I dont dislike wickedness and wretchedness more than pettiness and coldness. My own individual life is easy to lead. No doubt I shall have many stories to tell when we meet.—Could you and Frank know through how many scenes of cold and storm the muff and boa have[n] protected me, you would rejoice in the affectionate gift! What a note this is! worthy N. Y. but it is only meant to convey the loving remembrance of your friend

MARGARET.

ALS (MH: bMS Am 1417 [178]). Published in Wade, p. 573. *Addressed*: To / Mrs Sarah Shaw / West Roxbury / Mass.

Sarah Sturgis Shaw and her husband, Francis George Shaw, lived in Roxbury near Brook Farm. Close friends of Fuller's, the Shaws were involved in social reform movements.

boa have] boa ha⟨d⟩ ↑ve↓

1. That is, Sarah Shaw and her two sisters-in-law, who were frequent visitors: Anna Blake Shaw, who later married William Batchelder Greene, and Sarah Shaw Russell.

2. The *Phalanx* of 8 February reported the first annual meeting of the New England

Fourier Society, held in Boston on 15 January. George Ripley had been elected president; Shaw was one of four vice-presidents. The reporter for the journal wrote: "One of the most interesting and altogether effective speeches was made by Francis G. Shaw, a young and successful merchant, whose experience of the evils of a competitive state have led him to seek in agricultural employments a higher sphere of mental and moral culture. . . . A few such men as Mr. Shaw would ensure all that is needed—*A thorough experiment of Association*" (p. 316).

519.   To William H. Channing

[ca. March 1845]

I felt that you had learned much of your own heart and life through my friendly sympathy. May our Father lead you to your true home. He will infuse a glow of fervent light and steadfastness.

ELfr, from Frothingham, *Memoir of William Henry Channing*, p. 193.
Frothingham gives the approximate date.

520.   To James Nathan

Saturday Morng.
[ca. 1? March? 1845]

I sealed my letter last night and dont know what is in it, but it seems as if there was *nothing* no response at all, and yet my mind has been enfolded in your thought as a branch with flame. Now the branch, perhaps, too green, looks only black upon the hearth. Yet if there *is* nothing—wait.

Are you very busy? if not, walk up *through John St* toward the Dr's about twenty minutes past ten. But, if you are busy, dont disturb yourself. I go that way at any rate.

AL (MB: Ms. Am. 1451 [6]). Published in *Love-Letters*, p. 15. *Addressed*: Mr Nathan / 86 Cedar St.

521.   To James Nathan

[ca. 2? March? 1845?]

Though I wish to see you, yet come not on a cold cloudy day. Though you are farthest from what is commonly meant by a *fair weather friend,* I like to see you in the sunshine best.

AL (MB: Ms. Am. 1451 [7]). Published in *Love-Letters,* p. 17.
The highly conjectural date is based on Fuller's comment on the weather.

522. To Richard F. Fuller

Brooklyn, 2d March 45[n]

My dear Richard,

I come from the parlor, where they are telling anecedotes, of Quaker preachers to write to you. One word more about correspondence and then I will drop the subject. You are mistaken in supposing I write much to any person. I cannot. It is a physical impossibility. If you live to have sixty people or more write to you, and have a great deal of other script to do, you may see that I cannot. I feel sorry to have you take the view you do.

As to Mary Allen your conduct was very natural, yet be warned to more reserve another time.[1] You run the risk of exciting expectations in a young girl's mind, which cannot be realized, if her feelings are un-occupied, yours not. I am glad you have a friendship you value with Mary; and hope you will have many more such with women. You will aid them and they you. You can give them more dignity of aim and solid knowledge than our sex usually have; they will refine and expand your nature. Only, in such intimacies, be careful not to begin with a devotion you cannot continue. Neither break off without wounding the pride of the lady and subjecting her to misconstruction. Perhaps you did not, in this instance; but in those little country towns, it is necessary to be very careful; they are so fond of gossip.

I am glad you see Anna with so much freedom.[2] I would advise you to be so far guarded there, too, as to distinguish and improve yourself and show yourself worthy,[n] first and foremost. Yet it will do no harm to let her see, delicately, your strong regard. Give my love to her.

Anna Ward tells me you are greatly improved.[3] I have not, however, had any chance to talk fully with her. You can have no idea how one thing crowds upon another in my life here. You say you feel worthy and able to be my friend. That I believe this, I did not think any further proof was needed on my side than the great confidence I placed in you during the latter part of our sojourn in Cambridge. On yours I am inclined to ask of you to take so far as possible my place in the family. To show refined consideration for Mother, take judicious care of Lloyd. You have felt as if my honor and the development of my powers, was really precious to you. I have now a position when if I can devot myself entirely to use its occasions, a noble career is before me yet. I want to be unimpeded by cares which I cannot, at this distance, attend to properly. I want that my friends should *wish* me now to act in my public career rather than towards them personally. I have given almost all my young energies to personal relations. I no longer feel inclined to this, and wish to share and impel the general stream of thought   I really have nothing, at present, to communicate to any one, except what you may see indications of in print. I am observing my new field this occupies me. No doubt there is a great deal of incident in my life, and when we meet I shall have much to tell you. But I cannot write it, and do not wish to as it passes, for similar reasons to what made you burn your letter to me. I cannot do it justice.

I hear with regret from the Ws that Ellen is looking out for a farm. Penury and the narrow difficult life Ellery is ill fitted to bear. If they get a farm, I trust it may be a *little* one. I knew E. would not stay here permanently, but hoped he would earn a little money before going away[n] to begin the farmer's life with. Farewell from your ever affece sister

M.

Since finishing this letter I find Mr G. has de[cide]d he must part from Ellery next April, so E. *must* take the farm. I presume this is no disappointment to him, he could not have done as he has if he had wished to stay.

ALS (MH: fMS Am 1086 [9:111]); MsC (MH: fMS Am 1086 [Works, 2:757–63]). Published in part in Chevigny, p. 135. *Addressed*: To Richard F. Fuller / at the Law School of Cambridge / Mass.

2d March 45] 2d March ↑ 45 ↓
yourself and show yourself worthy,] yourself ↑ and show yourself worthy ↓ ,
money before going away] money ↑ before going away ↓
1. Mary Cole Allen (1824–45), daughter of Sylvester and Harriet Ripley Allen of Greenfield, died the following 9 October. Richard first met her at Brook Farm (Greenfield VR; Francis M. Thompson, *History of Greenfield, Shire Town of Franklin County, Massachusetts* [Greenfield, 1904–31], pp. 843, 855; Fuller, *Recollections*, p. 80).
2. Richard was at this time very much in love with Anna Loring.
3. Anna Barker, one of Fuller's closest friends, had married Samuel G. Ward, the man Fuller had loved in the late 1830s.

523. To James Nathan

Friday eveg
[7? March 1845]

I cannot, dear Mr Nathan, go with you to the Concert, because, before receiving your note, I had engaged to accompany another friend. But you will be there; and we shall, I hope, have beautiful music that will associate us in sympathy.

Perhaps you will be at the farm on Sunday.[1] I shall go out after dinner. But you must not let this intimation break up your Sunday; if you had planned any distant excursion. I know the charms of an unbroken day, indeed it always seems that I do not half enjoy any scene till I have had its presence through an entire day.

I am glad to have you wish to retain the book, but should sometime like to correct with my pen the little errors in the printing, of which I see too many, but hope to remove them all in another edition, for they begin to talk of that.

It pleases me that you feel so truly what is told of Panthea.[2] I believe there is nothing writ that is more to my mind. Can you doubt the possibility of such feelings? do they not prove themselves as soon as seen to be just what nature intended, if only we would not be satisfied with affection less fervent and less pure? à revoir

P.S. The reason of your not receiving my note earlier was that I did not send it. I wrote and carried it about, thinking, if we happened to meet, I would give it, but thought it too trifling to send. But that afternoon, which was of such blue sky and inspiring breezes, gave me an impulse to send it, as I passed through the city. A note will scarcely ever fail to reach me, in the course[n] of 24 hours, if left at the office.

AL (MB: Ms. Am. 1451 [2]). Published in *Love-Letters*, pp. 10–11.

Dated by the reference to the "concert," *which was probably that of the German Society of New York on Saturday, 8 March.*

me, in the course] me ⟨at once⟩, ↑ in the course ↓

1. The Greeleys' home in Turtle Bay. Lydia Maria Child described it to Anna Loring in February of that year: "It was as rural as you can imagine. . . . It is a very old house, with a very old porch, and very old vines, and a very old garden, and very old summerhouses dropping to pieces, and a very old piazza at the back, overgrown with very old rosebushes, which at that season were covered with red berries. The piazza is almost *on* the East river, with Blackwell's Island in full view before it. Margaret's chamber looks out upon a little woody knoll, that runs down into the water, and boats and ships are passing her window all the time" (Child, *Selected Letters*, p. 217).

2. In *Woman in the Nineteenth Century*, Fuller summarized and commented on the story of Panthea in Xenophon's *Cyropaedia*, "the most beautiful picture presented by ancient literature of wedded love" (*Woman in the Nineteenth Century*, p. 73).

524. To Eugene Fuller

N. Y. 9th March, 1845.

Dearest Eugene,

Your Arkansas letter was received with great joy. It was long since I had heard from yourself and, as usual, I cannot obtain much information from the family. It is true I deserve not from them, as the necessity of doing so much other writing makes me a bad correspondent to them and to every one.

I am glad too to hear of your health, and that, with the ennui of so long a journey at such a time, you were able to make some profit. Profit always sounds like your coming back to us, which, amid the whirl of a busy life, I cannot cease to wish, and which Mother has only too much leisure to dream about.

I do not know much of the family, except that Mother is still troubled with dyspepsea, but, in other regards, not sick. Ellen well, and the child, they say most lovely, Richard doing well. For me, I have never been so well situated. As to a home the place where we live is old and dilapidated but in a situation of great natural loveliness. When there, I am perfectly secluded, yet every one I wish to see comes to see me, and I can get to the centre of the city in half an hour. The house is kept in a Castle Rackrent style, but there is all affection for me and desire to make me at home, and I do feel so, wh could scarcely have been expected from such an arrangement. My room is delightful; how I wish you could sit at its window with me and see the sails glide by!

As to the public part; that is entirely satisfactory. I do just as I please, and as much or little as I please, and the Editors express themselves perfectly satisfied, and others say that my pieces *tell* to a degree, I could not expect. I think, too, I shall do better and better. I am truly interested in this great field which opens before me and it is pleasant to be sure of a chance at half a hundred thousand[n] readers.

Mr Greeley I like, nay more, love. He is, in his habits, a slattern and plebeian, and in his heart, a nobleman. His abilities, in his own way, are great. He believes in mine to a surprizing extent. We are true friends.

It was pleasant you should see that little notice in that wild place. The book is out, and the theme of all the newspapers and many of the journals. Abuse public and private[n] is lavished upon its views, but respect expressed for me personally. But the most speaking fact and the one wh satisfies[n] me, is that the whole edition was sold off in a week to the booksellers and $85 handed to me as my share. Not that my object was in any wise money, but I consider this the signet of success. If one can be heard that is enough! I shall send you 2 copies one for yourself and one to give away, if you like. If you noticed it in a N. O. paper, you might create a demand for it there; the next[n] edition will be out in May.[1] In your next letter tell me your address, that I may know what to do[n] when I wish to send parcels to you.

I wish you would write a series of letters about what you have seen in Arkansas and the S. West, that I might use in the Tribune, if I thought best. I think you would do this well. Write one, at least, about this late tour as a sample and tell about Wild Cat &c *out full*.[2]

I hear a great deal of music, having free entrance every where from my connection with the paper. Most of the Italian Opera corps is now at N. O. and I hope you will hear them perform Semiramide, with which I was enchanted I am glad you love music as well as ever. Farewell, and Heaven bless my dear brother is always the prayer of

MARGARET.

I am almost perfectly well at present.

If you see the Weekly Tribune you will find all my pieces marked with a Star. I began 1st Decr.

ALS (MH: fMS Am 1086 [9:116]); MsC (MH: fMS Am 1086 [Works, 2:763−71]). Published in part in Higginson, *MFO*, pp. 202−3, 208−9. Published entire in Wade, pp. 574−75. *Addressed*: To Eugene Fuller Esq / New Orleans / La. *Postmark*: New York Mar 11.

hundred thousand] hundred ↑ thousand ↓
Abuse public and private] Abuse ↑ public and private ↓
one wh satisfies] one wh ⟨interests⟩ ↑ satisifies ↓
the next] the ⟨first⟩ ↑ next ↓
address, that I may know what to do] address, ↑ that I may know what to do ↓

1. Despite the success of *Woman in the Nineteenth Century*, no other American edition was published in Fuller's lifetime.

2. No essay clearly ascribable to Eugene Fuller appeared in the *Tribune*, although one letter from Arkansas dated 17 March appeared on 2 May. The writer described the working of speculative state banks and their bonds—one form of the Western "Wild Cat."

---

525. To David Thom

N. York 12th March 1845.

Dear Sir,

I owe many apologies for having omitted to answer your letter recd early in Decr an unusually busy winter must be my excuse. The packages of which you speak were not from me and I have vainly inquired among those to whom your book has been lent whether they had sent you any books. With this letter I send, and hope you may safely receive a book just issued by myself. It has met with much notice here, and some acceptance. A friend commends to your care the accompanying package for the author of Festus.[1] I believe this also contains one of my volumes, but one which I did not esteem of sufficiently grave importance to send across the waters.

I am, at present, established in N York, in care of a literary department of the N. Y. Tribune, a journal as widely circulated as any in this country. I find it a very pleasant position: the editor is a man of honor, noble disposition, and fine abilities of a class much prized among our people. Should you write to me again please direct to the care of Horace Greeley, N. Y. Tribune.

The paragraph concerning your brother was interesting, and, as is the use of persons connected with the daily prints, I, at once, made use of it in that way. I should be glad now of any such items of literary intelligence and could give them immediate circulation here.

Forgive, dear Sir, few lines of M.S. as indeed[n] from one who sends you a volume in print, that may not be difficult.

With respect

S. MARGARET FULLER.

ALS (ViU). *Addressed*: Rev David Thom / St Mary's place Edgehill, / Liverpool, / England—. *Endorsed*: Miss Fuller.

David Thom (b. 1795?) was a Universalist minister and theologian who had begun his career in the Presbyterian church (*DNB*, under John Hamilton Thom).

M.S. as indeed] M.S. ↑ as indeed ↓

1. Caroline Sturgis had sent a package for Fuller to forward to Philip James Bailey, author of *Festus*, a poem that Fuller admired (Caroline Sturgis to Margaret Fuller, 29 January 1845, MH). Bailey (1816–1902) first published *Festus* in 1839, then revised it many times during the next half century (*DNB*).

526.   To Caroline Sturgis

N. Y. 13th March, 1845.

Your letter, dear Carry, is but just recd, because I have been away from home. With Anna's picture I am delighted.[1] It is even a better impression than the first I saw and it will be a cause of true happiness to have it.

What you say of my book is very true, mostly, especially is it true that there ought to be no cause for writing such a thing.[2] But that there is cause is too evident by the ardent interest it excites in those who have never known me. Those, you know, are the persons to whom it is addressed, and they do feel their wounds probed, and healing promised by it. The opposition and the sympathy it excites are both great, and you will laugh to hear that it is placarded here as "Great Book of the Age."

Are you not inconsistent to reproach me for writing such outside things, and then fear that I will reproduce, even in veils, what I have known that is most interesting?[3] Of what should I write then?

I am very glad you like Richard. And well content you should make the distinction between us, you do.[4] Perhaps a "substantial" intercourse may take place between you, for he is really of your kind, the simple kind.

Yes! I have had great pleasure in seeing Sam, and with Anna. He seemed dignified in himself, and their relation more dignified. S.'s translations from Goethe have been a fine study for him as all things are, still in the Come Mair chapter, though roselights may have been let[n] through his windows, by draperies from another home. As you say the Raphael time is quite over— Let it go.[5]

Georgiana is to go to the West in May. I have seen a man from the place (Alton, Illinois)[n] where she is to pass the summer and many letters from Mr Arnold, and I think she will have just the free various life she wants.[6] I will send you some of her letters when I can collect them.

Anna Ward, too, has put herself under Dr Leger's care. I have a very entertaining time with this. Nothing wonderful happens to me. I have no sleep, no trance, but seem to receive daily accessions of strength from this *insouciant* robust Frenchman, and his local action on the distended bones is obvious.[7] During this part, which occupies about twenty minutes, he talks to me, and as his life has been various, full of experience and adventure, entertains me much. He has lived ten years in Mexico, and if I wanted to write dramatic novels, I should get materials enough from what he tells me. Going to him takes great part of my morning, and makes the rest of my life too harried, but my passage too and fro and what I meet at the Mesmeric apartments affords a new view of life. On the subject itself I have as yet nothing worth your reading nor even the reading of the readers of the Tribune but by and by, I hope—

Seeress of Prevorst Dr Francis has and I believe James Clarke, too.[8] Memoir of Emily Plater is in Miss Peabody's library.[9] The newspaper editors, who have *not* read the Memoir, are more indignant at my praise of Emily than at any of my other sins. They say it is evident I would like to be a Colonel Plater!

I do not know any magicians— Miss Lynch parties are not pleasant;

too much second hand literary gossip.[10] Miss L. herself I like better than her guests. She is intimate with Fanny Kemble and wears her miniature as a pin, which immediately set my covetous mind to wishing I was wearing yours.[11] William's or Sam's I could not wear. But your picture waits a Festus. F.K.'s was [   ] ditto the Farm schools, insane hospital, (not Bloomingdale but pauper insane) and penitentiary.[12] They got out out of the boat with me at the farm and walked back to N.Y. together.[n] It was a queer combination of persons and objects, but, it was very pleasant for us three together, all reserves and obstacles seem to have melted away. [   ] view given me by others and I compassionate her much. Of new people or things no time to speak now— No time—no time; that is the cry all the time now. I suppose you know that Ellery returns in April. I often [   ] It is[n] the little all I can give just now Mrs Cranch sends love She thinks of you with a great deal of affection She says she will call on Susan.[13] [   ] you saw Mr Greeley's [   ] Your father's [   ] pamphlet.[14]

ALfr (MH: bMS Am 1221 [247]). *Addressed*: To / Miss Caroline Sturgis / Care Wm Sturgis Esq / Boston / Mass.

Caroline Sturgis, daughter of William Sturgis of Boston, was Fuller's closest friend.

been let] been le⟨?⟩t

place (Alton, Illinois)] place ↑ (Alton, Illinois) ↓

They got out out of the boat with me at the farm and walked back to N.Y. together.] ↑ They got out out of the boat with me at the farm and walked back to N.Y. together. ↓

It is] I⟨?⟩t is

1. Sturgis sent Fuller a daguerreotype of Anna Loring (Caroline Sturgis to Margaret Fuller, 4 March 1845, MH).

2. In the letter of 4 March, Sturgis wrote of *Woman in the Nineteenth Century*, "It makes me sad that it is necessary such an one should be written but since it is so it cannot but do good to lift the veil as you have done."

3. In the same letter, the nervous Sturgis had written: "How could you put that about the three Valentines in the paper? I begin to be afraid when I think how much has been told you. Is it quite fair to make your friends step before the public even in veils?" Sturgis probably objected to Fuller's published recollection: "A companion, of that delicate nature by which a scar is felt as a wound, was saddened by the sense how very little our partialities, undue emotions, and manias need to be exaggerated to entitle us to rank among madmen." The "companion" was probably Sturgis, who had accompanied Fuller to Sing Sing, the prison Fuller describes in this passage. The scene was part of Fuller's account of Valentine's day at the Bloomingdale Asylum (*New-York Daily Tribune*, 22 February 1845).

4. "I have a real respect for Richard, such as I have for very few persons," wrote Sturgis. "I find this difference between you & him, & that when he talks to me upon any subject he presents me with substantial food while you give me perfumes."

5. Sam Ward published his translations as *Essays on Art, by Goethe* (Boston, 1845). Fuller reviewed the book in the *Tribune*, 29 May 1845. She often called Ward "Raphael" because of his talent as a painter.

6. Georgiana Bruce (b. 1818) had lived at Brook Farm before joining the staff of the women's prison at Sing Sing. George Benedict Arnold, Marcus Spring's brother-in-law,

was active in reform communities, and became president of the North American Phalanx and of the Raritan Bay Union. First a minister at large in New York City, Arnold later became a nurseryman in Illinois (John Humphrey Noyes, *History of American Socialism* [Philadelphia, 1870], pp. 488–89).

7. Georgiana Bruce described how Leger treated Fuller: "She was seated on a convenient stool and the doctor held his right hand horizontally, close against the vertebral column, the fingers pointing towards but never touching it. Slowly he moved his hand from the very end of the spine to the base of the brain, charging it with his vigorous magnetism. There was a slight trembling of his arm as *willed* that power should flow from him to the patient. She described the sensation as like having a rod of iron worked into her poor spine." Implausible as it sounds, Bruce says that after two months Fuller could then walk the four miles from Greeley's home to Leger's office, that after five months she grew three inches taller, and that she had to discard the horsehair pad she normally wore under her dresses to equalize her shoulders, for now "they were perfectly flat and similar" (*Years of Experience*, pp. 213–14).

8. Fuller had discussed Justinus Kerner's *Die Seherin von Prevorst* in *Summer on the Lakes*. Convers Francis, once associated with the Transcendentalists, was on the faculty of the divinity school in Cambridge. Fuller had studied German in the 1830s with James Clarke, a Unitarian minister in Boston and one of her closest friends.

9. Emily Plater (1806–31), daughter of Count Xavier Plater, was a Polish nationalist. In 1831 she cut her hair and joined the nationalist army fighting the Russians for Polish independence. She died on 23 December, two months after the rebellion was crushed. Fuller, who found much of her own personality reflected in Plater, called her "Countess Colonel Plater" in *Woman in the Nineteenth Century*. She went on to say: "The dignity, the purity, the concentrated resolve, the calm, deep enthusiasm, which yet could, when occasion called, sparkle up a holy, an indignant fire, make of this young maiden the figure I want for my frontispiece" (*Woman in the Nineteenth Century*, p. 33). Fuller had read either Jozef Straszewicz's *Émilie Plater, sa vie et sa mort* (Paris, 1835) or the English translation he published under the pseudonym J. K. Salomonski, *The Life of the Countess Emily Plater* (New York, 1842). Elizabeth Palmer Peabody, a writer, publisher, and reformer, had a bookstore on West Street in Boston.

10. Anne Charlotte Lynch (1815–91) began her literary career in Providence, where she edited an anthology and began to hold salons. After settling in New York, she attracted such writers as Poe, Bryant, Greeley, and Parke Godwin to her evenings at Ninth Street. It was probably at such a gathering that Fuller met Poe. In 1855 Lynch married Vincenzo Botta, an Italian émigré (*NAW*).

11. Frances Anne Kemble, the English actress, was separated from her husband, Pierce Butler.

12. Fuller described her investigations of the charitable institutions in "Our City Charities. Visit to Bellevue Alms House, to the Farm school, the Asylum for the Insane, and Penitentiary on Blackwell's Island" (*New-York Daily Tribune*, 19 March 1845).

13. Susan Sturgis, Caroline's youngest sister.

14. William Sturgis, Caroline's father, was a prominent Boston merchant.

527. To James Nathan

Evening 14th March. [1845]

It is for me to regret now that I have troubled a gentle heart far more than was intended. I only wished to be satisfied, and when you told me how you had viewed the incident, I really was so. Do not think of it ever again.

It would be more generous to be more confiding, but I cannot you must see me[n] as I am. Trifles affect me to joy or pain but I can be absolutely frank. You will see whether you find me fastidious and exacting. Our education and relations are so different and those of each as yet scarce known to the other, slight misunderstandings may arise. Fate does not seem to favor my wish to hear more of your life and the position of your mind. But I do not feel that, whatever I may know, I can misunderstand what is deepest. I have seen the inmost heart, what the original nature is. I am thus far confiding.

Tell me, if it is not wrong for me to ask, what was the "severe loss." What has power to make you "heart-sick."

I hear my host and his sweet little wife singing together. If I were only alone with them, I should have urged your stay; you would like them, but there are so many corner-pieces beside in the parlor, with living eyes that are over busy in taking note, I do not invite any friend to face them, Lebewhol.

Do not fancy that I have lost this day by staying. I have been well engaged, and it has been still and sweet alone in my room, by the bright fire, with the rain falling so musically outside. One feels at home on the earth, such days. I am sorry that you should have come here in the wet, for naught; but hope your day, also, is closing pleasantly.

AL (MB: Ms. Am. 1451 [5]). Published in *Love-Letters*, pp. 15–17.

see me] see ↑ me ↓

528.　To Richard F. Fuller

[ca. mid-March 1845]

Dear Richard,

I thought to postpone writing to you, but finally I feel it will be of no use. I cannot write a good letter at present. I am unwell now the heat is coming on, have a weight in my whole frame which makes exertion painful. I do not like to write a word, but want to sleep or look merely at the green growing things. So soon as this passes you shall hear from me.

Am sorry you find Cambridge so dull and fear it will be the same with A Think you will enjoy seeing him. He seems very entertaining, greatly improved every way and full of generous kindly plans. You must try [to] induce him to take the rest he seems much to need.

How is Anna Loring she has never answered the note you thought she wished so much to get, ever affecly your sister

MARGARET.

ALS (MH: fMS Am 1086 [9:248]); MsC (MH: fMS Am 1086 [Works, 2:727–29]). *Dated by the fact that both Richard and Arthur are in Cambridge.*

529. To James Nathan

Wednesday.

19th March. [1845]

I dine today with Mrs Child, house of Isaac Hopper 20, Third St.[1] If you will come for me there at seven or half past seven, I will go with you. 'Tis said the third attempt never fails, but, if it should, in this instance we will not try again, but accept it as an omen that we are not to see Zion together For, though I dine in town one other day this week, it is at a place where I cannot easily excuse myself for going away in the eveg.

I have no time now for more, except to express happiness in the aspirations of my friend. May Heaven cherish them! I cannot ask this[n] for you in that ancient noble speech of the chosen people. Yet the prayer which He of Nazareth gave is true for the heart of all nations— "Lead me not into temptation and deliver me from evil." The Stars answer to that; while they reprove, they promise Ask *for me* in the words of your own poet, his original words, which I cannot repeat "Keep back thy servant also from presumptuous sins"—[2] If you receive this in time, let me know at Dr Leger's whether you will come, this eveg

AL (MB: Ms. Am. 1451 [8]). Published in *Love-Letters*, pp. 17–18. *Addressed*: To / Mr James Nathan / 86 Cedar St.

ask this] ask ↑ this ↓

1. Lydia Maria Francis Child had known Fuller since the 1820s, when they read history together in Cambridge. A novelist and ardent abolitionist, Child was editing the *National Anti-Slavery Standard*. She lived in the home of Isaac Tatem Hopper (1771–1852), a Quaker abolitionist and prison reformer (*NAW*). A leading Hicksite, Hopper was expelled from the meeting in 1841 for his abolitionist activities, among which was an early and extensive involvement in the underground railroad (*DAB*).

2. Ps. 19:13.

530. To Richard F. Fuller

[27 March 1845]

[   ]pated that if I have a lonely eveg as I had last night, when nothing presses, I want to read and rest my mind, instead of making any exertion. Last night I thought of writing Anna L. the promised note, but did not feel like it, so read a German book instead. I take great pleasure in the Daguerrotype they have sent me of her,— it is one of my dearest companions, and some night, when I have been looking at it, I shall write and send a letter[n] at the same time to Sister Ellen.[n]

I write from the Tribune Office on my way to Anna Ward, with whom I am going to spend a day and for the first time since she came too. The newspaper sallies are dying away about my book; many expressions of feeling from private sources come in; here as often before I have found the stranger more sympathizing and in my belief intelligent than some of my private friends.[1] It is a most lovely day; the weather here is much milder than in Mass and I feel better able than usual to enjoy the Spring. Ever affecy your sister

ALfr (MH: fMS Am 1086 [9:111]). *Addressed*: To / Richard F. Fuller. / at the Law School / Cambridge / Mass. *Postmark*: New York Mar 27.

send a letter] send ⟨one⟩ ↑ a letter ↓
Sister Ellen.] Sister Ellen ⟨too⟩.

1. Fuller had, for example, received a lively letter from John Neal, whom she did not know personally: "Many thanks to you for what you have done, and for what you are so qualified to do, in behalf of woman." He went on to describe the differences between their approaches: "You find a lion in your path at every step & instead of making faces at him, and bullying him off the field, you sit down by the wayside and begin magnetizing him. . . . I go for the whip and spur" (John Neal to Margaret Fuller, 28 February 1845, MH). Caroline Sturgis, however, was chilly: "Thank you for the pamphlet dear Margaret. I have read it through but the style troubles me very much. I cannot free myself from a feeling of great consciousness in all you write. There is a recurrence of comparisons, illustrations, & words, which is not pleasing. There seems to be a want of vital powers as if you had gathered flowers and planted them in a garden but had left the roots in their own soil" (Caroline Sturgis to Margaret Fuller, 4 March 1845, MH).

531. To James Nathan

Saturday Eveg
March 31st— [1845]

My dear friend,

I feel a strong desire to write you a few words at the close of this sweet day. And yet—there are no words, many or few, in which I can even begin to utter what there is to say. It is, indeed, true that the time is all too short. To feel that there is to be so quick a bound to intercourse makes us prize the moment, but then also makes it so difficult to use it Yet this one thing I wish to say, where so many must be left unsaid. You tell me that I may, probably, never know you wholly. Indeed the obstacles of time and space may prevent my understanding the workings of character; many pages of my new book may be shut against me. But to know the natural music of the being, what it is, will be, *or* may be needs not long acquaintance and this perhaps is known to her, better than to himself. Perhaps? *I* believe in the *Ahnungen*[1] beyond any thing.

Has this sweetest day been spent by you in busy life or doubtful thought? For that I grieve; it is so much more lovely than yesterday; the mood in Nature far tenderer and more expansive. I must again write you of the birds; it is in early morning that they are in such a rapture; their songs at other hours are cold and tame in comparison I perceive they have learned and lived, since I first wrote of them— then their notes were timid; they were not sure but they must perish with cold before they could enjoy the sunshine of this beautiful world, but now they have had some of it, and are content. Will you smile at such a trifle being written down? after all, what better can we tell one another than these little things; each is a note in the great music book, which historians and critics never opened, but which contains all that is worth our singing. The word[n] Weehawken was a strain from that book, between you and your friend. Oh there are glimpses in this world of a truly happy intercourse, simple as between little children, rich, various, intelligent as among perfected Men. Sometime— Somewhere— Meanwhile benedicite

AL (MB: Ms. Am. 1451 [17]). Published in part in *Love-Letters*, pp. 31–33.
The word] The ↑ word ↓

1. *Ahnungen*: presentiments, premonitions (which Fuller often had and took seriously).

532. To Anna Loring

New York,
2d April 45

My darling Anna,

I have wanted often to write you the little note, but a time *would* not come perfectly free. It surprizes me to find how much I love you. I was not aware how much when I used to see you often, but your image comes up before me oftener than that of almost any person, and the fond hope of seeing you unfold to excellence, through the desire after it, you have expressed to me in our little confidential talks, lies very near my heart. You remember how sad I was last Spring; that was from disappointment as to the delicacy, the tenderness, the intelligence of human beings. Finding then, that though no more a child, I was still so childish as to suffer such keen pangs of surprize and disappointment, I tried to wean myself from such close habits of personal relations, and have, in some measure, succeeded. Still hopes will spring up, as the buds in Spring, mindless of last Winter's frost, and I know not how to believe that these which bloom at thought of you will suffer an untimely blight.

The picture of you is very precious to me. I look at it often; it is a loved companion. These Daguerrotypes from your picture are the best I ever saw. But whose gift is the picture? mention, when you write. I told Carry how I wished for one, and I know that Mrs Child, too, begged one for me from your parents, so I do not know whom to thank.

I see Mrs Child often and they are, indeed, pleasant hours we pass together. She is so entertaining, and her generous heart glows through all she says, and makes a friendly home around her.

Richard often mentions seeing you. I hope you are a careful friend to him, giving him all those advices and hints which will help him. You are better able to do this than one older would be, as youths and maidens grow up together; it is their natural and holy office to refine and strengthen one another. I do not feel that I can be now of that benefit to any friend that I was in early years. Then having fewer ties, and fewer thoughts, I could give my time, my strength, my heart in generous measure to a friend, and the world being all new to me, I observed every thing. I miss Richard very much, when I have time to miss anyone. I may say he is one of my most valued friends, for it is not as brother alone that I value him. It is one of my chief regrets in leaving Massachusetts that I can no longer aid him, nor hear the ingenious expressions of his mind. My little niece and namesake, too, I can know nothing about her at this charming time in her life. Write me how she seems to you.

I send to your care a package of roots and seeds, which I want you to keep in a cool place till Mother comes, I believe the 9th or 10th April, then give them to Richard for her. Now she is to have a garden of her own, it will be a solace to her. You will go to see her; will you not? it will gratify me.

How lovely it is all around me. I cannot tell you. I feel exceedingly happy, really like the Spring. The sails are gliding by, clothed in visionary beauty by the setting sun. I have in my bosom a large bunch of English violets which I wish might shed their perfume over this letter; we have whole banks of them here, but I have to gather them for myself; if you were here, you would bring them to me. Farewell, much love to Father and Mother. I thank Augusta[1] for her love, give mine to her and Caroline, too, and tell dearest Jane that I think of her and bide my time. Your friend

MARGARET.

ALS (MWelC).

1. Augusta Gilman King, daughter of John Glen King of Salem, was a friend of Fuller's, a member of the James Lowell circle in Cambridge, and Jane Tuckerman King's sister-in-law.

533. To James Nathan

Wednesday
2d April. [1845]

I must not dear friend, try to answer your letter; it moves me too much. May good angels guide you! It was painful to see your letter curtailed of a part Yet I appreciate the cause that takes it from me. So would I have it; let all that is given to me be with the *full consent* of your mind, then shall I be at home in its permanent temper.

Though the veil of mystery must be sad for one who would like to come close in reliance, yet such is my belief in your honor,—and shall I not say your tender regard for me, that I shall not, voluntarily, seek to penetrate it, even by a *mental* question. Yet certainly it will be happier for me, if you do not leave me thus in the dark when you go for[n] so long and and so far a travel. The only part that can trouble me is to see you reproach yourself in some degree. Yet can I never look on you and believe that conscience is seriously "*gekrankt*,"[1] and you told me that you had "only broken through the conventions of this world." *That* I know a generous and ardent nature may do, and unwisely, without deep injury anywhere, yet much outward difficulty may ensue. But, again, only with the full consent would I hear ever a word more. You will act as the heart prompts in communion with me, and as to the circumstances of our outward intercourse, as there are influences unknown to

67

me, you will consult them as you have consulted them, and my trust will be in you.

Again, may our good angels guide you and foster daily the best and loveliest self! I shall expect you tomorrow but I wish it were today. Twenty four hours are a great many— More than enough to bring clouds, yet they will not come in the heaven of the Mind— not this time.

AL (MB: Ms. Am. 1451 [18]). Published in *Love-Letters*, pp. 33–35.

go for] go ↑ for ↓

1. *Gekrankt*: is suffering.

534. To James Nathan

Waverly Place
Sunday aftn 6th April 45

Can my friend have a doubt as to the nature of my answer?[1] Could the heart of woman refuse its sympathy to this earnestness in behalf of an injured woman? Could a human heart refuse its faith to such sincerity, even if it had accompanied the avowal of error!

Heaven be praised that it does *not*! Some of your expressions, especially the use of the word "*atonement*," had troubled me. I knew not what to think. Now I know all, and surely all is well.

The first day we passed together, as you told me of your first being here, when you came to the telling the landlord so ingenuously that you had no money, and said "the tears ran down my boyish cheeks"— my heart sprang towards you and across the interval of years and I stood beside you and wiped away those tears and told you they were pearls consecrated to Truth. You said[n] you "would not do so now" but I believed you *would* act now with the same truthfulness, though in a different manner as becomes *the man*, according to the degree in which circumstances should call[n] on you. And so it is,—there are no tears nor cause to shed any. I need not approach so tenderly as I might have[n] to the boy, but if it be of avail to bless you, to express a fervent hope that your great and tender soul may harmonize all your nature more and more and create to itself a life in which it may expand all its powers; this hope, this blessing take from the one in whom you have confided, and never again fear that such an experiment may fail.

Indeed I have suffered much since receiving the letter. I came into town yesterday with that winged feeling that often comes with the early sunshine. When the letter came, I could not wait, though there was only time for a[n] glance upon it. Then a cold faintness came upon me. I took off the flowers I had put on, expressive of my feelings a little hour before, and gave them to the blind girl, for I almost envied her for being in her shut up state less subject to the sudden shocks of feeling. For there I read at once the exact confirmation of what had been told me of your position, and could not read the whole to be soothed by its sense and spirit. For this day had been given to others, and the evening to a circle of new acquaintance. Not till I went to my room for the night was there any peace or stillness and all things swam before me. For I felt the falsity of the position in which you had placed yourself, that you had acted a fiction and though from honorable nay heroic[n] motives, had entered the path of intrigue I felt too, that he had, probably, been somewhat tempted by the romance of the position, and with a firmer clearer determination to act always with simplicity, might have found some other way. He will tell me whether I was wrong in this. But[n] I placed the letter next my heart and all day it seemed to comfort me, and assure me that when I could be once alone, peace would come; and it has come.

I do not see, my friend, how you can feel thus secure against this being generally[?] known. It came to me through the mistress of a lodging house wherever you are, must you be subject to such transmission. I cannot say more in my case, being bound by a promise, but only repeat what I before told you, that the way in which I heard was so purely accidental as not to argue any publicity *now*. But you say you use your own name, and if you did not your personality is too remarkable to fail of being recognized, beside do some of your male friends know where or how you live?

I say this because you say disclosure might be a source of misery to your[n] afterlife in ways I do not know of; what ways? say all to me —[n]

As to our relations,[n] I wish these circumstances to make no difference in them, private or as to being together in public. Now that I know all and have made up my own mind, I have no fear nor care. I am myself exposed to misconstruction constantly from what I write. Also there have been circumstances in *my* life, which if made known to the world, would judged[n] by conventional rules, subject[n] me as probably to general blame, as these could you. They will, probably, never be made known, but I am well prepared for the chance. Blame could not hurt me, for I have not done wrong, and have too much real weight of character to be sunk, unless by real stones of offense being attached to me: As I feel for myself, so do I for a friend. You are noble. I have elected to abide by you. We will act, as if these clouds were not in the sky." The case in which I asked your counsel was of another sort. I had proposed going about with the lady, not from any strong feeling of affinity or regard, but merely as a matter of convenience. On hearing afterwards that such public odium had been thrown upon her, I thought it might be more advisable for me to choose another escort, and I asked you, thinking thus to be enabled to judge. But *as to you* I *have* judged and have chosen.

But Oh, I wish nothing so grave had come up between us for judgment, thus early. My feeling with you was so delightful; it was a feeling of childhood. I was pervaded by the ardor, upborne by the strength of your nature gently drawn near to the realities of life. I should have been happy to be thus led by the hand through green and sunny paths, or like a child to creep close to the side of my companion listening long to his stories of things unfamiliar to my thoughts. Now this deeper strain has been awakened; it proves, indeed, an unison, but will the strings ever vibrate to the lighter airs again?—

And now farewell. Come to see me so soon as you will and may." The golden time is past, in which a female friend could so much have aided you, but tell me if there still remains any need in which such aid could benefit your charge. Farewell and love ever your friend—

I stay here today but go back to the Farm tomorrow morning. As to your letter I cannot yet part with it; at present it is safe as myself and before you go, shall be disposed of as you desire. I feel as if I had not expressed enough my deep interest in what you have done, but it was because of beginning with a sense that you must know *that* and the wish to satisfy you as to myself. You will read, I believe, what was left unwrit.

AL (MB: Ms. Am. 1451 [19–22]). Published in part in *Love-Letters*, pp. 35–39.

You said] ⟨Then⟩ You said

circumstances should call] circumstances ↑ should call⟨ed⟩ ↓

might have] might ↑ have ↓

time for a] time ↑ for a ↓

honorable nay heroic] honorable ↑ nay heroic ↓

But] *This word and the preceding sentence have been canceled by a later hand but are here recovered.*

    misery to your] misery ⟨in⟩ ↑ to your ↓

to me—] *Both this paragraph and the one preceding it have been canceled by a later hand but are here recovered.*

    to our relations] to our ⟨intercourse⟩ ↑ relations ↓

    would judged] would ⟨if⟩ judged

    rules, subject] rules, ⟨would⟩ subject

    the sky.] *The remainder of this paragraph and the first sentence of the next have been canceled by a later hand but are here recovered.*

and may.] *Save for the final sentence, the remainder of this paragraph has been canceled by a later hand but is here recovered.*

1. The details are unclear, but apparently Fuller had recently discovered that Nathan was involved with a young "English maiden." Fuller here responds to his apparent explanation that he had assumed responsibility for the rehabilitation of the woman, who must have been his mistress. Letters 579 and 603 (in which Fuller calls her the "English maiden") show that Nathan took the woman with him when he left New York.

535. To James Nathan

Tuesday eveg.
8th April. [1845]

The Cedar St merchant did well. Say, was that street selected from any association with Lebanon? How far the name wanders from the thing in this world!

Josey commends himself to you with a mild, but fond regret, if I read aright the glance of his eye when I told him of your enquiries.[1] He seems very content, but I marvel at him for it, for he is kept close a great deal. Sarah says she gives him a bath every day, but he does not look as he did with you. When you come out, perhaps you will give Henry some directions; he appears to have more respect for the toilette than any member of this family except myself, and I should be sorry to have your pet get the dilapidated air! He rejoices when he sees me and cries after me when I go, but I fear there" is no especial devotion in that, but that he is a general lover, and more affectionate than deep in his feelings. The only fine day since you were here I took him out with me, and for awhile we were very happy together, but, when I fell a dreaming he disappeared and I had a sad time looking for him. I was so distressed lest he should be lost, *and by me*. At last, I found the sun was burning me so, I went back for my bonnet which I had forgotten and beside it I found poor Josy looking as if he felt as disturbed about me, as I had about him. When he has a collar, I shall not feel anxious in having him with me.

This has been a sad day, so cruel cold; it hurts me. This morning all the flowers lay with their poor heads on the ground and ice clinging round them, the blue eyed flowers that looked up so trusting to the blue sky, the golden flowers that looked up so full of joy and sure of the sun. May tomorrow be more genial! With love gute nacht

It is, indeed, such a worthless little note. But I am sad! two such dissipated days! and here at night comes a thick book named "American

Facts" and forbidding me to look at that best fact the Moon.[2] Help me! my friend; be the Oasis! with its fountain and its palm! I go to seek you in the land of dreams!

AL (MB: Ms. Am. 1451 [23–24]). Published in *Love-Letters*, pp. 39–41. *Addressed*: Mr James Nathan / 86 Cedar St.

fear there] fear ⟨me,⟩ there

1. A dog that Nathan had given Fuller to keep.
2. George Palmer Putnam, *American Facts* (London, 1845), which Fuller reviewed coolly: "It is merely a compilation, from which those who have lived at some distance from the great highway may get answers to their questions, as to events and circumstances which have escaped them. It is one of those books which will be valued in the back-woods" (*New-York Daily Tribune*, 19 May 1845).

536. To James Nathan

Evening of 9th April. [1845]

I take the little sheet to answer the long and beautiful letter, not because there is not much to say, but because it does not seem that I can say it yet. The sweet ray touches my life, and I wish it might call out full and splendid blossoms, like the pink cactuses seen in the windows of the rich these bright spring days. But my thoughts lie, rather, deep in the ground like lily roots; not till the full summer time will they show themselves in their whiteness and their fragrance, but then— where they stand lonely in the confidential night, they will return a blessing for all that has been given.

I am with you as never with any other one. I like to be quite still and have you the actor and the voice. You have life enough for both; you will indulge me in this dear repose.

Sweetly you answer to my thoughts, and even in the same images in which myself had clothed them. I *will* trust you deeply. I will not recal my thoughts from an involuntary flight. But can there fail to be timidity?— Of the many who have stretched out their arms, there was not one who did not sometimes scare back the little birds to their nest. Often when they pecked at the window to which they had been invited the inmate was asleep, or, hearing, said "It is nothing but the wind" And on[n] one pure altar they could always alight, save that sometimes the fire burnt there too fiercely, and at others it was desolate with ashes. Long has it seemed they might not be permitted to soar and sing until a better world should offer freer and surer invitation. Yet the lark may never refuse her song if the true sun should dawn.

I hear the fire[n] bells, perhaps the happiness of hearths is being marred at this moment. Heaven bless all thy children and save them from the inexpressible ills for more than equal joys. I am full of pity to-night. I know not why especially. Farewell, dear friend, take the little incoherent letter in good part: if you are like me, you wish for one every day. But I wish still more to see you now and borrow courage from your eyes. I like to see the old fashioned Deutsche name written by your hand, and should like to hear it from your lips, but would rather myself not sign but come unannounced, and depart informally as if *at home*.

AL (MB: Ms. Am. 1451 [25]). Published in *Love-Letters*, pp. 41–43.
And on] And ↑ on ↓
the fire] the ↑ fire ↓

537. To James Nathan

Monday April 14th [1845]

My dear friend,

What passed yesterday seems not less sad to day.[1] The last three days have effected as violent a change as the famous three days of Paris,[2] and the sweet little garden, with which my mind had surrounded your image lies all desecrated and trampled by the hoofs of the demon who conducted this revolution, pelting with his cruel hail-stones me, poor child, just as I had laid aside the protections of reserve, and laid open my soul in a heavenly trust. I must weep to think of it, and why, O God, must eyes that never looked falsehood be doomed to shed such tears? It seems unjust, as other things in my life have seemed, though none so much as this.

Yet in that garden must be amaranths flowers "not born to die." One of these should be a perfect understanding between us, and as "spirit identity", on which you relied, did not produce this, we will try words. For I perceived yesterday in you a way of looking at these things, different from mine, more common sense, and prudent, but perhaps less refined, and you may not, even yet,[n] see my past as truly as I do myself, *now*.

73

I have felt a strong attraction to you, almost ever since we first met, the attraction of a wandering spirit towards a breast broad enough and strong enough for a rest, when it wants to furl the wings. You have also been to me as sunshine and green woods. I have wanted you more and more, and became uneasy when too long away. My thoughts were interested in all you told me, so different from what I knew myself The native poetry of your soul, its boldness, simplicity and fervor charmed mine, of kindred frame.

But this is *all* that can be said of my feelings up to receiving your confidential letter a week ago. I enjoyed like a child the interest with which a growing personal interest clothes common life, and the little tokens of outward nature. You enjoyed this with me, and the vibrations were sweet. I received, indeed, with surprize the intelligence that you would go away. It startled me for the moment, with a sense that you did not prize me enough. I had felt that I could be so much to you to refine, expand, and exalt, could it be[n] I thought you did not feel this?[n] But then your words assured me that you *did* feel it, and I easily forgot pride and self-love. I was thinking more of you than of myself, and I hoped the travel was, indeed, just what you wanted.

But when I received from you the mark of truth so noble, and that placed your character in so striking a light, also seeming to attach so religious an[n] importance to my view of it my heart flew open, as if with a spring, and any hidden treasure might have been taken from it, if you would. I can never resist this kind of greatness. I may say, it is[n] too congenial. At such times I must kneel and implore ever God to bless with abundant love the true heart that consoles me for the littleness I must see in my race, elsewhere.

Afterwards I thought of you with that foolish tenderness women must to men that really confide in them. It makes us feel like mothers, and we wish to guard you from harm and to bless you with an intensity which, no doubt, would be very tiresome to you, if we had force to express it. It seemed to me that when we should meet I *should* express to you all these beautiful feelings, and that you would give me a treasure more from your rich heart. You know how we *did* meet; you seemed dissatisfied. I had an undefined anxiety to do something, and I spoke of being as a bark that fears to leave the shore. This was partly in reply to what you had said, so beautifully, in your letter, of never recalling my thoughts when they naturally rested on you, and of trusting to nature and providence. I wanted to do so, but felt afraid lest pain should ensue, such as has already[n] ensued and which my heart, born for the most genial confidence, knows not well how to bear from a cherished hand.

When you approached me so nearly, I was exceedingly agitated, partly because your personality has a powerful magnetic effect on me, partly because I had always attached importance to such an act, and it was asked of me so as to make me conscious, and suddenly, partly because this seemed the moment to express all I had felt for you, but I could not. As to what I said of a brother, I felt distaste to[n] the use of the word; I have seen too much of these *brothers*.[n] I do not doubt they think for awhile like brothers, but they do not always, and I think it is fairer to have a nameless relation, which cannot be violated and may grow to what it will.

Truly the worldly and *manly* way in which you spoke of circumstances so delicate and which had moved me so much, was sad for me to hear, yet was I glad to know what could pass in the mind even of the dear one who had claimed,— *and merited*, so large a trust. My guardian Angel must take better care of me another time, and make me still more timid, for truly nothing but perfect love will give a man patience to understand a woman, even such a man as you who have so much of feminine sweetness and sensibility.

After receiving your little note of Saturday, I again looked to you to make my feelings perfectly tuneful when I saw you. I do not think any human being ever felt a lovelier confidence in the pure tenderness of another than I did when we left the church. When you said what you thought necessary to say, it struck upon my heart like a blow. Something in your manner seemed to mark it *for me*, and yet I *could not believe it*, yet the weight pressed and I could not rest till our final conversation made all clear.

O was *that* like angels, like twin spirits bound in heavenly unison,[n] to think that any thing short of perfect love, such as I myself am born to feel, and shall yet, in some age and some world, find one that can feel for me, could enslave my heart or *compromise* a lover?

My friend! believe what I say, for I am self-conscious now. You have touched my heart, and it thrilled at the centre, but that is all. My heart is a large kingdom.

But *your* heart, your precious heart! (I am determined to be absolutely frank,) *that* I did long for. I saw how precious it is, how much more precious may be. And you have cruelly hung it up quite out of my reach, and declare I never shall have it. O das ist hart. For *no* price! There is something I am not to have at *any* price. Das ist hart. You must not give it away in my sight at any rate, but you may give away all your prudence and calculations, and arrangements, which seem so unlike your fairer self, to whomsoever you like.

It seemed the work of an evil angel making you misread a word in my letter, but since it could lead you to think it needful so to act, I am glad you did since I thus became apprized of these things in your mind, else my little birds might have flown to you in too thick flocks. You said; "what shall our relation be now?"[n] I say, most friendly, for we are really dear to one another; only it is like other earthly relations, poison plants will sometimes grow up in the night. But we will weed them out so soon as possible, and bear with them, since only perfect love casteth out fear. Think of me with love and honor. I deserve them. So do you, and shall ever have them from me. To the inspirer of all just thoughts and holy hopes commending you, farewell, my friend.

For the sake of every thing dear, dont misread any words in *this* letter. I must tell you why I was so slow to understand you yesterday, it was because you made use of the word *hope*. "Has any circumstance led to a *hope*" etc. Ah, Gretchen![3] has thy really proud and sacred life only led to such an episode where thou are supposed and by a most trusted friend[n] to be "*hoping*" about such things? Where is the fault in thee, that can lead to conclusions so humiliating? Thy own mind does not appreciate it.

Yet again I am glad my friend used the very word that could come into his mind. Truth is the first of jewels,— yet let him feel that if Margaret dared express herself more frankly than another it is because she has been in her way a queen and received her guests as also of royal blood. *What* her vanity[n] was you may see if you read how ingenuously it was said "Tell me and I will love you" as if promising a boon. Alas alas she must go to Heaven. And the journey is long.

AL (MB: Ms. Am. 1451 [27–29]). Published in *Love-Letters*, pp. 43–50.

even yet,] even ⟨now⟩, ↑ yet ↓
exalt, could it be] exalt, ↑ could it be ↓
thought you did not feel this?] thought ↑ you did not feel this? ↓
religious an] religious ↑ an ↓
it is] it ⟨it⟩ is
has already] has ↑ already ↓
distaste to] distaste ⟨at⟩ ↑ to ↓
I have seen too much of these *brothers*.] ⟨too many⟩ ↑ I have seen too much of these ↓ *brothers* ⟨have approached me⟩.
heavenly unison,] heavenly ⟨love⟩, ↑ unison ↓
be now?"] be?" ↑ now ↓
supposed and by a most trusted friend] supposed ↑ and by a most trusted friend ↓
her vanity] her ⟨view⟩ ↑ vanity ↓

1. While the details are unclear, it is evident that Nathan made an explicit sexual overture to Fuller. Probably emboldened by her response of the previous week to the news of his mistress, he made a proposition of some kind that caused the distress evident in this and her next letter to him.

2. Fuller refers to the "July Revolution," which led Charles X of France to abdicate in favor of the duc d'Orléans, who became the "citizen king," Louis-Philippe. "On 27 July [1830], the first of what came to be called the 'Three Glorious Days,' simple resistance

turned to revolt" in Paris (André Jardin and André-Jean Tudesq, *Restoration and Reaction, 1815–1848*, trans. Elborg Forster [Cambridge, 1983], p. 98).

3. Probably a reference to Gretchen (that is, Margarete) in Goethe's *Faust*.

538. To James Nathan

Tuesday.
[15 April 1845]

Yesterday was, perhaps, a sadder day than I have had in all my life. It did not seem to me an act of "providence," but of some ill demon that had exposed to what was to every worldly and womanly feeling so insulting. Neither could I reconcile myself to your having such thoughts, and just when you had induced me to trust you so absolutely. I know you could not help it, but why had fate drawn me so near you?

As I walked the streets "the piercing drops of grief would start into mine eyes" as the hymn book promises they shall *not* in heaven, and it pained me to see the human beings. I felt removed from them all, since all was not right between me and one I had chosen, and knew not where to turn my thoughts, for nature was stript of her charms, and God had not taken care of me as a Father.

But, in the evening, while present at the Antigone, my heart was lightened by the presence of this darling sister, even in such disguise.[1] The straight forward nobleness of the maiden led her to Death; we, in modern times, have not such great occasions offered us, we can only act out our feelings truly in the lesser ones, and die, if needs be, by inches; but it is the only way, for one grain of distrust or fear is poison to a good nature, felt at once through every vein." I hoped to wake this morning blessing all mankind, but it was not so. I woke with my head aching, and my heart cold and still, just as on the day before. But a little while after on my way through the town, there came to me the breath I needed. I felt submiss to heaven which permits such jars in the sweetest strains of earth. I saw a gleam of hope that the earth-stain might be washed quite away. I thought of you with deep affection, with that sense of affinity of which you speak to me. and as I said this morning that it was suicide to do otherwise." I felt the force of kindred draw me, and" that things could not be other than they were and are. Since they could be so let them; I cannot do other than love and most deeply trust you, and will drink the bitter part of the cup with patience.

Since then, I have your note. Not one moment have I sinned against you; to "disdain" you would be to disdain myself. Can I be deceived, then am I impure! Yet forgive if I say one part of your note, and some particulars of your past conduct seem not *severely* true. Your own mind, strictly scanned, will let you know whether this is so. You have said there is in yourself both a lower and a higher than I was aware of. Since you said this[n] I suppose I *have* seen[n] than lower; it is, is it not? the man of the world, as you said you see *"the dame"* in me. Yet shall we not both rise above it? I feel as if I could now, and, in that faith, say to you dear friend, kill me with truth, if it be needed, but never give me less. Indeed I have a soul to bear the[n] [   ] die of truth.[n] I will never wish to draw any hidden thing from your breast unless you begin it as you did the other day, but if you cannot tell me all the truth, always, at least tell me absolute truth.

The child, even when its nurse has herself given it a blow, comes to throw itself into her arms for consolation, for it only the more feels the nearness of the relation. And so I come to thee. Wilt thou not come with me before God and promise me severe truth, and patient tenderness, that will never, if it can be avoided, misinterpret the impulses of my soul. I am willing you should see them just as they are but I am not willing for the reaction from the angelic view to that of the man of the world, nor[n] [   ] at[n] the effects with the material eye. Yet the time is past when I could protect myself by reserve. I must now seem just as I feel, and *you* must protect me. Are you equal to this? Will an unfailing reverent love shelter the "sister of your soul"? If so, we may yet be happy together some few hours, and our parting be sad, but not bitter. I feel today as if we might bury this ugly dwarf changeling of the past, and hide its grave with flowers. I feel as if the joyous sweetness I *did* feel in the sense of your life might revive again. It lies with you,— but, if you take up the lute, Oh do it with religious care; on it have been played hymns to the gods, and songs of love for men, and strains of heroic courage, too, but *never* one verse that could grieve a living breast and should it not itself be treated delicately? With sorrow but with hope farewell.

These letters you will destroy now, if otherwise they are not in absolute safety, but, if they will[n] be, keep them till your departure, when we will mutually exchange all[n] our letters.

AL (MB: Ms. Am. 1451 [10–11]). Published in part in *Love-Letters*, pp. 22–25. Addressed: Mr James Nathan / Cedar St.

Dated by the reference to the performance of Antigone.

every vein.] every ↑ vein. ↓

me. and as I said this morning that it was suicide to do otherwise.] me. ↑ and as I said this morning that it was suicide to do otherwise. ↓

me, and] me, ↑ and ↓
Since you said this] Since ↑ you said this ↓
I *have* seen] I ⟨see⟩ ↑ *have* seen ↓
bear the] *This sentence has been canceled by a later hand but is here recovered. The sheet is cut at the bottom of the page.*
of truth.] *The last three words of this sentence have been canceled by a later hand but are here recovered.*
world, nor] *The final word has been canceled by a later hand but is here recovered. The sheet is cut at the bottom of the page.*
at] *This word, which is inserted above the line, has been canceled by a later hand but is here recovered.*
they will] they ⟨are⟩ will
exchange all] exchange ↑ all ↓

1. Fuller reviewed the performance of *Antigone* staged at Palmo's Opera House by John Vandenhoff. The production included music by Mendelssohn in an attempt to approximate the Greek theater. "We went," said Fuller, "to see this attempt at a performance of the old Greek drama, fearing it could inspire only disappointment and distaste, but the result was so favorable that we hope it may be carried further, and think a sincere satisfaction might be produced" (*New-York Daily Tribune*, 16 April 1845). The production played twelve nights before closing. Of his effort, Vandenhoff said: "It was truly a beautiful and highly interesting tragedy, aided by grand music. In Berlin and London, it drew crowded audiences; in New York, it never paid expenses" (Ireland, *Records of the New York Stage*, 2:445).

539. To James Nathan

Evening.
[16? April 1845]

I am seized with feelings of regret for thee, and seem to enter into thy mind. How selfishly *I* fret for loss of my pet dream, to walk like a child with its brave playmate. Is not *yours* broken just as much, finding so much of mortal in your angel? "And yet," said Beethoven at such a time, there *is* the godlike in man"![1] There is also[n] the angel-like in woman— she is thus angelic long before she is angel. We love what is pure. You, I believe, will never regret aught that makes your poetic soul more conscious of its hidden treasures. All shall yet be so sweet, gaining, like the plants, beauty and fragrance from these cold rain storms. The blossoms, for which I begged you to stay, are opening on the trees; will you not take me into the country the first fine day. The dust will now be laid and the air pure after the storm.[n] Will it (or rather will you wish it?)[n] be inconvenient to you on Saturday, if the weather is fine? I stay in town that day to attend the Philharmonic Concert in the evening.

Mr and Mrs Spring wished me to go to Staten Island on Sunday, but I have not said yet, whether I would go, and hate the thought of going[n] thinking it might be the only day on which I could see you. But you said *last* Sunday, you had parting visits to make; perhaps it will be so *next* Sunday. Let me know about this on Saturday morning whether you will take me on Saturday, and if not, whether I shall see you on Sunday that I may know how to arrange And will you let the little messenger be in waiting for me at Dr Leger's at 9, or a few minutes before, Saty morng.

I feel a growing persuasion that we shall now meet most sweetly, and that our minds will be tuned in the same key and tuned with nature. So as you have begged of me not to *grieve or be weary*, let me pray of you not to be *oppressed or embarrassed any more*.

AL (MB: Ms. Am. 1451 [39]). Published in *Love-Letters*, pp. 67–69.

Fuller's reference to the Philharmonic concert puts this letter in the week of April 13–19, for the last concert of the season was on Saturday, 19 April. The letters to Nathan on 14 and 15 April precede this one; had this letter been written on Friday, she would have said "tomorrow," not "Saturday." Wednesday is a reasonable conjecture, for Fuller is still tense over the emotional confrontation of the previous Sunday.

is also] is ↑ also ↓

The dust will now be laid and the air pure after the storm.] ↑ The dust will now be laid and the air pure after the storm. ↓

it (or rather will you wish it?)] it ↑ (or rather will you wish it?) ↓

go, and hate the thought of going] go, ↑ and hate the thought of going ↓

1. Fuller found the passage in Anton Schindler, *Biographie von Ludwig van Beethoven* (Münster, 1840). She quoted it in her "Lives of the Great Composers," *Dial* 2 (1841): 189.

540.   To Caroline Sturgis

17th April. 45

My dear Caroline,

You will remember Honora Sheppard whom you talked with in the hospital at Sing Sing.[1] You may see by the accompanying letter what Georgiana has been doing for her and proposes to do. G. went up to Albany last Saty and got her pardon from the governor at once. I can hardly tell you how much I feel the generosity of G. to be willing to take with[n] her such a charge into her new field of action wearied out as she is, craving rest and freedom for herself. It is[n] an act of which myself would be wholly incapable. G. is now anxious to get some money for Honora's travelling expenses, and can you aid a little and would Anna Shaw and perhaps Ellen help?[2] Ten or even five dollars would help. Anna Ward will get a little for me here, but I do not myself know many people with purses, and Mr Greeley is prejudiced against Honora. G. will go, probably by the 25th, if you can do any thing, write to your affece

MARGARET.

A letter from Sarah Clarke but nothing special in it.[3] Ah it is most lovely here now; whole beds of violets and mountain myrtle all starred with its blue flowers, trees just leaving out.

how many associations with these days last Spring. The dates speak powerfully even to me.

I enjoy much being with Anna Ward now; she is in a beautiful tone —We go every Sunday together to church. At Miss Lynch's was introduced to me Headly author of those letters from Hamilton County with quick glancing eye and hawk nose, you would like him a little[4] O Sullivan, too, whom I like and another pleasant man, unknown to fame![5] I am a[n] good deal interested in Miss Lynch. Winty Whitemore is in town and remembers you *with force*.[6] I hear you are "lovely" now Heaven help you!

ALS (MH: bMS Am 1221 [248]). *Addressed*: Miss C. Sturgis / Boston.
take with] take ⟨her⟩ with
It is] It ⟨a⟩ is
am a] am ⟨or⟩ a

1. Honora Shepherd, a convict in whom both Fuller and Georgiana Bruce took an interest, was pardoned by Governor Silas Wright. According to a correspondent in the *Tribune*, Shepherd was the child of a family of forgers. She had previously escaped from jail disguised as a man. Her pardon, which was instigated by a group that petitioned the governor, was bitterly condemned in the press (*New-York Daily Tribune*, 22 and 23 April 1845; *New York Herald*, 22 April 1845).

2. Ellen Sturgis Hooper, a poet and early friend of Fuller's, was Caroline's sister.

3. Sarah Ann Clarke, sister of James Freeman Clarke, was a painter. She accompanied Fuller on her trip to the West in 1843.

4. Joel Tyler Headley (1813–97) was a prolific writer of biographies, histories, and travel books. The "letters from Hamilton County" are unidentified; Headley wrote nothing with that title. Fuller reviewed his *Alps and the Rhine* (New York, 1845) and his very popular *Napoleon and His Marshals* (New York, 1846). Of the former she said, "He will be found well worth knowing if only for this singularity—he is never dull (in the English sense of the word) and therefore not likely to make [readers] so (in the American)." However, she took Headley severely to task for his praise of Napoleon: "A godless, reckless, daring Ambition is to our view the worst possible trait in the character of one appointed to play a chief part on the world's great stage" (*New-York Daily Tribune*, 24 December 1845, 1 May 1846, and 18 June 1846).

5. Probably John Louis O'Sullivan, editor of the *Democratic Review* and, since 1844, also of the *New York Morning News*.

6. Winty Whitemore was Elizabeth DeWindt Cranch's nephew (Cranch papers, MHi).

541.   To James Nathan

Saturday
19th April, 45

My beloved friend,

Your hand removes at last the veil from my eyes. It is then, indeed, myself who have caused all the ill. It is I who by flattering myself and letting[n] others flatter me that I must ever act nobly and nobler than others, have forgot that pure humility which is our only safeguard. I have let self-love, pride, and distrust creep upon me and mingle with my life blood. All unawares I have let experience corrode the virgin gold. I came from the battle field fancying my self a victor, and now in my arrogance have fallen beneath the just hopes of a kindred spirit, and grieved it and put this same darkness into its clear life

I need not say pardon "long since" hast thou pardoned. Nay! thou wilt bless our father for making thee the instrument of good to me, in that only religion which restores our innocence to us by making us weep for its beauty and implore a restoration through the divine original.

I will now kneel, and, laying thy dear hand upon my heart, implore that, if pride or suspicion should hide there again, the recollection of this day may rise up, and, with its sharp deep pulse, make them flutter their wings. And when I know they are there, indeed, indeed there is nothing she will not offer herself to endure to drive them out.

I have indeed always had a suspicion that I was not really good at all, and have longed for *a baptism*[n] *without* to wash off the dust of the world, *within, a deep rising of the waters* to purify them by motion. And yet while I wished, I feared it. Pain is very keen with me. I cannot help fearing it. Yet Oh[n] Father, against whose love as against the trust of man I have sinned, in this sane moment I submit and say, when and how much thou wilt— thou wilt proportion it to my strength to bear.

My beloved friend. I will not say forget these days; we cannot and we need not, but I think, receding in the distance the rough crags, with their serpent brood, will not misbecome the landscape. You will not feel that I am incapable of faith because I have not yet[n] shown it, nor misdoubt the light which shone on you through me, because it does not yet pervade me. Fain would I never again give you pain or disappointment, but you are noble enough to be willing to take me as I am. A higher will must govern and make my faults perhaps subservient to its purpose. Your trust in human nature will not be shaken; you have the vouchers in your own breast.

If I ever fancied you other than "severly true," I do not now. I have now taken of the kernel of your life and planted it in mine. We have now been embraced in the eternal goodness and truth, and a certainty, a reality has supersceded hope, and I trust fear, at all events that which has been, *a certainty*, must ever be.

You complain of being bodily sick, but I think you must be better now. Do not regret the "nightmare" or distrust the words, poor[n] blind messengers though they be from the true home; this time they found their way, and shed the light on all that came before. We *shall* now, I think, be "Gods good children," and I shall be like a child, otherways than in fancies and impulses and childish longings.

I too have been sick and though seeming cheerful these last three days; it was outward and wilful. The Spirit nestled not softly, saying All is well. I was *ueberspannt*;[1] the feeling of alienation was dreadfully unnatural to me.

Indeed I was alienated from *myself* how could it be borne? But coming home today with your letter, I could not forbear falling asleep though it was broad daylight. There was such repose in those convictions; it gave me the power of sleep at once, which has not really been before[n] since Sunday. I rested on thy heart, which is so good and noble, and which must surely find repose for itself, also, now its painful task is done. Yet tonight it shall be the last thought with me, to wish it, though by me it cannot be given. I have not been good and pure and sweet enough. I have no words wherewith to say farewell my brother, *Seligkeit*.[2]

Evening.

The afternoon has been of such tender sweetness; the little frequent showers so musical, and drawing from the earth and every leaf and bud fragrance, till the air seemed full of soul. The clouds were very thin, with a faint glow on the horizon. The great tree is far more glorious today. I have worshipped it much.— and very soon it will be all starred over with blossoms. The world may be wicked, but it is impossible on such a day not to rejoice that we have been born into it.

AL (MB: Ms. Am. 1451 [30–32]). Published in *Love-Letters*, pp. 50–55. *Addressed:* To / Mr James Nathan / 86 Cedar St.

and letting] and let ↑ ting ↓
a baptism] a ba⟨b⟩ptism
Yet Oh] Yet ⟨one⟩ Oh
not yet] not ↑ yet ↓
words, poor] words, ⟨b⟩poor
been before] been ↑ before ↓

1. *Überspannt:* overexcited, overstrained.
2. *Seligkeit:* bliss.

542. To James Nathan

Tuesday eveg 22d
April. [1845]

Your aid, dear friend, is all you ought to give and more than I would receive, knowing that the claims on[n] one placed as you have been, and with your heart, must be numberless and boundless, did I not take especial pleasure in receiving it *from you* in this matter.[1]

I have written to Boston for the rest, as there are a circle of young and rich persons whose purses were always open to my call and who are desirous I should appeal to them in the same way from this distant sphere, when I think best. But I shall do it sparingly and only hope that the same affinities will draw to me here[n] similar sponsors for my good desires. For at home I did not suffer that worst evil of narrow circumstances, inability to do any good in extreme cases; others being willing to do what was pointed out by me. I wish you would remind me to give you some particulars about this, as there is a sweet picture of generous sympathies which you would enjoy.

There are innumerable pleasures worthy your acceptance and which I often wish to give you of knowing the good and beautiful in books and men. I could bring you facts that would embellish all your mortal years,—but ah! still this daily grief *there is not time*. This very day have I been reading somewhat I long especially to impart, but it would take you a deep silent night hour to enjoy it— and will you have such an one to spare?

The little notice gave the glad certainty that you will remain a good part of the blissful May month. Last night, which was so beautiful, I thought sadly that I had not enjoyed this moon with you, and should not any, but you will, at least, see the May moon grow with us. I am willing to see her wane alone. If you are here some moonlight evening I shall bring you up here, and show you the loveliness I see from my window,— to me enough to repay my coming to New York. I keep your guitar by this window; if only I could play upon it!

Mit *Sehnsucht*, ja infinite, exquisite, tremulously lovely, as this light upon the waters! But *Wehmuth*?[2] ah! the word is faint to express the depth of shadow which yet the soul would not be without, for is it not the *over* shadowing of a heavenly birth?

I had this morning the fairest rose, which my little lover, Eddie Spring, sent me, the only child of his rose bush. I wanted to send it, to you as[n] the reply to your note, but his mother was by and I could not act out the perfidy of my heart, so it went home with me in the hot sun and withered so.

This day has been one rapture; nature had decked herself during the rain with a thousand new charms, the most tender and delicate. The trees are in their fragrant veil of blossoms, the green deepening, the leaves opening each moment, every flower awake. The winds and waves full of happy inspiration. You can have no idea of the beauty of the myrtle bed as I[n] pass to go down where we have been together[n] low on the rocks; it is now one heaven of blue flowers. I gathered two buds, one for you, and one for me. While I sat there; it seemed too bad that you were, probably, in the midst of dust, and[n] of what your generous soul rejects far more painfully than the body can its kindred earth. But soon, soon you will be where you can expand, and let your own life grow. When I sit alone on these rocks I shall, at least, think it is well with you or[n] *besser*! As you tell me of this uncongenial life, I feel it all, but long to lay a soft hand on your forehead, there between the eyebrows, where it makes you knit them so.

Say have not I the force to bless you from the distance? At evening you occupy me much. I know you are freer and often it seems that you are thinking of me. But *the morning* is the time I am most drawn towards you, often the image comes as the light first salutes my eyes, sometimes I have[n] a rush of feeling that seems like the passage of a spirit through me, and ought to flow to you like blessing. This is the most beautiful feeling I ever experienced; it is indeed divine, and too much for mortal force; there is no music for it; it can never, I fear me, be expressed. I have abjured dread, and yet with it comes dread lest it return no more. Like sunset it cannot be remembered. Farewell, dear friend, bless me, if you can.

P S.
Since finishing, I receive nearly forty dollars from Boston I send you a leaf of the note that you may see *my* daughters are as good as *yours*. My friend, Mrs Ward, gave me five dollars, that with yours is enough!

The moon has just risen, oh it is almost too beautiful. I hope you feel as happy as I do this moment; it is so happy when human beings are kind and do not jar with nature.

AL (MB: Ms. Am. 1451 [33–34]). Published in *Love-Letters*, pp. 55–59. *Addressed:* Mr James Nathan / 86 Cedar St.

claims on] claims ⟨of⟩ on
me here] me ↑ here ↓
it, to you as] it, ↑ to you ↓ ⟨in⟩ as
but as I] but ⟨we⟩ ↑ as I ↓
been together] been ↑ together ↓
dust, and] dust ⟨without⟩, and
you or] you ⟨a⟩or
I have] I ⟨feel⟩ have

1. Apparently Nathan contributed to the fund that Fuller was raising for Honora Shepherd.

2. *Sehnsucht:* longing, desire; *Wehmuth:* sadness.

543. To James Nathan

Thursday.
[24? April? 1845]

Yesterday I was able to be industrious, and to go to rest singing, if not with that sense of deep peace with which we would lie down in the bosom of Night, saying as our sufficient prayer "All is well" But today your letter, with its tone of sweet pure reproach, comes to touch the hidden springs of feeling

—Art thou indeed yet better, lovelier, truer than thou seemest to me? If so do not expect me to blame myself for the clouds. I shall be too happy to find a being rise beyond my expectations, one whom I must improve and expand to "understand." I shall have no time to blame myself.

Yet forgive if I have done amiss, forgive when I shall do amiss.

And *I too* "do not understand"!! From so many beautiful dwellings whose doors stood hospitably open, myself must turn away into the shivering muddy street, because they would not let me in in my true dress and manner—and now am I to repel *thee*? *O no!* it will not be so; *I shall understand yet*; have patience.

And yet, Oh dearest friend, indolent, cowardly that I am, I do wish that I had not begun to read the book, but only learnt the title page by heart and left a happy kiss upon the cover. How sweet it would have been just to walk on with thee through the winding ways, without hope, without doubt or fear, gathering the flowers of the new day or mosses from the old rocks for one another, with sometimes a mutual upward look to sun or star. I needed no future, only that there should be no precaution or limitation as to the future, nothing to check that infinite hope which is the only atmosphere for Spring. Those winding ways would have led us to the beach, and there we should have parted, and I would have watched the white sail, with unwearied eye and salutation, till it was a dark speck in the blue, and then I would have wept away a portion more of this earthly life, and wept myself to sleep when Absence and Duty would have taken me again[n] and placed me on the spot where I ought to awake, and all would have been past except a fair picture on the wall of my dwelling.

Now it is deeper, and we cannot get out of the labyrinth, nor my heart find what it craves, sweet content with thee. God grant that a pure high ministry may compensate for this loss which to me is unspeakable. I do so long for childish rest and play, instead of all the depths which never will go deep enough; can it not be again? You promised the lighter chords should yet again vibrate.

You speak of the "cataract;" when I get *down here*, I do always hear its plunge and almost see its white foam. But I know little about the mystery of life, and far less in myself than in others. I inclose you two little poems addressed to me which seem to point at what you have in mind; do they not?[n] yet the echo from them is not homefelt. Your voice awakens a longer echo through the subterranean chambers, yet not long enough to teach me where to go. The one signed S. was given me last autumn, the other by my brother W. E. Channing and like that I partly repeated from my brother Richard pleased me as it is always pleasing when the common intercourse of daily life does not destroy, but enhance, poetic interest.[1]

And *you* I must cause to "stoop"; that is uncongenial, indeed, nor could we have expected it. But truth,— truth we have resolved always to accept I await the letter finding myself always your friend

Late eveg I hear tonight of a generous action which gives me so much pleasure I wish to say to you that I am happy; will you remind me to tell you about it when we meet.

From W. E. C. to Margaret

> I mark beneath thy life the virtue shine
> That deep within the star's eye opes its day;
> I clutch those gorgeous thoughts thou throwst away
> From the profound unfathomable mine,
> And with them this mean common hour do twine
> As glassy waters o'er the dry beach play,
> And I were rich as night, them to combine
> With my poor store, and warm me with thy ray.
> From the fixed answer of those dateless eyes
> I catch bold hints of spirit's mystery[n]

As to what's past, and hungry prophecies
Of deeds today and things which are to be;
    Of lofty life that with the eagle flies,
And lowly love that clasps humanity

S. to Margaret—1844.

Each sat alone, girt round with plastered[n] walls
Of little rooms; how different from halls
Which we should build, possessed we the delight
To bring the treasures of our thoughts to sight.
But our thoughts were not these; they soared away,
I know not whither thine, but if I may,
Mine will I tell thee

Thou art the Wind, the Wanderer of the Air,
The Searcher of the Earth, and every where
Art unappalled; the dizziest heights are thine,
Thy force is felt across the foaming brine;
Unbaffled thou dost dash aside the wave;
Thou art not awe-struck by the loneliest cave
Whose hollow sides reverberate thy voice;—
With eager swiftness wilt thou now rejoice,
To emulate the cataract's uproar loud,
Then dancest on into the city's crowd,
Who stand astonished at thy wayward play,
And seek a shelter where they sought the day.
But when at length thou sinkst to gentleness
Thou art an angel's whisper sent to bless,
And while thou art caressing the fair child,
He smiles to meet thy touch so soft and mild.
By thee the flames are fanned unto their height
The air is purified by thy swift flight;
Thou mournest round the grave unvisited,
To hollow ruins all thy sighs are paid;
The lonely harp that hangs upon the wall,
Attuned by thee, shall not neglected fall,
But who shall e'er attune thy symphony
Thou art a Voice, but not a Melody.
Where is thy home?

The writer of this is a person all intellect and passion, no loveliness of
character; impetuous, without tender symphathy; hard and secret,

when not strongly moved, yet keenly sensitive to a wound from others, noble in the absence of little faults; ignoble in want of confiding sweetness. Such a picture do I draw; the subject would, probably, no more accept it as a genuine portrait than I do this of me.

AL (MB: Ms. Am. 1451 [14–16]). Published in *Love-Letters*, pp. 25–31. *Addressed:* To / Mr James Nathan / 86 Cedar St.

Dated by the contents and tone. Although Fuller still feels the shock of the confrontation of the week of 13–19 April, her language is more moderate. The letter might have been written on 17 April than the 24th, but the later date better fits the tone.

me again] me ⟨away⟩ ↑ again ↓

you have in mind; do they not?] you ⟨do,⟩ ↑ have in mind; do they not? ↓

mystery] *Here Fuller marked the sheet as a reference for this comment:* Is not this what causes the cataract? And *need* the cataract be dangerous either as action or passion, if its rock walls stand but firm?

with plastered] with ⟨little⟩ plastered

1. With slight changes, these lines appear in the "Sonnets" section of Channing's *Poems* (Boston, 1843), p. 148. The poem signed "S" was probably written by Sam Ward.

544. To James Nathan

Friday evening
[25? April? 1845]

I feel the need of writing just to say good evening, dear friend, good night,— a good day I cannot suppose you have had. But that *was* a good day along the river side. I have felt so contented since, scarcely one little wish yet. When there has been time a cloud of thoughts have floated over, thoughts suggested by the inspirations of your mind, but it was not a dark cloud; but one silvery white full and volumed, such as we see in the days of early June upon a bright blue sky. But there has been little solitary time: I have with me the two girls, Georgiana and Honora; they are preparing for their pilgrimage in a happy spirit. I brought Honora out with me today and had a full talk as we were walking. The love and trust shown her by many seem to have given a new development to her mental history. Her eyes are full of a good young herzlich look. I think she is *naturally artful*, in the sense of having a great deal of tact, but that it may all be turned to good. They leave me tomorrow. The Springs are again prevented from going to Staten Island, and will be, I think, be prevented[n] for several Sundays, probably till after I lose you: this is a relief to me. Even when I do not see you I had rather not go out elsewhere, especially to ride. But I hope I shall

see you next Sunday. We will worship by impromptu symbols till the religion is framed for all humanity.[n] The beauty grows around us daily
the trees now are all in blossom and some of the vines; there is a *Crown
Imperial* just in perfection to which I paid *my*[n] evening worship by the
light of the fire which reached to us, and there are flashes of lightning
too. But I do not like the lightning so well as once, having been in too
great danger. Yet just now a noble flash falls upon my paper, it ought
to have noble thoughts to illume instead of these little nothings but indeed tonight I write only to say thou dear dear friend and we must
meet soon.

AL (MB: Ms. Am. 1451 [4]). Published in *Love-Letters*, pp. 13–15.
Dated by the reference to Bruce and Shepherd, who left late in the spring for Illinois.
think, be prevented] think, ↑ be prevented ↓
We will worship by impromptu symbols till the religion is framed for all humanity.]
↑ We will worship by impromptu symbols till the religion is framed for all humanity. ↓
paid *my*] paid ⟨the⟩ *my*

545.   To James Nathan

Sunday evening 27th April [1845]
My beloved friend, for from its short and dissatisfying flights my
mind returns to rest on the broad certainty that such you really are.
The mists have given place to a lovely shower which refreshes the trees,
while it makes the blossoms fall. I have a fire in my own room, and the
evening light falls on the pictures, gifts of a most cherished hand,
which have been my companions ever since my earthly father died. I
feel quite happy now; it seems domestic in the stillness, and my heavenly father it is that makes the home. He, I feel, will care for me. He
will make me to bear the want of the soft mother's arms, and father's
sheltering breast, and the music of love's heart beat tuned to perfect
melody He will help me not to misjudge my fellow men, and to bear the
weight of spirit's mystery, though it[n] must turn me pale.

> "The beautiful are never desolate;
> For *some one* alway loves them, God or Man.
> If man forsakes God himself takes them."[1]

And I am, surely, one of the beautiful so far that the soul is full[n] of
beauty.

This day has been like life as it is, in the blossoming sweetness of outward nature, and the equally sweet promises of the eye,[n] the brutal attacks of wicked men, and the shrewd comments of worldly ones, no less than the Tantalus cup filled for one another by two who really meet, — if not enough. The life that will be is the fruit of this worm-assailed flower.[n]

Fate will not grant both at once,[n] it seems, the joys of absence and of presence. The day we passed together (Wednesday)[n] I enjoyed thoroughly presence, except the hour we spent, I know not why, in mining in one another's hearts. Perhaps we found treasure by doing so, and yet the rest of the day had been passed merely in culling what grows on the surface of the earth, and *that* is so entirely sweet! Yet that day[n] ended in satisfaction, too, and I drew nearer to you. I did not wish to speak of it today, but never have I felt anything like as near as that night after writing the note, which you so clearly saw was but an evasion. What I felt that night was worth our knowing one another for it was beautiful and full, indeed. But these times of pure soul communion are almost too much for my strength. All is so rapid; in real intercourse, such as that of the day we rode, life proceeds with a gentle tranquil step, and her fresh green garland is better than the halo, till one be to that crown of light *gewachsen*.[2]

My friend, I send you a book with which more than any except Wilhelm Meister, I have sympathized.[3] These two books express something of the peculiar life of this age, of which we are part. I know not what it is; on us lies the weight of giving it to the light. Tennyson knows some things about it, but none like this man. Keep it by you a week or two; there is much that might tire, but your eye may fall on passages that go deep and which you may understand as well as I or better. The person, who called me *unnatural,* or rather my way of viewing things so, said that if I had the experience of passionate life, it would alter my view. Such an experience has this Festus, and you, too, I suppose; perhaps that is what you mean by unlikeness in our experiences. We parted in the lane and went our opposite ways, and I thought my brother wishes to make his existence more poetic. I need mine should be more deeply real; must we go opposite ways in the same road? I send the little gift, but you will not wear it for a daily companion;[n] yours to me is also something that I shall lay aside, to look at only now and then, but it is a thing exquisitely fair and pure and mine to you is a memento of that truly human heart which first[n] turned mine to you, for I saw you had a heart for all mankind. Just so when you told me you had carried so many poor women across the mire, I was glad you had carried me.

In return let me say one thing— the sadness that lingers in memory of that period, when your spirit-life took its painful birth is almost gone. These are the last bitter drops which I drink with you.

I cannot bear to write any more except God bless you and protect me!

Tuesday evening this morning brought on its glittering wings your letter written at the same time with mine *(I expected to receive it this morning)* As always you express yourself with more simple force than I can, but the mood was identical in both of us when writing.[n] I had *your* flower by me; well did I understand when you likened yourself to that flower. The passage in yours beginning "O for wings" receive back in echo, for even in words I said it to myself also. Now I will not send you "Festus"; there is no time for books, and no poem like the poem we can make for ourselves. This day has been to me one of rapturous joy; the earth has decked herself in such beauty as if for the fairest of festivals; it is impossible not to meet her, it is incredible the dawning of sweetness since yesterday. Many deep things have also dawned in my thought which are yours but tonight they cannot be expressed, for I feel subdued My head is heavy; let me lean it on your shoulder, and you divine these deep things A sweet Goodnight.

AL (MB: Ms. Am. 1451 [35–36]). Published in *Love-Letters*, pp. 59–64.

though it] though⟨t⟩ it

is full] is ⟨fill⟩ full

nature, and the equally sweet promises of the eye,] nature, ↑ and the equally sweet promises of the eye, ↓

The life that will be is the fruit of this worm-assailed flower.] ↑ The life that will be is the fruit of this worm-assailed flower. ↓

both at once,] both ↑ at once ↓ ,

together (Wednesday)] together ↑ (Wednesday) ↓

that day] that ↑ day ↓

it for a daily companion;] it ↑ for a daily companion ↓ ;

first] *Here Fuller marked the page and commented on a separate sheet:* first turned here is not the exact truth, and yet it seemed so, while writing

us when writing.] us. ↑ when writing ↓

1. Slightly misquoted from *Festus*, p. 48.

2. *Gewachsen:* form of *wachsen,* to develop, to grow into.

3. Fuller was fond of both of Goethe's *Wilhelm Meister* novels. The book she mentions here is *Festus.*

546. To James Nathan

May day. [1845]

This bleak morning is like those by which the hopes[n] of the children in my native state, (of the rock-bound coast and terrible climate) are almost always disappointed. The world is full of blossoms, but they are not happy in this cold air. I meant to have sent you some of the fairest, but now will not; let every thing be alike in so bleak a day; you too will pass it in the midst of car-men.

After you went away the other night, I felt unusually grieved not to have shown my soul more. I felt so deeply all *you* felt about this mistuned life, and longed to express my sympathy in a thousand sweet ways, but the things that come to me to do are so childish. I have not courage, being grown up, and we sometimes meeting with the forms of the world. But the thoughts I had, with the swell of their religion, kept me awake all night, and thus I was unfit to meet a very fatiguing day, and last night, tired and with headach, could not write. Thus it so often is; feeling keeps from doing what would show it. The Editor is gone away till Sunday and the evenings are open to music; will you not come tomorrow evening you know there was to be one with the guitar and there may not be such another free opportunity Farewell mein liebste — shall I not find a letter I want one.

AL (MB: Ms. Am. 1451 [37]). Published in *Love-Letters*, pp. 64–65. *Addressed:* Mr Nathan / 86 Cedar St.

the hopes] the ⟨p⟩ hopes

547. To James Nathan

Friday evening.
[2? May? 1845]

You come not, dear friend. The day was full of golden sunlight, and kind words and deeds as well, for the thought of you stood at the end— but you come not. My head has ached ever since you were here, and needed you to take away its pain— but you come not. You said once I was too sensitive and that such little disappointments would affect me; it is, indeed, the absence of the light, but would never affect me any other way, where I am sure of love as I am of yours, but that absence is sad. The shadows and damps of evening settle down upon me as they do upon the earth, for where is the torch that was to cheer the indoor retirement? You come not— and now I realize that soon will be the time, when evening will come always, but you will come no more.

We shall meet in soul; but the living eye of love; that is in itself almost a soul, and that will beam no more.

O Heaven, O God, or by whatsoever name I may appeal; surely, surely O All Causing thou must be the All Sustaining *All-fulfilling* too. I, from thee sprang, do not feel force to bear so much as one of these deep impulses— *in vain!* Nor is it enough that the heavenly magic of its touch throws open all the treasure chambers of the Universe, if these enchanted doors must close again.

My little rose-tree casts its shadow on the paper. They bade me *cut it down to make it blossom,* and so have I done, though with a reluctant hand. So is it on this earth; but not so will it always be; the soul protests against it and sometime, somewhere claims its own *in full.*

Wilt thou search out such mysteries in the solitude of thy cave? Wilt thou prepare for men an image fair and grand enough of *hope!* Give that to men at large, but to me send some little talisman that may be worn next the secret heart. And let it have a diamond point that may pierce when any throb swells too far to keep time with the divine frame of things. We would not, however, stifle one natural note, only tune all sweet.

My head aches still and I must lean it on the paper as I write, so the writing goes all amiss. Ah I really needed you tonight and you could not come yet you are not away from me;— are you?

I long to hear whether the most wearisome part of your winding up is not now over. May [day] morning, after thinking it was unfit to send the flowers; I changed my mind for[n] it seemed perhaps they might not be uncongenial in the evening after the fret and dust of the day were over. Farewell.

AL (MB: Ms. Am. 1451 [38]). Published in *Love-Letters,* pp. 65–67. *Addressed:* Mr James Nathan / N. Y.—

Dated by the contents, which place the letter early in May.
flowers; I changed my mind for] flowers; ↑ I changed my mind for ↓

548. To James Nathan

Sunday afternoon.
[4? May? 1845]

The true lovely time is come at last. The leaves and grasses are out, so that the wind can make soft music as it sweeps along instead of the rattling and sobbing of winter. A dear little shower is refreshing the trees and they grow greener and fairer every moment in gratitude. (I write so badly because the wind shakes my paper too as well as the other leaves, but I cant bear to shut the window.)

You must use your moderation about our interviews, and as you know best. I like best to rely entirely upon you, yet keep time as much as possible with the enchanting calls of outward nature. It is nothing to be together in the parlor or in the street, and we are not enough so among the green things Today the lilacs are all in blossom, and the air is full of a perfume which causes extasy.

I hear you with awe assert the power over me and feel it to be true. It causes awe, but not dread, such as I felt sometime since at the approach of this mysterious power, for I feel deep confidence in my friend and know that he will lead me on in a spirit of holy love, and that all I may learn of nature and the soul will be legitimate. The destiny of each human being is no doubt great and peculiar, however obscure its rudiments to our present sight, but there are also[n] in every age *a few* in whose lot the meaning of that age is concentrated. I feel that I am one of those persons in my age and sex. I feel *chosen among women.*[1] I have deep mystic feelings in myself and intimations from elsewhere. I could not, if I would, put into words these spirit-facts, indeed they are but swelling germs as yet, and all I do for them is to try to[n] do nothing that might blight them. Yet as you say you need to forget *your*[n] call, so have I need of escaping from this overpowering sense. But when forced back upon myself as now, though the first turnings of the key were painful, yet the inner door makes rapturous music too upon its golden hinge. What it hides you perhaps know, as you read me so deeply; indeed, some things you say seem as if you did. Yet *do not*, unless you *must*. You look at things so without their veils, yet that seems noble and antique to me. I do it when you hold me by the hand, yet when I feel[n] how you are thinking, I sometimes inly say Psyche was but a mortal woman, yet as the bride of Love, she became a daughter of the Gods too.[2] But had she learned in any other way this secret of herself, all had been lost, the plant and flower and fruit.

But it is impossible to say these things at least for me. They are myself, but not clearly defined to myself. With you, all seems to assume such palpable reality, though you do not forget its inner sense either. I love to hear you read off the secret, and yet you sometimes make me tremble too.

I confide in you, as this bird now warbling without confides in me. You will understand my song, but you will not translate it into language too human. I wish,[n] I long to be human, but divinely human. Let the soul invest every act of its abode with somewhat of its own lightness and subtlety. Are you my guardian to domesticate me in the body, and attach it more firmly to the earth. Long it seemed that it was only my destiny to say a few words to my youth's companions and then depart. I hang lightly as an air plant. Am I to be rooted on earth, oh choose for me a good soil and a sunny place, that I may be a green shelter to the weary and bear fruit enough to pay for staying.

A revoir à dieu

AL (MB: Ms. Am. 1451 [9]). Published in *Love-Letters*, pp. 18−21; Miller, pp. 203−4; and Chevigny, pp. 136−37.

Dated by the references to the advanced spring vegetation. On 17 and 19 April Fuller says the trees are just beginning to leaf out, so this letter was not written on the following Sunday, 20 April. On 22 April she mentions the flowers that are in full bloom, but this letter cannot have been written on 27 April because one to Nathan exists for that date. On Tuesday 29 April she again mentions the beauty of spring. May 4 is thus the only available Sunday that fits the description of trees, flowers, and lilacs.

are also] are ↑ also ↓
to try to] to try ↑ to ↓
forget *your*] forget ⟨my⟩ *your*
I feel] I ⟨think⟩ feel
I wish,] ⟨?⟩I wish,

1. An echo of the greeting given to Mary: "blessed art thou among women" (Luke 1:28, 42).

2. After incurring the wrath of Venus and suffering the misfortune of her own curiosity, Psyche weds Cupid and drinks a draft of immortality that Jupiter gives her (*The Golden Ass, Being the Metamorphoses of Lucius Apuleius*, trans. William Adlington [London, 1924], pp. 185−285).

549. To James Nathan

Wednesday eveg 7th. [May 1845]

Mein liebste do not reproach yourself as the cause of what I suffered yesterday for the fault was with my own imprudence. I knew I was not so well able to stand or walk as usual, but there was no good place to sit still and I was so bent on hearing you out I could not bear to say this. Indeed, I do not mind the pain, except that it has put me back a little; and I wish much I were strong that I might be a fit companion for you and not weigh upon your motions. Coming home, I lay down in the dark room, and the dark was what I wanted. Shutting out all outward objects the thoughts seemed to grow upon me and clothe themselves in forms and colors so glorious. Much, much appeared before the closed eyes. Mein liebste, you tell me to rest, but how can I rest when you rouse in me so many thoughts and feelings? What good does it do for you to stay away, when, absent or present, every hour you grow upon me and the root strikes to my inmost life. There is far more repose in being with you when your look fills my eye, and your voice my ear than in trying to keep still, for then these endless thoughts rush upon me. And then comes, too, that tormenting sense, of only a few days more shall we be together, and how can I rest, though indeed I am desirous to do as you desire. It was hard for me to have you pass from the door unseen by me. I would have given much to call you to me for one cheering moment, but that the customs of this strange world did not permit, and I was unable to rise and go to you. It is impossible now for me to express the many thoughts born in my mind from yours, but time and unison will perhaps perfect them and enable me to do it; if not, it is no matter as they are all yours and must at any rate bloom in your garden, perhaps far larger and fairer. Yet the birds from your own bosom should return perfected in beauty and song to their nest. I send you within a little poem; it is one of those I wrote last summer when living quite alone in a country house, near a thick wood where I passed many sweet hours. It seems to me a prelude to this time. How much in the past so seems, were but one full strain permitted O my God! My friend, unspeakably affecting to me was your appeal to the angels. I also bow the head to their commands, to their prohibitions. But that is only o[n] one side; on the other, life seems so ful[l] so creative; every hour an infinite promise, — I cannot keep in mind prohibitions or barriers or fates. You said, write with out concentration, and surely I have done so, written I know not what, for the sense of all that has flowed through my mind confuses it, and makes my head ache again. But take it gently, and take me near your heart. I must stop now and make one of these attempts *to rest.*

I will be out at quarter past ten will walk towards Bowling Green and then back again.

AL (MB: Ms. Am. 1451 [40]). Published in *Love-Letters*, pp. 69–73. *Addressed:* Mr James Nathan / 86 Cedar St.

550. To James Nathan

Friday evening, May 9th. [1845]

Dearest,

I must begin by "babbling of green fields".[1] Though it be true as you say that this region of beautiful symbols is not the highest. I do find such relief in the soft trance, the still rapture they can give. I live in their life and am nourished by it, as the infant from the mother's breast. Do you not cease to love this region too. You shall upbear me to the stars, when your energies overflow, and I feel sure that you will not find me incompetent to receive in the region of Ideas. But let me sometimes hold you by the hand to linger with me here, and listen while the grass grows; it does me so much good, the soft warm life close to the earth. Perhaps it is that I was not enough a child at the right time, and now am too childish, but will you not have patience with that?

The tulips are out now and the crimson ones seem to me like you. They fill gloriously with the sunlight, and the petals glow like gems, while the black stamens in the cup of the flower look so rich and mystical. I have gathered two and put them in my vase, but the perfume is almost overpowering. There are also two golden ones that have rooted themselves on the edge of a grassy bank. I do not know how they could get there; it was a strange elopement from the regular flower bed, but the effect is beautiful of flowers so *vornehm*,[2] willing to be wild.

I have been sitting in the twilight in the spot where we have been several times: always[n] something unpleasant occurred when we were there, but it has all endeared us to one another and ennobled the relation. And now a shrub has starred itself all over with white flowers and bends over the place. The young moon lent[n] her pure crescent above the rocks, my parapet behind; the waves stole in vibrating the silence with insidious murmurs. Spülen!—[3] how expressive is the German word, we have none like it. In this enchanting solitude, I thought of thee, of thy great thoughts. I have well understood all that has been told me— do not hesitate to unfold the whole, only, indeed, in the musical order, so as to feel satisfied. *I* feel sure of being equal to it; indeed, it seems as if there had been a gradual and steady preparation in me to hear it all. It will not be in vain that we have met; whatever be your destiny whether you be born to give form to these ideas, or are only the harbinger, the father of him who is to come, that they have been uttered on earth and found their due vibration predicts that their fulfilment is near. Man shall stand upon the earth as Man, and no more content himself with specific titles and partial claims.

My dearest, I feel a deep desire to utter myself, to answer the inspirations of your life from my inmost soul, but I cannot. The easy powers, the superficial eloquence all fail me here. The little wings on my feet upbear me in the world but they are not strong enough for here. You would have to take me to heart and read my silence, but I believe you will. Since I began to write I grow more powerless, whether that you are thinking of me now or from[n] the sense of your thoughts that have been poured upon me I do not know this time. But often I feel that you are thinking of me and it takes away all power of thought or motion. You say it will not always be so, that by and by it will stimulate me to be more myself; this may be; there is at present so much for me to assimilate and absorb. Could I indeed but let it rest in me till I grow to the stature of what I feel. You know how it will be; since you have the secret of this vital energy; you must know how it works in all forms of life, especially in mine, with which you are now in conjunction. I feel the most tender reliance, and also faith that I shall never be a trouble to you. I observe that it is with you, as it has been with me in many cases. You attract beings so much that after a while it is too much for their good or your pleasure. Then comes the painful retrograde motion. But I feel confident that my angel will not let it be so with me. I have never been able to go a step where you did not take me; now, when I want you most, I feel that I cannot seek you,[n] unless you do me. So not even by a thought shall I be permitted to follow you, where I cannot accompany. The Pyrus Japonica, and some[n] other vines, fall at first, if they lose their support, but they do not perish; they have strength to raise themselves and become shrubs, though they are not so beautiful so.

Now there is more, and far better to be said, but again I cannot. Yet it is delightful to know that you will read all that is left unsaid. Then why say any thing?— but it is sweet to express all one can.[n]

Michel Angelo whenever he paints a great form full of soul, paints young cherubs near, so powerful radiant and gentle; these are the thoughts of that soul at that moment. May such attend you now, my friend! and in love good night.

do not come into Wall St for me Sunday morning till 20 minutes past 10 and then I will come so soon as I can, but sometimes they *will* keep me, talking.

If it rains Sunday morng I suppose I shall go to church as then I could not see you this proposed way. But I do hope for sunshine

AL (MB: Ms. Am. 1451 [43–44]). Published in *Love-Letters,* pp. 76–80; published in part in Chevigny, pp. 137–39. *Addressed:* Mr James Nathan / 86 Cedar St.

times: always] times: ⟨there⟩ always
moon lent] moon ⟨Gr⟩ lent
me now or from] me ↑ now ↓ or ↑ from ↓
cannot seek you,] cannot, ↑ seek you ↓
and some] and ↑ some ↓
one can.] one ⟨again⟩ ↑ can. ↓

1. *Henry V,* II.iii.16.
2. *Vornehm:* noble, eminent.
3. *Spülen:* to wash against.

551.   To James Nathan

Thursday afternoon.
[15? May 1845]

I will not this time wait till the dark night before I open my thoughts to the loved soul who has brought me so much sunlight. Thou hast brought me so much and I would gladly make return. But I know you ask nothing of your moon except a pure reflection and[n] in a serene sky. When I listen to your many perplexities I long for the privilege of "wise counsel in cumber," but it comes not. Yet I have— have I not? power to soothe *for the moment* by listening understanding, loving, and you have force and honor and aspiration to find your way out of them all— in time.

You have force; and take with you the sense that I am thus deeply in your debt. The sense that has always been mine that I should not be restless sad or weary with one who combined force with tenderness and delicacy has become certainty. This is much; it is an assurance, also a promise. Yes there *is* one who understands, and when we are separated and I can no longer tell the impulse or the want of the moment; still I will not forget that there *has been* one.

But I feel that you begin to go, that you are much taken from me already by your plagues and your preparations.

I have been very ill; last night the pain in my neck became so violent that I could not lie still and passed a night suffering and sleepless. There were in the house no remedies and none to apply them. I went crying into town this morning; my nerves all ajar and the pain worse than ever; it was a sort of tic douloureux. I brought out a very strong remedy, and since applying it, have been asleep. Now waking almost free from pain earth, too, seems almost as good as heaven. Still, it hurts me to lean down my head and write. I must look rather out of the window on the soft shadowy landscape which stills me. Put me in mind then when we meet to say two or three little things I had meant to write and lebewohl—

O how dull reads this letter, burn it "take the heart from out the breast"[1] read that.

Let me say in reply to your last that you had better leave my letters. You will not find it of any use to take them with you. They have been like manna, possible to use for food in their day, but they are not immortal like their source. Let them perish! let me burn them; keep my image in the soul, without such aids and[n] it will be more livingly true and avail you more.

AL (MB: Ms. Am. 1451 [42]). Published in *Love-Letters*, pp. 73–75. *Addressed:* Mr James Nathan / 86 Cedar St.

reflection and] reflection ⟨?⟩ and
aids and] aids ↑ and ↓

1. From Tennyson's "Adeline": "Thy rose-lips and full blue eyes / Take the heart from out my breast" (*Poems of Tennyson* [London, 1936], p. 30).

552. To James Nathan

Friday evening.
[16? May 1845]

I have been quite unwell, so that I could not go to town today, but hope to tomorrow. Yesterday I wrote some lines, but think they will not come with this; lest they be morbid or languid. It were best to write only when well to my friend who is well. Hoping news of you in the morning no more tonight, for the mood is not brighter than the skies without. May yours be more so; and daylight be seen amid all your perplexities is the last thought!

Saturday morng

I remain here a little while, twenty minutes, perhaps, cannot you send a note to tell me, whether you still expect to go early in the week. I thought you would write to me this morng, you cannot be less able just now than I.

AL (MB: Ms. Am. 1451 [45]). Published in *Love-Letters*, pp. 80–81. *Addressed:* Mr Nathan / read this first.

Dated by her reference to Nathan's approaching departure.

553. To James Nathan

Monday evening, 19th May. [1845]

Dearest friend, for such I cannot choose but have thee. Oh it was a waste of this heavenly day to walk upon that terrace away from the gentle growing things and talk about those barriers that keep us apart. Better to forget them! better be blest in the affinities while we may!

And then you have so much more energy and spirit for the fight! I must try not to throw down the poor little silk glove again in defiance of the steel gauntlet. And you, Oh set up no mental limits against me: *do not,* I pray.

Is it not hard on my side? You can think what thoughts of conquest you will, and I cannot disprove them to you. On the other side you must be as the stone, if I give way to feelings of love and reliance, and you have your mysterious reasons against me there. You talk to me with such cold wisdom, sometimes, I do not know the brother of my soul, to whom I had but just flown. Next time we must go to Hoboken; it is not so confined there. You must tell me things, and I will forget myself; that is always the best way. I look up the free and noble river. I feel myself associated with you in the new religion, and that suits me, but today you put me in the dust, and a hundred miles from you, too.

This afternoon, though, a singular change took place in my feelings. I am curious to know whether induced by you, or rising in myself, and shall ask you, so soon as we meet.

There has been the most glorious thunder shower. I hope you have enjoyed it. Now the moon is shining queenly. I must be with you one more moonlight evening. She seems to bless so purely. I feel all fears and piques melt as I look upon her. Yet through pain, through pain, sweet Queen, must we come to where thy pale Mother's smile calls. As says Novalis

> No angel can ascend to heaven
> till the whole heart has fallen
> to the earth in ashes.

Might these be the right lines. I cannot remember what they are. Come tomorrow morng without fail.

AL (MB: Ms. Am. 1451 [46]). Published in *Love-Letters,* pp. 81–83. *Addressed:* Mr James Nathan / 86 Cedar St.

554.   To Ralph Waldo Emerson

N. Y. May 22d.45.

Dear Waldo,

Thirteen copies of Summer on the Lakes were sent to your address in Boston, five for you, four for Caroline, four to be sent to Sarah Clarke through James, if you will take the trouble

Charles Newcomb has been here and we have had a good meeting[1]
Your Mrs Black has been to see me, and I liked her pretty well, consid-
ering she claims to belong to the sacred bard.[2]

Did you go to the Wachusett? I have not yet seen Elizh[3]

Your friend

MARGARET.

ALS (MH: bMS Am 1280 [2377]). Published in part in Higginson, *MFO*, p. 199. *Addressed:* To / R. W. Emerson / Concord / Mass. *Endorsed:* Margaret Fuller / May 1845.

1. Charles King Newcomb of Providence had lived at Brook Farm and written an essay for the *Dial*.

2. On 10 March 1842 Emerson described Mrs. Rebecca Black to Fuller: "[She] would
have been more admirable to me several years ago, but now, as soon as I found she was
serene and self sufficing, I propounded to her the cases of those high unhappy persons
whom we so often meet & cannot assist; and found instantly it availed nothing; the spiritual life did not as it ought convert itself at the first need into the intellectual" (Rusk, *Letters of RWE*, 3:29).

3. Elizabeth Sherman Hoar of Concord, Fuller's close friend, had been engaged to
Charles Emerson at his death in 1836.

555. To Sophia and Nathaniel Hawthorne

N.Y. 22nd May [1845] eveg

Dear Sophia and Mr Hawthorne,

I received your letter and read it with attention, then laid it aside and
thought I would not reply, for so much had been said and written
about my pamphlet, that I was weary of it and had turned to other
things. When my interest revives, I shall, probably, make reply, but I
hope viva voce.

Yes! I hope to see you once more at the dear old house, with the
green fields and lazy river and have, perhaps, sweet hours [   ] of
last summer [   ] [i]f things work well, I hope to come. Una alone
will be changed, yet still I think the same.[1] Farewell, dear friends, now,
for this is only meant as a hasty sign of affection from

M.

ALS (NN-B). Published in Rose Hawthorne Lathrop, *Memories of Hawthorne* (Boston
and New York, 1898), p. 189. *Addressed:* Mr & Mrs Hawthorne, / Concord, Mass.

1. The Hawthornes' daughter Una, with whom Fuller was much taken on her visit to
Concord in the summer of 1844.

556. To James Nathan

Friday evening, May 23d [1845]

dear friend, I do not, just now, find any thing to write; the fact of an approaching separation, presses on my mind, and makes me unable to make the best use of the hours that remain.

I will therefore borrow from the past. Many little things have made me feel as if there had been a gradual and divinely moved preparation for our meeting. Today I took out of the portfolio some leaves written last autumn among the mountains and found there these lines which will impress you from their consonance, in some respects, with what you have since uttered to me. Many such things I write down; they seem dictated to me, and are not understood fully at the time. They are of the things which are received mystically long before they are appreciated intellectually.

Perhaps you had better destroy them, not now, for you will hardly be at leisure for them yet, but sometime when you feel ready, as they are so intimately personal.

I wish you would ask me to explain the difference the Greeks made between the moon as Hecate and as Diana, and the allusions to the girdle of Apollo, and at the conclusion to Tantalus; there are beautiful things in the Greek mythology which you will appreciate.

I feel it is true what you say that in the new and greater religion we shall rise above the need of this mythology, for all which they intimated in poetry we must realize in life, but as yet I cling to these beautiful forms as I do to the green and flowery earth, and again will say, linger with me here awhile.[1]

Our friend, here, asks anxiously *whether you are gone yet?*[2] She expresses a great desire to hear you play on your guitar once more, and I am glad you left it; we will pass an hour together so. She is really quite content about us now.

I am not well. You cannot bend your mind on me now. I know it is not because you love me less but because there are necessarily so many things, at present, to distract, but I feel it; the strength that was only given is gone. Or rather it was not given only lent, but you would have given it if you could, I know.

Later

I have copied out the poem and hope there are no words miswrit, but cannot read it over, do not smile at all, liebste, I am a little afraid of your smiles, and it is only in the deepest recess of our mutual life I could have shown it you, for to me it is prophecy

Among the mountains, October 1845.

Afternoon in the dell where was a broken fall and many-voiced
With evergreens and red and golden trees,
At varying elevations grouped around,
   Its basin hid and cool and circular,
On which the leaves rested as dreamily
   As if the stream could never wake again;
The mountains towered around, purple and rose,
The Sun, still climbing, vainly sought to peer
   Into that still recess.
     My soul sank there
A prayer that Intellect with its broad light
   Will ne'er reveal, nor even clearly know
But Nature holds it to her secret heart.

Evening, moonlight.

       To the Face seen in the Moon.
   Oft, from the shadow of my earthly sphere,
I looked to thee, Orb of pale pearly light,
   To loose the weariness of doubt and fear
In thy soft Mother's smile so pensive bright.
   Thou seemedst far and safe and chastely living,
Grace-full and thought-full, loving, beauty giving;
   But, if I steadfast gaze upon thy face,
   A human secret, like our own, I trace.
For, through the woman's smile looks the male eye
   So mildly, steadfastly, but mournfully,
He holds the *bush* to point as to his cave
   Teaching anew the truth so bright, so grave.
"Escape not from the riddle of the Earth,
Through mortal pangs to win immortal birth,
   Both man and woman from the natural womb
Must slowly win the secrets of the tomb
   And then, together rising, fragrant, clear,
The worthy Angel of a better sphere.
   Diana's beauty shows what Hecate wrought,
Apollo's lustre rays the Zodiac thought
   In Leo regal, as in Virgo pure,
As Scorpio secret, as the Archer sure.

In unpolluted beauty mutual shine
Earth, Moon, and Sun, the Human Thought Divine.
For Earth is purged by tameless central fire,
   And Moon in Man has told her hid desire,
   And Time has found himself eternal Sire,
   And the Sun sings All on his ray-strung lyre."

   Steady bear me on
   Counting life's pulses all alone
Till all is felt and known and done.
   Thus far have I conquered Fate
   I have learned to wait.
Nor in these early days snatch at the fruits of late.
   The man from the Moon
Looks not for an instant noon,
But from its secret heart
   Slow evolves the Art
Of that full consummation needed part.
   For thee, my Apollo.
     The girdle I weave,
   From whose splendid hollow
Thy young breast shall its impulse receive.
   I am the mother of thy spirit-life,
   And so in law thy wife
   And thou art my sire.
For all this treasured fire
   Learns from thee
   Its destiny.
And our full mutual birth
Must free this earth.
From our union shall spring
   The promised King
Who, with white sail unfurled
Shall steer through heavens of soul an unpolluted world.
   In that world
Earth's Tale shall be
   A valued page
   Of poesy.
As Grecian bards
   Knew how to praise
The kingly woes
   Of darker days,

And Tantalus, soaring where the mist is over blown
Meets on his hard-won throne a Juno of his own.

AL (MB: Ms. Am. 1451 [48]). Published in *Love-Letters*, pp. 85–90.

1. Perhaps an echo of the well-known line in *Faust*: "Verweile doch! du bist so schön!" ("Linger awhile, you are so beautiful"). With this line Faust seals his compact with Mephistopheles. Should the philosopher surrender to this longing, his soul would be lost. He repeats the line in his dying vision (Johann Wolfgang von Goethe, *Goethes Werke*, ed. Erich Trunz [Hamburg, 1949], 3:57).

2. Mary Greeley.

557.   To James Nathan

Monday afternoon, 26th May [1845]

Mein liebster. I will use the word again and correct my mistake. And yet was not that mistake an instinct, seeking the woman in you, when myself was in the melting mood. I have come in while the sun still shines and the warm airs blow, pleasing myself to give up to you a part of the first beautiful afternoon we have had for long, since you, probably, are not enjoying it, neither will I this day any longer. You say the sadness has been on you for sometime, so has it upon me, and nature has reflected our feelings, instead of, like a good mother, displaying sweet love to win us from them; it has been either too damp or cold to a degree which to my frame is absolutely *cruel,* but now the mild winds have come again! pray heaven they may continue! and we both may have sweeter brighter hours and moods. Yet *this* is sweet to me that you come to my heart to soothe away your sadness; it would be to me the dearest office. I have felt so[n] often that I could find comfort in you and wished to fly thither like a bird, and I would have you come to me like the sick lion and let me see if I cannot take out the thorn and if I cannot, let me at least soothe to rest for awhile

You bid me, on[n] beautiful evenings, if I sat alone in our bower, call you and you would presently be there; if it should indeed be sad on the wide waters, will you not, on your side, call me and I will hasten there, wherever I be or howsoever engaged.

Yes! dearest, the sadness will crystalize more and more the burning coal or what was burning to diamond, and what was the heat of life shall be turned to permanent light, this[n] was what I forgot to say to you that the Greek thought about Hecate and Diana seemed to me the same that had risen in your mind about the volcanic nature of the moon and her pure white light. White! we will be worthy to wear white. La dame blanche vous regarde; we will not act lightly or faithlessly. I like much your way of writing to me on the music; it binds me with the past, beside seeming so appropriate now. I was also much pleased to hear you speak of looking for the moss rose again: that is the most modest and yet most full of all the roses; may it bloom again for you! I do not wish the past eclipsed or forgotten, but I do long to see you entirely consoled and[n] that the deep wound should seem to be a mine which opened such precious treasures as to make the violence with which it was done forgotten. Yet I prize you more that this may not easily be done. You have asked me not to cross my letters, so I will not now write any more. Shall I not see you tomorrow, if it is still lovely and come so as to have some sunshine with me, as well as evening dusk.

The baby has just brought me two sweet roses.[1] I wish I could send you one fresh.

AL (MB: Ms. Am. 1451 [50]). Published in *Love-Letters*, pp. 91–93. *Addressed:* Mr. James Nathan / 86 Cedar St.

felt so] felt ⟨too⟩ so
me, on] me, ↑ on ↓
light, this] light, ⟨?⟩ this
consoled and] consoled ⟨for the past⟩ and

1. Arthur Young Greeley (1844–49), called Pickie by Margaret and the Greeley family (Greeley, *Genealogy of the Greely-Greeley Family*, p. 671).

558.   To James Nathan

Tuesday eveg
[27? May 1845]

My dear friend,

I have just had with Mrs Greeley a talk in full which may, I hope, be of use, so that before you go an interview will, indeed, leave things straight.

I believe I ought to have been angry with you the other evening for asking whether I had ever told her what you had communicated to me in confidence. How could such a thought cross a mind like yours? The scene was so beautiful and I so moved, I could not bear to be angry, but ought I not to have been so?— would not *you* have been so at such a doubt from me?

Today has been very lovely, fragrant and fresh after yesterday's shower, a new era, too, of blossoms. But I was up at five oclock to write for the paper, and have been in society ever since, up to this date, half past nine. Yesterday it was just the same, so I have no thoughts to give you. I have not had time to let any grow. You, too, have been engaged in just such dissipation of thought and feeling ah! it is painful when we might be so much to one another. I look to another meeting to cherish life anew. Tomorrow *at farthest!* let it be! Now there is only one little week left. Yes! the memory of Sunday evening is sweet to me. If a flow of gentle love be *natural,* surely there was nature. But why do you say you were less the *genuine man?* You must always instruct me very clearly. I am a dull scholar, though perhaps a good atmosphere.

About the evening I feel simply

"There is no silence; it is music ceased."[1]

But all you said to me in the *morning* lies distinct in my mind. I understood that deeply; the history! My friend, take this note kindly, though it be not much. Find nothing to "jar" in it. There is nothing in my mind. I seek inspiration from your thoughts, life from your life. I seek repose upon your heart. One little week; it is long enough for a dreamer; but to the good children might it not be one hymn!

AL (MB: Ms. Am. 1451 [47]). Published in *Love-Letters,* pp. 83–85.
Dated by the reference to Nathan's departure, which was Monday, 2 June.
1. From *Festus:* "There was no discord—it was music ceased" (p. 48).

559. To James Nathan

Wednesday eveg.
[28? May? 1845]

dear friend,

to my great joy Mrs Greeley appears to be satisfied and, I trust, all will go sweetly to the end. Thus I take the sheet with the little heartsease to repeat once more what resounds so constantly in my heart. God bless you!

AL (MB: Ms. Am. 1451 [26]). Published in *Love-Letters,* p. 43.

560.   To James Nathan

Evening of 30th May 45.

I was disappointed, dear friend, to receive no token from you this morning, for it had seemed as if you, like myself, would not be happy till our minds were again tuned to acknowledged harmony. Perhaps you think I did not myself do what I ought last night to produce this result. Indeed, I wished to do so. Long before you went, I felt that the tone which had for a moment repelled me was caused by the mood of the hour, the trials of the day, and, above all, by the presence of a third person. Had we been alone, I should have dropped a few tears, as I think from something you said you felt I needed to, and then the sun would have shone again and have lighted to the higher ground far more natural to us. But as it was, I could not act as I felt, and the warm tide of sympathy with which I had begun the evening was turned back upon me and seemed to oppress my powers of speech and motion. Yet it was very sad to me to have you go forth from the place whither you came in hope and trust into the dark night and howling wind. So far as the fault of this was mine, forgive me, dear friend. I feel as if such difficulties would not occur after longer acquaintance had tempered us to one another, and made that faith, which is already so deep, pervade the character more thoroughly. But, perhaps it might not be so; perhaps, I am, as you say, too sensitive, and in that case, it it well we are to separate now, for we are already too near to be easy or well if the unison be broken.

You reproached me for not stating with distinctness the difference betwixt us, last night. I did not feel able to do so then, but will try now. The view you stated had undoubtedly a foundation of nobleness, of manly honor and independence. It would well become a relation which began *from without*, where the parties were to become acquainted by gradual test and trial. But you have proposed to me to become related *from within*. You have claimed me on the score of spiritual affinity and I have yielded to this claim. You have claimed to read my thoughts, to count the pulses of my being; often to move them by your heart or will. You have approached me personally nearer than any other person, and have said to me words most unusual and close to which I have willingly listened. After this, could there remain doubts that we should sympathize with the griefs of one another; would it, indeed, be possible to conceal them, if there is that unity you have supposed? If there is that faith you have demanded, could we wish it? I felt that you went back from ground to which you had led. I also felt that it was not well to talk of there being only one perfect relation, in these parting hours, when I naturally wish to do all I can for you. I want to cast soft light over these hours; why say to your moon that there might be a better light? She admits it, but when told that hers is *of no use even at present*, what can she do but veil in cloud the pallid beams?

Yet I speak of this with reluctance for again I say it was the mood of the hour and not your deepest self I believe. You would really wish to trust me just as I wish to trust you, and do, in fact, hold me as dear as at any hour you ever thought you did. Your mind will not repent but revert with joy to what has been sweet and generous in our intercourse, to the confidence you have put in me as to the ills that beset, the thoughts that engaged you, to the hidden aspirations of your soul. Nor will the flowers we have been enabled to gather from the moment be forgotten; if not *perfect*, they were lovely and innocent, nor must the violet be cast aside, because she is not a rose.

This is, probably, my last letter, and I have written it with the inclosed pen, which I wish to give you and hope it will pen down some fine thoughts and passages of life during your journeyings. It also contains a pencil. I send it today, thinking you will have your initials put upon it, that you may be the less likely to lose my^n parting gift. A small copy of Shelley's poems I wish also to make your companion, but keep that till I can give it into your hand and point out some passages.

I feel, as you may see, rather subdued to night, having been unwell all day. But it seems as if tomorrow would be better. With you, at any rate, may it be so, with you be energy and light and peace and love! You in your turn, have patience with the Psyche, and draw the best music you can from the Lyre.

Reading over my letter it seems too^n restrained. Believe that my whole soul utters God bless you, and feels that your whole soul returns the same. May we meet as we feel!

AL (MB: Ms. Am. 1451 [51–52]). Published in *Love-Letters*, pp. 93–97.
lose my] lose ⟨your⟩ ↑ my ↓
seems too] seems ⟨to me⟩ too

561. To James Nathan

Saturday morning.
[31 May 1845]

I have slept sweetly; the sun rises bright, yet still I feel sick at heart.

May I find just the right word in town from you, or rather see you; if I do not, it will seem very dark. But this is your last day in the busy mart amid the falsehoods. I will cheer myself beneath that sad word, *the last* by thinking you will soon be on your way to scenes more conge[nial] to one of Grossmuth, Sanftmuth und Wahrhei[t][1]

"Nature *never* did deceive The heart that loved her"[2]

This will not, I believe, by my *last letter*, as I wrote; there must be a better fuller, deeper tone.

AL (MB: Ms. Am. 1451 [53]). Published in *Love-Letters*, pp. 97–98. *Addressed:* Mr. Nathan.

Dated by the reference to her "last letter."

1. *Grossmuth, Sanftmuth und Wahrheit:* generosity, gentleness, and truth.
2. A modification of the passage from "Lines Composed a Few Miles above Tintern Abbey": "Nature never did betray / The heart that loved her" (*The Poetical Works of William Wordsworth*, ed. Ernest de Selincourt and Helen Darbishire, 5 vols. [Oxford, 1940–49], 2:262).

562.   To James Nathan

Thursday evening.
5th June, 1845

I will no longer delay my letter of regrets for one such, I feel must be written, before the mind can shake off its weight of sadness and turn to brighter things. To be sure, before you can receive it, these hours will be past with you, yet come back with me, and sit down here by my window, and share the feelings of this hour.

Ever since you went, it has been the most beautiful weather, such as *we* never had at all. I do not think, my friend, fate smiled upon us; how much cold and storm there was; how little warm soft air when we could keep still out of doors in peace, how much interruption throughout from other affairs and relations, and the cloud of separation threatening from the distance from the very first. One good month, containing unbroken days of intercourse, and with no thought of the future would have been worth, in happiness, these five that we have known each other in such a way. But then, as we have met in common life, and amid all its cares and interruptions, all we do possess from one another is a more precious possession, for it is tested gold.

Yet I do wish we might have had together these glowing hours of the season's pride. Everything is so rich, so full, and fragrant with the warm breeze sighing all the time in excess of happiness. The roses are all out now, and the enchanting magnolia, too, and oriental locust. All the fruit is turned red in the sunlight; that on my tree, to which you so sweetly likened yourself, glances like cornelians and corals among the leaves. All is full and lustrous, as it has not been and will not be again, for these first days of June are the bridal days of the year, but through all breathes to me a tone of sorrow, over all droops a veil, for I have lost my dear companion, the first I ever had who could feel every little shade of life and beauty as exquisitely as myself, whose strength gladdened and whose gentleness soothed me, and wanting this finishing note, Nature herself pleases no more. It will not be so long, I trust, but *it is so now.*

Morning of the 6th,—When I had written the last words, I could write no more; all seemed too sad and heavy, and I went to take counsel of my pillow. Here I never fail to find comfort. Night seems to me the gentlest mother. We are taught, in our childhood, verses to which I know not if you have anything corresponding in German they begin

"Receive my body, pretty bed,

Dear pillow, thou receive my head."

And this feeling of trust in the confidential, gentle Night, that she will drive away dusky thoughts and needless cares, and bring sweet counsel and hope for the morrow, deepens in me year by year. It pleased me much when you told of your Father taking the flowers to bed with him; he must have had the same feeling. And I was not disappointed, but awoke brightly this morning. But it is daily a sadness to me again to go to the town and know I shall not find the little messenger with your letter. Out here I want you to enjoy the beauty of the solitude, in the city I feel alone among the multitude of men, because you are gone. Strange that there should be just one with whom I could hold deep sympathy, and just that one of all the thousands must go as I came. Ah well! I will fret as little as I can, but this sighing is of some use just to exhale one's—

The day you went, I was interrupted by visits all the time. At night I had promised to accompany Mrs Child and Mr Benson to the Park Theatre.[1] There an actress, once beautiful and celebrated, whom Mrs Child had raised from the most degrading fall was to reappear before a N. Y. audience[2] Mrs C., after attending her as a sister till she learnt to love her as one, had secured her engagements in the other cities, and from the gutter (as one may say,) she had come into the enjoyment of an honorable independence and respectable relations. But she had never revisited N. Y. which was the scene of her former degredation till now, and was very nervous in the fear of being hissed. Mrs C. had engaged me and other friends to be present to sustain her by our sympathy. But we were there only to heighten her disgrace; the poor woman, unable to sustain her anxiety, took some stimulant, and it set her quite beside herself. It was the saddest sight to see her robed in satin, and crowned with roses, ruining with every word all her hopes of future ease or peace, till no resource seemed left her but suicide, (for she is unfit for any thing but her profession to which she was educated,) and dealing such blows on hearts which had shown her real disinterested love. Although I had felt averse to going, because it was the day of your parting, and it would have been best to be alone and still, I became painfully interested. But in the very midst my heart beat suddenly, your image rose before me. I could think of nothing else for a long time; you must, I think, have called me that evening as you looked out on the blue waters. Afterwards as I witnessed Mrs C's trouble I thought of you, and that your labor of love to which you have sacrificed so much and me and this summer among others, was at least likely to end well. That is a rare blessing in this tangled world, to bring a good to fulfilment, even by great sacrifices. Write me all you can about this, for I feel deeply interested. Since you went I have been looking over the "The Crescent and the Cross" a book of Eastern travels;[3] there are in the *Appendix* "*Hints to travellers in the East*" you may possibly not know all he mentions. Mr Delf will easily get you the book, and it is worth your looking at.[4]

Mrs Greeley thinks a great deal about you; she was left with a perfectly sweet feeling in which I rejoice. She has been in these days very tranquil

I take Josey out with me; he is very gay, but does not mind me well. I cannot get him to go into the water at all; last night I had to ask some boys to throw him in. I shall not *cross my letters much, though you did ask it,* because I know you will enjoy reading them more if I do not. I have arranged all yours in company with the white veil and the memorandum book and some dead flowers that once bloomed sweetly in hours of sweet life, but have not had courage to read them yet. To our Father's care commending you lebewohl.

After all I forgot to say to you what I meant about Mrs C's marriage.[5] And it comes apropos to this event. It was this that with great affectionateness and love of disinterested action, she had not the surest instincts as to selecting objects or occasions, so that much she has done, has been of no good except to her own heart. I know not, however, that in either of these cases, she had much choice; she married very young, before she knew much of herself, and in the case of the actress, she could not choose but do all she could for one whom none else would help, and so she did it nobly, with the whole heart!

Please mention the receipt of each of my letters that I may be sure none of them are lost.

AL (MB: Ms. Am. 1451 [54]). Published in part in *Love-Letters*, pp. 98–104. *Addressed:* To / James Nathan / Care Mr Thomas Delf / 16 Little Britain / London /England. *Postmark:* 28 Ju 28 / 1845.

1. According to the New York directory, Benjamin W. Benson was a clothing merchant in New York City.

2. Anne Henry Barrett (1801–53) was an actress who first performed in New York in 1824. Twice married and divorced, she drank heavily, but was, as Fuller says, rehabilitated and eventually resumed her career. At the Park Theatre on 2 June she played Lady Gay Spanker in Dion Boucicault's *London Assurance*. Though contracted for six nights, Barrett did not continue beyond the first evening. "On her first entrance on the stage, she was received with general applause, but after the ceremony of introduction to Sir Harcourt, she became quite overwhelmed with embarrassment, and lost every word of her part. The side scene unfortunately shut out the prompter's voice and her embarrassment became very painful" (*New York Herald*, 3 June 1845; Ireland, *Records of the New York Stage*, 2:437; Odell, *Annals of the New York Stage*, 5:101). The *Herald* blamed the problem on "the injudicious and boisterous manner in which she was applauded after speaking the first sentence or two, by some gentlemen in the boxes with Mrs. Child, and a few other ladies, who now regard Mrs. Barrett as their *protege*. Their well-meant, but rather *bizarre* way of supporting the fair actress, attracted the notice of the house, and evidently appeared to annoy Mrs. Barrett." As Fuller says, she was one of the party with Lydia Child.

3. Eliot Warburton, *The Crescent and the Cross; or Romance and Realities of Eastern Travel* (London, 1845). In her review, Fuller said that Warburton "wants vivacity and individuality of expression," but that he gives "a better wholesale account of 'manners and population' in the East, than other more captivating books" (*New-York Daily Tribune*, 7 June 1845).

4. Thomas Delf was an Englishman who worked for the publisher D. Appleton (*Love-Letters*, p. 188).

5. Lydia Child.

563. To Elizabeth Hoar

Thursday June 12th [1845]

Dear Lizzie,

Anna Ward is in town, will stay till Saturday, would like to see you at her grandmother's *80 Beekman St*[1]

I shall go there tomorrow morng at 10 from the Dr's, if Mamma[2] does not come today, could she not with you then and join me at *80* half past eleven or 12 then you could have your visit after we were gone and then come to our house.

AL (MHarF). *Addressed:* Miss E Hoar / Care Wm Emerson Esq / 60 Wall St.

1. Anna Ward's maternal grandmother was Anna Rodman Hazard (1761–1845), daughter of Thomas and Mary Borden Rodman. In 1780 she married Thomas Hazard

(1758–1839) (Charles Henry Jones, *Genealogy of the Rodman Family, 1620 to 1886* [Philadelphia, 1886], pp. 27, 42).

2. Ruth Haskins Emerson, Waldo's mother, who was visiting her son William's home on Staten Island (Rusk, *Letters of RWE*, 3:285–89).

564. To James Nathan

N Y. 12th June, 1845—

After those three days of intense heat we usually have in June comes one shadowy, sighing,[n] cool, which seems very suitable for writing to you. You will not find too many letters in London, if you feel like me. I thought when you went letters would be nothing after the fulness of living intercourse, but already I begin to want them very much and be disconsolate to think I can receive none for near a month yet. I hope you will have written on the voyage. But we are on unequal terms in this; all around you is new, while every object here is associated with you, and the more lovely the scene, the stronger my regret that you are not beside me. Into the wood it seems as if I could no more go at all.[n] Yet you seem to be much with me, especially now the moonlight evenings have again begun. Last evening I had no lamp lit[n] after the sunset and lay looking at the moon stealing through the exquisite curtain of branches which now overhangs all my windows. You seemed entirely with me, and I was in a sort of trance as on evenings when you used to sing to me. At these times heaven and earth seemed mingled as in twilight[n] But when I was roused I did not feel so happy as after those evenings. I have really suffered in my health as I feared. It is no imagination my being much less strong, and my head has ached constantly, but today I begin to hope to be better again. I try to picture you where you are and enter into your new hopes and plans, but somehow I cannot. You seem still to be here. Almost I hear your voice. But after your letter comes perhaps I shall be able to imagine your new life and wean my thoughts from all this.

Last Sunday I passed at Staten Island; oh it was most lovely; the long drives in the wooded lanes and still breezy spots on the hills. It is a pity we could never go there. You forgot to tell me which was the drive you were fond of there; mention when you write its name, as I shall go there on a visit, by and by. There a beautiful moss rose bud was given me!! All the evening riding home and in the boat, though people were taking to me and I answering mechanically, I was really conversing with you.

But this is a dull song to send so far— I have been thinking you wanted me to write of the people and things that interest you here and how shall I? for I do not know them by name. When you have told me stories you have not told me the names of the actors. What has been the main subject of our talk has been personal to ourselves and life and re-ligion in general. If there are special subjects, you want to hear about, will you tell me? And write whether you ever get that letter from Mr Polk. If you do not, let me try and get it and send to your address in time for the use you wish. I forgot to beg you would let the friend you commissioned to receive it apprize me of the result, and now I have no way of finding out[n] do not fail yourself, dear friend, to tell me. I know at this distance you must feel so affectionately, you will like to have me do it for you; say, is it not so?

Many, many things I forgot to ask and say; many questions now oc-cur I wish I had asked you, many words, some as good as wine or honey, I wish I had said. But the effect of our intercourse was to make me so passive, sometimes I wonder it was so interesting to you, and yet I do not, for I seem a part of yourself. We were born, surely, under the same constellation[n] You found much of yourself in me, though veiled by a light haze, there was a long soft echo to the deepest tones. Some-times you doubted whether I fully comprehended you, and, probably, I did not, but I felt able to, and it was so pleasant to be led on and sup-ported at the same time. Whenever there was dissonance between us it ended as being so superficial

"It seemed but tuning of the breast
To make the music better."[1]
I never had these feelings at all towards any other

And now, loved friend, I find myself just so passive, waiting. You have told me much of your history and[n] of the inward call of your heart. This seems to be the crisis in your life. I cannot at all look for-ward to the result. Whether it will lead you inward or outward, to pil-grim sorrows or a small harmonious sphere of earthly uses and bles-sings?— I long to know but only from yourself can I know! Impart *all you can* to the chosen sister. I never did like to ask you questions and now shall still less, but know that I always want to know. And forgive should my letters be somewhat reserved. I am afriad it will make me timid that my letters must go so far and be so long of getting answered and through many hands and public offices. When they only went by the little foot-page a street or two and I could presently add with lips and eyes all that was wanting to explain them, I had more courage than I can have this way. You I hope, I trust will draw to you in the spirit what is best and truest. But you are a man, and men have the privilege of boldness; put your soul upon the paper as much as you can.

Your amiable townsman, Mr Benson, as if he had an instinct that I was forsaken, came the day you sailed to offer me all kinds of kind offices.[2] Would I go to Long Branch, to Rockaway; he knew all the prettiest places in the neighborhood and would take me in his gig, he would come out with his boat and take me; He has been out in the boat[n] one aftn, but I was sick and did not see him. Alas! how full the world is of persons and kind ones, too, but how few with whom we can make music. But you find such an one in Mr Delf; do you not? you will find yourself at home with him in London? Mrs Storms is coming on Saturday with a set of Ionian distingúes to dine here![3]

I am to break off for a time with Dr Leger. He says while my head aches I had better not come, but change the scene and air and I mean to make some excursions. Matters go on here in their usual disjointed fashion Mr Greeley is, I believe, really going to the West soon—[4] I am trying to devote myself to the paper so as to make it easy for him. Little Arthur grows pretty and mischievous; his mother is in better spirits. A thought comes into my mind which I will not write; divine it and much else from your—

I may not be able to write by the Western as there is much to be done these next coming days, but will the last of the month.

AL (MB: Ms. Am. 1451 [55]). Published in *Love-Letters*, pp. 104–10. *Addressed:* To / James Nathan / Care Mr Thomas Delf / 16 Little Britain / London / England. *Postmark:* 28 Ju 28 1845.

shadowy, sighing,] shadowy, ⟨silent⟩ sighing,

Into the wood it seems as if I could no more go at all.] ↑ Into the wood it seems as if I could no more go at all. ↓

no lamp lit] no ⟨light⟩ ↑ lamp lit ↓

At these times heaven and earth seemed mingled as in twilight] ↑ At these times heaven and earth seemed mingled as in twilight ↓

result, and now I have no way of finding out] result, ↑ and now I have no way of finding out ↓

We were born, surely, under the same constellation] ↑ We were born, surely, under the same constellation ↓

history and] history ↑ and ↓

out in the boat] out ↑ in the boat ↓

1. From "The Temper" in George Herbert's "The Church" (*The Works of George Herbert*, ed. F. E. Hutchinson [Oxford, 1941], p. 55):

> Yet take thy way; for sure thy way is best:
> Stretch or contract me, thy poore debter:
> This is but tuning of my breast,
> To make the musick better.

2. Edmund Benzon (d. 1873) was a German businessman who often contributed money to Lydia Child's abolitionist causes. He later left New York for London, where he became wealthy. Though Fuller misspells his name here, she corrected herself in later letters (Child, *Selected Letters*, pp. 166, 517).

3. Jane Maria McManus (1807–78) was an aggressive worker for American expansion in Mexico, the Carribbean, and Central America. She and her family were involved in a scheme to colonize the Texas coast, the first of her many adventures into colonial empire building. In 1825 she married Allen B. Storms, whom she divorced in 1831. At the time of Fuller's letter Mrs. Storms was writing for the *New York Sun* (*NAW*).

4. Several Michigan Whig supporters of Henry Clay came to New York in 1845, "bringing wondrous accounts of the riches of the Superior region in copper and silver, if not also in gold." They quickly ensnared Greeley in a mining company, which he apparently was planning to visit (Horace Greeley, *Recollections of a Busy Life* [New York, 1869], pp. 242–43).

565. To Richard F. Fuller

[13? June 1845]

My dear Richard,

Your letter before this last was most pleasant to me, giving more feeling of being with you than I had had since we parted; write such another now and then. Augusta King has just been here. I was sorry to see so little of her, but it was one of my headach days. Now I am very well again. Give my love to Anna Loring, say I want her to write to me one of these beautiful days: tell her I look at her picture often; it lies near me in my delightful chamber. I wish she could see this place it is so lovely now; and I wish m[ore?] that you, too, could be with me. Shall write to Mother soon, now must sent off in haste. Much love to Arthur; say I recd his speech; thought it very judicious and even in newspaper report, remarkably well expressed.[1] Think he must have made a very favorable impression. Do you receive the Weekly Tribune regularly; dont omit to answer your ever affect sister

M.

The first oppory I want Mother to send me my bathing dress.

Augusta K. spoke with much friendsh[ip] of you and what she said was good and just too. E. Hoar has been spend[ing] a day with me.

ALS (MH: fMS Am 1086 [9:124]); MsC (MH: fMS Am 1086 [Works, 2:777–79]). *Addressed*: To / Richard F. Fuller / at the Law School / Cambridge / Mass.

Dated from the contents. Fuller had not seen Elizabeth Hoar by 22 May, and Mrs. Fuller did not arrive in New York until the middle of June. Since she invited Hoar to visit on 13 June, Fuller probably wrote this letter on the same day.

1. Arthur Fuller gave a speech to the Sunday School Society, whose annual meeting was held during "anniversary week" in Boston, 18–24 May (*Christian Register*, 31 May 1845).

566.   To James Nathan

No 1

New York, 24th June, 1845.

This beautiful summer morning finds me free to write to you, dear
friend, but a good hour of it, have I wasted, lying here, thinking which
of the many things I have to say shall be selected for the letter. They
are so many and yet so little; none seems well worth[n] writing down by
itself, though I should say them all to you, if you were here.

If you were here, alas! that you are not. The softness and splendor of
every thing round me, the musical sweep of these breezes still suggest
that melancholy *if*. You would enjoy them all soo fully, and there is
none else who could enjoy them so, except me, and now having had
you with me, I cannot be happy as I should have been, if I had not had
your companionship at all. Now I must miss you. I try not, but cannot
yet help it.

I do not now go out in the afternoon or evening which was the time
we used to be together, but choose the morning rather. I have got a
new place on the rocks which is delightful in the morning, much more
so than the one where we used to go. It is more shadowed and retired,
yet the water comes up to my feet.

—But you, I fear, will never see it. Every thing looks as if our hosts
would not remain here another year, and as if[n] you, having lost the
pleasure of being here this summer, will not have it another, even if
you should come back.— I will not tell you more about them at present; but the same griefs keeps breaking out with violence, and I feel[n] as
if no peace or security could be expected from connection with persons
so circumstanced. My dear mother is staying with me now; her sweetness and elegance make the house seem a very different place from
what it ever did before. While she stays, I feel it almost[n] like home but
she will leave me early in July.[n]

I have had many visitors, and been about a great deal, for the last
month of your stay, I used to put all such engagements off till you were
gone, and they have accumulated. I take some pleasure in these for
Mother; to her they are fresh and amusing.

I have also tried to revive[n] my energies about the paper, and have
succeeded in doing a good deal. Mr Greeley told me that he could not
bear to urge me, but unless I took more interest he should not feel that
he could go away; however his journey seems still in the distant perspective. I doubt his going before Septr—

This is the day of the great procession to[n] pay funeral honors to

General Jackson, honors with which I do not sympathize, except on this score, that the flaming old warrior was so downright.[1]

There is also a new movement against the Texas annexation, but which will not, it is to be feared, raise a very full wave.[2]

What else shall I tell you? nothing has happened that interests me, except that the Prison Association have[n] taken a house in Twelfth St, as a temporary asylum for released female convicts while finding them employment. I have written an appeal to the public, to procure aid to this house, which has interested a good many.[3] Last Sunday I went there, found ten of these women, one about eighteen whose face you would like; her eyes were brown and very soft, around the mouth signs of great sensibility. She seems to be in consumption. It pained me to see the poor things so bowed down, much more so than they seem in their prisons; some *pious* ladies were exhorting them, bible in hand. I had some pleasant chat with them. I like them better than most women I meet, because, if any good is left it is so genuine, and they m[ake] no false pretensions, nor cling to shadows. Bu[t] then, in talking with me they do not show the contamination and painful images that must haunt their lonely hours; they are pleased and cheered, and show only the womanly and self-respecting side.

We have had one interesting book, Longfellow's Poets and Poetry of Europe; look over it, if you have a chance any time; it contains a good course in these charming studies, and there are some things, I wish I could read with you.[4]

Little Arthur grows very handsome and engaging. He walks firmly and lightly now, and his figure is full of spirit. He likes much to run into my room and have me show him pictures, and understands all the stories I tell him about them. He has learnt from my lips to say several words, but, manlike, he will only say them at his own time, and not when I ask him. The first one was *bird*, which is a good one to begin with. — Josey is thriving; we have now an excellent man who will take good care of him.

Now, dear friend, I have told you all the gossip. I wish I could do better, but I cannot. Indeed there *are* soul realities. I feel a perfect stream of life beneath all this. But it is not one of the times when I could fathom it, it carries me on. I know not whither but only feel borne by the stream, and fanned by the gales. But it seems as if in our bond, these deep things you will easier know untold, than the little outward things. Indeed

> "A weary time thou'st been away
> But yet I feel thee near."

And when I am tempted to sing sometimes the other song "O say dost thou love me yet." I seem to be answered, "Yes! I love and know thee, even now my thoughts enfold thee with that intelligence that was so sweet, so cherishing, nor can we become unknown to one another." If it is really so thou knowest well how great the life that is growing up within me and what sweet strange music flows in upon me at times. But I do not count these things or seek to detain them. I am passive.

turn to the next letter.

24th [June 1845] No 2.

Continued from another letter

We have been much to one another, and, should we never meet again in bodily presence, precious realities must ensue to both of us from the past meeting.

But not more of such things now.— I feel as if my power about writing to you would be much decided by the character of your first letters. Once you intimated that you should not want a real correspondence with me while on your pilgrimage, for you needed to be "unaccompanied," and quite free to receive new impressions. I thought this very natural and acquiesced. But later you wished it otherwise; yet this, perhaps, was only the pain of parting. When I see what direction your feelings permanently take, then shall I be drawn or repelled accordingly. Your first letters I shall have before you receive these, I hope, and those will tell me, too, many things, outward at least. I shall know how you fared on the waters (never do I see the sails pass without thinking of *that*) what thoughts rose uppermost, whether the *Angels* did not console you for sickening realities that had disturbed your last days here, and shown you how such are in the end tuned and melted into a sublime music, the melody of the Earth, heard from due distance. Or were entirely new thoughts revealed, or confirmation given of what had passed before. Or were you listless and sick, needing more amusement. Or did new sources of interest spring up? I long to know what news you find in London, whether you will be permitted to pursue your journey, or obliged to go to your home— There you will see your mother, too, and what a holy hope it must be after such a long separation. I think from traits you have told me, she is in some respects like mine.

I want to copy for you two pieces which have fallen under my eye since you went; 'tis no matter if I do make such use of this sheet as it will probably find you in London; indeed you are there now, it may be. But when the paper has to travel after you I shall be more avaricious of it. The first is a *Volkslied* of your adopted nation, and deeply expressive of that deepest sadness in life that, though blessings come, they so often come too late

Mutter, ach Mutter! Es hungert mich
   Gieb mir Brodt, sonst sterbe ich.
      Warte nur mein liebes Kind!
   Morgen wollen wir säen geschwind,
Und als das Korn gesaët war.
   Rief das Kind noch immerdar;
Mutter, ah Mutter! Es hungert mich,
   Gieb mir Brod, sonst sterbe ich.
      Warte nur mein liebes Kind!
   Morgen wollen wir ernten geschwind,
Und als das Korn geerntet war.
   Rief das Kind noch immerdar.
   Mutter ach Mutter &—
Warte nur mein liebes Kind
   Morgen wind wir dreschen geschwind.

And so on through the threshing, the grinding, the baking till

      als das Brod gedbacken war,
      Da lag das Kind schon auf der Bahr.[5]

This is from Shelley and was not, I feel pretty sure, in your volume. Even if you do not like him generally you will the exquisite pensiveness of this

      When passion's trance is overpast
      If tenderness and truth could last
      And live, while all wild feelings keep
      Some mortal slumber, dark and deep,
      I should not weep, I should not weep.

      After the slumber of the year
      The woodland violets reappear,
      All things revive in field and grove
      And sky and sea—but two which move
      As for all others life and love.[6]

Perhaps the haze of his style and want of clear finish in the expression of his thoughts will prevent your liking him.[n] I feel in copying his verses that he must be harder than others for a foreigner to understand

Now I will stop for this day. I sent no letter by the Western, in consequence of an oversight, but two by the Boston steamer which I hope reached you safely though they contained little beyond the words of love and regret.

Evening of the 25th your companion, Mr Miller, has just been here. I thought I recognized traits of which you have told me, but he had with him a talkative gentleman that would not let him say much. I wanted to ask if he knew the name of your ship. (I never asked you and am disturbed, because you would have been willing to tell *me* and now, if you do not write at once, I shall have no way of knowing that you arrive safe.) but I think you cannot fail to write at once, you will feel that I shall be anxious— A poor pretty young girl, a cousin of Mrs Greeley's who is staying here has just heard of the death of a brother of her own age by drowning. To me it always seems so: we tremble constantly on the verge of separations; I do not feel steeled against them yet, so that I can forbear clinging to what I hold dear.

26th Again a day of the most splendid beauty. I have been walking; every thing is so full of fragrance; all objects so joyous. I feel happy too. I have just finished some essays for the paper one little one on "The Irish Character" I wish you were here to read; you would like its scope and character.[7] Perhaps you can give me some hints from what you observe in London as to matters that will interest in this country, too.— Now I am going away for two or three days and expect to have no further chance to write, before it is time to send by the steamer You cannot think how touching it is to me to see the fruit ripened which was in flower when you were here. Now the blackberries are ripe where tender white-flower buds you used to gather for me. May all you hopes bear fruit as well!

Adieu, a month is past, in it I have written you four letters; this one is the continuation of another. They are more long than good, but you will take them kindly from your friend who commends you ever a Dieu

AL (MB: Ms. Am. 1451 [56–57]). Published in *Love-Letters*, pp. 110–21. *Addressed:* To / James Nathan / Care Mr Thomas Delf / 16 Little Britain / London,— England. *Postmark:* 15 Jy 15 1845.

well worth] well ↑ worth ↓
and as if] and ↑ as if ↓
I feel] *The remainder of this sentence has been canceled by a later hand and is here recovered.*
feel it almost] feel ↑ it almost ↓
in July.] *Fuller here turned the sheet and added:* I take pleasure too in being the means that some persons weary of the city and to whom it is a delight to come here can come
to revive] to ⟨resume⟩ ↑ revive ↓
procession to] procession ↑ to ↓
Association have] Association ⟨has⟩ ↑ have ↓
liking him.] liking ⟨them⟩. ↑ him ↓

1. Former president Andrew Jackson died on 8 June. The *Tribune* reported that a very large crowd waited six hours on a hot day for the long procession to make its way "through Chatham-street and East Broadway to Grand-street, down Grand-street and the Bowery to Union Square, thence down Broadway to the Park" (*New-York Daily Tribune*, 21 and 25 June 1845).

2. Not only was Horace Greeley denouncing the move to annex Texas in his *Tribune* editorials, but William Henry Channing was using his pulpit for the same purpose. On 22 June he said in a sermon quoted in the *Tribune*: "The annexation of Texas is the deliberate destruction of the constitutional compact—we therefore go back to the original Declaration of Independence—and we demand of the Legislatures a Convention of the people of the U. States to carry out the original purposes of that Declaration" (*New-York Daily Tribune*, 23 June 1845).

3. Isaac Hopper and his daughter, Abigail Hopper Gibbons (1801–93), were active in the creation in 1844 of the Prison Association of New York, which had a "Female Department" that sponsored "The Home," a shelter for newly discharged women prisoners (NAW; Sarah H. Emerson, ed., *Life of Abby Hopper Gibbons* [New York, 1897], pp. 251–53). Fuller described the home in "Asylum for Discharged Female Convicts," in the *Tribune* for 19 June, where she urged the public to donate furniture, books, and clothes.

4. Longfellow's *Poets and Poetry of Europe* was announced as "just issued" in the *Tribune* for 11 June. Fuller reviewed it on 17 June, calling it "a most valuable collection."

5. "Verspätung," from Ludwig Achim von Arnim and Clemens Brentano, eds., *Des Knaben Wunderhorn* (Frankfurt, 1806–8).

6. Shelley's "To—," in Mary Shelley's edition of *Posthumous Poems of Percy Bysshe Shelley* (London, 1824).

7. Fuller wrote a sympathetic essay on Irish immigrants for the *Tribune* of 28 June. She described the intense family affections among the Irish and wished that they had a better welcome in the United States. In her writings on the Irish, Fuller followed Greeley's lead, for he denounced the "nativist" attitude taken by both the conservative Whigs and the Democrats in New York (Glyndon G. Van Deusen, *Horace Greeley, Nineteenth-Century Crusader* [Philadelphia, 1953], p. 101).

567. To Richard F. Fuller

New York
29th June 1845.

Dear Richard,

Though Mother does not go for several days, I write some short letters ere[n] this, lest I have not time again. She will tell you all the outwards about me; and how I feel, too. Her visit has been a great pleasure to me.

Though she speaks of you most affecy I infer from some slight things that you do not entirely by her as I could wish. She does not complain, but happened to mention that you took now no interest in a garden. I have known you would do what you thought of to be a good son, and not neglect your positive duties[n] but I have feared you would not show enough of sympathy with her tastes and pursuits. Care of the garden *is* a way in which you could give her genuine comfort and pleasure, while regular exercise in it would be of great use to yourself. Do not neglect this, nor any the most trifling attention, she may wish, because it is not by attending to our friends in *our* way but in *theirs* that we can really avail them. You know your pursuits and thoughts lead almost wholly away from her at any rate, and now that she has no daughter with her, this is more palpable. She is living there more for you than for any one else, and the garden is almost the only pleasure she can have, while you, full of your studies and your hopes, have many.

It will not be long now before I see you, and seeing *you* will be one of my main objects in going to Mass. But I know not yet whether I come in August, or not till Octr. I will let you know by the time your term is out, that you may arrange about going to Groton. I think of you much, with love and pride and hope for your public and private life. When I come we will go once to Watertown and the walk along the river's bank, and have some real intercourse, I hope. I cannot write. Lizzie Hoar showed me your letter to her, and one you have written me shows me what your mind is *innerlich*—[1] It is only some of the household virtues sense of the gentler sympathies that I fear your neglecting[n] till it is too late and I know you take all counsels kindly from your friend and sister

M.

W. Channing is coming soon to Boston. I hope you will go and see him.

ALS (MH: fMS Am 1086 [9:117]); MsC (MH: fMS Am 1086 [Works, 2:771–77]). *Addressed:* To / Richard.

letters ere] letters ⟨by⟩ ↑ere↓

son, and not neglect your positive duties] son, ↑and not neglect ⟨many of⟩ your positive duties↓

your neglecting] your ne⟨c⟩glecting

1. *Innerlich:* intrinsically.

568. To Sarah Shaw

New York
1st July 1845.

My dear Sarah,

Today the cheap postage law begins its sway and I think you will be willing to pay a little for a letter from me, even if it contains *but* little.[1]

I have been wanting to write ever since the little girl came.[2] Heaven, I think, must have some important task before us for women, it sends so many little girls. Bobby will have a good deal to do to balance the female influence at this rate; he will have to blunt his sensibilities. I hope Josephene will not be obliged to retire into the back-ground, if she is as sweet as when I saw her.[3]

Now I think you will be able to do little except take care of the children, and that, though it is so good a life, and *may* lead to so many good thoughts, seldom *does* with Mothers because they do not get enough of other life to wake them to the good thoughts. In this respect, as most others, mortals who have most, seldom realize anything, so, in fact, possess nothing. But it is not so with Sarah.

Often I think of your place and the woods near. I have just been staying at Staten Island and there are quite long wood-walks, and, as you go up and down them, for they are on hills[n] you catch glimpses of the sea and of the narrows with the processions of ships gliding through and Coney Island with its long strip of silvery sand[n] that cleaves the waters with such beautiful effect. I have also had delightful drives along the North River. But I like best to stay at home here. I always like best to stay in one place. I do not get tired but only to love it more, and I like this place better than any I ever lived in; only there are no walks away from the place. I can only sit here on the rocks, or walk in our own little paths amid the thick trees and shrubbery. Perhaps there would not be variety enough for another year, but for this one, I am perfectly content and should never care to be away a day, if I could help it, but I have to be away many days.

I heard of Frank through W. Channing, of his confirmed hope and faith. I am glad he is translating Consuelo; it will be a gift to the world.[4] Sarah and Anna are well I hear "tell them, I love them yet" as the song hath it, and hope they will be glad to see me, when I come, which will be either in August or October, the former, I hope. Then I shall come to see thee, also. The little crucifix hangs always in the recess where my study-table is, and where I have, too, a drawing by Sam Ward and a picture of the Countess Emily Plater. Adieu, always dear Sarah, write me a little, if you can sometime   Your friend

Margaret

I thank you all much about *Honora*; she behaves thus far perfectly well; and has got good employment at Alton as a dressmaker.

It is very right for Frank to translate Consuelo when he has so many daughters.

ALS (MH: bMS Am 1417 [179]). *Addressed:* To / F. G. Shaw Esq / for Mrs Shaw / ⟨West Roxbury / Mass.⟩ / Cape Cottage / near Portland / Maine. *Postmarks:* New York 2 Jul; Boston / Mass / Jul 4.

them, for they are on hills] them, ↑ for they are on hills ↓
silvery sand] silvery ⟨l⟩sand

1. On 3 March 1845 Congress voted a reduction of postal rates, which had not changed since 1816. A one-sheet letter that formerly cost 25 cents could now be sent for 10. Fuller wrote a spirited, ironic essay on the new rates for the *Tribune*: "Not only there is a limit set to human strength and activity, but from the pressure of care and excitement which has already begun to deteriorate the race from generation to generation here, it arrives unusually quick with us. And now, in addition to all the other demands upon our energies, comes this inducement to write many and long letters" (*New-York Daily Tribune*, 24 February 1845).

2. Ellen Shaw (1845–1936), fifth and last of the Shaw children, was born on 1 June. In 1867 she married General Francis Channing Barlow (1834–96), son of Almira Barlow, another of Fuller's close friends (*Sturgis of Yarmouth*, p. 51; MVR 1936; *DAB*).

3. Other Shaw children, Robert Gould and Josephine.

4. Frank Shaw retired as a young man from his lucrative Boston trading house. He began to translate the novels of George Sand and to pursue an interest in Fourierite socialism. His translation of Sand's *Consuelo* was first published in the *Harbinger*, vols. 2 and 3 (1845–47). It went through four editions, the first in 1846.

569.   To [?]

New York, 2 July 1845

I am interested in the paper. Mr. Greeley is a sagacious and a wonderfully good man and his paper worth retaining [?] while we are waiting for the better state.

MsCfr in Higginson's hand (MB: Ms. Am. 1450 [18]).

570.   To Elizabeth Hoar

New York,
Sunday 6th July, 1845.

My dear Lizzie, I may truly say it planted a thorn in my breast, when I found that you came to town and I disappointed you. Though it will do little good, I must, for my own relief, tell you how it happened

You know I sent you word to come, if it was fair. About 2 it continued to rain hard and I thought there was no chance of its stopping, so sent word to town for them to send back my order upon the theatre and the tickets in exchange for another eveg. I did this, thinking the weather would certainly not let you come from the Island. I was in that state when it is dangerous for me to get wet, though it is not at other times, and I wanted to send back the tickets while the box office was yet open, as I thought if I kept so many places without using them or writing any thing about the opera I should not like to ask for them another night.[1]

About half past four it was so far fair that I could have gone to town. I then regretted that I had sent, but, having done so, reasoned thus. Lizzie will not consider this *"fair"*; it clears up too late for her to get over from the Island. As to the Cranchs it is no matter; I can ask them to go another eveg. We *cannot* go *this*, because the Theatre office will be shut up, before I can get there and, if I could, the tickets are probably disposed of. Beside it is still very damp I am unwell; it is too late &c &c.

But when I found that you really did come, I felt that I had acted very indolently I thought I ought at least to have gone to town and seen if you were there, and if you were, have gone down to our office and one of the gentlemen would have gone with me to the Theatre door and probably got us in. I could not forgive myself for not doing what I ought or could[n] to insure your pleasure and especially when I may not have another opportunity in the same way. I never acted in this sort of lazy, fearful way but two times before and one of them was at your and Waldo's expense, about Waltham, you remember. And yet, Lizzie, there are no persons in the world I would be less willing to pain and disappoint. Indeed, I would have gone through wet or any thing, if I had thought you would be there, but the truth is I was tired and engaged in my writing and did not think enough about it, or act with the energy I ought. On Wednesday, I went, hoping your departure might have been delayed till Thursday to Mr E's office to see whether you could not be got to see Robert le Diable.[2] My only comfort for your departure was that the French company I found so poor and that I could wish your first introduction to Operas[n] might be to the *Italn* Opera. If you could come on next autumn for a few days, and stay[n] with me in this sweet place, where I hardly hope to be another summer and hear Ole Bull's farewell strains and go with me to the Italn Opera I should be consoled for my derelictions.[3] Is this wish too much like a dream could it not be realized. Farewell, dear E, if I sometimes feel that I could bear the loss of my friends, I do not when I have acted ill by them; what a deep shadow it casts!

M.

ALS (MHarF). *Addressed:* To / Miss Elizabeth Hoar / Care Hon Saml Hoar / Concord / Mass. *Postmark:* New York 8 Jul.

ought or could] ought ↑ or could ↓
introduction to Operas] introduction ↑ to Operas ↓
and stay] and ⟨?⟩stay

    1. Hoar and Fuller probably missed the performance of Donizetti's *La Favorite*, which the French Company from New Orleans staged at the Park Theatre on Monday, 30 June (*New York Evening Post*, 30 June 1845).

    2. The company performed Giacomo Meyerbeer's *Robert le diable* (1831) in French on 2 July (Odell, *Annals of the New York Stage*, 5:105).

    3. Ole Bornemann Bull, a Norwegian violinist, had toured in the United States in 1844. Fuller was enthusiastic about his music, especially his own compositions on American themes. She had reviewed him in the *Tribune* on 20 December, remarking on the "cold and dull reception given him by the audience." On 30 December she reviewed him for a second time.

571.   To Richard F. Fuller

New York, July 8th 1845

My dear Richard,

    I hope you will always write and speak to me when it can do you good in any way.[1] You know I always had time and strength for you and trust I always shall.

    I cannot judge at this distance of Anna's feelings. I know her parents, at least, her mother, are persons not likely to see a youth and maiden like to be together so much, without thinking of something beyond friendship. By Mrs L's permitting or rather encouraging your attentions to Anna I thought such a connection might be pleasing to her. I have felt surprized at her doing as[n] she did, as A is so young and an only darling; as[n] it would have been easy for her gently and indirectly to prevent[n] your being alone together so much.— Now, it seems to me as if Mrs L. may have talked with her daughter in a way to make her prematurely conscious or warned her perhaps not to compromise herself by any early engagement. I was afraid that she would disturb the natural course of Anna in such affairs

    This we may well suppose without inferring that Mrs L. is not fond of *you*. I have no doubt she is so, but it is really undesirable for Anna to form any engagmeent so young.

    Yet what A said is certainly pointed, and what she said about being "compassionate" pains me, because it seems as if old and worldly people had really been too[n] near her. I wish much to see her again.

    Has any one been with her to whom she especially referred in speaking of *flattery*?[2]

    I should think you had acted just right about your manner to her, when she is cool, but now this conversation has taken place I would stay away a little longer than usual, not long enough to seem marked or strange but a little longer than usual. And now she has said this, avoid any remarks that she might construe into expressions of love for herself at present. When I come, I may have oppory to see what is acting on her mind.

In true love ever your sister

M.

If you mention receipt of[n] this letter to dear Mother say we are all well, and miss her much[n] But you need not unless you think best. I shall write to her in a few days.

You cannot suppose that such persons as Anna says, such as W. Story for instance, will fail to rally her[n] on your attentions.[3] And little girls feel a kind of terror at the idea of being the object of serious addresses though they make like homage and the person who renders it.

ALS (MH: fMS Am 1086 [9:120]). *Addressed:* To / Richard F. Fuller / ⟨at the Law School / Cambridge / Mass.⟩ Groton. *Postmark:* New York 13 Jul.

doing as] doing ⟨it⟩ as
darling; as] darling; ↑ as ↓
to prevent] to ⟨f⟩prevent
been too] been ↑ too ↓
mention receipt of] mention ↑ receipt of ↓
well, and miss her much] well, ↑ and miss her much ↓
rally her] rally ⟨Anna⟩ ↑ her ↓

1. In a despondent letter written on 6 July (MH), Richard began by saying that he had been reading *Woman in the Nineteenth Century*: "I hit upon the thought of writing to you which made me feel relieved."

2. Anna, said Richard, "wanted to see you; for she feared a love of flattery was wanting in her—that she had cried much over it. . . . In coming home, she said she thought she never should be married; for she had never seen one she could marry."

3. William Wetmore Story, a Cambridge native whom Fuller had known from childhood, was then practicing law in Boston. He was a member of the circle gathered around James Russell Lowell.

572. To Caroline Sturgis

New York, 10th July 1845.

Dear Caroline, I begin now to wish much for some words from yourself, (of your whereabouts I have heard all along from others) But as I have been silent so long I shall have no right to complain if you feel no immediate readiness to answer when at last I call. Yet do so if you can.

I hardly know, now that I feel inclined to write, what to say to you, so much has passed in my mind since we met. A flood has passed over the country; it was a mild and warm one, but it has uprooted some objects that used to be landmarks there, has planted the seeds of new growths and effected some change in the climate though the main features of the country I suppose are still the same.

All this passes, as deep^n passages of inward life have with me, without making any show outwardly. My activity, so far as necessary to secure leave of stay in this world, has been continued independent of it. Separation from all old habits and intimacies has saved from all casual and partial confidences; all has passed in a beautiful seclusion.

I believe this true life will never with me take form in art or literature The more its treasures accumulate the less am I inclined to do any thing with them in such ways. Sometimes I wonder they do not so express themselves, for I feel that these shadows, so precious to others, would not injure their substance in its vitality. But there is no impulse to it, and I do not care, and never shall care any more. I believe I am the mother of a genius, more than a genius. It seems as if I was learning every thing, that every element of beauty and power was being reproduced in my frame, but only in my son shall they appear not in me, his unknown but happy mother.

Do you remember that night last summer when we fell asleep on the bed and we were like Elizabeth and Mary.[1] I have often wanted to express what appeared to me that night, but could not, only every day I understand it better. I feel profou[nd]ly bound with you and hope you wear my ring.

My days pass at present in the most tranquil sweetness. You cannot think how beautiful it is in this place; the winter-sight gave no idea of what it is in its nuptial robes. I very seldom go away, and never wish to for a day. You know I thought of travelling to^n many places but shall not to any this summer, for we may not be able to keep the the place another, and I feel as if it were appointed me for a brief repose from my wearinesses and wanderings. My room is delightful with its side view to the water and the great willow which contains the other windows. This is far more beautiful than the one we saw^n at Mr De Windt's and the waving of its^n boughs— whether in sunlight, moonlight,— or best in starlight only, has been to me more than the speech of any other tree ever.[2] The branches fall and make a bower trailing on the ground like the fringes of a tent. I have most charming places on the edge of the rocks; in one a wall of some forty feet of rock rises behind me; it is the best place I ever had to sit in. I have a fine Newfoundland dog, who is my companion on the rocks; he is as much to me as the willow.

Shall you not be here this summer? I should like to have you see these places, and have your spirit touch them too. Do you like your new abode? I should think you might be having a good time there. You will write, if you can to

Margaret.

Intelligens has silenced Aspirans for the present. But I feel afraid the time of peace will vanish now it has been spoken of. But the spirit prompted so to do.

ALS (MH: bMS Am 1221 [249]). *Addressed:* To / Miss Caroline Sturgis / Care of William Sturgis Esq / Boston / Mass. *Postmark:* New York Jul 11.

as deep] as ⟨all⟩ deep
travelling to] travelling ↑ to ↓
we saw] we sa⟨y⟩w
of its] of ⟨the⟩ its

1. Elisabeth, mother of John the Baptist, and her kinswoman Mary, mother of Jesus. Fuller had referred to them in letter 477.
2. On their vacation at Fishkill Landing in the autumn of 1844, Fuller and Sturgis met Christopher Cranch's mother-in-law, Caroline Smith De Windt, who was the granddaughter of John and Abigail Adams.

573. To James Nathan

*

New York 22d July, 1845

dear friend,

with pleasure inexpressible I have at last received your letters. At last!— I hope there may not be cause for so long an interval of silence again. And yet it cannot again be so hard to bear, seven weeks was so cruelly long after the habit of almost daily intercourse had been formed. It was an inevitable pain, and so I have tried to bear it well but all this month, since I began to look forward to hear, it has been very hard. This morning I wrote to Mr Bancroft, but hardly expect to get an answer so as to let you know by the 1st, for I do not know that he is in Washington; he has lately been absent. I did not think before of the probability of being refused, as I never was any trifling favor by Mr B. But it may be that "honors will change manners" as the proverb threatens, the rather as I can be of no use to him, am connected with a paper of the hostile party and in which, unfortunately, was[n] published a ludicrous anecdote about him three or four days since, and one which, if he

133

chances to see it, will make him very angry.[1] But, if he refuses, it will affect me no other way than with regret because *you* cannot have what might be useful to you. I have been a frequent guest at Mr B's house, and treated by him with a marked courtesy that gives me a right to feel I do not intrude in making the application. This being the case, refusal will not mortify me, though it would prevent my ever asking him for any other favor. On the other hand, I should have no right to resent a refusal he owes me nothing; all the favors hitherto have been from him to me, if he does not see fit to add this to the list, it will not, as I said before, affect me any how, except that I have it not to send to you. So, however it ends, have no trouble on my account. If I write nothing further by this steamer, leave orders to have the letter[n] sent after you, in case I should get it to send by the 15th. I mentioned last winter another friend, of influence in the party, but as he has not taken office, and I know not where he is, shall not attempt to do any thing by his means, as it would be too long a process to be of use. I wish I had acted before, but supposed the Sun Editors far more likely than I to get it done to advantage,[n] and supposed it beside, too trifling a favor to be refused.[2]

Most sweetly breathes your spirit to me through your[n] words; it is indeed what I felt, and felt as if you were feeling, but it is a great satisfaction to see it written down, to hold it in my hand and to my heart. The moss-roses bear transplanting well; they will grow in either climate. It is true, as you say, that the precious certainty of spiritual connexion, which will bear the test of absence and various influences, is worth great sacrifices, but— our sacrifice was premature. We needed the suns and moons of this summer to ripen our knowledge of one another (to say nothing of the loss of happiness) I always felt and feel that at the end of a few months more, separation would have been more natural, and that, though circumstances on your side seemed to command it now, yet their doing so seemed sad and of evil omen.

Yet oh! may we at least ever keep pure and sweet the joys that have been given, and the tender and elevated strain of your letters makes me trust we may. Me, too, it moved tearfully to read what you say of laying down to die that you might not ever by your presence abet falsehoods.[n] When this heart-sickness comes again, may I not draw nigh and lay my arms about your neck and my cheek to yours, and will you not then [feel] that, in a world where such true affection still find a home, there must be salt enough to keep the whole from corruption, and that we must *live* to be as good as we can, a comfort and earnest of better things t[o one] another and to other vexed and [   ] spirits, born for love and light, st[   ] walking and working in the dark [   ] You are, indeed, continually present with m[e;] other voices are silent, yours is soon heard. I only need to be alone and undisturbed. But sometimes the sense of communion is more deep and sweet and things are told that I much admire, indeed, hardly understand them yet. I do not know whether it is that seeds planted in the spring-time are growing up now in the green solitude of summer, or whether there is a rush of our souls to meet at the same moment in time, as used to be the case, and I want you to date the times when this happens with you, and I will do the same that we may know.

I am very sorry that I did not write the 16th, but yourself, I thought, told me to write up to the 1st July and not again till I heard from you. You will be disappointed, I know, since you had forgotten this. But I shall be faithful, when I understand about writing. The only[n] difficulty is the same as yours *where to begin*. I might as well write all day long as any one hour. Of outward event little has occurred of late. In the city the great fire of which you will read in the papers, by which you, I trust, are no loser, for even where there is so much suffering selfishness impels to think first and most of dear friends.[3] The still smoking ruins looked really sublime last night by the setting sun. Many chimneys and balconies are left standing in picturesque blackness upon this large area. A gazing crowd animated the foreground; it gave some notion of the miseries of war. Our friend, Mrs Greeley[n] is more dejected than ever, indeed she has much cause, but I cannot now speak of this. I gave her all from your letters I could, and all your messages except what related to going abroad. It only unsettles her to think of that and I fear Mr G. would never consent now they have the child. Also I did not speak of your writing or not writing to her; she does not now expect it, but I thought the message would irritate her towards me now and whenever I receive a letter from you. She wishes her feelings to be quite sweet towards me and is not conscious that they are not, but so it is. I hope and think they may in time become perfectly[n] so, of this eternal silence! for I could not say it elsewhere.

Sunday 27th I am anxious you should take pencil notes as you used to sometimes of things as they rise in your mind and then write them out for me. I want the little thoughts and little feelings as well as the great results. Now, dear friend, farewell! May we be *tender and true*, it was the motto of the noblest house of a noble race, and one that would do honor to any one and any relation.[4] Farewell. 27th—The letter from Mr Bancroft is recd and accompanies this in an envelope from me. I hope it will not fail to reach you, if it should by any chance Fate must have determined to leave you entirely to the impression made by your personal presence.

I will now begin upon another letter rather than spoil this by crossing

A man lost his young wife to whom he had been married only four months in the fi[re]. He is seeking her remains, half-distracted among the ruins. A girl was found in convulsions in the Fulton ferry house. Having been burnt out and lost every thing she wandered awhile homeless and then took laudanaum to kill herself. A corpse has been disinterred grasping in one hand charred ledgers, in the other some gold, a clerk they suppose The Chevalier of the counting room, vowed to *duty* to the last moment of his life.[n]

* 2d

New York, 22d [July] 1845

Our friend[5] would wish to be perfectly generous and affectionate towards me; generally she is, but at times, she compares herself with me, which I think would never have been, had it not begun in thinking of you, she then seems to think me an unduly privileged person, forgets or does not see the dark side of my lot, of which once she thought with so much tenderness, as if it would be the privilege of her life to free me from pain and care. She wishes then to make me feel my faults, and told me the other day, (it seemed her own opinion,) that you thought I could not bear being told of them. *Do* you think so?— I do not wish to hear about them constantly, especially from those whom I think younger in mind than myself, for I do not think they can apprehend me as a whole, enough to be of use to me, and I do not like a great deal of that sort of intercourse, for I think, as a general thing, we improve most by being loved and trusted and by loving and trusting. But I think too[n] with one whose judgment I valued I should receive fault-finding in the spirit in which it was meant, and, if it gave me pain, should be more likely to mend than many who take it more easily. I knew you thought me too sensitive, and *I* have thought about it, and admit it to be so, now if you think I could not bear fault-finding, as a seeker for truth ought, perhaps that is true also. You need not however answer upon this point, if you have not leisure or inclination to do it to your mind, it will not rest upon mine, except to make me examine myself more strictly. I rather wished at the time it had not been told me, but you know I promised you to hear only yourself about yourself, which promise I shall not find it difficult to keep, for I feel that we are so much more deeply known to one another than to others, that anything you could say or do would always seem entirely different to me from yourself to what it would coming through another. I also make it my request that you will *never* speak to her of this. Her main feeling is one of warm affection for both of us; she yielded to a sudden impulse in telling me this. She is sometimes satirical on the deficiencies in my care of Josey and indeed, there is room, for I do not know enough about such things to take the best care of him. He grows, however, strong and handsome, swims nobly, and is very fond of me, without regard to my faults or my unwillingness to hear about them, and I believe his master also will be indulgent. I confess I want indulgence from those I love, but it seems to me, it is not that I want blind idolatry, but as a child never finding repose on the bosom of love, I seek it now, childishly, perhaps. God knows all about it—

One trifle let me add. I dont know that any words from your mouth gave me more pleasure, a strange kind of pleasure, than these, "You must be a fool, little girl" It seemed so whimsical that they should be addressed to me who was called on for wisdom and dignity long before my leading strings were off and so pleasant too. Indeed thou art my dear brother and must ever be good and loving as to a little sister. Dear Mother left me more than a fortnight since. The only drawback on her visit was that she could not conceive of my being content here. She could not fully see how far the outward beauty of nature, and my confidence in the real goodness and honor, which both my hosts have at bottom, outweigh with me the want of^n order, comfort, and, far worse, mental harmony. Their dissensions troubled her deeply and scarce less the confusion of the household. At first, she could not forbear trying to put things to rights. At last she found upon trial what I saw from the first that they would never "stay put" and contented herself with the enjoyment of the place and of being with me; the 4th July, we spent on the rocks; reading; it was a soft cloudy, dreamy day. I felt very happy with this sweet Mother; you would love her, for she, at least, is all gentleness, and she would understand your noble human heart. She is much taller than I, and larger and prettier and kinder.— While she was here I went about with her a good deal, but since have been absolutely still and secluded, for the heat has been too great for me or any one to go about; steady intense heat for a fortnight, such as has not been known in N. Y. for many years. The nights, however, have been enough to make up for the sufferings of the days, so warm that you could be out all night and floods of that mellow moonlight that is seen only in such warm weather. If She came to you "laden with my love" before, what must she now when the whole scene was but one thought of love's earthy sweetness transfigured in celestial light; One night when I was out bathing at the foot of the tall rock, the waters rippling up so gently, the ships gliding full sailed and dreamy white over a silver sea, the crags above me with their dewey garlands, and the little path stealing away in shadow. ah! it was almost *too* beautiful to bear and live.

I have had my hammock slung on the piazza. I lie and swing there with the baby in the day-time, in the evening alone, while the breezes whisper and the moon glimmers through the stately trees, and am very sorry it was not so while you were here that I might have heard you sing there some happy evening; it is just like being in a cradle. The baby has been a great pleasure to me since I have been at home so much and grown very fond of me; when I propose taking him he says *yes* and is very gay; he is an arch child and good to frolic with, but also he likes to be talked to and understands the tones, if not the words. I carry him about and talk to him in the most wonderful way; he clings to my neck and says little assenting sounds to the poetic remarks, and looks straight in my eyes; the look in a child's eyes at this time is heavenly, so much dawning intelligence, yet so unsullied; while they are the object of unbroken love from those older they seem as if tended by Gods and fragrant with their thoughts, when they begin to play much with other children they lose it gradually. My dear friend, I say so many little little things, it will never be done. It gratifies me deeply you feel so to "Summer on the Lakes" for that is just a piece out of my common summer life; it seems as if I might write just such a volume every summer, only one lives so fast there is not time to write it down. I wish I might write something good before you come back, but really the paper when I attend to it as much as Mr G. wishes, takes all the time I feel disposed to read or write. He is now quite content again. I write often and at length; some of the pieces have attracted a good deal of attention and reply especially pieces on Swedenborgianism which I should like you to have seen, and two upon the Irish character.[6] But the merit of such things is for the day— Mr G. still intends going to the West, so whatever you write for the Tribune you had better inclose to me, or it will fall under the care of his clerks, and be treated accordingly, indeed, you had better always inclose it to me, if you wish to make sure of my seeing it before it comes out. Now how many many things beside I have to say, but must stop for this time.

Evening

More little things occur to be said; what you remark of Mrs Child is very correct, except I do not understand what you imply by connecting "deep passion" with "having no offspring" is not most fruit ripened in the warmer climates and does not the spiritual cause produce the same result in the human as in the natural sphere? I wish you had explained these things more to me; you meant to, I think, and then forgot it, for many things you began to tell me are left unfinished, and if you do not come back to me I shall never understand them, and I wish to these most of all, for their meaning seems to lie at the foundation of every thing.

I think with the utmost pathos of your poor maiden returning to her parents; though the faults of a child are generally traceable to the mismanagement of parents, yet it must be no better to return under such circumstances. I hope Heaven will teach them to be wise and tender to her and that you may have every reason to look back with happiness on your work. But she must suffer greatly to part from you, you who have been a friend to her such as it has been given few mortals to find *once* in this world and surely none could hope to find twice![n] May Heaven forever bless you for it![n] And she must bid you farewell. I shall always regret that I did not in some way see her so as to have in my mind her image, for now this want torments me when I think of her.

27th It is the still sweet Sunday, just two months since you went. How many things have I thought of since that I might have said that night but it is always impossible to do as you wish at such times. In looking over this letter it seems almost wrong to Mrs G. to send what relates to her, but it is so mixed up with the rest I cannot take it out. Yet let me add these clouds are slight the effect often[n] of undue heat from other causes and I doubt not will always yield soon to her great affection for both of us. Perhaps I will not write about such any more. I like to write just as I used to talk with you of whatever is uppermost in my mind at the moment, but when I do not have a chance to explain and qualify as when we were near it may be right to practise reserve where others are concerned.

AL (MB: Ms. Am. 1451 [58–59]). Published in *Love-Letters*, pp. 121–35. *Addressed:* To / James Nathan / Care Mr. Thomas Delf. / 16 Little Britain / London / England. *Postmark:* New York Jul 30.

unfortunately, was] unfortunately, ↑ was ↓
have the letter] have ⟨it⟩ ↑ the letter ↓
done to advantage,] done, ↑ to advantage ↓
through your] through ⟨the⟩ ↑ your ↓
abet falsehoods.] abet ⟨in⟩ falsehoods.
The only] The ↑ only ↓
Greeley] *The name had been canceled by a later hand but is here recovered.*
become perfectly] become ↑ perfectly ↓
his life.] *Fuller cross-hatched this paragraph over the description of the fire.*
think too] think ↑ too ↓
want of] *The remainder of the sentence has been canceled by a later hand but is here recovered.*
world and surely none could hope to find twice!] world! ↑ and surely none could hope to find twice ↓
for it!] *The remainder of the paragraph has been canceled by a later hand but is here recovered.*
effect often] effect ↑ often ↓

1. George Bancroft was secretary of the navy in the new Polk administration. On 19 July the *Tribune* reported a cabinet quarrel that pitted Bancroft, Secretary of War William Marcy, and Secretary of State James Buchanan against Polk on the questions of the tariff and the Oregon situation. "Mr. Buchanan," said the correspondent, "will, therefore, certainly resign, but Messrs. Bancroft and Marcy are too fond of the loaves and fishes to follow his example."

2. In 1834 Moses Yale Beach (1800–1868) joined his brother-in-law, Benjamin Day, who owned the *New York Sun*. In 1838 Beach bought control of the paper and made it into a journalistic and financial success (*DAB*).

3. Early on the morning of 19 July, a fire broke out amid loud explosions. It raged through the business district of New York City, eventually destroying hundreds of residences and businesses (*New-York Daily Tribune*, 21 July 1845).

4. Though not the Douglas motto, the phrase was associated with the clan. "O Douglas, O Douglas! tindir and trewe" (Richard Holland, *Buke of the Howlat*, stanza 31).

5. Mary Greeley.

6. Fuller wrote twice on the Swedish philosopher Emanuel Swedenborg: "Swedenborgianism" and "Swedenborg and his Disciples" (*New-York Daily Tribune*, 25 June and 7 July 1845). The first two of her three pieces on the Irish had recently appeared: "The Irish Character," 28 June and 15 July.

574. To James Nathan

Saturday, July 26th. [1845][n]

Mr Bancroft attended to my request at once and accompanied the enclosed with a most cordial note expressive of his pleasure in doing so. As I told him what had been done previously and that it was said a private letter would be sufficient, he sends such an one, and though it is addressed only to persons connected with the navy, I suppose it will prove sufficient as such consuls or officers will give you other letters if you need them. I could, no doubt, procure good letters to the consul at Rome, and one from a cousin of his, my intimate friend, to Mr Langdon, a distinguished merchant at Smyrna,[1] to[n] whom many Americans go, if you need any thing further:— you will answer fully on this score, whether this is enough and whether you want more, will you not, dear friend. Every sweet will have its sour, and the same post which brought me a bit of paper that may be of use to thee, brought, also, the news that my poor Georgiana had lost the brother whom she adopted and brought to this country. The poor boy died alone, among strangers. He had kept at work to the last moment he was able to sit up; indeed, much too long, yet his sickness, funeral &c leave a[n] debt to his sister which embittered his last thoughts. She says "I cannot sleep at night for thinking how he must have longed, ah more than that— to see me, of his working when so miserable from sense of necessity. I try to drive away such thoughts and believe that he is now in good society where he is bound by no fetters but those his own spirit imposes,— but how shall I tell Mother. I could wish to lie down and die, too"— O, my friend, how often that wish must come to all of us, yet it would be useless, *we must pay our ransom out of our own earnings either in this world or the next,* and the Beethovens the heaviest

I have been thinking of you today more than ever; I have been entirely alone, all the others gone to Coney Island and no sound except the murmur of the summer wind to invade the deep sweet stillness. All day it was sweet, yet toward nightfall it grew oppressively sad. I longed to be summoned by your voice catch animation from your eye. Yet today my thoughts have been concentrated on our relation as never before. It seems to me not only peculiar but *original.* I have never had one at all like it, and I do not read things in the poets or anywhere that more than glance at it; they do not touch that[n] which is especially its life. Your thoughts are growing in my mind, the influence of your stronger organization has at times almost transfused mine, and has effected some permanent changes there, there have been moments when our minds were blended in one, yet what I mean is the inner fact the[n] kernel, of whose existence these are only the tokens. It has never made me so deeply sensible of its presence as today[n] beating like a heart within me, a heart that seems strong enough to cast aside this weed of flesh and clothe itself anew. If others enjoy the same, they nowhere speak of it. And is it not by living such relations that we bring a new religion, establishing nobler freedom for all? for that which takes place in us must, by spiritual law, widen its circles till it embraces all. But I talk to thee of what thou knowest better than I, yet indeed, I feel when known to me it will be angelic knowledge. Farewell, du Bester, take me to thyself in that deep sincerity which is prayer and God's will be done!

Sunday eveg As I lie thinking, I begin to be troubled lest the enclosed should not suffice for what you want as one from the President or Secretary of State would. It is, of course, credentials as to who you are, but you may not always wish to make use of it, when you want such.

In this case let me name persons from whom I could get letters that might supply the want.

Mr Glidden not known to me, but much indebted to some of my friends. Dr Howe, well known to me and to Greece— Mr Edward Everett, who will soon be on his return, and who though he has left office might have the desirable connexions abroad.[2] He has shown me much kindness and would, I doubt not, still do so.

If any of these can be of use, name it to your sister who is best entitled of any here to act for you, since you say you love her best and she is most anxious you should have the full profit of your travel and not be exposed to interruption and useless annoyance.

A letter from Mr Bancroft seems more appropriate to one with professions of literary objects in travel than one either from the President or Mr Buchanan. I left it at his own discretion what to do, and suppose he did what was easiest, but it will, I think be sufficient.

I have shown the utmost senselessness in writing this envelope, forgive, if it costs you pence additional to put another. I forgot what I was about and have not time to copy. imagine you economized enough by my omission to write the 15th to pay for the additional envelope. I never did anything so clumsy before.

I draw my pen through the above for how silly it seems to jest at such a distance, even in this flat heartless way, it is too uncongenial.— Next week I hear from you and shall then know whether I am to write again. Alway I begin to feel like it.

Even if you wrote to me that you wanted any thing and circumstances should then have so changed that I could not with perfect delicacy and propriety apply I would not, because I know you would not in such case be willing to have me, so do not again scruple to speak; for I do not know the case clearly enough to divine—

I am sorry that I have scrawled so all over the thick letter which accompanies this. I fear it will hardly be legible to you and will try not to do so any more, but one thing came to hand thick after the other till I had irregularly covered almost every inch.

AL (MB: Ms. Am. 1451 [60]). Published in *Love-Letters*, pp. 135–40.

1845] *Fuller apparently was writing two letters to Nathan at the same time, for the previous letter to Nathan overlaps with this one.*
Smyrna, to] Smyrna, ↑ to ↓
leave a] leave⟨s⟩ a
touch that] touch ↑ ⟨you and⟩ ↓ ⟨that⟩ that
fact the] fact ⟨life⟩ the
presence as today] presence ↑ as today ↓

1. George Washington Greene (1811–83) of Rhode Island had been United States consul at Rome since January 1837. Ironically, his appointment ended the day after Fuller wrote this letter. Greene attended Brown University, became a historian, and taught modern languages at Brown. His "cousin" was Albert Gorton Greene of Providence, a writer whom Fuller often met when she taught there in 1837–38 (*DAB*). Langdon is probably Joseph Langdon (bp. 1799), whose father, John Walley Langdon (1772?–1854), had established the tea trade at Smyrna with his brother, Thomas Walley Langdon (1783–1861). John Walley Langdon was the uncle of Amelia Greenwood, Fuller's close childhood friend (Stillman Foster Kneeland, *Seven Centuries in the Kneeland Family* [New York, 1897], pp. 108, 131–32; *New England Historical and Genealogical Register* 15 [1861]: 185).

2. Dr. Samuel Gridley Howe, director of the Perkins Institute for the Blind in Boston, had fought in the Greek revolt against the Turks in the 1820s. He was the husband

of Julia Ward. Edward Everett, clergyman, scholar, and a former governor of Massachusetts, soon returned to the United States after serving as the ambassador to England.

575.   To Georgiana Bruce

[27? July 1845]

Some persons seem the mark for the darts of destiny, but then the gods appear to love them specially too.[1] It seems very hard that this grief should come, and thoughts of the poor child's lonely death be your companions, just as there was a chance that free nature and new impressions should bring you refreshment. For him I trust his position may be improved. My dear Georgiana, invite every peaceful thought that shows any willingness to come, and live on courageously as you can, for us who cherish and the many who will yet need you. I can say no more; this is all the consolation I have been able to find for myself at certain dark periods of my life, yet have lived after to beautiful moments, and successive daybreaks of glorious light.

But if not inly, outwardly I may aid you. I see from Mr. D.'s letter that you now have a considerable debt in Cincinnati; this will trouble you too much. I have a sum now in Boston, from which I can draw it, and I want you to write me exactly how much you need, and how I shall remit it, from Boston, when I am there in September or October— whether to you or Mr. D. in Cin.

I do not wish you to consider this as a debt. I can easily earn it again before ever I shall have occasion for it, and my desire is to enable you to feel free. It is this which would give me pleasure and solid satisfaction in sending it to you, that it may be a help to peace and repose.

On the other hand, should there come a time when your debt to Brook Farm is off your mind, and you have had rest and some of those pleasures and opportunities—of which life has brought me more than my share,—and then have it to spare, you may give it back to me if you wish, for as I am older than you, and may not always be able to use my talents for lucre, by that time I may need it. This is a fair arrangement, I think; at least it is one that I should acquiesce in with a sisterly friend, as I am to you, am I not?

Always affectionately yours,

S. M. F.

Loud shrieks just took me down into the little wood, there to see finely dressed, painted courtesans playing at being insulted by swear-

ing men, whose lightest repartee was, "God damn your soul!" Oh, these
are woes cancerous, horrible, of which *we* know nothing.

ELfr, from Kirby, *Years of Experience*, pp. 228–30.
Dated from the reference to Bruce's brother.
1. Bruce's brother had just died.

576. To Richard F. Fuller

New York, 6th August, 45.

My dear Richard,
    I put off writing to you, merely because I was too unwell and tired
the night I wrote to mother to think clearly. I really loathe my pen at
present; it is entirely unnatural to me to keep at it so in the summer,
looking at these dull blacks and whites so much when Nature is in her
bright colors is a source of[n] great physical weariness and irritation. I
cannot, therefore, write you good letters, but am always glad to get
them. That of yours from Groton was good. I am glad you feel so, for
the time was come.[1]
    As to what you say of my writing books that cannot be, at present, I
have not health and energy to do so many things, and find too much
that I[n] value in my present position[n] to give it up rashly or suddenly.
But doubt not, as I do not, that Heaven has good things enough for me
to do and that I shall find them best by not exhausting or overestrain-
ing myself.[2]
    About your coming, you cannot doubt it would be a true pleasure to
me, and if you had money enough to come often, I should urge your
setting out at once.[3] But as you have not, perhaps you would rather,
when you cannot see me any other way and have some plan which you
could combine with this. Next summer I may not come to Mass. I cannot take more than a month's recess in the year and may prefer giving
that time to some new place or longer journey. But, if you think you
could come then and now too, you had better. Travelling can never be
cheaper, you can come here, stay a few days, see all you want to you being able to walk a good deal[n] and return for seven or eight dollars, but
had better bring *ten* We want you to stay here; Mrs G is truly desirous
you should and there is a room in which you can be comfortable enough
for a short time. I should like much to see you and have you see this

place where I have had sweet hours and where we *may not* be next summer. If you do come, I will expect you in a few days.

When you go to Mrs Loring's will you ask W. Story if he has any of Robert[n] *Browning's poems* to lend me for a short time. They shall be returned safe. I only want them a few days to make some extracts for the paper.[4] They cannot be obtained here. Give my love to Mr and Mrs L. and Anna.— I wrote you a letter the same night I recd that of yours about *yr side* and a few lines by Mother, none others I think, so it probably, was not mine that Lloyd lost. Pray see that dear Mother has ale, fruit, sea-bathing, and [whatever] her health requires. I will provide money if necessary. Every affecy yr sisr,

M.

ALS (MH: fMS Am 1086 [9:121]); MsC (MH: fMS Am 1086 [Works, 2:783–89]). *Addressed:* To / Richard F. Fuller / at the Law School / Cambridge / Mass. *Postmark:* New York 7 Aug.

is a source of] is ↑ a source of ↓

much that I] much ⟨too⟩ ↑ that I ↓

present position] present posit⟨s⟩ion

to you being able to walk a good deal] to ↑ you being able to walk a good deal ↓

of Robert] of ↑ Robert ↓

1. In his letter of 18 July (MH), Richard described his Groton visit: "I see it sympathising with the regret you used to feel, that you were here buried."

2. Richard urged her to continue to write: "Mother said you hinted that you might not do much more except your miscellaneous pieces. Do not thus think! Let not that fine organism be laid in the dust till it has borne a fruit worthy of your God!" She ignored his tart observation that "Emerson is not your true friend. I know that thoroughly, & I rejoice you are away from him. His influence is bad, & he does not know you. I was pained by his saying of your book, that you ought not to write, you talked so well."

3. "If you do not come on this next month," wrote Richard, "I should like three weeks from now, to come & see you."

4. Which of Browning's books she wanted is unclear. He had published *Pauline* (1833), *Paracelsus* (1835), *Sordello* (1840), *Pippa Passes*, and the first number of *Bells and Pomegranates* by this time. *Dramatic Romances and Lyrics* appeared in November 1845. She may not have received the poems, for no excerpts appeared in the *Tribune*. She first reviewed Browning on 1 April 1846.

577. To James Nathan

N. Y. 12th August, 1845.

My very dear friend,

It is true that I have been indulging myself day by day in writing to you. But *that letter* has swollen to such a bulk, that it really seems wrong to send it, when it may have to travel after you from station to station till it comes to[n] cost its weight in gold. Yet This[n] circumstance seems but an outward obstacle expressive of the will of the Spirit that it will rather be trusted to communica[te] in full between us what is there stammered out with childish prolixity.

I will not, however, destroy the letter, perhaps on[n] some future occasion I may send, or show it you. The Cambria brought yours with wonderful speed, full four days before I hoped. But now I fear I must wait a long time, to pay for this favor of Fate; The Great Britain brought in all its mighty bulk, not one little seed for my garden. I did not expect it, yet was disappointed, so unreasonable is affection.

The letters for the Tribune appeared on 8th August.[1] By a mistake which I did not forsee, they mistook your J. for an A. and the signature stands *A. N.* This shall be amended in future. They are under the head *"Wayside Notes Abroad."* I have kept 6 copies for you. They did not need copying; and[n] needed but little retouching which I easily gave to your *M. S. Pan* is literally *the All*; it is the Universal Spirit[n] best known in the solitudes of Nature. As this did not correspond with what you wished to express, I substituted the *Oreads and Dryads.* These are nymphs representing the first[n] the lights and shadows that play upon hills and open fields,— the second the secret recesses of the woods; the trees and fountains. There is no God who stands *both* for free nature and agriculture and these nymphs represent the aspect of a cultivated country, interspersed with woods. These first letters are written with freedom and sweetness; the facts selected are of a leading character; the second a beautiful poem; truth to tell, I rather grudged it to the Public— Mrs G. was charmed with the letters. Foster, one of our Editors, asked *if I had read them*![2] expressed admiration of them and said the image of the Moon passing the pillars of her palace was entirely original yet reminded him of Shelley!

I hope you will follow it up by letters from *London and Paris.* Dr Lardner writes us quite good business accounts of matters in Paris, but different things from his would strike you.[3] I have been much interested by the letter of the Carpenters and the homage paid to the *Mother of the Carpenters by them*![4]

My loved friend, I am deeply sorry that the affair that has troubled you so long finds not a definitive and peaceful issue.[n] There is somewhat, also, in the course of the Maiden that strikes me painfully, but, perhaps, imperfect knowledge of the circumstances makes me unjust. Is it not possible I might aid you? My friend, Mrs Farrar is English; her mother a benevolent old lady, widely acquainted with good people, lives in London.[5] My pupil, Maria, who has been two years on the Continent will be there this autumn in the house of this her Grandmother.[6]

She loves me much and would, I think, act energetically for me, if without acquainting her with the other[n] circumstances, I told her of a fair girl who had been in this country and[n] in whom I was interested needed friends and employment. So would Miss Martineau if in London.[7] But perhaps they could not do better than the friend under whose care you have left her. But if you think they could, give me her name and address and tell me just what to say about her. She may need female protection and the old lady, a Quaker, would be a refuge to her.

Whatever else this affair brings, believe that it has brought you a portion of *immortal love*. It is not only your noble frankness towards me, but, though you avowed to me the thoughts and possibilities which prevented your first action in this case from being wholly disinterested, and though the falsehood and other circumstances of your position were painful to me, yet I know that your main impulse was always noble, and that the latter part of the time you acted solely from fidelity to the duty you had undertaken,[n] and disinterested regard to its subject. The sense of this is immortal with me.

Yet I do ardently hope that you will now be able to find a clear path. *Now* is the crisis. You have great experience, great ideas, a religious heart and unbroken manhood. You ought to have one where you can act freely, and, so far as is given to men, bless and be blest. And now is the crisis! We all ascend the mountain.— some, after conquering the obstacles near the base, find a distinct path amid lofty trees, and though they may have to climb over terrible rocks, and be beset by wild beasts or fretted by thorns or hungers, still they have a distinct path, and are often comforted and animated[n] by wide outlooks or bright sunlight visiting them through the branches. But others have to cut wearily their course day by day through the thicket and never know their way nor their journey's aim, till they see the stars from the top. May my brother be of the first! he would know how to use and enjoy a free life for himself and others. You will laugh perhaps, but, whenever I meet one of those wagons labelled Rockland Lake Ice, I think it will all be well; that you will be the bearer of some thing as clear and refreshing, in a more suitable vehicle, and I myself shall drink it in with the water and milk every day earth affords. Much did I write of these and other matters in the big letter, especially was a deep mood while staying last week in New Jersey noted down. That was the 6th and 7th August. I made a request to you in the end, we shall see if you will not comply, without being asked in words.

Your pictures are all correct, except that I do not go to the little wood. I have never even with Mother. I have[n] been to the wall, but you always used to take me over, and now to get over by myself and walk there alone is too sad. I could not go. I pray for you sometimes on the rocks, but they are little fluttering prayers that may not rise very high. Your self will be your own prayer, but I, if indeed your Muse, may help inspire you to make it earnest. I wear my^n prettiest dresses at those times that I go to think of you^n as if you were here, but when I take Josey, he gets salt-water all over them. I have not the heart, however, to be angry, he looks up with such loving eyes. When he is in the water, ever so far off, if I make the least sound, he turns them right upon me. I am much troubled about him; his eyes looked so badly two or three weeks ago, that I began to take all the charge of him, but he seems as yet little be[tter] and a gentleman who was here yesterday said they had an expression as if he^n would not live long. Would it not be a great grief to you to come back and find him not? Can you tell me what to do? the people round here say he should take Sulphur, but Mrs G. is not willing.

She has been quite ill and I now think it was nervous irritation that occasioned some appearances of which I wrote you. She is better. The baby [   ] now.

In each letter you have spoken as if you *might* remain in Europe; is any thing new influencing you? You always said to me, you felt yourself permanently a Citizen of the U. S.

You expressed some care about me in addition to your other perplexities, but do not feel it. Nothing threatens near; there are causes that might break the domestic relations, but do not seem likely to the business ones. I fee[l] fixed here for the present.

` I passed some days last week in N. Jersey, of which was also some notice in the big letter. During my absence Mrs S. staid here. This lady does not improve upon me; Her conversation and temper of mind bear traces of much low converse.

I have had some congenial hours, for Mr Emerson has been here two days, full of free talk and in serene beauty as ever. He went yesterday.[8]

I am going tomorrow eveg with Mr Benzon to hear "The Huguenots", since you did.[9] It seems whimsical or like the influence of a Star to go thus with your townsman. He is the bodily, you the spiritual presence of that Hamburgh influence. I am inclined to scold Fate that has given him all the money and the broad place to stand in and you chiefly the cares and scruple that haunt the life of trade. And certainly I see no propriety in her keeping him here and sending you there!

Yet are you with me more than ever, especially when I wake, so that I do not like to rise and break it all up. Always we were nearest at early morning and are so still; is it that we have met in dreams or only that the mind has been refreshed by sleep?

I told you in the big letter of the next scene in the life of Mrs Barrett and how she was befriended by one who had been her schoolboy lover But I shall have occasion yet to tell you all these little things, for surely we shall yet sit together in the [gre]enwood shade and reveal these fin[e f]acts or signs of life that others do [not] appreciate

Keep by me I pray let me not go till the whole mystery be known. And now, at least with this pen farwell. Could but the words become instinct with the soul, how sweetly would they beam and breathe upon thee liebster Freund.

By last Steamer I sent 2 large letters from me and a Circular from Mr Bancroft, not all you need I fear, yet hope it came safe.

Eveg of 12th Mrs Greeley has just come in and sends her love, but I in vain suggest a kiss in return for the one she received by Steamer last.

Another thing I must quote from the by gone letter now you are in the region of Artists, will you not have your picture taken If a good miniature on ivory is too great an extravagance I have seen excellent likenesses in colored crayons of large miniature size. But do not have it taken at all unless it can be excellent well done.

AL (MB: Ms. Am. 1451 [61–62]). Published in *Love-Letters*, pp. 140–49. *Addressed:* To / James Nathan / Care of Mr Thomas Delf / 16 Little Britain / London / England. *Postmark:* New York 13 Aug.

it comes to] it ⟨become⟩ ↑ comes to ↓
Yet This] ↑ Yet ↓ This
perhaps on] perhaps ⟨I shall⟩ on
copying; and] copying; ↑ and ↓
Universal Spirit] Universal ⟨s⟩Spirit
representing the first] representing ↑ the first ↓
peaceful issue.] *The remainder of the paragraph has been canceled by a later hand but is here recovered.*
the other] the ↑ other ↓
girl who had been in this country and] girl ↑ who had been in this country and ↓
undertaken,] untertaken,
comforted and animated] comforted ↑ and animated ↓
I have] I ⟨alw⟩ ↑ have ↓
wear my] wear ⟨your⟩ my
dresses at those times that I go to think of you] dresses ↑ at those times that I go to think of you ↓
if he] if ⟨th⟩ he

1. The two letters were printed in the *Tribune* on 8 August. The changes Fuller describes appear in the first letter.

2. George C. Foster (d. 1850) wrote several books about New York.

3. Dionysius Lardner (1793–1859), an Irish scientist and inventor, edited the *Cabinet Cyclopaedia*, which was completed in 133 volumes in 1849. The *Tribune* had often excerpted his lectures when he spoke in America from 1840 to 1845, and Greeley had published several volumes of them. From 1845 until his death, Lardner lived in Paris (*DNB*). Fuller's comment suggests that he is the correspondent who signed himself "P. A. R." in

several reports from Paris. Such dispatches appeared in the *Tribune* for 15 and 31 July and for 12 August.

4. In Paris 5,000 carpenters held an illegal strike, demanding a daily wage increase from four to five francs. In "The Social Movement in Europe," Fuller published her translation of a letter signed "Journeymen Carpenters of Paris," which had originally appeared in the *Deutsche Schnellpost (New-York Daily Tribune,* 5 August 1845). On 12 August, a report from P. A. R. in the *Tribune* described the arrest and release of a woman called the carpenters' "mother," the title given to a woman who received union money and provided food and shelter for the strikers. In July one such woman had been arrested for "exciting the workmen to coalesce." She was greeted in triumph upon her release by a crowd of carpenters, whom she called her "sons."

5. Eliza Farrar's mother was Elizabeth Barker Rotch (1764–1857), daughter of Josiah and Elizabeth Barker of Nantucket (John M. Bullard, *The Rotches* [New Bedford, 1947], p. 112).

6. Maria Rotch was traveling in Europe with her brother, Francis Morgan, and their parents, Francis and Ann Waln Rotch.

7. Fuller had met Harriet Martineau in Cambridge in the 1830s.

8. After lecturing at Wesleyan College, Emerson went to New York to visit his brother (Gay Wilson Allen, *Waldo Emerson: A Biography* [New York, 1981], pp. 450–51).

9. Meyerbeer's *Les Huguenots,* first performed in Paris in 1836, had its New York premiere on 11 August (*Annals of Opera,* col. 777).

578.   To Ellis and Louisa Loring

New York, 22d
August 45

To Mr and Mrs Loring
Dear friends,

Mr Greeley has recd a letter from a slave-holder in Kentucky making this proposal. This person, Lindsay by name, is the owner of a mulatto girl, who, being hired out to service in the City, became a mother at a very early age of a little girl now 4 or 5 years old. This child, he says, is very handsome and sprightly, and by all strangers considered a white child. He says "as it is impossible she should here be brought up in a virtuous manner, or, in fact, receive any education at all, I am anxious to give up all right or title to her, pay her expenses on to the East and there give her up to the care of some one who will furnish evidence of being able and willing to act toward her as a parent or guardian and see that she has a fair chance of education for whatsoever place in society her abilities may fit her to occupy."

Foreseeing natural suspicions that may arise, he offers "any amount of evidence to show that this offer is entirely disinterested, and that I stand in no other relation either to Mother or child than that of Master, and shall not that long to either." He furnishes references at to his general character.

Ellis G. Loring. Courtesy of the Massachusetts Historical Society.

Louisa Gilman Loring. Courtesy of the Massachusetts Historical Society.

He is desirous the origin of the child should not be made known, but that she should be educated as white, and it would, I think, be an interesting task to[n] one who feels or wishes to settle doubts as to the tendencies of African blood, of Amalgamation &c. I wished myself, much, to try a half-breed child of white and Indian descent, to ascertain how far the common objections to such[n] unions are founded, but I am not in a situation to undertake any such charge. Do you know of any one who is? Mrs Child recommended that I should apply to you as the persons most likely to know of some place for her and to take an interest in inquiring. She also mentioned *Mary Chapman*, as one likely to take such an interest.[1] Wd you answer soon, if you can, with convenience.

Mrs C. showed me a note from Anna, which says you think of coming here this Autumn; that will be in Septr I hope, for the last days of that month or the first of Octr I go to Mass on a visit and want to see you both there and here. I want much that Anna should pass a day with me here, and see my beautiful rocks, where I have been so happy and which I shall not have next summer. Do come in Septr.

In haste but always Affecy Yours

S. M. FULLER.

ALS (MWelC). *Addressed:* To / Ellis Gray Loring Esq. / Boston / Mass. *Postmark:* New York Aug 22.

task to] task ⟨as⟩ to
to such] to ↑ such ↓

1. Mary Chapman (1799?–1874) was the daughter of Henry and Sarah Green Chapman of Boston. Like her brother, Henry Grafton Chapman, and his wife, Maria Weston Chapman, Mary was a Garrisonian abolitionist (MVR 267:244; Suffolk probate, no. 56306).

579.   To James Nathan

N. Y. 31st August, 1845.

We said farewell the first day of summer and now it is the last. It is again Sunday, the same hour in the evening. I am by the window in the little study recess with the tree looking in, and the stars looking through *it*, "but where art Thou!"

It is gone forever, the beautiful summer when we might have been so happy together, and happy in a way that neither of us ever will be with any other person. Oh it is very sad! My friend, shed some tears with me.

Why, why, must you leave me? If you had staid, I should have been well and strong by this time, and had so much natural joy and so many thoughts of childhood! And you! have you gained much thus far?

I will write no more tonight. I am heart-sick about it all. I am wishing so much for a letter, yet when it comes, how little it will be; letters are so little and you do not love writing; that makes it worse yet. O the summer! "the green and bowery summer"! gone, irrecoverably gone!

Yet, all through it, have I been growing in the knowledge of you. You would be surprized to find how much better I know you than when we parted. But I should have been so much more happy in real than in the ideal intercourse! Why! Why? Yes I must fret, *must must* grieve.

5th Septr—

Last night came the wished for letter, dated Paris, 12th August; but, dearest, it seemed cold and scanty. It was five weeks since I had had one; that is a long revolution for an earthly moon she needs then to come into full light.[n] You say "be embraced" but this letter is not an embrace, and that was what I needed to feel the warmth of your heart and soul; it would have enlivened me at once. Yet I do feel as if I lived in your thoughts constantly, as you do in mine, but the need of some outward sign is only the same as that you express about having with you no letters, "nothing to kiss";— it would be such a relief and "cast a light upon the day/—a light that would not go away/A sweet forewarning." I acquiesce in what you say of the dissipating influence of travel and that you will ever with me be truthful nor profane the pen, by writing from any but the mood you are in; this truthfulness, which has made us to one another all that we are, shall ever be welcome to me, however bitter the truths it may bring; but is[n] it not *true* that you were chilled by not receiving a letter from me when you expected? now this was in consequence of your own directions that I "should write by the two next steamers and not again till I heard from you" I pray thee, if any disappointment of[n] this kind occur in future, attribute it to misunderstanding or accident; I must change indeed, more than seems now possible, if I can voluntarily omit writing; on the contrary it is a painful repression that I cannot write[n] far oftener. I feel peculiarly anxious in this point, because Mr G. has twice now mislaid my letters when they were of importance and in both instances I have only discovered his having done so by accident. There is no help for this, as he is far more careful of my affairs than his own, and only[n] at times when he has some piece of writing in his head is so incurably careless. Promise me, then, that if any gap of silence should occur you will attribute it to some such cause.

I, on my side, have deep confidence in your honorable and tender care of me. I know if you give yourself to other influences, it is not likely to be lightly or suddenly, for your nature is not light or shallow,ⁿ and you are now a mature man, so I shall not *lightly* believe in your silence. I feel more apprehension on this subject, for once in my life, two consecutive letters, intercepted on their passage to me, occasioned great unhappiness to another,ⁿ and in my mind would have left wonder and sadnessⁿ always, but for an accident that cleared all up. So my loved brother, believe ever I hold thy hand, though the veil of darkness may have fallen so that thou canst not see where I am. And then,ⁿ remember, that, only a day or two before you went away, you talked of "whether a man of honor ought to seek *"hingebung"*[1] unless *sure of being able to feel as much"* And that sometimes when sadness oppresses me, and I might like to give way to all the impulses of my soul, I cannot but remember that if sometimes you have called on me to do so, as celestials would, at others there have been on your part careful limitations as to yourself, doubting the extent or permanence of your feelings for me,ⁿ which would give to the overflow of a soul the shame of infatuation, if received with such. Dearest, Heaven grant that all this may be tempered betwixt us to a permanent music: we have reason to hope it may be so, for Heaven alone has brought us near; no earthly circumstances favored it at all. Yet again we may only be lent to one another for a season and then withdrawn for other duties and relations; the sense of this sometimes checks my feelings on their sweetest flight. *All* the flowers are worth cultivating; those which have on them the doom of mortality are even more touchingly beautiful that we must prize them today, for they have no tomorrow; but only *the amaranth* is worthy to be watered, the purple with our life-blood, the white with our holiest tears. Yet let not Chance snatch any thing from us; she is a wicked Goddess and would not be especially kind to us, who have never been willing to trust her. For in this we are alike, looking forward, planning life.— Enough! You will love me as much, as long, and as *carefully* as you can, will you not? For though the essence be indestructible, the crystal that encloses it may be broken and the perfume escape far:— into another life perhaps. I, on my side, will be equally careful, for though you are a strong man, I do not think you, in this sense, less delicate than I.

I wish that I had written, if only that the letter might go with you into Switzerland. I think of you now beside those torrents or looking up to those sublime peaks, for which I have so longed in vain. You will have these holy places much to your self at least I see that a great proportion of the professed Tourists and Sketchers who usually infest these beautiful scenes have been kept away by the agitations of the country. And

Rome— greet the Sistine and the halls of the Vatican for me! and say that I am no longer favored to see them for Rome has grown up in my soul in default of the bodily presence nor could the interval of space hinder[n] my communion with Dominichino, Raphael, and Michel Angelo. I am glad you begin to love pictures; that is a world by itself, and the true comfort from the strifes of this world to see human nature represented as it ought to be, as, yet, in some serene world, it must and will[n] be. In Michel you would find an echo to the deepest tones of Jewish inspiration, men and women sublimed to children of God and masters of Eternity

In my letters of 1st and 15th August (three in all long and, pardon me, too heavy, at least in a material sense) you will find what I say of your letters to the Tribune; the same applies to these; *they are very good.*[2] I shall, however, remodel them I have now[n] a little leaving out some particulars that are better known than you suppose. Already you write well, and a year or two of composition for such purposes would correct trifling faults and give you full command of English. I hope you will continue as often, and earnestly as you can. Give, next, letters from Paris (*in full*) from Switzerland, beautiful as that on the moon at sea. Rome is an all hacknied theme and by the most accomplished pens, but you will find somewhat of your own, no doubt. Do not describe outward objects there in detail we[n] know every nook of St Peters, every statue, every villa, by heart almost. But what you see characteristic and your own thoughts will interest.

Now if you want the particulars from "The Crescent and the Cross" I must fill up my letter with them. I am sorry you did not look at it, both on this account and because it is too long to copy all and I shall have to select particulars according to my own judgment, which may fail as to what you most want.[n]

After finishing this copy I lay down and fell asleep for awhile when that happened, which has several times while you were here, when I had seemed to be put from you during an interview. The next time I fall asleep, my spirit would seem drawn to yours and there soothed and cherished like a pet dove till it came back in its native bouyancy and peace. I feel quite happy now and I have you with me as a river that has passed through another rushes joyous and enriched on its course. Yet the time of words and discussions must come again, but do thou, O Father, lead us through and bless thy children.

You do not speak to me of the deep things of the spirit, but you will in due time. And of *the promises*. But I will write no more, for there is neither time nor word— as yet. But sometime, surely I shall have beautiful things to tell and to hear.

How rejoiced was I to hear that the maiden is like to do so well. I had cumbered myself much since hearing that she could not go to her home, that I had not urged to see her and persuaded her to stay here, for I felt sure I could have had her well placed in Masstts. But now it is well;[n] thy deed of love will yet, I trust bear worthy fruits.

I live here still in extreme seclusion, too much, I believe for my spirits. I have only been to Rockaway a few days; these I enjoyed much; it was transcendant moonlight all the time and then by day in the surf or riding fleetly on the noble beach. At home the baby is my chief company; he grows more and more lovely and begins to talk; it is enchanting to see the faculties developed one after the other and learn yourself in the clear eyes of a child. His mother is well again. I am going to Mass soon for a month and I need it, for there I shall be obliged or induced to keep in bodily motion all the time and not use my eyes for reading or writing. Josey is pretty well. I have given him up to the man again after taking care myself for some weeks. I had too much trouble not with but about him.

AL (MB: Ms. Am. 1451 [63–64]). Published in part in Miller, p. 219; published entire in *Love-Letters*, pp. 149–58.

moon she needs then to come into full light.] moon. ↑ she needs then to come into full light ↓

but is] but ↑ is ↓

disappointment of] disappointment⟨s⟩ of

cannot write] cannot ↑ write ↓

and only] and ↑ only ↓

not light or shallow,] not ⟨so⟩ ↑ light or shallow ↓

unhappiness to another,] unhappiness, ↑ to another ↓

wonder and sadness] wonder ↑ and sadness ↓

And then,] And ⟨you⟩ ↑ then, ↓

yourself, doubting the extent or permanence of your feelings for me,] yourself, ↑ doubting the extent or permanence of your feelings for me, ↓

space hinder] space ⟨?⟩ hinder

it must and will] it ⟨ought to⟩ ↑ must and will ↓

them I have now] them ↑ I have now ↓

describe outward objects there in detail we] describe ↑ outward objects there ↓ in detail ⟨there⟩ we

want.] *A two-page excerpt from* The Crescent and the Cross *is here omitted.*

well;] *The paragraph to this point has been canceled by a later hand but is here recovered.*

1. *Hingebung:* devotion.

2. Nathan's next series of "Wayside Notes Abroad" appeared in the *Tribune* for 10, 12, and 16 September.

580.   To Richard F. Fuller

[31 August 1845]

[   ] of our correspondents. He acquiesced with his usual generous readiness. He wrote formally, but expressed affection. Said they were at Beverly.

Take good care of dear Mother. I feel all the time anxious about her and grieved that I cannot see whether she wants any thing.

I hope our poor Lloydie can go to Brook Farm soon. Poor, *poor* Lloyd! Most deeply do I feel fo[r] him! he is likely to suffer far more from his partial inferiority than he would, if it were complete; I want to hear directly whether Mother has got entirely well. My love to her A. and L. I am sleepy and sad tonight. Sometimes I get very tired of my lonely and comfortless life, and forget to look on the best side it has been so for a few days back. You, dear R. may good Angels guide and bless!

ALfr (MH: fMS Am 1086 [9:253]). *Addressed:* To / Richard F. Fuller / Law School / Cambridge / Mass. *Postmark:* New York Sep 2. *Endorsed:* Aug. 31 / 45.

581.   To James Nathan

13th Septr 45

Dearest,

I must begin all the leaves this time with the sweet word— I feel so confiding and affectionate Last night came your book Foscolo on Petrarch.[1] I have read this book but am very glad to own it, and to feel with what thoughts you sent it. It was delightful, too, to receive something unexpectedly. I touched my lips to the well known characters and felt that we were together. There came, too, a book from Mr Delf. It was translations from the Nova Vita and Convito of Dante with a fine head of him on the first leaf.[2] The Vita Nova has been one of the most cherished companions of my life. Dante has made a record which corresponds in some degree with my intuitions as to the *new life of love*, although I have an idea of much beside what he mentions, for he loved from afar and never entered into for the most intimate relations. But both Dante and Petrarch, though they truly loved, did not keep themselves sacred to the *celestial* Venus, but turned aside in hours of weakness to a lower love. Michel Angelo alone was true to his ideas of love, even when he could not hope the possession of its object. But all three of these great Italians seem to me to have discerned the true nature of Love, enough to have received some of its almighty revelations.

I was glad, too, to have the book from Mr D. for I would like to have your best friend become mine. Yet, have no confidant as to our relationship! I have had and shall have none. I wish to be alone with you in strict communion.

I feel much happier, now, about your absence; in this sense, if it is improving you, I ought to be willing. And, now the summer is over, it is not so much matter; we could not have such happy times together in the winter, even[n] if you were here, as when we could wander through the woods, and fields. I will try to do without you now, only earnestly, fervently hoping you will not be debarred from visiting the East, but that Nov or Decr will see you on the lotus bearing Nile. By the way, I wish much I had told you the story of Isis and Osiris; it is like *your religion.* But a time may come. Yet, yesterday, a proposition was made me, which, if accepted, might take me to Europe just as you come back.[3] Would not that be like all the rest of the Angels' management? But I do not think it will happen so.

I want you *very much* to write so that I shall get letters every two or three weeks, whether you hear from me or not, for when you do not it will always be that I do not get your address in time and as mine is always the same you might write as often to me, *do.* Your letters to the[n] Tribune are printed except the last which will probably be in the Daily of 16th. The others are 10th, 12th. The first 3d and last 5th[n] are best, there is most of your direct observations in[n] them. If you could mix in them[n] personal life still more; it would improve them. Send these too as often as you can that the interest may be kept alive. I expect very good ones about Paris, as you will see through veils, and want you to give free play to your feelings in writing of Switzerland and beautiful nature every where; there is strong practical sense enough to give enthusiasm the needed relief.

Not having heard from Mr Tobler I went yesterday and spoke to him, but he had nothing as yet to say, if he had would write me a note for you[n] tomorrow.[4]

I have had a most lovely letter from my loved brother Eugene. Brighter prospects seem dawning on him. He is now to be co-editor of a very good paper in N. O. and in part[n] proprietor, by and by, when he wishes. His love and devotion for me seem even greater than ever and there is now a prospect of our playing into one another's hands and by and by meeting. May you experience the joys of sympathy when meeting those of your blood! may they prove such that you can meet in deep

congeniality of intercourse! I often wonder when I think how entirely
you have been debarred of these sweet charities that you are so generous and good in the inmost heart, and so warm and tender in life as
you are! But the Angels had a care of you! For to day with them I leave
you—

Sunday eveg 15th
I have kept open the letter, hoping to have news for you from Mr
Tobler, but he has sent no note.

This has been a very happy day with me. A dear friend came about
noon to announce a joyful change in his fate and has only just left me,
feeling very happy in the crisis that brings a noble being liberation
from many woes and perplexities, but over excited! My head throbs; it
is time to go to rest, but I fear I shall not sleep and the hand trembles so
I can hardly write. I feel grateful for something manifestly right[n] and
more noble, more confidence in God than usual. I blame myself for
writing in[n] the within. Let us love carefully. I ought not thus to shrink
from giving or receiving pain. Yes, it is most true the fault you find in
me; I am faultily sensitive. I ought to have more noble faith. I will try;
we both will; will we not, loved brother, to be constantly nobler and
better.

I know not that I can write more tonight, many little events have
occurred to me and I have been away; last moon at Rockaway on the
noble beach with the surf rushing in, I thought of thee, every night and
in a sense all the time, so near wast thou And to night when her holy
rays steal through my willows I bless thee and pray that life may purify
and perfect thy noble nature until the message of thy soul be fully spoken. God grant this prayer and make it a solace to the pilgrim to know
that it lives always and more and more warmly in the heart of his *Muse*.

I looked all through the life of Petrarch for your pencil marks, but
had to fancy them.

AL (MB: Ms. Am. 1451 [65]). Published in *Love-Letters*, pp. 158–63. *Addressed:* To /
Mr James Nathan.
    winter, even] winter, ↑ even ↓
    to the] to ↑ the ↓
    first 3d and last 5th] first ↑ 3d ↓ and last ↑ 5th ↓
    observation in] observation ⟨up⟩ ↑ in ↓
    in them] in ↑ them ↓
    note for you] note ↑ for you ↓
    and in part] and ↑ in part ↓
    manifestly right] manifestly ⟨w⟩right
    writing in] writing ↑ in ↓
    1. Nathan probably sent Fuller Ugo Foscolo's *Essays on Petrarch* (London, 1823).
    2. Charles Lyell, trans., *The Lyrical Poems of Dante Alighieri* (London, 1845), which

Fuller reviewed on 18 November. Of the *Vita nuova,* she said it "is the noblest expression extant of the inward life of Love, the best preface and comment to every thing else that Dante did."

3. Marcus and Rebecca Spring invited Fuller to go to Europe. She was to tutor their son in return for her lodging and travel expenses (Borchardt, "Lady of Utopia," p. 54).

4. The New York City directory lists a John Tobler, importer, at 86 Cedar Street, the area where Nathan had his business.

582. To Pliny Earle

Wednesday
24th [September 1845]

To Dr Earle,
Dear Sir,

If it would be agreeable to you to have me come to Bloomingdale this week, I can" come, and will be ready on Saturday any time after eleven in the morning. If otherwise, I will postpone the visit till my return from Massachusetts, whither I am to go next week.[1]

With much regard yours

S. M. FULLER.

ALS (MCR-S). *Addressed:* To / Dr Earle / New York Asylum for the / Insane at Bloomingdale. / by Omnibus / paid. *Endorsed:* Miss Fuller / Sept 25 / '45 / S. Margt Fuller, / Countess D'Ossoli.

Pliny Earle (1809–92) graduated from the medical school of the University of Pennsylvania in 1837. An effective doctor of the mentally ill, he was in charge of the Bloomingdale Asylum in New York City from 1844 to 1849. He was later on the staff of the New York City Insane Asylum (*DAB*).

I can] I ca⟨m⟩n

1. Fuller twice wrote about Earle's clinic: in "St. Valentine's day—Bloomindale Asylum for the Insane" and then in a review of Earle's annual report (*New-York Daily Tribune,* 22 February 1845 and 11 February 1846). In the first she said: "The Bloomingdale Asylum for the Insane is conducted on the most wise and liberal plan known at the present day. Its superintendent, Dr. Earle, has had ample opportunity to observe the best modes of managing this class of diseases both here and in Europe, and he is one able, by refined sympathies and intellectual discernment, to apply the best that is known and to discover more."

583. To James Nathan

The Farm. Sept 29th 45

Here I am still, dear friend, although next Saturday will see me in Masstts. These are the loveliest days, of the American year, the breezes are melody and balm, the sunlight pours in floods through foliage itself transparent gold. The water is so very blue and animated; the sail-boats bound along, as if they felt like me. I have been inexpressibly happy these last few days. The weather within has been just the same as^n without. I am generally serene and rather bright, but *these* feelings are joy. Even for thee, I seldom feel regret; sometimes indeed I turn suddenly, my heart full of something I want to say and long to meet thine eye, but oftener I feel thou art indeed here much of the time and the rest looking on what is beautiful and full of rich suggestions; thou art living and growing and in all this I have my part. Yes, in all that enriches and dignifies thy life I have my part. And say, dear brother, brother of my soul, have I not been much with thee in beautiful Switzerland and Italy? Had I been with thee *indeed*, often we might have shared the same quick glance, the same full gaze, and every joy of sympathy where nature, at least, and the memories of human greatness are worth sympathy. But then there would have been many rough and difficult places, where thou must have upborne me in thy strong arms, or else I could not have gone. So I should have been in fact sometimes^n a burden, but in thought, in memory I have been altogether a sweet companion, have I not? one who gives no trouble and shares all joys?—

If I had written you any letters that were good, I should think you had just recd such an one, from this joy I have in being drawn to you. But I know too well, how frivolous, feeble, and inexpressive of what I really thought all mine have been. I think it must be merely that you are happy in grandeur and beauty you have seen and that your feelings of happiness extend to me.

I feel as if we were both within the pure white veil. I have kept my promise and never thought why you gave me that token, but whenever I have these lovely feelings as if we were both in an atmosphere of love and purity, I take it out and look at it, and then again I vow to trust our God and what is deepest in the impulses he has given. He will protect and the pure silver haze he will cast around shall be more efficient than armor of triple brass against all evil powers.

And amid that silver haze I am with thee, my brother, and repeat the holy vows, I made when thy generous soul was most made known to mine, and I meet the full look of thy eye, and it *is not tearful* and thy voice in its rich persuasive tones answers to the vow.

At such times there is no more age or sin or sadness. O may the immortal births of them— those creatures of our true selves, grow daily in strength, in sweetness and in purity!

I will not write any more; it is all in vain. I cannot relieve my heart; it craves expression, but cannot find it in words.

30th Septr

This is a most lovely pensive evening. My great willow shakes its long graceful locks with deep sighs, warm breezes sweeping slowly by. I have taken infinite pleasure in that tree and hope it has some[n] consciousness of what it has been to a human heart. I shall see it no more in beauty, for when I return from Masstts its leaves will have fallen and not dress it again by the time we go next Spring. For it is decided that we go and no more shall my brother and I meet on the rocks where the waves lapse up so gently or in the little paths of our dear wood. I have never been there yet since Sunday 1st June.[n] last Sunday it looked tempting, but I would not. I have made no vow lest I be forced to break it by some chance, but feel as if I should never go there again, unless with you.

To night is the anniversary of my father's death, just about this time he left us and my hand closed his eyes.[1] Never has that hand since been employed in an act so holy yet it has done so much, it seems as I look on it, almost a separate mind. It is a pure hand thus far from evil; it has given no false tokens of any kind. My father, from that home of higher life you now inhabit, does not your blessing still accompany the hand that hid the sad sights of this world from your eyes[n] which had begun to weep at them. My friend, I think it[n] does. I think he thus far would bless his child. We have both upright and pure men to our fathers; is it not a great happiness? I realize it more and more. Our star had some[n] benign rays.

AL (MB: Ms. Am. 1451 [66]). Published in *Love-Letters*, pp. 164–68. *Addressed:* To / Mr James Nathan / Care of N. S. Nathan / Hamburg / Germany. *Postmarks:* [Par]is 17 Nov 43; Hamburg 22 / 11 / 1845.

same as] same ↑ as ↓
been in fact sometimes] been ⟨only⟩ ↑ in fact sometimes ↓
has some] has ⟨there⟩ ↑ some ↓
yet since Sunday 1st June.] yet. ↑ since Sunday 1st June ↓
world from your eyes] world ↑ from your eyes ↓
think it] think ⟨h⟩it
had some] had ↑ some ↓

1. Timothy Fuller died of cholera in 1835.

584. To Sarah Shaw

Cambridge Octr 8th
1845

Dear Sarah,

Here I am! and want to see you. Should you like to have me come next week and what day would you prefer? I am going to Concord to-morrow, but expect to return Monday or Tuesday at farthest.[1] Cannot Anna come too when I am with you so that I may see all three at once. I shall stay awhile in this region, but there are a good many and many good, friends to see. Affecy ever

MARGARET.

9th

Can it be Friday or Saty of next week dear Sarah please answer through post office to Old Cambridge Care R. F. Fuller

ALS (MH: Ac 85. St 317. p. 164). *Addressed:* F. G. Shaw Esq / for Mrs Shaw / West Roxbury / Mass. *Endorsed:* Margaret Fuller. *Postmark:* Cambridge MS Oct 10.

1. Concord was hardly serene: Ellen Channing was pregnant with her second child; an anti-Texas convention was held there late in September; and Sarah Ripley was staying with Emerson, who was working on his lecture series "Representative Men," which was to begin in December (Rusk, *Letters of RWE*, 3:305–6).

585. To Sarah Shaw

Boston
Friday 17th Octr [1845]

My dear Sarah,

Ole Bull is here and gives a Concert tomorrow eveg, to[n] which I want to go, so think I will not come to you as we agreed, tomorrow; nor will I fix any time precisely again.[1] Perhaps I can come out Sunday, but if I am prevented will come the first day I can and then if it is inconvenient for you to have me stay a little with you, will go on to the Farm or go back. Shall you not, perhaps, be at the Concert? Where is[n] Anna? at Savin Hill? I want much to see her while here. ever affecy

M.

ALS (MHi).
eveg, to] eveg, ⟨s⟩to
Where is] Where ⟨I⟩is

1. Bull had begun a series of Boston concerts prior to his return to Europe (*Boston Daily Advertiser*, 17 October 1845).

586. To Sarah Shaw

26th Octr 45

My dear Sarah

The Chinese herb came safe and I doubt not I shall think of you while inhaling its fragrance, though you are by no means a person to have *mandarin* associations withal.

I think, dear Sarah, the cares and anxieties you expressed when I saw you were, like your langour, only an effect of your situation. However, they may haunt you much and at such times the presence of a friend may be cheering. Should you at any time desire mine, for this reason or any other that you think important, do not fail to let me know that I may come to you who when *I* have been unable to move about were so willing to bestow your animated and affectionate presence on me. I always have time for my friends when they need me.

Your friend

M. F.

ALS (MH: bMS Am 1417 [180]). *Addressed:* Mrs F. Shaw / West Roxbury.

587. To Richard F. Fuller

New York,
10th Decr [November] 1845

Dear Richard,

I feel painful regret that I could not devote myself more to you while in N. E. I wish we had had some beautiful walks, more thoughtful talks. I wish I could have made a full mental return to your confidence. But my thoughts were continually dissipated and my body wearied. I felt that in meeting so many, I could be nothing to any.

Continue to love me as your worthy friend and intelligent companion, for I am sure you will yet again find the[n] same satisfaction as of old in meeting. Next spring or summer, if you come here, we will have some undisturbed and full hours of communion.[n]

I have today the unexpected pleasure of receiving from England a neat copy of "Woman in 19th" &c republished there in Clarke's Cabinet Library.[1] I had never heard a word about it from England, and am very glad to find it will be read by women there; as to advantage to me the republication will bring me no money but will be of use to me, here, as our dear country folks look anxiously for verdicts from[n] the other side of the water.

I shall get out a 2d edition here before long, I hope, and wish you would translate for me and send those other parts of the story of Panthea you thought I might like. Please write them out legibly, that, if I use, I may not need to have them copied for the press.

Lane's notice (in a newspaper) was left, I believe, with Mother.[2] If she has it, I shd like it sent me when W. Channing comes, or by any other good opportunity. I hope it is not lost, being the only notice that ever appeared of the book, I thought worth keeping.

I am staying tonight with Mrs Child and take a few minutes to write, while she is with a visitor. I have no lines and cant write with her pens, so burn the letter, only let rise from the ashes a breath of sympathy from yr sister and friend.

AL (MH: fMS Am 1086 [9:126]); MsC (MH: fMS Am 1086 [Works, 2:793–97]). *Addressed:* To / Richard F. Fuller / at the Law School / Cambridge / Mass. *Postmark:* New York 11 Nov. *Endorsed:* 10 Nov / 45.

Despite Fuller's date, the postmark puts the letter in November.
find the] find ⟨ever⟩ ↑ the ↓
of communion.] of ⟨meeting.⟩ ↑ communion. ↓
verdicts from] verdicts ↑ from ↓

1. This may be the copy sent Fuller by Thomas Delf (Joel Myerson, *Margaret Fuller: A Descriptive Bibliography* [Pittsburgh, 1978], p. 22).

2. Charles Lane reviewed the book in *Herald of Freedom* 11 (5 September 1845): 1.

588. To Georgiana Bruce

[ca. 15 November 1845]

My Dear Georgiana:

I have seen much of Mr. Lane lately.[1] He is staying at the Springs, and is a charming companion just now, the mellow side being uppermost; his wit, conversational powers, and warmer feelings being in play. The qualities he lacks, as you say, he can scarcely obtain here, I know. He wants living experience, which should have verified principles and expanded the nature, and it is too late for many of the most precious things. There are but few who have lived a too intellectual life, but he is one of them.

I have seen somewhat of Ole Bull, who is just in the reverse case, all nature and genius, instinct and feeling, full of comic power, full of tremulous sadness. An exquisite being, but without a serene home in thought.

Some persons come and go, and only the light that shows them is our own. Yet other souls there are, which, passing, drop a seed in our own life and grow with us forever till we have mortal, and, I hope and think, immortal companions.

ELfr, from Kirby, *Years of Experience*, pp. 207–8.

Dated from the reference to Ole Bull and Charles Lane, who was then in New York City.

1. Charles Lane had moved to New York from the Shaker community in Massachusetts.

589.   To Anna B. Ward

New York,
16th Novr 1845,

My dear Anna

I came back just as you went away; surely that was not luck to be away all the time you were at home here.

I worked too hard at human intercourse while in N. E. to enjoy myself much. I need long intervals between of "skiey influences and solemn concentrations"!! and there were too many people to see and things to do to allow of any such matters.

I staid several days at Concord, did not enjoy being with Waldo as usual; our moods did not match. He was with Plato, and I was with the instincts.[1] Of the Hawthorn-tree I saw the blossom, lovely still, but not so much so as in first bud.[2] Ellen and Ellery were in their new house; it is very pretty, convenient, and beautifully situated. It is too far from the village for Ellen, in this way, that she can never go there without riding,[n] which, as she has no domestic companion,[n] except her little daughter, leaves her very lonely and unhelped, now that she is much unwell, for she is to have another little one in Spring.[3]

Ellen spoke gently of Sam's letter; said she did not think she had deserved to be placed in so humiliating a position; that she had really supposed you loved and cared for her for herself as well as for being Ellery's wife and thought she had had a good deal of reason for her mistake. I did not see the letter; do not know whether it is still in existence. Ellen showed it to Cary, who thought it very good and just and wanted to talk with E. about it, but he declined all conversation upon the subject. I did not attempt it, but suppose he feels bitterly or has felt so, from some verses he sent me, on such subjects. He seems unhappy. I fear his dark will know rarer intervals of bright even than heretofore.[n] His ill success here, though willingly incurred, has pained him; so easy is it to find poison in the field.

Ellen Hooper I saw at Woburn; she was full of grace as usual, but still more pensive than usual. She talked a good deal of you both.

I passed a last half hour with Anna Shaw at the window of her delightful room, where we have had so many good talks. She is full of pleasure at the thought of leaving Beacon St. and living among real farmers, draws a long breath whenever she speaks of the promised *half a house*, for in such they choose to live for the present in South Brookfield. Mr Shaw is as well pleased as if he had made the match, all by himself.[4] I had a pleasant time at West Roxbury, all things much as they were.[5] Little Baldwin seems happy and they say is getting regulated, though the little Shaws told me one time when he was there one of[n] the boys had to sit on his head to keep him from throwing stones at the girls. I wrote a note to Dr Howe in behalf of Ole Bull, who was in Boston and wished to visit the asylum and play to the blind, signed it *S. M. Fuller* and recd an answer beginning[n] *Dear Sir.* Julia, they say, is very graceful and playful; people in general around see no more.[6]

I was two days at N. Bedford, saw Mr and Mrs Tucker there and came back with them to Boston[n] in the cars; they really seem to have the domestic happiness untiring.[7]

I meant to write more and better, but I am too tired. Keep *Festus* as long as you wish and Tell[n] me of some way by which I can send you books, if any come that you would like. I suppose you are in the beautiful new house now. I saw Russell's drawing and Waldo showed me in what respects it failed to give the true idea—[8] The state of Mr and Mrs Farrar was dolorous beyond description; we must not think of the ugly things.[9] Now forgive this unconnected scribble; you evoked an account of my visit, and I have only given one or two items but can do no better now

Goodnight, dear S. and A, from that other affece letter of the Alphabet

M.

ALS (MH: bMS Am 1465 [925]).
without riding,] without ⟨hav⟩ riding,
domestic companion,] domestic ⟨ar⟩ companion,

bright even than heretofore.] bright ⟨yet hereafter⟩. ↑ even than heretofore ↓
there one of] there ↑ one of ↓
answer beginning] answer ⟨y⟩ beginning
them to Boston] them ↑ to Boston ↓
Keep *Festus* as long as you wish and Tell] ↑ keep *Festus* as long as you wish and ↓ Tell

1. Emerson was reading Plato in preparation for his lecture series "Representative Men."

2. Una Hawthorne, about whom Fuller often wrote in her letters of the autumn of 1844.

3. Caroline Sturgis Channing (1846–1917), the Channings' second child, was born on the following 13 April. In 1865 she married Follen Cabot (1839–1905) (L. Vernon Briggs, *History and Genealogy of the Cabot Family, 1475–1927* [Boston, 1927], pp. 655–56).

4. Anna Blake Shaw married William Batchelder Greene (1819–78), a former army officer and a graduate of the divinity school at Cambridge. Greene was ordained at Brookfield in 1845 (Arthur W. Hodgman, "Elias Parkman of Dorchester and His Descendants," New England Historic Genealogical Society, p. 55; *General Catalogue of the Divinity School of Harvard University, 1901* [Cambridge, 1901]).

5. West Roxbury was the home of the Frank Shaws and of Brook Farm.

6. Fuller had known and liked Julia Ward Howe for several years.

7. Probably Charles Russell Tucker (1809–76) and his wife, Dorcas Fry Tucker (b. 1810). He was a prominent merchant, banker, and member of the Society of Friends in New Bedford (Ephraim Tucker, *Genealogy of the Tucker Family, from Various Authentic Sources* [Worcester, Mass., 1895], p. 305; Bolton VR).

8. Possibly Sarah Shaw's brother, Nathaniel Russell Sturgis (1805–87), whom Fuller knew as a child. Sturgis was a wealthy China trader who joined the banking firm of Baring Brothers in 1849 (*Sturgis of Yarmouth*, pp. 50–51).

9. John Farrar had been ill for several years.

590. To Richard F. Fuller

New York
Decr 3d 1845.

My dear Richard,

At last I have had a still time to read over the translation by Lear and enjoyed it much. I shall begin soon to prepare the new edition though it will not come out till Spring. I shall *give* you 2 copies, one for you and one for Anna. I have given Anna in my letter a hint for a discussion with you on the subject of filial love.

I have reflected on all you said to me the last time we talked and am satisfied that you might take views on this subject more profound and tender, more worthy of your best self. I do not wish on this subject or any other to have you coincide with me (though of course it is pleasant to have you) but to have you think out the best in your own way, and I think talking with Anna in whom a religious state on these subjects is natural will be of use to you someway. I wish, though, you would show her the verses you wrote about Mother once, there could be nothing more sweet or just than those were.[n]

I suppose the leisure is past, before I read your offer of reading over Woman &c to mark misprints If you have time I should like it much.

Ever affecy

MARGARET

I shall write to Arthur next time I write home, whether by post or Mr Greeley I shall keep your letters "among the safest things"

ALS (MH: fMS Am 1086 [9:125]); MsC (MH: fMS Am 1086 [Works, 2:789–91]). *Addressed:* To / Richard F. Fuller. *Endorsed:* Dec 3. / 45.

just than those were.] just. ↑ than those were ↓

591. To Anna Loring

New York,
3d Decr 1845.

I should have written to my dear Anna earlier, but thought I might have something interesting to tell her about Ole, if I waited. However, he sails today without ever having given me an afternoon out here, as he said he should, and I have seen him very little. The first time I did see him, after coming back here he asked about you, said he had sent you his March in honor of Washington and expressed his affection for the soul that shone through your eyes.[1] I believe he will remember you and expect much goodness and loveliness from you.— I told him about the flowers growing *musty* and that you said, if they had only withered, it would have been no matter,— but musty flowers!! He laughed a great deal, but he was touched, too.

He has shown a good deal of regard to the Sedgwicks one of whom I told you is so beautiful. They are a *poor* branch (in money I mean) of the Sedgwick family and are also, on the mother's side, related to various persons of wealth and fashion, none of whom, as is the wont too often[n] with such people, wish to aid their own relatives, even by seconding their efforts at independence.[2] Thus, though young, they have been much thrown on themselves; this has developed in them much character, self-reliance, and a strong pure affection for one another. Ole saw all this very quickly and was anxious to mark his regard for them in some way. So he not only went to see them several times, but offered to bring his violin and play to the children in their school. When he did so, many of the children were delighted and came round him, wanting just to touch him; these girls said it was a lovely picture and I think it was one of the sweetest things I have known of him, worth far more, than public giving of Concerts for the sake of widows and orphans &c which, if not done for show, are still showy.

I did not enjoy his last concert much; his orchestra plagued him and I was not agreeably placed. But I heard the Washington piece to tolerable advantage and the impressions were confirmed I had recd from hearding him play it on the piano. You will have seen my notice in the Tribune of the last Concert, with various tender effusions of devotees to Ole.[3] Miss Lynch's verses were thrown to him with a laurel crown. One of the musicians tried to clap it on his head, but Ole resisted and would only hold it in one hand. So adeiu to the child of genius whose image we will always cherish the same as now; shall we not, Anna? for the good we have known of him has been indubitable, and the impression of beauty so peculiar that other forms beautiful and good need never efface or eclipse it.

To day is one of the sullen, brooding days of early winter. The sky is full of snow[n] clouds, only waiting for nightfall to clothe the earth in a shroud. I feel quite ready, for all seems ready now for the funeral, the trees are bare; my rocks, stripped of all their garlands, look desolate, and on the leaden waters not a sail is in sight. I tremble in every joint with cold for the air is full of frost and, in such weather, we cannot keep this old dilapidated mansion warm.

I am waiting for some German gentlemen who were to call and see me on business this morng. I think they have lost their[n] way and are now shivering in some unknown road or field, and wishing they had never seen me, or at least that they had never wished to see me again. I, on my side, am the gainer by their defection, as it has given me time to read the translation of the story of Panthea, in which Richard's pen was aided by your Mother and father and you as judges and reformers. I have not had a still time before since it came. I think the translation is beautifully done, though I may make some slight exceptions; whether I shall or no, am not quite sure. Is it not the most exquisitely told history of married love. To me it is ever *satisfactory*.

Richard writes that he has very happy times in visiting you now, and I am rejoiced at it; he deserves to be happy. His life is generally in a noble direction and growing better and better. About one thing I wish he agreed with me more nearly; he does not cherish filial love *as a sentiment*. I think he needs some revelations on this score; perhaps you, who are differently constituted and whose feelings come much nearer mine, might lead to his receiving them. He does not see enough that in living with persons who are older, whose habits are more formed and who have suffered more than we, we must learn to throw ourselves into their feelings, tastes, and states of mind, and show our affection for them in *their* way, rather than *ours*, if we would make it contribute much to their happiness. This too must be free and flowing sympathy, coming from a deep conviction of soul that so it ought to be, or it will not avail. It is not enough to esteem our friends and resolve to serve them; we need to delight to do it. Do not show this part of my letter to any person unless it be Richard himself. Others might not understand it. Mother has good and dutiful children, yet her life is lonely, and she needs that her sons should learn to be, in part, daughters also. I *have* seen men that could act the part of women with poetic appreciation when occasion called, as Wallenstein took care of Max Piccolomine when a baby in the freezing camp.[4] But even the good and wise and delicate may fail. Charles Emerson was as good as a daughter to his widowed mother, but Waldo is only a good son.[5]

And now à Dieu, dear child! What I always want of you, you know, that you should grow into all the excellence Nature intended, and keep yourself unspotted from the world. I should also like from you the special good act, of writing to myself of yourself, but I fear you will fail me here. If you do write, mention among the trifles what became of the little German Johanna, and how Lucia Peabody goes on and the prospects of the Anti-Slavery fair.[6]

The name of Lucia reminds me to ask you to get Anna Parsons to tell you about her swimming out to save her mother.[7] The simple nobleness of her conduct was just what I should think of her from her face. Write me too of dear Jane. Remember me with much affection to your father and mother. I was very happy while in their house this last time. In love always your friend

MARGARET.

I send you a Tuberose and Hyacinth root. I hope both will bloom for you in the sunshine of the lengthening days.

ALS (MCR-S). *Addressed:* To / Miss Anna Loring / Winter St / Boston. *Endorsed:* Margaret Fuller.

wont too often] wont ↑ too often ↓
of snow] of ⟨?⟩ snow
lost their] lost ↑ their ↓

1. At Bull's concert she heard for the first time a complete version of his "Tribute to Washington" (*New-York Daily Tribune*, 28 November 1845).
2. The family of Roderick (1785–1864) and Margaret Dean Sedgwick (d. 1850) of New York. A broker on Wall Street, Sedgwick had five daughters, some of whom con-

ducted a school that Fuller praised in the *Tribune* on 25 August 1845. The wealthier, prominent member of the Sedgwick family was Theodore Sedgwick III (1811–59), whose law practice was lucrative. Margaret Dean Sedgwick's father, Stewart Dean, was a soldier and merchant (Hubert M. Sedgwick, *A Sedgwick Genealogy* [New Haven, 1961], p. 139; *DAB*).

3. Of the final Bull performance in New York, Fuller wrote: "We need unspeakably the beautiful arts to animate, expand, and elevate our life which rushes dangerously toward a coarse utilitarianism" (*New-York Daily Tribune*, 28 November 1845).

4. Fuller refers to Schiller's play *Wallensteins Tod*. In act 3, scene 18, Wallenstein, who is trying to enlist Max Piccolomini's aid, describes their past:

> Max., remain with me.
> Go you not from me, Max.! Hark! I will tell thee—
> How when at Prague, our winter quarters, thou
> Wert brought into my tent a tender boy,
> Not yet accustomed to the German winters;
> Thy hand was frozen to the heavy colours;
> Thou wouldst not let them go.
> At that time did I take thee in my arms,
> And with my mantle did I cover thee;
> I was thy nurse, no woman could have been
> A kinder to thee; I was not ashamed
> To do for thee all little offices,
> However strange to me; I tended thee
> Till life returned; and when thine eyes first opened,
> I had thee in my arms.

(Friedrich Schiller, *The Works of Friedrich Schiller*, trans. Samuel Taylor Coleridge [Boston, 1901], pp. 268–69).

5. Two of the Emerson brothers: Charles Chauncy, who died in 1836, and Ralph Waldo.

6. Lucia Maria Peabody (1828?–1919), daughter of Augustus (1779–1850) and Miranda Goddard Peabody (1793–1871), lived in Roxbury (MVR 1919 4:360; Selim H. Peabody, comp., *Peabody (Paybody, Pabody, Pabodie) Genealogy* [Boston, 1909], p. 71). According to the *Liberator* for 19 December 1845, the annual antislavery fair was to open at Boston's Faneuil Hall on Tuesday, 23 December, and run for ten days. A petition opposing the annexation of Texas was to be displayed for visitors to sign.

7. Anna Quincy Thaxter Parsons was a friend of Fuller's who often engaged in mesmeric experiments, during which she "read" characters while under hypnosis. She was a frequent visitor at Brook Farm. Her mother, Anna Quincy Thaxter (1791–1879), married Nehemiah Parsons (Haverhill VR; MVR 312:88).

592. To William H. Channing

[14 December 1845]

[   ] I feel in an indifferent state, not caring even for the things that have hitherto animated me, music for instance. So I use the days merely to work and look around and bide my time for better things.

Mother writes that my dear old grandmother is dead.[1] I am sorry you never saw her. She was a picture of primitive piety as she sat, holding the "Saints Rest" in her hand, with her bowed trembling figure and her emphatic nods and her bright sweet blue eyes.[2] They were bright to the last, though she was 90. I went to see her just before I came back here. It is a great loss to Mother who felt a large place warmed in her heart by the fond and grateful love of this aged parent.

Mr Lane is here now and we had some eloquence at the meeting of your people last Sunday eveg.[3] We were to have met again tonight if it had not stormed. They all think of you with constant affection and reverence.

I send a little book belonging[n] to Julia as I hear she is with you. Remember me to her and to Fanny.[4]

Adieu, my ever dear William. May our Father watch over you and bless you with a double blessing! We have never spoken of it, but I think if you were very ill at any time, you would send for me no less than if I were your sister by birth— But you will not be very ill now! I look with hope for the news of your being better. A Dieu

I shall consider my saying this to you as implying a promise on your part— unless you write me to the contrary

ALfr (MB: Ms. Am. 1450 [56]). Published in part in *Memoirs*, 2:121, and Higginson, *MFO*, pp. 17–18. *Addressed:* To / William H. Channing / Mt Vernon St. / Boston / Mass. *Endorsed:* 15 Dec 1845.

Fuller's this evening *implies that the date was Sunday, 14 December, the day Channing's people would meet.*

book belonging] book ↑ belonging ↓

1. Elizabeth Jones Weiser Crane died on 2 December 1845 (MVR 21:75).

2. Richard Baxter's popular *Saint's Everlasting Rest* (London, 1649) existed in many editions.

3. In April 1843, Channing had formed a society of "Christian Union" in New York City; the group included Fuller, the Cranches, Horace Greeley, and Isaac Hopper. Channing led the group until he left New York for Brook Farm in September 1845 (Frothingham, *Memoir of William Henry Channing*, pp. 186–97).

4. Julia Allen Channing, William Henry's wife, and Frances, their daughter.

593. To Mary Rotch

[25? December 1845]

Dear Aunt Mary

I feel tonight like writing a little note just to say I wish you both a happy Xmas. Alone here in the boarding house this freezing night[n] I feel "lonesome" to the extent of the Yankee meaning of the word and think this little process will make me less so.

"For to know that here and there upon the earth ball somebody is caring for us &c"

Imagine how glad I am that I did not fail to go and see my dear old Grandmother She died about a fortnight ago and if I had staid another day in N. Bedford I should have lost my last chance of seeing her sweet precious blue eyes that never had in all my life looked other than affecy on me. It is a great loss to Mother stopping up for the present a fountain of sweet feelings that cannot be replaced by others. I feel very sorry that I cannot see Mother for a day or two. [   ] for indulging myself and drink my health Xmas eveg (since you no less than Mr Parker still claim a share in the privileges of the day!!) in a cup of tea poured out in the beautiful red China.[1]

I wish Mary could see the shops here now in all the splendor of holiday preparations. Mere [   ] things!

I am *very* sorry Waldo will not see you this winter.[2] Did you know W. Channing had had a fever? I always want to hear of your health every now and then; you wont fail to write me a few lines will you? And tell me sometimes what you think of the books and topics of the day.

To both very affecy

ALfr (MH: fMS Am 1086 [9:53]).

house this freezing night] house ↑ this freezing night ↓

1. Probably Theodore Parker, whom Fuller admired even though the two were temperamentally unlike. He contributed often to the *Dial*.

2. On 17 November, Emerson wrote William J. Rotch (Aunt Mary's brother) to refuse an invitation to speak at the New Bedford lyceum because the society had voted to exclude blacks from membership. "This vote quite embarrasses me," wrote Emerson, "and I should not know how to speak to the company. Besides, in its direct counter-action to the obvious duty and sentiment of New England, and of all freemen in regard to the colored people, the vote appears so unkind, and so unlooked for, that I could not come with any pleasure before the Society" (Rusk, *Letters of RWE*, 3:312). Fuller denounced the lyceum in the *Tribune*: "Our readers may have noticed the act of exclusion by which the citizens of New-Bedford have shown the illiberal prejudice against people of color with an unblushing openness unusual even where it exists in its most unchristian form. The black population were denied, even in the case of the most respectable persons, the privilege of membership, and only allowed to hear lectures if they would confine themselves to a particular part of the house.— A minority protested in the strongest terms, but the majority persisted in the act of proscription." She went on to praise Emerson and Charles Sumner, who had also refused to address an audience "whose test of merit, or right to the privileges of a citizen consists not in intelligence or good character, but the color of the skin" (*New-York Daily Tribune*, 9 December 1845).

594.   To Richard F. Fuller

New York,
27th Decr 1845.

You said in your last, dear Richard, that you should write again directly I therefore have not written, wishing to hear all before I said anything, but as I do not, will wait no more.

I never meant to advise your speaking to Anna yet. I said (or meant) before she went to Europe, so that there might be in her mind a certainty of your attachment to help defend it against other impressions, also because uncertainty for so long a period and in absence would have been unbearable for you.

But I am sorry you have spoken to her *now*, because, whatever be the state of her mind, doing so cannot but place barriers to your free intercourse with her. By too much haste to get some outward token, you have robbed yourself of a long period when you might have had happiness in being with her and might have strengthened her attachment in a thousand ways without alarming her. Now her conscience and all her feelings must be set on the guard. Giving such a permission as you asked could not to an honorable mind be less binding, or less oppressive than an engagement. It must force one back on one's self, force one to analyze feelings in this case probably, prematurely. Were it of any use I should be sorry you had done it. What is the use, you think, of saying so now. It is because *I* think I see both here and in your intercourse with the Allens too much impetuosity and a readiness to go to extremes which places you in false positions and may make you the agent of much pain to others. And though you may be willing, with the bravery of a generous nature, to accept whatever flows from your character, there is no reason why you should not mellow and improve that character so that its fruits be better and better with the passage of time.

You have[n] lost temporary youthful happiness, such as time cannot restore, but if Anna really feels towards you as you[n] have supposed during Novr, no harm will be done to your cause eventually. She knows you love her, and knows what you are, and time will reveal herself to her, so that she will know whether she can love you. Perhaps the result may be good, if you can *now* be faithful, whether she feed your feelings with smiles or not.

As to the rest, I think denying you at the door must be accidental and and that, if you saw unhappiness in Mrs L's face, it must be from some other cause. No person of common sense ought to be surprised at such a result, after promoting intercourse between a youth and maiden as she has done, and she has surely too much sense of justice to punish you for her own fault— I want much to hear from you again as soon as possible and beg dear Mother to write to me so soon as she feels able of her own health, feelings, and plans for the winter and fully of Ellen and Greta Ever most affecy your sister

M.

ALS (MH: fMS Am 1086 [9:128]). *Addressed:* To / Richard F. Fuller / at the Law School / Cambridge / Mass. *Postmark:* New York 27 Dec.

You have] ⟨Thus⟩ You have
as you] as ↑ you ↓

595. To James Nathan

New York, 31st Decr.
1845.

I have waited till the last moment, dear friend, hoping to hear from you again before writing.—ⁿ I have recd only one letter in the course of more than three months. That was dated Florence 27th Septr, but did not reach me till 1st Decr, nor till I had felt much troubled by so long a pause. You had not then had any letters from me since leaving England, but as I knew by a letter from Mr Delf that they would reach you in Rome by the middle of October, I have been expecting ever since to hear from you in answer to them. But not a word! I feel entirely unlike writing without hearing, nor would I, but that you express a strong wish to find letters in Hamburg on your arrival, and now the semimonthly steamers have stopped for the winter, I shall not have a chance to send quick again before 1st Feby, if I do not write by this one.

You said in the letter from Florence that you told me you "would not be able to keep up a real correspondence with me while absent"— But, on the contrary, while here you used always to be telling me that you could not write because people interrupted you at the office, or because you had a person with you at home whom you did not wish to see you writing the letter. I often felt as if you sacrificed both writing to me and seeing me to trifles and wished it had been otherwise for I thought the greater was sacrificed to the lesser, even according to your own view of our relation. Still I did not listen to these feelings, as they were superficial compared with the thatⁿ of the inevitableness and deep root in the character of both of the bond between us.—But when urging me

177

to write at our last meeting you said expressly "I have not been able to write as I would, but I *shall now* I shall answer in full, if you will write."

You are your own master, at present, you have no companions, unless from choice, nothing to interrupt you. You are amid the scenes and impressions, it seems to me, most congenial with the thought of me,— and if you cannot write now, *when*, my friend, could you?—

I am deeply touched by what you say of not finding help as to repose of mind or religion. Many considerations have occurred to me as to the burning pain which the wrongs and woes of men cause you. But I will not write them yet, hoping we shall meet again, when they can in full be expressed and you see whether you find any worth in them.

I feel much disappointed to find that you cannot, after all, go to the East this winter. It was all useless then for you to hurry away. You might have staid longer and last summer not have been lost! And how will it be now? Shall you not return here in the Spring? Shall you go to the East another autumn? Shall you give it up altogether? Write me of this as soon as possible![1]

I am glad but not surprized that the great works of art have become familiar to you. But you will find deeper and deeper senses as you look more. I am glad *and* a little surprized that the Medicean Venus did not please you. I want much to know what you saw in Rome. And Naples you are going there surely. *There* and in Switzerland it was my place to have been with you.

We have lately had published here books of travel very minute about Switzerland, by Mr Cheever who saw a great deal, but mixed it all up with sectarianism and books,— and by Mr Headly who has a real love of natural beauty and picturesque power in describing it. Mr Headly is one of the few entertaining persons I know here; he is full of vivacity and feeling quick if not deep, and sparkles along in talk very pleasantly.[2]

I am boarding in town for the winter in an excellent house in Warren St for the present. I find it a most agreeable change in point of order and comfort. The people in the house are such as you, I suppose, have have seen constantly, I scarce ever at all,— men of business who seem like perfect machines. No wonder they wearied you to death![n] I see but little of them, however, only at the table.

I devote myself a great deal to the paper, as I am more and more interested by the generous course of Mr G. and am desirous to make my own position important and useful. As I shall find no longer a home in the house of Mr G. except for a brief space in the Spring and must therefore live at much more expense, if I remain, they are to make me a new offer, as soon as they have settled up their affairs this New Year.

Mr G. said they should do all they possibly could for me. I shall remain till Septr at any rate, as he wishes much to be at liberty during the summer.

As to other things now I am in town I make many acquaintance and see many amusing people, and some who are very friendly to me, but none of deep interest. I feel very lonely, sometimes very sad, and I still pine for you, my friend, and that home of soul where you used to receive me and strengthen me, and all the flowers that grew from frequent meeting.

I do not, indeed, feel separated from you, your silences, or the want of personal intercourse does not seem to have that effect at all. When I am alone, your image rises before me, or indeed in the presence of others I sometimes am suddenly lost to them and seem absorbed by this communion. But I do not feel refreshed or invigorated enough by this— there is a void, and I can only commend myself to the care of Heaven.

I want to think that you feel the need of me in the same way and surely you must,— yet I do not know how to understand some things in your letter; it was as if you said "do not think it is *you* I want" and then you say "do not *mis*understand" so I will not *mis*understand, and therefore must let it all go, but that is difficult.

I feel inclined to write no more unless we can have "a real correspondence"; what is the use of any other. I feel sick and my head aches at this moment. Do try to have things better. I beg you by that time when I left off taking care of myself and put it all into your care in holy keeping You then gave me the veil, and whenever I look at it, it seems like peace, and that thou must bring to me.

I suffer writing this letter; when it is gone, I may receive one that may make me feel so differently. I cannot help feeling jealous of you, knowing your nature, knowing you went away on your Wanderings, *seeking* new impressions. I never did and never shall feel happy any way but in *answering* you. When you draw me I like to come. I do not like to come of my own accord.

You are now to be among your kindred I do hope you will find joy in it, and that it may be possible to take up the ties as if all these years had not passed between. May you be happy with Mother and bretheren, your sisters by blood I cannot permit to take the place of the sister of your soul.

I want you to write me how they all strike you, but do not, loved friend, speak to them of me, except outwardly as you have to Mr Delf and others. I want the mysterious tie that binds us to remain unprofaned forever, and that if in this cruel fatal sphere we are in, we have to bury the sweet form of the Past, that we should do it quite alone, we the only ones that could appreciate its budding charms, how lovely it was, and of capacity how glorious. Then we would weep together and part, and go our several ways alone but we would tell no man.

Promise me this.

This is the last day of the year in which I have known you. It is just a year since we met. May our Father bless you and give to your other years joys hopes and sorrows no less pure than these have been.

O may he add tranquillity and fruition! Do you bless me when you receive this and bend your mind to have me feel it.

Mrs Greeley has been in a sad state mind and body, but seems a little better now. Her boy is beautiful,— the picture of health and gayety. Shall I send you at Hamburg the copies of Tribune, containing your letters— How many and *how?*— Did you know my book on Woman &c had been republished in England.

AL (MB: Ms. Am. 1451 [67–68, 68a]). Published in *Love-Letters*, pp. 168–75.

again before writing.—] again ↑ before writing.— ↓
the that] the ⟨deep one⟩ ↑ that ↓
No wonder they wearied you to death!] ↑ No wonder they wearied you to death! ↓

1. Nathan answered this and two other Fuller letters on 5 June 1846 (MH). He reported that he had been to Jerusalem, Cairo, and Constantinople and asked Fuller to "find some liberal journalist, for whom the narration of my journey is of sufficient interest to allow me for it, what you may think it worth." He ignored her emotions beyond saying coolly: "Your three letters . . . are duly received and from the great anxiety about my safety therein impressed."

2. George Barrell Cheever, *Wanderings of a Pilgrim in the Shadow of Mont Blanc* (New York, 1845), which Fuller did not review. She called Headley's *Alps* "charming" (*New-York Daily Tribune*, 24 December 1845).

596. To Georgiana Bruce

[1846]

The grand features of a scenery, and the presence of a Destiny as grand, which makes its large strokes daily on the canvas, were far more propitious to a deep, inward life than is the mixed existence of the East. Then, in the West you have great chances: interesting characters occur rarely and unexpectedly; but you do sometimes meet them, and when you do, it is far easier to get into full intercourse with them.

ELfr, from Kirby, *Years of Experience*, p. 230.

The contents show that Fuller answers a letter from Georgiana Bruce, probably written in 1846, though 1845 is possible.

597. To Mary Rotch

New York, 9th Jany
1846.

Very dear Aunt Mary,

How shall I get done thanking your two letters, the first such a nice long one, and then the New Year's fount of ruby wine, open for me as if I were a Prince of the blood!

You must not think me disobedient though, if I turn some of the wine into a new dress. Having but one of the class Mrs Farrar calls *tightum* and being much invited out now I am in town, I was grudgingly reflecting on the necessity of getting another Grudgingly,— for you have no idea how much, in this dirtiest of cities, it costs a poor scribe (what it costs the Pharasees Imagination shrinks from counting) who is far from all aid of unpaid affection in the line of sewing getting up clothes &c even to^n keep herself neat in the tightum line. [   ]

Mrs Child will not go out at all, either to^n evening party or morning call. She says she cant afford the time, the white gloves, the visiting cards or the carriage hire. But I think she lives at disadvantage by keeping so entirely apart from the common stream of things. I shall never go out when busy, or to keep late hours, but to go sometimes is better and pleasanter for me. I find many entertaining acquaintances and some friends. So I mean to steal from your money at least ribands and lace for the inevitable dress, and that will leave me more of the grape juice than I should drink betwixt now and another Christmas.

I talk of gaieties, but shall not have much of them, if I do not get well. I have had for a fortnight a very bad cold, which has ended in absesses or boils in the glands of one cheek and side of the^n throat. From these I suffer much, from the pain and because it is of a burning, irritating kind that I cannot forget a minute. I have thought much of you, how patiently you bear an infliction of a similar kind all the time, while I think it hard for a week or two,— and then I fret not. You probably have observed how little I write, for the paper. I have felt really unable to write or do any thing, but better times are coming I hope.

181

You ask if my pieces in the paper will be published in a volume. I hope sometime they may, or at least those worth preserving, but know not when.[1] My Miscellanies would fill several volumes, if collected, but nobody thinks it worth while to propose this.[n] Whether they ever will depends on how far M. may win the favor of the public (without making it her object as most of the others do!)

The boarding-house is a very good one, neat, orderly, still. They have been kind, as people generally are to me, urging my having my meals sent to my room &c instead of thinking, because I kept up and exerted myself, that I could not be sick, as so many would have thought.

Farewell! I look forward to the Spring visit. I hope there will be Italn Opera then and Miss Gifford and I will go together. Give much love to her A Miss Wells has called on me who was with Mrs Rotch, Frank and Maria in Rome. She gives very pleasant accounts of both the jeuveniles, but liked Frank best. I ought to tell you also that Mrs and Miss Dewey propose to call on me.[2] With patience great mercies may be expected! Affecy ever

MARGARET F.

ALS (MH: fMS Am 1086 [9:123]); MsC (MH: fMS Am 1086 [Works, 1:47–51]).

even to] ⟨f⟩ even to
either to] either ↑ to ↓
and side of the] and ↑ side of the ↓
propose this.] propose ⟨d⟩ this.

1. Her plans were fulfilled with the publication of *Papers on Literature and Art*, which Wiley and Putnam published in September.

2. Louisa Farnham Dewey (1794–1884) was the wife of Orville Dewey, minister of the Church of the Messiah in New York City. Their daughters were Mary Elizabeth (1821–1910) and Catherine Sedgwick (b. 1838). Fuller probably met Mary (Adelbert M. Dewey, ed., *Life of George Dewey, Rear Admiral, U.S.N.; and Dewey Family History* [Westfield, Mass., 1898], pp. 948–50; MVR 1910 13:231; *DAB*).

598.   To Evert A. Duyckinck

4 Amity Place
N Y.
2d Feby 1846.

To Mr Duyckinck,
Dear Sir,

Mrs Ellett tells me that you lent a willing ear to a plan for the publica-

Evert A. Duyckinck. Courtesy of the Art, Prints, and Photographs Division, The New York Public Library, Astor, Lenox, and Tilden Foundations.

tion of some of my essays.[1] This would be very agreeable to me, as copies of them are continually borrowed and I think, if more accessible, they would command a good deal of sympathy. I should be glad if this took place under your auspices, for I have thought from what I observed that[n] your ideas, as to movements in the literary world, are what I can truly respect. I should like an opportunity to talk with you fully: can you call upon me? If you will, by a note sent through the Tribune Office, appoint an hour I will be at home and most happy to receive you.

With respect yours

S. M. FULLER.

ALS (ViU).

Evert Augustus Duyckinck (1816–78) was the editor of Wiley and Putnam's Library of Choice Reading. A biographer and critic who graduated from Columbia in 1835, he edited the magazines *Arcturus* and, beginning in 1847, *Literary World (DAB)*.

observed that] observed ⟨with ↑ of ↓ your movements⟩ that

1. Elizabeth Lummis Ellet (1812?–77), wife of William Henry Ellet, a professor of chemistry, lived in South Carolina but was on an extended visit to New York City. An accomplished writer, Ellet became a rival to Frances Osgood for Poe's attention (*NAW*). According to Sarah Helen Whitman, Fuller was involved in a struggle between the two. At the instigation of Mrs. Ellet, Fuller and Anne Lynch went to Poe to retrieve a letter that Osgood had written him. In a rage, Poe "called the fair embassadrisses 'Busy-bodies!' & added injury to insult by saying that Mrs. [Ellet] had better come & 'look after her *own* letters.'" This episode presumably added to Poe's disdain for Fuller (John Carl Miller, ed., *Poe's Helen Remembers* [Charlottesville, Va., 1979], pp. 20–21; John Ward Ostrom, ed., *The Letters of Edgar Allan Poe* [Cambridge, Mass., 1948], pp. 406–9).

599. To Evert A. Duyckinck

[ca. 5 February 1846]

To Mr Duyckinck,
Dear Sir

I was so much interrupted last eveg, as not to be able earlier to send you the list you desired. I have made out as fully as I could[n] an account of the pieces I wish to publish. I may alter or enlarge somewhat[n] as limits suggest or permit.

Among the earlier pieces there is not one that has not excited a good deal of interest in this country and many of them have in England. I judge of this from the correspondence and acquaintance they have brought me. Of the degree of interest the portion that is to be taken from the Tribune may have for your public yourself can judge as you have seen them.

Should Messrs Wiley and Putnam desire or incline to make these a part of their series I should like to know as soon as may be what terms they offer and at what time they would wish to bring out the book, for I should have a good deal to do in arranging the materials and writing some new morceaux.

I request your acceptance of the illustrated copy of Summer on the Lakes and the Engh copy of my volume on Woman.

With respect yours

S. M. FULLER.

Mr Emerson informed me that the terms offered by you to him, for his poems, with every desire to be liberal on your side, were inferior to what he could make for himself in N. England.[1]

ALS (NN-M).
Dated by the contents, which place the letter close to the previous one.
as I could] as ⟨accoun⟩ ↑ I could ↓
enlarge somewhat] enlarge ⟨it⟩ somewhat

1. Emerson's negotiations with Duyckinck were protracted. Duyckinck wrote on 13 August 1845 to solicit a contribution from Emerson for Wiley and Putnam's Library of Choice Reading. Emerson later offered a book of poems, but Duyckinck's response was not financially satisfactory. The New York firm offered to sell the book for 31 cents and to pay a royalty of 6 cents. Emerson replied: "It seems to me you make me a very liberal offer on the part of Messrs Wiley & Putnam for my book of Poems; and yet it does not in fact promise me the advantage I had expected from the book, nor an equal advantage to that I do derive from my prose books, which may be presumed to be less popular. . . . I print them at my own risk, & Munroe & Co have 30 per cent as their commission." Munroe published the volume in December 1846 with an 1847 date (Rusk, *Letters of RWE*, 3:297, 301, 307–8, 366).

600.   To Rebecca Spring

4 Amity Place,
12th Feby 1846.

Dear Rebecca,

If the Dr comes before Saty, could you not make an arrangement with him to make his next visit after on Monday 16th Feby. Then I would come on Sunday p.m. that is next Sunday[n] and stay till Tuesday

morng and we would have time to talk over all our bright thoughts,
whether night or day thoughts. Be at Miss Lynch's Saty night, wont
you?

    Affecy

S. M. F.

I hear Mr. Lane wants to see Harro Harring[1] Ask Mr. L. to be at Miss
L's on Saty eveg and Harro Harring will be there.

ALS (MHarF). *Addressed:* to Mrs. Spring / Care Wells & Spring / Pine St / N. Y. *Endorsed:* S. Margaret Fuller.

    p.m. that is next Sunday] p.m. ↑ that is next Sunday ↓

    1. Harro Harring (1798–1870) was a writer and revolutionary who was often expelled from European countries (Henry and Mary Garland, *The Oxford Companion to German Literature* [Oxford, 1976]). In the summer of 1846 he sued Harper's over the publication of his novel *Dolores.*

601. To Richard F. Fuller

[ca. 13 February 1846]

[   ] You ask of me, my plans &c. I was ill nearly all the month of
Jany and since getting well, have been hard pressed, because of the enforced indolence of that month. Else had I answered a letter you wrote
me about Mary Allen, as I much wanted to, but now that must wait
some day of Italian leisure.[1]

    I have been much distressed by a letter recd from Ellery, in which he
informs me that he is going to Europe in March, as Ellen is to be confined in April and "he is only a bugbear in the house at that time and
during the first year of a child's life; it will be best for him to be absent"
and "Ellen wishes it as much as he does" that *I* shall sympathize with the
absolute necessity to his mind of seeing works of art and as he has
never before asked me to do any thing he expects me now to do all I
can to secure him employment in order to pay his expenses and make
up as heavy a purse as possible from my friends. Among other things
he wishes the situation of foreign correspondent to the Tribune! and to
receive a hundred dollars in advance!![2]

    I need hardly tell you what my feelings were on receiving this epistle.
I had meant and hoped never to feel indignation and aversion towards
Ellery, but the unnatural selfishness of a man who, having brought a
woman into this[n] situation of suffering peril and care, proposes to

leave her without even knowing whether she lives or dies under it, is a little too much for my nerves.

He has also written to the Curtises to accompany him.[3] They are thinking of it, meanwhile have written to say that his estimate of expenses is entirely too low. I think I shall not write to him, till they get an answer to their letter. I fear to do something that may exasperate him to Ellen's disadvantage in her present state, as he writes me "he is in a very bad state." Meanwhile I wish, so soon as you receive this that you[n] would write and tell me whether you know any thing about the matter, whether Ellen knows it, how she feels and what proposes. If he goes, I think it must be a crisis between them. Do not delay answering, tha[t] I may get yours before writing.

I recd last night a letter from Mr Spring, saying that his offers to[n] his partners in business had been accepted and he should be free to go to Europe. He requested silence as to people in general for about a fortnight yet, as the papers are not yet formally made out.

But he knows you know about it and that you intend writing him a letter. So now the sooner you do it[n] the better. Tell him in full your views and feelings about my going and what you feel you can undertake. Only do not undertake too much.

Entre nous, *strictly*, Greeley and McElrath have not acted as I could wish the last few weeks. The blame lies wholly with the latter.[4] He has devoted no attention to the 2d edition of my book, he delays making me a proposition as to the future, he acts towards me in a way that makes me think perhaps the boldness of my course does not suit his narrow mind. At any rate, his course is such that I doubt his making me a liberal offer for letters to the Tribune. I do not wish to encounter the labor of writing them unless I can do it on good terms. I would rather make notes and on my return publish[n] a book of travel mixed with stories and verses, quite fresh.

I should be glad therefore if Marcus would advance what money I may need and be repaid it gradually by me and you.

These clouds between me and the Tribune may be transient. I think it the best way to keep on the reserve, and see how things turn out. I shall not speak to them again till the last moment, and if they do not act as I had hoped and expected shall still not forget that to the paper and the freedom I have enjoyed in it I owe standing on some vantage ground now. The other periodicals make me good offers, and if[n] I leave the Tribune by and by I think I can do well. But *while* I remain, I shall devote myself to it[n] as I have done, and shall certainly remain until Septr as I promised Mr G. I would.

The literary[n] advisor of Wiley and Putnam is in treaty with me to publish a selection from my essays. This also^n is at present a kind of secret, but I am much pleased about it.

And so the sweet and sour alternate with me. I enjoy, when well, the use of my faculties and making some good strokes in a good cause. Happiness shall yet be ours, but the full draught is far off. I might tell you many more things, but there is no more time and room except to say myself with love and benediction your sister

M.

ALfrS (MH: fMS Am 1086 [9:249]); MsCfr (MH: fMS Am 1086 [Works, 1:113–19]). *Dated from Richard's reply of 16 February* (MH).

into this] into ⟨th⟩ this
you receive this that you] you ↑ receive this that you ↓
offers to] offers ⟨by⟩ ↑ to ↓
do it] do ⟨?⟩ it
return publish] return ⟨f⟩ publish
and if] and ↑ if ↓
myself to it] myself ↑ to it ↓
The literary] The li⟨b⟩terary
This also] This ↑ also ↓

1.   On 21 January Richard wrote to tell Margaret of Mary Allen's death. "I wish you would mourn with me," he said, "for I cry much over her beautiful letters. . . . I wish you would write me some thing beautiful descriptive of Mary Allen" (MH).

2.   Richard replied on 16 February: "Mother wrote to me that 'Ellen wished her to stay with her while Ellery has gone to the continent.' So you see Ellen knows of it. It would be heinous, but Ellery's presence is so torturing, that perhaps it is not to be deprecated. I have given up Ellery." Channing solicited money from the family, from several friends, and from former acquaintances (Hudspeth, *Ellery Channing*, pp. 31–32).

3.   George and Burrill Curtis of Providence, who had been at Brook Farm and who lived for a time in Concord, went to Europe, but not with Channing (George Curtis to Almira Barlow, 11 March 1846, MH).

4.   Thomas McElrath (1807–88) was Greeley's partner and business manager for the *Tribune* and the publishing firm (*DAB*). As Fuller implies, he was a close and careful businessman.

602.   To Evert A. Duyckinck

4 Amity place
Friday 27th Feby. [1846]

To Mr. Duyckinck,

I accept the offer of Mr Wiley and could be ready to begin next week on Tuesday.

I am sorry not to have been able to see you and that you should find a fireless room on so cold a day. I hope you will come again soon and to give you a more cordial reception

S. M. FULLER.

ALS (NN-M). *Addressed:* To / Mr Duyckinck. / 20 Clinton place.

603.   To James Nathan

[ca. 28 February 1846]
Evening by my bright fire
in the prettiest little room
imaginable wh I tenant
for the present in Amity place.

My dear friend

Last month brought me a letter which repaid for long waiting, —your letter from Rome, full of soul and sweetness as ever was your-self in the best hours of our life together last Spring.

How do I wish I could answer to it as I ought, as I would, but unhap-pily this last day before preparing for the March steamer has brought me one of my bad headachs, of which I have not before had one for sometime, and I feel paralyzed, not myself. I think, however, you may prefer having such a letter as I can write to none at all. I feel hope that you may by this time be at home with mother and bretheren and that the next steamer may bring me a leaf to tell of your pilgrimage, and how the home of your childhood looks after it, and after the long sepa-ration. I feel as if it *might* be a sad survey, the changes must have been so very great, but I want to hear all.

I hope to have this past, before you can receive this, but when you do, write quick in reply, and tell me of your plans. When do you return to the U. S.? A plan which I mentioned to you in an earlier letter is now matured and if nothing unexpected intervenes, I shall with Mr and Mrs Spring leave here for England by the middle of August. We are going also to Germany France and Italy. I expect to stay a year; *they* may travel longer. Shall I not see you all that time? Shall you not return here before I go, or if not shall we not meet in some place the other side of the water?[1]

I rather think the latter by your sending for Josey Answer decisively

189

whether you will have him sent the 1st May. The Gs break up from our dear old place then. Mrs G. will have no objection to parting with him. She views him almost with hatred. Oh my friend what a singular chapter I should have to narrate if we met. But I do not wish to write; it is impossible with the pen to be just and tender enough. Suffice it to say I have paid dear for your love. Let it be immortal and if we meet no more, let it shine on me from the distance with a steady and cheering ray. It was pure and fresh as the blossoms amid which it grew and if it never comes to fruit let it, at least, forever bloom as they in memory.

Yes, do write to Mrs G. a good and full letter, but do not, I counsel you, speak of her coming to Germany. But write as a friend. I believe the fact of my hearing from you and she not[n] renews constantly the bitterness.

Her child is one of the finest imaginable. I love him[n] much, and he me no less.

I send through Mr Benzon Tribunes containing your letters. The last describing ancient Rome I did not publish; every object in the eternal City is too familiar to the reading public. I wish you had sent, instead, the letter on Modern Rome, for your observations on what you personally meet are always original and interesting. I hope you will write *yourself* out in letters on Egypt and Palestine and not describe objects which, there also, have already been described many times.

Yourself, yourself. —

The rose from Shelley's grave would have been dear to me, but somehow in opening the letter I lost the rose and when I had finished could find only the green leaves. Is not that rather sad?

Your *picture* I shall see abroad, if not yourself.

I have been in town ever since 1st Jany when I wrote to you. I have had an outwardly[n] gay and busy life, made many new acquaintance and two or three friends Among these number two men of heroic blood, Cassius Clay, who was here in Jany and Harro Harring, the Dane, a stormy nature, but full and rich and with a childlike[n] sweetness in him at times when the vexed waves recede.[2]

All the little demons warn me not to send this letter. First the headach, then I have dropped ink upon it, then let it go against the candle. But if thou be minded towards me as in thy last, all these threats will go for nothing, thou wilt take it in good part and turn the soiled and blotted leaves to precious purpose.

Unless I hear from you again I shall not write by steamer of 1st April I want to know first that you are at home and how you are feeling. I want too that you should receive this. Nevertheless, if I have a letter from you in March that draws an answer, it will come in April. I shall now be overwhelmed with things to do for awhile. I am to bring out my Miscellanies in 2 vols, which[n] will be a constant care as they claim revisal and additions. I am also to keep on writing for the Tribune up to the last. I have some family troubles that keep obliging me to write to Masstts. In fine, if I saw you, I could say much, but at this crisis I cannot get repose of mind for it.

When you receive this breathe a prayer that I may be sustained and aided by the Angels, for just now I need aid. On you my blessings always wait.

I have a few days since a note from Mr Delf. He had not heard from you How is the English maiden?[n]

AL (MB: Ms. Am. 1451 [69–70, 72]). Published in *Love-Letters*, pp. 175–79.
Dated by the reference to her book.
you and she not] you ↑ and she not ↓
love him] love ⟨it⟩ ↑ him ↓
had an outwardly] had ⟨a⟩ ↑ an outwardly ↓
with a childlike] with ⟨at l⟩ ↑ a childlike ↓
vols, which] vols, ⟨and⟩ which
maiden?] *This sentence has been canceled by a later hand but is here recovered.*

1. Nathan replied on June 5 (MH): "Your coming to Europe is of the next interest to me and I am heartily glad of it, but how singular!" After saying that he had no firm business plans but that he certainly would not return to the United States before her departure, Nathan concluded that he would write to her by Delf in London: "You will certainly find something with Mr. Delf in London, from me, if not myself and then thanks to god! in all probability shall we meet either there or here [i.e., Hamburg]."

2. Cassius Marcellus Clay (1810–1903) was a Kentucky abolitionist who founded the newspaper *True American* in Lexington in 1845 (*DAB*). In reporting a speech Clay made in New York City, Fuller said: "Whoever saw Mr. Clay that night, saw in him a man of deep and strong nature, thoroughly in earnest, who had well considered his ground, and saw that though open, as the noble must be, to new views and convictions, yet his direction is taken, and the improvement to be made will not be to turn aside, but to expedite and widen his course in that direction" (*New-York Daily Tribune*, 14 January 1846).

604. To Samuel G. and Anna B. Ward

New York.
3d March, 1846.

My ever dear friend,

I was glad, indeed, to get your and Anna's letters after the long silence. Indeed, of your health and outward life I had heard in other ways, but my heart had often turned towards you and wished for sight of your handwriting at least.

Yet I do not feel able to answer the good part of your letter, I mean the thinking part, unless I do so in the Tribune. I may, very likely, take it as text, if I can find a suitable form for my reflections.

At present I am not fit to write a good letter. I cannot spare time or feeling. All the month of January I was sick in a way that unfitted me for any serious effort. Ever since I have been toiling in vain to make up at the same time for my forced derelictions and to meet new demands. *Now* I am on the point, in addition to my usual work of getting out two vols of my Miscellanies (pieces from Dial and Tribune wh will require a good^n deal of revision; they are to be published in Wiley and Putnam's series) and getting ready to go to Europe in August, wh will be hard work, as Mr Greeley is to be absent most of the summer and I have promised to stay by the Tribune till the last. Add to this the perplexity and grief as to home affairs that Ellery's last freak has brought upon me—

But it is not of this I want to speak, but of my going to Europe. It is now ten years, since I was forced to abandon the hope of going at the time when I felt that my health and mind required it as they never could again.[1] Still more I felt that in not going with you at the time when our minds were^n so in unison, and when I was drawn so strongly towards your peculiar province, I lost what life could never replace. I feel so still.

At every step I have missed the culture I sought in going, for with me it [was] no scheme of pleasure but the means of needed development. It was what I wanted after my painful youth, and what I was ready to use and be nourished by. It would have given my genius wings and I should have been, not in idea indeed, but in achievement far superior to what I can be now. Fate or Heaven, or whatever we may call it, did not will it so, and in entering other and less congenial paths, I do feel that I have tried to make the best of life in every sense I could. Many sweet fruits has it brought me, fruits of spiritual knowledge and a liberal communion with the woful struggling crowd of fellow men. I have accepted my lot, such as it was, and while I have not cast over it any veil of commonplace resignations I have not complained inwardly or outwardly. I have, indeed, had my periods of morbid suffering, because the perpetual stress upon me has been beyond my strength to bear, and at this present time I feel threatened with one, because the day is thronged a great deal too thick with tasks and perplexities and I have not the chance for repose that I ought.

I hope however to avoid it, for I have grown wise and now seek physical remedies for irritated nerves, rather than struggle with them mentally, which I formerly augmented the ill by doing.

I do not look forward to seeing Europe now as so very important to me. My mind and character are too much formed. I shall not modify them much but only add to my stores of knowledge. Still, even in this sense, I wish much to go. It is important to me, almost needful in the career I am now engaged in I feel that, if I persevere, there is nothing to hinder my having an important career even now. But it must be in the capacity of a journalist, and for that I need this new field of observation.

I want to go in a way not too laborious for my strength and it is with this view that I apply to you. I have about a thousand dollars secured for my absence. But from all calculations I seem likely to want five hundred more. Can I through you or your father have a credit abroad to that amount, in case I need it.[2] I wish to be in debt to a friend, that in case I live and return, I may pay it gradually as I earn it and not feel oppressed by it. I should like it to be a debt in regular form, and pay suitable interest for the use of the money. If I live I could probably earn that sum soon, if I die, the lender would not eventually be a loser, as seven or eight hundred dollars will come to me when Mother leaves this world from which she seems likely to be driven prematurely, though truly I wish I might go first.

I think I remember something of your saying you never meant to *lend* money If you have any vow or resolution of that kind that will interfere, or if I am mistaken in thinking that yr fathers relations abroad would make this easier to you than any one else, write soon, dear Sam, and say so, and I shall apply elsewhere. If I cannot get it otherwise I can take upon me correspondences with periodicals here, only too much of that will give me so much labor as in good measure to deprive me of the benefit of the journey

Dearest Anna, I thank much for the sweet picture of your life It will be repose to think of it, in dust and rush of a different one. I have no time to answer except about my visit. I wish *very* much, to come but do not feel sure of being able and if I am, the visit must be short. I should like much however to come, if I can, and should[n] be glad to meet Cary as else I cannot see her again. Will you ask her for the last of June or first of July and I will come then, if possible. I am glad we saw so much of each other last summer, we may not meet much again for a good or bad while.

I feel sorry not to have the books you name, they came out in my sick time and not being noticed by my hand do not belong to me by rules of the office I send such as I have.

Dear Sam I look to see you. Shall be here 4 Amity place, Mrs Elwell's till 12th March, after that time inquire at[n] Tribune office.[3] I have been interrupted forty times while writing and now am so again, but ever yours

MARGARET.

ALS (MH: bMS Am 1465 [927]).
a good] a ⟨d⟩ good
minds were] minds where
and should] and ⟨if I⟩ should
inquire at] inquire ⟨in⟩ at

1. Timothy Fuller's death in 1835 ended his daughter's plan to go to Europe with the Farrars and Ward.
2. Both Ward and his father, Thomas Wren Ward, were associated with the London banking house of Baring Brothers.
3. The New York City directory lists Mary Elwell, a widow, at 4 Amity Place.

605. To Richard F. Fuller

[7 March 1846]

My dear Richard

You will, perhaps, be disappointed on cracking this nut to find how small a portion of its kernel is for you, but I cannot help it. I have out gone my poor little strength entirely.

In answer to yours whose contents were every way interesting to me I say as to one part of its contents you cannot write too minutely of your affairs. Uncle H. is a slippery customer, but if the death of Mr Stone acts on hi[s] circumstances as you supposed, you wil[l] be more likely to do well with him. At any rate I am glad you incline to stay in Boston.[n]

But, Richard, I grieve to see how great the chance is of your making the miserable mistake that has wrecked so many of my best friends in marriage. I conjure you not to be so rash and impetuous. If you had acted with patience and judgment, as to Anna you would, I think, have had a great chance of happiness there. At any rate I conjure you not to ruin your whole life by any rash engagement of this sort. You could not be *a little* unhappy; you would be utterly miserable in a bad connection.

Among the gifts I send you only a transient trifle, intending before my return to find for you an engraving of some beautiful subject that you will always like to keep with you.

I send Anna L. a trifling gift and a little note at your desire, otherwise I should not have written, as, though I doubt not she thinks of me, she never exerts herself to write, and I have to exert myself every way within an inch of my life Ever affectly your friend and sister

I want to observe one thing, dear R, as to Anna Loring Were she my child I should advise her for the sake of the other party no less than her own not to bind herself at this age or at all before she returns from Europe. That experience will have a great effect on her character and she ought to go through with it before binding herself in any way. This remark may be quite needless but I thought it would do no harm to make it. Take all kindly remember I cannot write deliberately or express fully what is in my mind.

AL (MH: fMS Am 1086 [9:247]). *Addressed:* To / Richard F Fuller / Office H. H. Fuller / 6 State St / Boston, Mass / Kindness of Mr Cowden. *Endorsed:* 7 Mar. / S. Margaret Fuller.

I am glad you incline to stay in Boston.] ↑ I am glad you incline to stay in Boston. ↓

606.   To Caroline Sturgis

9th [March 1846]

My dear Cary,

After receiving your letter I wrote you one, chiefly about Ellery, but finally concluded not to send that or one I had written to him. They were of use to me, as enabling me to calm my mind and dismiss the subject, and could have been of none farther to any one. I will speak briefly to you on the subject when we meet.

I did not see him while here, but understand he went away sad, and he is, no doubt, suffering now, body and mind. [The pa]rt that cuts me is Ellen's being thrown on the sympathies of my poor frail Mother *She* is to be the one sacrificed and after so many years of steady effort I find my poor little schemes for her peace all baffled I am going to let every thing go in this world and scud where the wind drives.[1]

I shall have no chance to think of any body but myself, as I have to exert myself laboriously and unremittingly, or give up going to Europe. I expect to go, if indeed it be permitted, in August, and must work all the time and stay in the hot town till then.

My prospects are good, as to *advantages* of various kinds. I must come back, if I come, in debt, but if as well as I am now, shall be able to pay it in time.

I shall[n] want to see you before going, and have asked the Wards to invite you, (they had previously spoken of having us at the same time,) in case I am able to go to Lenox for two or three days. If I am not, you say you will come here.

Give my love to Waldo and say I go.

My life is, at present, oppressively rich. I need to die and rest. I will not speak of it now.

Write when you can to yours ever

MARGARET

Do write me word how Ellen is.

ALS (MH: bMS Am 1221 [251]).
Dated by the reference to Channing.
I shall] I ⟨wa⟩ shall

1. Sturgis had given a bleak portrait of the Channings in her letter (MH): "I suppose you think his scheme of going abroad a wild & even ruthless one, but if you could talk to Ellen about it you would agree with her, that he had better go. He cannot keep himself peaceable in the house, even now when she has a girl, & it will be worse in the summer. . . . It is very sad for Ellen, sadder than anything she could have had to expect."

607. To Mary Rotch

N. Y.
9th March, 1846.

Dear Aunt Mary,

I was truly glad to get your little letter and will write a few lines to tell you of myself.

I have been very well since I wrote you and perfectly happy in the place where I have been living. I would give much to stay here permanently (4 Amity place), but money considerations oblige me to go away, at least for the present.

I very seldom care for having so little money, but I do now when want of it circumscribes and hampers me in my preparations for going to Europe and will make my life too laborious while there, thus robbing me of many benefits of the journey. I shall however scramble along as well as I can, for after all I often find green and flowry places to look upon along a difficult and fatiguing path.

I am going in August (if Heaven pleases) with Marcus Spring and his wife. You have, probably, heard Mrs Follen speak of them.[1] They are excellent people. All particulars I will tell when you come here. I hope you will stay, *at least*, a week. Will it be in April or May? I want to plan a little so as to have time. Then I[n] shall have to abide by the Tribune up to the day of departure, I believe. No more of this now. I have had only too much thinking and discussing about it of late.

You will like to hear about my tightum dress. It was a light green silk, which I had before and had never worn except on two or three festal occasions But it required alterations.[n] I had it altered and trimmed with blonde lace and this and natural flowers which I have worn with it every time I took from your money and know you will be glad, as I have had very pleasant times, wearing it. I wore it at a party which I myself gave. I asked all those who have asked me and many pleasant gentlemen. I wish you had been here at the time. Mary would have come and enjoyed it, as there were many people worth seeing. The lady with whom I live made every arrangement for me as prettily and with as much interest as Mother might and every body declared that it was remarkably pleasant.

I do not write much for the Tribune just now, as I am trying to get ready my Miscellanies which are to be published by Wiley and Putnam in two volumes. They require a good deal of arrangement correction and some new writing and as Spring comes on I am sadly inert.

I shall not, however be too much so to talk when you come and hope we shall have some happy hours With love to both my friends, ever dear aunt Mary your affece Margaret, who wishes she had any time to write letters of worth. But she prizes your affection not the less that she cannot do more to prove her own.

I think it is since I wrote to you that I have had a letter from Maria, a very good one She was about to be presented at the French Court; have I mentioned it?

I bethink me, now, I have and you have answered.

ALS (MH: fMS Am 1086 [9:130]); MsCfr (MH: fMS Am 1086 [Works, 1:51−55]).
Then I] ↑ Then ↓ I
required alterations.] required ⟨?⟩ alterations.

1. Eliza Cabot Follen was an author and antislavery activist whom Fuller had long known.

608. To Richard F. Fuller

[ca. 10 March 1846]

[   ] I want them directly, by Monday or Tuesday's express, if pos-

sible, as I am only waiting for this matter to begin printing my Miscellanies. Wiley and Putnam have taken them for their series, are going to print two numbers, at fifty cents each, and allow me 12 per cent. on all copies after expenses paid[n] or half profits as I choose. As it takes two thousand copies to pay expenses, I may make nothing or very slowly. Still I shall be content, as it is an object to me to get the pieces in an accessible form. I consider the offer a fair one under the circumstances and am anxious to get the book into press, so soon as may be.

Should the key not prove the right one, I wish you would try to get one from a locksmith and open the trunk; I think the magazines will be there but, if not, look in the box where you found my Bible. I cannot begin without them as the nos on the Engh poets are to come first in the book.[1]

I wish very much I could find the lines on the death of Charles Emerson, to put in, but have no idea whereabout the copy is.—[2] Even if Mr Greeley is not gone, when you receive this, it would be better to send by Harnden's or Adams's express, as Mr G. is sometimes careless, and if I lost my own[n] I know not where to go for these numbers. Direct to me care Tribune Office Corner Spruce and Nassau Sts. N. Y. and write a line by post to tell me you have sent the parcel.

You have, I suppose, a letter from Mr Spring. He was pleased with you and your proposal,[n] but prefers giving a part to lending the whole, and I, too, am satisfied that it should be so. I shall have to borrow a sum, but think I shall be able to repay it through my journey, if I should die, or be otherwise incapacitated, I will appeal to your future. The debt is not likely, at most, to be over five hundred dollars.

We expect to go in August. I shall want to see and talk with you, before I go. Perhaps we will meet at Lenox; by and by we will write of this.[n]

If I cannot come on to Masstts I shall want dear mother to come and be with me a few of the last[n] days. I shall be gone a long time and there is always the possibility of never returning, when one goes so far and across an ocean

I have long since done all I could to induce Ellen to give up having Mother, but I could not, and even if it were of use have[n] not the heart to write to her now on the subject. I expect it will do Mother great hurt. She, like all the gentlest and best, is sacrificed to others. I am glad you feel how frail her state is; We must do what we can to sweeten her life, but efforts to effectually shield her seem vain. God, I hope, has a rest and joy for her, but I fear she will be taken from us first.

The fire at Brook farm[3] will probably ruin them and make it necessary for L. to go, without a chance of returning, but for the present, all that is needed is to say that Ellen wants his help and they will make no objection If you want to know just how they are situated and what is best to do, speak to W. Channing; he is, I understand, in Boston and will act for me.

The little book that I send to make the parcel give to Arthur with my love. Say to dear Mother I will write again to her, so soon as I have more peace of mind and rest of body. Tell her to hope for me good things. Write me word how all is at home. I feel sad always when I cannot know. [   ]

ALfr (MH: fMS Am 1086 [9:135]); MsCfr (MH: fMS Am 1086 [Works, 1:123–27]). *Addressed:* Richard.

Dated by the reference to the Brook Farm fire.
cent. on all copies after expenses paid] cent. ↑ on all copies after expenses paid ↓
my own] my ⟨ow⟩ ↑ own ↓
your proposal,] your proposa⟨s⟩l,
will write of this.] will ⟨talk⟩ ↑ write ↓ of ⟨?⟩ this.
few of the last] few ↑ of the last ↓
use have] use ⟨c⟩ have

1. Fuller wanted her copies of the *Dial* to use for her *Papers on Literature and Art.* Her essay "Modern British Poets" became the sixth essay in the book.

2. Apparently Fuller did not find her copy of the poem she published in the *Boston Daily Centinel & Gazette*, 17 May 1836, for it does not appear in the book.

3. For several months the residents at Brook Farm had been building a "phalanstery," an apartment building with a kitchen, dining hall, and chapel. Shortly before nine o'clock on the evening of 3 March, an overheated stove set the uninsured building on fire. In less than two hours it was totally destroyed, a $7,000 loss. Despite the efforts of many of the community's creditors (who included Greeley, Marcus Spring, and Richard Manning) to keep the commune intact, the association voted on 4 March 1847 to rent the farm to outsiders. George Ripley's utopian experiment came to an end on 18 August 1847, when the property was formally transferred to a board of trustees (George Ripley, "The Fire at Brook Farm," *Harbinger* 2 [1845–46]: 220–22; George Willis Cooke, *John Sullivan Dwight* [Boston, 1898], pp. 111–14; Octavius Brooks Frothingham, *George Ripley* [Boston, 1882], pp. 194–95).

609. To Evert A. Duyckinck

Wednesday 18th March [1846]

To Mr Duyckinck,
Dear Sir,

I send, as I suppose, a volume or more for the press. When I see how it comes out in the new print, I can tell better about the 2d volume. I have so much matter that I am afraid of sending *too* much.

My file of the Tribune has not been sent to me entire, so that I have not the notice of Milnes and Landor and one or two other little pieces that ought to go into this volume. But I shall, probably, be able to send them, as well as the notice of Browning and of the Purgatory of Suicides, by the time they are wanted.[1]

I shall have new matter for insertion in the second volume.

Tomorrow p m. between five and six I go out to Mr Greeley's house to remain till Tuesday morng, when I go for a week to the house of Mr Spring, State St, Brooklyn. If, while I am there, the proofs could be sent me at night, I could send them back next morng—or what arrangement shall be made about them?

I shall be here (4 Amity place) tomorrow. Perhaps, if there is anything that needs saying or suggesting, you will call to see me between three and five p. m.

Most truly yours

S. M. FULLER.

ALS (NN-M). *Addressed:* To / Mr. Duyckinck / 20 Clinton place / N. Y.

1. Fuller wrote a two-part essay on Monckton Milnes, Julius Hare, and Walter Savage Landor that appeared in the *Tribune* on 4 and 28 March 1845. It was not, however, reprinted in *Papers on Literature and Art*. Her first review of Robert Browning's work, which appeared in the *Tribune* on 1 April 1846, became the third essay of the second volume. Thomas Cooper (1805–92), a worker with Chartist sympathies, was jailed for his labor activities. While in prison, he wrote *The Purgatory of Suicides. A Prison-Rhyme* (London, 1845) (*DNB*).

610. To Horace Greeley

Friday 20th [March 1846]

Dear Mr Greeley,

Enclosed is a notice of Mr Dwight which may, I hope, go in tomorrow morng as Saty is the last lecture.[1] He wants to come out to the Farm when you are there, if he comes.

Perhaps you will send me by David the proof this p.m. I want thirty dollars from the office, and I want David to do a little errand for me that will take a quarter of an hour. Will you send me *Typee* and *Titmarsh's journey*.[2] Mr Duyckinck wished me to look at them. Could David come by three or[n] four this aftn?

I shall take a cab for me and my goods and go out to the Farm[n] Saty morng

M. F.

If there are any letters for me will you send them by David?

Horace Greeley. Courtesy of the National Portrait Gallery, Smithsonian Institution, Washington, D.C.

ALS (NN-B). *Addressed*: To / Mr Greeley / Tribune Office.

by three or] by ↑ three or ↓
out to the Farm] out ↑ to the Farm ↓

1. John Sullivan Dwight, an old friend of Fuller's, was a graduate of Harvard Divinity School, a contributor to the *Dial*, and a Brook Farm resident. After the fire at the community, he lectured on music in New York City. Fuller, who was apparently still at Amity Place, working on the proofs of her book, probably did not hear Dwight on Thursday (the 19th). A notice, not marked with her star, appeared in the Friday *Tribune*.

2. Michael Angelo Titmarsh was Thackeray's pseudonym for his *Notes of a Journey from Cornhill to Grand Cairo* (London, 1846). His book and Melville's were Fuller's subject for an essay in the *Tribune* on 4 April. She found Titmarsh "amusing" but "flippant"; Melville wrote "a very entertaining and pleasing narrative."

611. To James F. Clarke

28th March [1846]

Dear James,

Here are your letters which you wished to read, but remember they are *mine* and that it will be larceny if you dont return them.

Here is another letter for Cincinnati, and if you dont find conveyance soon tell me, for I suppose I shall keep on writing them.

I could not talk with you the other night, and I cannot till we have had some quiet meeting by ourselves, and marked out the ground. Meanwhile in assured friendship yours

MARGARET.

ALS (ICHi). *Addressed:* Rev. J. F. Clarke / 9. Central Court. *Endorsed*: This note was written to me / by Sarah Margaret Fuller, / (afterward Madam Ossoli) / not long before she went to / Europe in 1846 / James Freeman Clarke / Nov 20th 1865 / Boston—

612. To Mary Weeks Manning

Sunday eveg
[29? March? 1846]

Will you excuse me, dear Mrs Manning, if I do not return this night and break off my visit to you with seeming bluntness. I expected to return to you, but making a mistake in the Dr's day, I had to come here again last night. This morng I went to ride and this p. m. have had a book to examine preparatory for a notice which must be made[n] directly and wherever I am shall have to spend this eveg upon it. I think therefore I had better not change my place especially as Mrs Spring will bring me down in the carriage tomorrow and take me to the Fulton ferry with my baggage. I should think it impolite to act thus, if I was not to return to you but then we shall see one another freely and make up for[n] all deficiencies and now you will all excuse me, will you not? for doing as is most convenient to me I am very glad to hear that little Henry is better.[1] I shall see you a few minutes in the morng and now am with remembrances to Mr and Miss Manning,[2] yours affecy

S. M. FULLER.

ALS (PHi). *Addressed*: To / Mrs Manning / Middagh St.

Mary Weeks Manning (b. 1815) was the third wife of Richard Henry Manning (1809–87), a Brooklyn merchant who was active in religious and social reform. She was the daughter of Cole and Eliza Weeks of New Hampshire (William H. Manning, *Genealogy and Biographical History of the Manning Families of New England and Descendants* [Salem, Maine, 1902], pp. 747, 749).

notice which must be made] notice ↑ which must be made ↓

make up for] make ↑ up for ↓

1. Henry Swan Manning (1844–1921) served in the Civil War, became a businessman and an engineer, and then rejoined the army (Manning, *Genealogy*, p. 763; *New York Times*, 10 July 1921).

2. Richard Henry Manning began his business career in Boston, then moved to Philadelphia and finally to New York. With a genius for friendship, he helped organize the Second Society (Unitarian) in Brooklyn and worked to bring William Henry Channing to the church. An abolitionist and a Fourierite, he bought shares in Brook Farm (ibid., pp. 747–49). Miss Manning is Abby Adeline Manning (1836–1906), Manning's child by his first wife, Frances Moore (1813–39) (MVR 1906 11:550).

613. To Sarah Shaw

Eveg of 17th April
1846.

My dear Sarah,

The departure of a friend for your neighborhood prompts me to send this bit of paper begging you will write to me, and tell me of yourself and Anna and Sarah Russell— all that I hold dear in "your connection." Or rather I wish you would come here *Ask* Frank if he will not come *and induce you to come!* If I go to Europe, as I expect, in August, I shall not see you a long time unless you do.

Your little bag I carry very often, and like to have what you have made. It is a household love I have for you, dear Sarah,— good solid stuff.

I have no time to write thoughts so stop here with, your friend ever

S. M. F.

I saw your brother Russell; it seemed strange but pleasant the face that used to peep out of the window in Mt Vernon St. when I was oh so strangely young.

ALS (MH: bMS Am 1417 [181]). *Addressed*: Mrs Sarah Shaw / West Roxbury / Mass.

614. To James Nathan

Sunday, 25 April 1846

Dear Friend,

Lost too soon, too long; where art thou, where wander thy steps and where thy mind this day?

This day, the last of leisure, I shall pass in the place that was the scene of our meeting when our acquaintance grew with the advance of spring, knew indeed its frequent chills, blights and delays, but also its tender graces, its young joys and at last its flowers.

This place, I think, will always be lovely in my memory. But alas! we shall meet here no more. Strangers to us will haunt the rocks and little green paths, where we gave one another so much childish happiness, so much sacred joy.

Hast thou forgotten any of these things, hast thou ceased to cherish me, O Israel!

I have felt, these last four days, a desire for you that amounted almost to anguish. You are so interwoven with every thought of this place, it seemed as if I could not leave it, till we had walked and talked here once more.

This is such a day as came last year after our reconciliation, when the trees had put on their exquisite white mantles and you gave me the white veil. That evening you went home and wrote me the sweet little letter, in which you likened yourself to the cherry-tree by my window. The tree has again decked itself with blossoms and I see it in its best loveliness before my departure.

But thou dost not return; could you but be here all this day, only one day. So many things have happened, such a crowd of objects come between us! Alas! there is too much to be said we cannot say rightly in letters.

I say Alas! and Alas! and once again Alas!

I send a leaf and flower of the myrtle that grew at the foot of the rock, of which I gave you some the day we seemed to be separated for ever. But we were not.

Where are you? What are you doing? I have not heard from you for more than four months. I do not know whether you passed safe through the East, I do not know whether you have ever reached your home. And I do not know what has been or is in your mind. How unnatural! for such ignorance and darkness to follow on such close communion, such cold eclipse on so sweet a morning. Is it the will of the Angels? Have they drawn the veil between us and given us to other duties, other ties?

We leave this place the last day of April. Mrs. Greeley goes with her child to Brattleboro (Vermont), for the summer. I have taken lodgings in Brooklyn near the heights for the summer or rather till the 1st August, when I expect to go to England. We intend to go in the steamer from Boston 1st August, on arriving in England to travel about, see Scotland and Westmoreland and be in London in September. Then the plan is to go to Hamburg and from there to see a little of Germany. Then, on the last of September or first of October, if you are there, I shall see you again, at least for an hour or two.

But do write, the moment you receive this, if you have not long before, and tell me everything good and bad. I thought surely to have heard before this, if only to know what to do about sending you Josey. He is now to be left, I don't know how. Mrs. Greeley has seemed more kindly towards him of late. She has sometimes even fed him herself. He is strong and seems tolerably well now, but he will never be the intelligent and fine creature he might, if you had not left him.

Farewell! for to-day, I have no heart to write any more.

16th May.

Still no letter from you, I do not yet know that you are safe. And in one fortnight it will be a year, since you went away.

The spring is now at its loveliest. I am not, where I can enjoy its loveliness as at the Farm, yet am happier, for I have a home now, where peace, order and kindness prevail.

Poor Josey remains at the Farm. I suffer much annoyance by continual questions from Mr. Greeley whether I have not heard from you, so as to let him know what to do with the dog, who remains only on suffer-ance with the new occupants and is exposed to loss or injury.

The affairs of this country are at present disturbed by wars and ru-mours of wars.[1] Still there seems no likelihood as yet of our being pre-vented from going to Europe the 1st August. We expect to go in the mail-steamer from Boston. Farewell. Unless I hear from you I shall not write any more. If I do not hear at all, I shall feel great anxiety and shall write to Mr. Delf to ascertain whether you are safe, as there is no one here that can inform me.

Wherever and however you are, that God may bless you always is the prayer of

MARGARET.

EL, from *Love-Letters*, pp. 180–84.

1. Matt. 24:6, in which Jesus says: "and ye shall hear of wars and rumors of wars: see that ye be not troubled: for all these things must come to pass, but the end is not yet." Slightly different versions occur in Mark 13:7 and Luke 21:9. Conflicts at this time were imminent with both Mexico and England. The failure of John Slidell's mission to Mexico and the movements of General Zachary Taylor along the Mexican border made war an immediate possibility. Greeley had written in the *Tribune* for 20 April: "That Mr. Slidell has returned disappointed and mortified from his Mexican mission is generally known; that Messrs. Polk and Buchanan are now concocting war measures or war fulminations to be submitted to Congress thereupon is highly probable." The Mexican war began on 12 May. The same issue of the *Tribune* had a report on the Oregon problem that had evolved from Polk's determination to oust the British from joint occupancy of the terri-tory: "If any attempt is made to possess Oregon by force, the result will be the horrible alternative—War! To this point affairs are daily drifting." On 23 April the Senate passed a resolution to terminate joint occupancy. The quarrel was, however, settled peacefully in June 1846 (Richard B. Morris, *Encyclopedia of American History* [New York, 1953], pp. 193–96).

615. To Evert A. Duyckinck

[Early May? 1846]

To Mr Duyckinck,

Could you come to see me on Tuesday or Wednesday morng of next week? I will be at home on both from 10 till 12.

When I saw Mr Mathews he proposed coming with you, but *this time* I should like to see you alone.[1] I am but little way from the Fulton ferry; 43 Middagh St; R. H. Manning on the door. With much regard,

S. M. F.

ALS (NN-M).

Dated by the reference to her residence with the Mannings, which puts the letter after 1 May.

1. Cornelius Mathews (1817–89) graduated from New York University in 1834 and was admitted to the bar. He never practiced law, however, but became a writer instead, the most contentious of the Young America group. He wrote poems, plays, and criticism and was tireless on behalf of an international copyright law. His tragedy *Witchcraft, or the Martyrs of Salem* (1846) was a successful play (*DAB*). Fuller described it as "a work of strong and majestic lineaments." She praised "the attempt . . . in making an aged woman a satisfactory heroine to the piece through the greatness of her soul" (*Papers on Literature and Art* [New York, 1846], 2:135). She published a portion of the drama (without attribution) as an appendix to her book (2:177–83). A friend of Elizabeth Barrett, Mathews gave Fuller a letter of introduction to the poet.

616. To Richard F. Fuller

Brooklyn,
May 17th 1846.

My dear Richard,

I have been puzzling my mind in vain to think of the right boarding house for you I have been too long absent from Boston to know about families. I meant to wait and ask my friend Mrs F. Shaw, who would be a good person to know and who will be here the 1st June, but Mother writes that you want to go into town *next week*. I thought it was not till the autumn.[1]

Though I do not know myself, the following persons will be likely to. They can suggest and describe places and then you can look for yourself. Any of them whom you do not know would be glad to advise with you if you say I asked you to go.

Ednah Littlehale Bowdoin St. I think most likely to know of any. Mrs Dr Hooper Summer St. Anna Parsons, La Grange Place, Mrs. Colburn, Mrs James Clarke.[2] All of these know a great many people in different circles, and have discrimination. Without being too expansive tell them you want a pleasant place, that will be like a home to you and get them to describe what they[n] know till you find the desired requisites This is the only way I can ever get a pleasant one for myself, as it is impossible for another to judge how things may affect us.

Belinda will also be likely to know of some herself, and through her friend Mrs Lewis. I do not, personally, know any one likely to accept a boarder unless[n] possibly Mrs Bond and that place you would not like, if she would take you.[3]

If you do not get suited, write again and I will talk with Mrs Shaw, when she comes.

I do ardently hope Mother may get a girl, on whom she can rely, so that she may feel free to leave home and get away from care and labor of which a very little seems to be such poison to her. If she can come here before I go and then to M. D'Wolf's it will do her good.[4] I see she is very weak, enclose half a dollar, want you to get[n] her a bottle of Port and see that she takes it every day and every drop; it always does her good at this time of year. She mentions her garden as if it was balm to her, what you and A have done for her there will meet its full reward.

I am sorry you have made up your mind against coming here; could not Uncle H. if you asked him get you a little business here that would pay the expense of coming on. If you do not, we shall have no chance to talk at all. Ask Mother to keep the garments for the present, but if they are marked to send them to me when a good oppory offers. These books are for her.

Ever affecy yr. sister

M.

ALS (MH: fMS Am 1086 [9:127]); MsC (MH: fMS Am 1086 [Works, 1:129–31]).

what they] what ⟨you⟩ ↑ they ↓

accept a boarder unless] accept ↑ a boarder unless ↓

to get] to ⟨see⟩ get

1. Fuller is answering Richard's letter of 7 May (MH), in which he said: "Next autumn I shall make some stroke or other. I may go to the West, though I do not feel as if I should." He asked her help with a boardinghouse: "Now you are powerful here in Boston, & I thought you might help me to a fine place where I should be feted out of nepotism & favoritism."

2. Ednah Dow Littlehale (1824–1904), daughter of Sargent Smith and Ednah Dow Littlehale of Boston, had been a member of Fuller's conversations in Boston, and later became a writer, philanthropist, and abolitionist. In 1853 she married the artist Seth Wells Cheney (*NAW*). It is not clear if Fuller refers to the mother or the daughter. "Mrs. Dr. Hooper" is Ellen Sturgis Hooper; Anna Parsons is the mesmeric seer Fuller admired; Mrs. Colburn probably is Temperance Horton Colburn, widow of Warren Colburn, the mathematician; Mrs. James Clarke is Anna Huidekoper Clarke.

3. Belinda is Belinda Randall, Fuller's friend since childhood; Mrs. Lewis and Mrs. Bond are unidentified.

4. Mary Soley DeWolfe, another friend from childhood, lived in Bristol, Rhode Island.

617.   To Richard F. Fuller

[6? June 1846]

My dear Richard

I am very glad you think of coming on for every reason.[1] I think it will do you good in point of health, and that, beside, it is desirable for you to see some other region than N. England and will be worth a great deal more to you now[n] than by and by.

It is no disgrace to any one to get run down. Every one needs frequent refreshment in this pilgrimage and nothing is gained by sticking too closely to the oar. I see no objection to your accepting this from Uncle. Father did all such things for him and the indulgence of a right and generous feeling can only do him good. Beside, you will have it in your power to requite the kindness at another time.

As to me, I think we could really meet now in a way to enjoy it, as we possibly never may again. I think, if we did not meet before my going to Europe better than we can amid the interruptions of my short visit home we should become strangers I have become quite discouraged about writing to you at all, by some things you say in your letters and the impossibility it seems to be to you to comprehend the hurry of my life and in which my short scrawls are inevitably written. I feel that I cannot be always wise and judicious, or even delicate, when I have not time to write or concentrate my feelings upon your mental position, and that if you cannot make allowance for this I ought to cease to write at all, for it can only annoy you and lead to answers that grieve me. Once when I *did* insist on having time to write "you thank me for my[n] copious and obliging letter"[2] I should not have written another to any other friend who had answered in that sarcastic way to what I said whether felicitously or otherwise. And the other day when you talked about[n] my wishing to influence you and in that patronizing[n] way about its being "perhaps unconsciously to myself" I did feel quite repelled and as if I could not write any more. I think, however, if we talk together, we shall soon come to a perfect understanding as we have always done on former occasions. The weather promises to be very beautiful, and[n] the foliage in perfection thanks to these eternal rains; we should enjoy going about very much; fortunately I have put off going up the North River I will depend on seeing you and set right to work now to ransom time wh I can by working well till you do come. The Sedgwicks have a Recitation party next Thursday eveg; it would be pleasant for you to be here *then*.[3] But you must think about Sunday in making your arrangements; I suppose no train goes from Albany on that day, so, in order to your further journey we should have to go up the river on Friday or wait till Monday if you got here Thursday morng. You need one or two days just to see N.Y. city.

In arriving put up somewhere, (Arthur will advise you) where you can have comfortable lodging cheap, and not pay for your meals in the house, as you may often take them with me, it will make it more economical.

Best call in at the Tribune office and see Mr Greeley but in case you want to come straight here, cross *Fulton* Ferry to Brooklyn.

I am going up to Lennox a week from next Tuesday if[n] I hear that Anna Ward is well enough. How I wish you could come on Monday 26th[n] by L. I. rail-road; and go up the North[n] river with me, Tuesday to Albany We could have just such a good time as I want to have Cannot you? [   ]

How I wish you could be as pleasantly situated as I am now. I have got rested and tranquil and am ready for the work that is coming Had I been here all the time I could have done twice as much. [   ]

ALfr (MH: fMS Am 1086 [9:127]); MsCfr (MH: fMS Am 1086 [Works, 1:119–23]). *Dated from Richard's letter of 4 June 1846 (MH).*
you now] you no⟨a⟩w
for my] for my⟨"⟩
talked about] talked ⟨of⟩ about
that patronizing] that p⟨re⟩atronizing
beautiful, and] beautiful, ⟨tran⟩ and
Lennox a week from next Tuesday if] Lennox ↑a week from next↓ Tuesday ⟨next⟩ if
Monday 26th] Monday ↑ 26th ↓
the North] the ↑ North ↓

1. Richard had proposed a visit: "I might come to N. Y. week after next, or the last part of next, & go up North River with you, & come home across the country, if so would be agreeable to you. Uncle Henry very generously wishes me to go at his expense; as he imagines I am somewhat run down at the heel."

2. Richard used this language to open his letter to her of 16 February (MH): "Your copious & very obliging letter came duly to hand." Startled by her anger, he replied on 8 June (MH): "You write I sound 'in a patronising way', which surprises me; as a thing so supremely ridiculous as my *patronizing* you as not in my mind certainly. As to the 'long & copious note', that was merely from my bluntness, I had no idea of there being anything sarcastic about it."

3. In his letter, Richard had asked specifically to meet the Sedgwicks.

618.   To Charles Edwards Lester

New York
Sunday morng
4 Amity Place.
[14 June 1846]

To Mr Lester,
Dear Sir

Harro Harrings process against the Harpers[n] comes to trial unexpectedly soon, a week from tomorrow.[1] His counsel attach great importance to being able to say then that the work (Dolores)[n] is in press. I wish very much to see you either this eveg or tomorrow morng but at any rate must solicit an immediate reply as to Baker and Scribner.[2] Forgive my trespassing on your time. I venture to do so because the cause is the cause of freedom one in which the generous cannot spare either time or trouble and I hope to be able to show myself not ungrateful for the bestowment of yours

With respect

S. M. FULLER.

ALS (ICHi). *Endorsed:* Miss Fuller.

Charles Edwards Lester (1815–90), a great-grandson of Jonathan Edwards, studied law but became instead a Presbyterian minister. A prolific writer, he was an active opponent of slavery (*DAB*).

Dated from the reference to Harring's trial, which was held during the week of 22–26 June 1846.

the Harpers] the Harpe⟨r'⟩rs
work (Dolores)] work ↑ (Dolores) ↓

1. According to Emerson, Harring, with the help of Sam Ward of New York (not Samuel Gray Ward of Boston), had contracted with Harper Brothers to publish his novel *Dolores*, but the publisher later backed out. "At much expense [Harring] got it translated into English, copied &c. and some *foreign* or some religious influence came in & they sent the MS back to him" (Rusk, *Letters of RWE*, 3:382). The original contract, signed in December 1844, called for the novel to be delivered to the publisher in January 1846. Harring was to pay half of the costs for a run of 10,000 copies and share half of the profits. After the Harpers found the manuscript to be "irreligious," they refused to honor the agreement. Harring then sued to recover his claim of $8,000 in damages. In reply, the publishers said that the law "prohibited them from publishing any work that had a tendency to sap the religion and morals of the community." In his charge to the jury, the judge ruled that if the book was blasphemous, then Harper was free to break the contract. The "nearly divided" jury could not arrive at a decision and was discharged on 26 June (*New-York Daily Tribune*, 24–27 June 1846; *New York Herald*, 24–27 June 1846; *New York Evening Post*, 27 June 1846). Fuller used the situation to denounce censorship in "Publishers and Authors" (*New-York Daily Tribune*, 3 February 1846).

2. In 1846, Charles Scribner (1821–71) joined with Isaac Baker (d. 1850) to form the publishing firm of Baker and Scribner. Baker was a drygoods merchant before joining with Scribner. An 1840 Princeton graduate, Scribner studied law but turned instead to the book trade, specializing at first in theological titles (Derby, *Fifty Years among Authors*, pp. 441, 443; *DAB*).

619. To Evert A. Duyckinck

43 Middagh St
Thursday. [25 June 1846]

Dear Mr. Duyckinck,

I was summoned for some purpose or other in Harro Harring's case and detained there great part of yesterday to *little* purpose. Today they send for me again so that I cannot be sure of being at home and ready for your visit in good season. Still I think to be so by 5 p. m. but, if you can, would prefer your coming tomorrow.

Please thank Mr Mathews for the loan of Brownings *"Luria"* is new and I hope a pleasure from reading it.[1]

Truly yours

S. M. FULLER.

ALS (NN-M).
Dated by the reference to Harring's trial.

1. Browning's "Luria" and "A Soul's Tragedy," no. VIII of *Bells and Pomegranates*, was published in London by Edward Moxon on 13 April 1846. In Fuller's review of 10 July, she said that Browning shows "a mind which soars in the creative element, and can only be understood by those who are in a state of congenial activity."

620.   To Evert A. Duyckinck

June 28th [1846]

private

To Mr Duyckinck

I received a note yesterday from Mr Wiley, requesting that I would omit the article on Festus from the forthcoming volumes and "all other matter of a controversial character or likely to offend the religious public."[1]

Now you well know that I write nothing which might not offend the so-called religious public. I am too incapable of understanding their godless fears and unhappy scepticism to have much[n] idea of what would offend them. But there are probably sentences in every piece, perhaps on every page, which, when the books are once published, will lead to censure.

I consented to take counsel as to the selection of pieces with *you*, because you can understand. As there is a superabundance of matter, and whatever is not published now will be hereafter I was willing to take counsel as to the selection from the pieces. But I hope it is clearly understood that in those I *do* publish, I shall not alter a line or a word, on such accounts[n] They will stand precisely as they were originally written and if you think Mr Wiley will not be content to[n] take the consequences you had better stop the transaction now.

Also in the department of Foreign literature I must be guided by my own judgment. The articles on Goethe and others, probably[n] contain things far more likely to offend than those in the piece on Festus, but I will not omit them, if I publish at all, for they are some of my best pieces, and I do not wish the volumes to be made up of indifferent matter.

I could[n] not, if I would, act in this temporizing manner; it is too foreign to my nature. But I do not believe in it as a matter of policy. The attractive force of my mind consists in its energy, clearness and I dare to say it, its catholic liberality and fearless honor. Where I make an impression it must be by being most myself. I ought always to ignore vulgar prejudices, and I feel within myself a power which will sustain me in so doing and draw to me sufficient and always growing sympathy.

I do not believe it is *wise* to omit the piece on Festus or that on Shelley. Those who care for what I write at all, will care most for such pieces. It seems unhandsome towards Mr Bailey, who is now the first of the younger[n] living English poets, to omit him and name others. There is only one consideration that makes me willing in that case, which is that, on looking the piece[n] over, I find the extracts make it too long and could not well be omitted. I consent then in the case of those two pieces.— I would also like to have you if you think it desirable[n] hold counsel with Mr Wiley, as to the articles on Swedenborgianism and the Wesleys. There is nothing in them controversial as, of course, there could not be in any thing I write, viewing all sects, as I do merely as expressions of human opinion and character. But they are on matters theological, though not viewed from a theological point. I wish to publish them because they have some merit, but I do not care particularly about it. Only make[n] Mr Wiley understand that where I *do* care I shall insist, and that I give him no vouchers that there shall be nothing to offend his religious public in the book. I shall publish the articles just as they stand, without any attention to such considerations or not at all. If he is not content with that, we had better stop now. If we do, however, I shall publish an account of this transaction for I wish in every way to expose the restrictions upon mental freedom which threaten to check[n] the progress of genius or of a religious sentiment worthy of God and man in this country.

I have read the play with great pleasure. The view of character and statements of magnetic influence from soul to soul is truly noble. The accounts by the girl of her love are fine poetry, so are those of the sympathizing aspects of nature with[n] those dark mental seasons. There is *no metre*, rhythm[n] though the poem assumes to be written in it. Tell the author's name; is it yours? I shall prize it.

I have recd only two proofs, as yet. I shall expect a note from you tomorrow night.

If we go on, (and I suppose we shall, only I want it to be on a firm and honorable basis) I can supply all the rest of the Engh lite[rature] part on Tuesday. Farewell, my good friend, for I feel as if you were such to me, though we have not seen much of one another yet. But I know your soul is truly liberal and fair.

S. M. F.

ALS (NN-M).
have much] have ⟨any⟩ ↑ much ↓
word, on such accounts] word, ↑ on such accounts ↓
not be content to] not ↑ be content to ↓
others, probably] others, ⟨in fact,⟩ ↑ probably ↓
I could] I ⟨would⟩ could
of the younger] of ↑ the younger ↓
looking the piece] looking ⟨it⟩ ↑ the piece ↓
you if you think it desirable] you ↑ if you think it desirable ↓
Only make] ⟨And⟩ Only make
to check] to ⟨oppose⟩ ↑ check ↓
nature with] nature ⟨in⟩ with
metre, rhythm] *metre*, ↑ rhythm ↓

1. John Wiley (1808–91) was the co-owner of Wiley and Putnam, publishers. His father, Charles Wiley, established the firm in 1803 and had been Cooper's first publisher (*New York Genealogical and Biographical Record* 22 [1891]: 110; Derby, *Fifty Years among Authors*, p. 292).

621. To Richard F. Fuller

N. Y.
4th July 1846.

My dear Richard,

I have been much sick since you were here; it rains all the time and this continuous damp hurts me. Beside I seem to have recd a chill that dreadfully cold day we went to Albany.

This has made me forget that I ought to write to you about the money you were to get for me of Uncle A &c. Mr Spring will take it and leave it with his own where it will be bringing in 7 per cent till[n] wanted. He will leave it and draw the sums as wanted—[n] I am afraid that, owing to my carelessness he may call on you before the receipt of this letter from me, requesting you to give it to him. The money you wish to pay me and that for the daguerrotype, you can keep separate till you see me. Send me a note what the exact sum is that you deliver over to him.[1] Mr. Plumbe has sent to ask me, if I would let him take a daguerrotype of me for his galley and I shall try for those for you and Eugene at the same time.[2]

I see that Ellery has returned, hope this will not interfere with my seeing Ellen and Greta before I go.[3] I I am not sorry[n] on the whole Mother resolves against coming here. I think she would not enjoy it and that I should have but little time to see her. But I hop[e] she will not go to Canton without hearing from me first. There is some doubt, now, whether we sail from here or Boston on 1st August. If from here I may[n] come home to pass Saturday 18th and the following Sunday instead of being there at the very end of the month. So, if she intends to stay some time, I hope she will not *go* till she hears from me again. I *may not* come till the last Sunday in the month.

From the force of habit in writing for the press, I passed over this page.

I am very glad to think you have been here, took sincere pleasure in your visit and feel as if we should understand one another much better for it. If all did not happen just right and especially I mourned that the weather on the river was unfavorable, yet *some things* happened right and the weather was better than it has been since. Today it pours to the disappointment of every body, and especially of the poor children, for great preparations had been made in their behalf and they are robbed of a promised Eden. There was to be a Floral Fete on Randall's Island to which Adeley and her Aunt were going with me and where we were to have met the Sedgwicks.[4] I have not seen them since you were here and now cannot today on acct of the weather The children were much pleased with your messages and with the poem which Mrs M. read to them. She herself shed many tears over it.[5] and has copied it to keep.[n]

I shall write again soon to say when I shall be at home Ever affecy yr sister

M.

I hope you will call on the Springs while in and near Boston and get acquainted with them. They are there today and mean, I believe to remain through next week.

ALS (MH: fMS Am 1086 [9:132]); MsCfr (MH: fMS Am 1086 [Works, 1:131–35]). *Addressed:* To / Richard F. Fuller / 6 State St / Boston / Mass / care Henry H. Fuller. *Postmark:* Brooklyn N. Y. July 4.

cent till] cent ⟨if⟩ ↑ till ↓
He will leave it and draw the sums as wanted—] ↑ He will leave it and draw the sums as wanted— ↓
not sorry] not sor⟨y⟩ry
I may] I ⟨shall⟩ ↑ may ↓
and has copied it to keep.] ↑ and has copied it to keep. ↓

1. In his reply of 9 July (MH), Richard reported that he transferred her assets of $404.53 in three notes and interest to Wells and Spring in New York.
2. John Plumbe (1809–57) was born in Wales, emigrated to the United States in

1821, and became a railroad man. Beginning in 1840, he developed the "Plumbeotype," a process that put daguerreotypes on paper (*DAB*). His photograph of Fuller is the frontispiece to vol. 1 of this edition.

3. Channing left for his European trip on 3 March, stayed sixteen days in Rome, and returned to Concord full of distaste for all things foreign (Hudspeth, *Ellery Channing*, p. 32).

4. Abby Adeline Manning.

5. In his letter of 28 June (MH), Richard enclosed a translation of an ode by Anacreon for the Manning children.

622. To John Wiley

> 43 Middagh St
> Brooklyn
> 7th July 46

Will Mr Wiley direct the Printers to make more haste?— At the rate proofs are sent, I cannot get more than half through before I leave
Respectfully

> S. M. FULLER.

ALS (OMC).

623. To Richard F. Fuller

> N. Y. 14th July, 1846.

My dear Richard,

It is finally settled that we go in the Cambria. I think I^n shall return home the 29th of^n this month, a fortnight from to morrow. If by the Long Island route, I shall be there that night, if by the boat not till next morng. I may possibly come^n the 28th, but do not much think I can get ready.

The 28th is, I believe, a fortnight from tomorrow, (Wednesday)^n You will not get this till the morng of Thursday (16th) Probably, then, you will defer going into the country till I am off the stage, as you would not have a fortnight to stay. I want very much you should meet me in Boston when I arrive, as I shall have much baggage. I should be glad, too, if you were in Boston during this interval, that I might communicate with you, if needful. Yet, if you need it, you must go, only letting me know previously to whom I can write.

About boarding, methinks it is unwise for you to go into town in summer. Your clients can wait till autumn, and while Mother has that house in the free air, it is a great pity to do so. Tell uncle it hurts[n] your health to make this change in the heat of the season and that you will come in in Octr I shd think this would be much wiser

Have you found my plates and had the cards engraved for me? It will save me a good deal of trouble as I cannot write cards neatly.

I send a novel, *Klosterheim*, wh Mother can keep.[1] *Monte Christo* I wish her to read before I come and not let it out of the house as I want to take it in the ship.[2] The package to President Everett, I want Arthur to deliver and leave his address that Mr E. may, if he pleases, send me some letters of recommendation. It is what I have asked for in the letter.

I want Mother to tell Mrs Farrar with my love, when I shall be at home and that I hope she will come and see me then. Shall not have time to write to her. I enclose a pretty and good letter from Eugene wh keep for me.

I want to have Lloyd come down and see me when at home, dont fail to let him know this I am continually unwell now. The sense of having a greal deal to do seems to hurt my head and unfit me for doing it. I have just been with Mr Godwin to his lovely place on Hempstead Harbor and bathed.[3] I feel better, but not well. Headach harasses and uses up my time. I could not get through at all, but that Mrs and Miss Manning are so kind. I sympathized entirely with you about the Commercial.[4] I hope you will always have these feelings. More when we meet Ever affecy

M.

ALS (MH: fMS Am 1086 [9:133]); MsC (MH: fMS Am 1086 [Works, 1:135–39]).
I think I] I ↑ think I ↓
29th of] 29th ⟨J⟩ of
possibly come] possibly ⟨return⟩ ↑ come ↓
tomorrow, (Wednesday)] tomorrow, (⟨Yes⟩ Wednesday)
it hurts] it ⟨?⟩ hurts

1. Thomas De Quincy, *Klosterheim; or, the Masque* (Edinburgh and London, 1832).

2. Alexandre Dumas's *Le Comte de Monte-Cristo* originally appeared serially in 1844–45 in newspapers. English translations were published in London and New York in 1846. In her review, Fuller said: "Dumas is a liberal and sumptuous nature, and his African blood is warm; but he has no depth, and his characters can have none" (*New-York Daily Tribune*, 21 July 1846).

3. Parke Godwin (1816–1904) was William Cullen Bryant's son-in-law. A Fourierite

and antislave reformer, Godwin had edited the *Harbinger*. He was a writer and editor for Bryant's *Evening Post* (*DAB*).

4. In his letter of 9 July (MH), Richard reported his move from the Commercial Hotel to the United States Hotel.

624. To James Nathan

New York,
14th July 1846.

My friend, I have been absent from town and unable to act upon your request of getting the papers to send by Messrs Appleton to Mr Delf.[1] I will 1st August take them myself, and send them on arriving in Liverpool[n] straight to Mr D. that he may send them to you. Tomorrow morng is the last time I shd have before the steamer goes and I probably shall not be able to go to town and see about it, having imperative engagements I have hardly a minute to write this line which is of importance for you to receive. I have talked with Mr Greeley about the narrative of[n] your journey. He says you had best make it brief and vivid and look into the many books of travel in that region that have been published lately, so as to repeat no information. That, if you have it written out fairly and send to him, he will do as well as he can in getting it published for you, but could not expect *much* pecuniary profit, as your name is not known as a writer.

I suggested Noah's Weekly Messenger, thinking the information would be of special interest to the Jews, but Mr G. said there would be no pay there.[2]

I think you may find Mr Delf could get it published in London to better advantage, as to money, than here, where the reward of the writer is so very little. But, if you prefer sending to America, I should think Mr G. could and would do as well for you, as almost any one, only no doubt, if I were here I might put more zeal into the affair than a mere business friend would. I am sorry on that acct, to be gone. Your[n] old acquaintance, Mr Miller, is in the employment of Wiley and Putnam, with his aid and that of Mr Delf and Mr Greeley, you certainly have a very fair chance for one who is served by *men alone*.

I am overwhelmed with things to be done in the last days. We go in the Cambria first August, and I to Boston for a few days previous to bid farewell to my family and friends After arriving in England we travel a while and shall not be in London till early in September[n] I will there expect to hear from you in some shape. I shall notify Mr Delf of my arrival.

Mrs Greeley I have seen only once since we left the Farm, as she is far in the country. She was much pleased with your letter and I was very glad

15th, Morng

Interrupted last night and only time to add a word. I was about to say that I was glad you wrote to Mrs G. and repeated your invitation to Germany. She cannot accept it, being soon to become a mother, but, no doubt, it would please her that it should be given.[3] Adieu, may happiness and good be with you.

Great part was written almost in the dark, but I hope will not be illegible. I do not like to write so, but know you needed to hear of the book.

I will hope to find a good letter if not yourself in London, early in Septr

AL (MB: Ms. Am. 1451 [71, 73, 73a]). Published in *Love-Letters*, pp. 184–86. *Addressed:* To / Mr James Nathan / Care of E Nathan M. D. / Hamburg / Germany / By Boston Steamer of 16th. *Postmark:* New York 15 Jul.

in Liverpool] in ⟨London⟩ ↑ Liverpool ↓
about the narrative of] about ↑ the narrative of ↓
gone. Your] gone⟨,⟩. ⟨but y⟩ Your
in September] in ⟨Septr⟩ ↑ September ↓

1. In his letter of 5 June (MH), Nathan had asked for copies of the *Tribune* that contained his travel essays.

2. Mordecai Manuel Noah (1785–1851) was a lawyer, journalist, and editor. In 1825 he founded a colony on Grand Island in the Niagara River as a haven for Jewish refugees. He edited *Noah's Times and Weekly Messenger* from 1843 until his death (*DAB*; Frederic Hudson, *Journalism in the United States, from 1690 to 1872* [New York, 1873], pp. 287–89).

3. Mary Inez Greeley was born on 1 November 1846 and died on 7 May 1847 (Greeley, *Genealogy of the Greely-Greeley Family*, p. 671; *New York Evening Post*, 7 May 1847).

625.   To Evert A. Duyckinck

Tuesday eveg
July 14th [1846]

Dear Mr Duyckinck,

Mr Wiley sends me word he wishes to restrict the narrow limits of the vols thirty pages more each. It was, before, impossible to adhere to the original arrangement, or make any thing like an adequate representation of what I have written and now I dont know how to arrange at all.

Could you come to see me tomorrow (Wednesday.)[n] for a short time, and I hope not to have occasion to trouble you again

S. M. FULLER

I shall be at home any time after one or before eleven.

ALS (NN-M). *Addressed:* To / Mr Duyckinck / 161 Broadway.
me tomorrow (Wednesday.)] me ⟨today⟩ ↑ tomorrow (Wednesday.) ↓

626. To Ralph Waldo Emerson

N. Y. 15th July
1846.

Dear Waldo,

I was very glad to get your note, for it began to seem as if you meant to let me go and make no sign. I leave Boston in the Cambria 1st August. Shall be at home at my mothers in Cambridge Port, the morning of the 30th July.[n] Can see you either that day or the next three, as I shall not go out. Please write to care of Richard 6 State St. Boston, which day you will come

I should like to take the letter to Carlyle, and wish you would name the Springs in it. Mr S. has been one of those much helped by Mr C. I should like to see Tennyson, but doubt whether Mr C. would take any trouble about it. I take a letter to Miss Barrett and am likely to see Browning through her.[1] It would do no harm to mention it, though.— I have done much to make[n] him known here.

Could you get me any other letters like to be of use. I write in killing haste but as ever yours

MARGARET.

ALS (MH: bMS Am 1280 [2378]). Published in part in Higginson, *MFO*, p. 220, and Rusk, *Letters of RWE*, 3:339. *Endorsed:* Margaret Fuller / July 1846.
30th July.] 30th ↑ July ↓ .
have done much to make] have ⟨made⟩ ↑ done much to make ↓

1. Emerson wrote a letter of introduction to Carlyle on 1 August (*Emerson—Carlyle Correspondence*, p. 408). She saw neither Tennyson nor Barrett, who was on her honeymoon with Robert Browning. Elizabeth Barrett's first response to Fuller was disdainful. On 4 January 1846 she wrote Browning that she had received "'Woman in the Nineteenth Century' from America from a Mrs. or a Miss Fuller—how I hate those 'Women of England,' 'Women & their Mission' & the rest. As if any possible good were to be done by such expositions of rights & wrongs." She was no more enthusiastic in the summer: "I have another new fear. . an American lady who in her time has reviewed both you & me, it seems, comes to see me. . is about to come to see me . . armed with a letter of introduction from Mr. Mathews—& in a week, I may expect her perhaps" (Elvan Kintner, ed., *The Letters of Robert Browning and Elizabeth Barrett Barrett, 1845–1846* [Cambridge, Mass., 1969], pp. 361, 961). Despite this beginning, the friendship between the Brownings and Fuller flourished in Italy.

627.   To Evert A. Duyckinck

43 Middagh St
20th July. [1846]

I return Mr Duyckinck's books with thanks. I retain only the works of Mr Mathews as I may have occasion to look into[n] them again for a moment and will send them to Wiley and Putnam's with the last proof. I should like to hear whether Mr Duyckinck receives the M. S. safely. Will he give the little parcel to Mr Mathews and oblige

S. M. FULLER.

ALS (NN-M). *Addressed:* To / Mr Duyckinck / 161 Broadway.
look into] look ⟨at⟩ ↑ into ↓

628.   To Caroline Sturgis

N. Y.
20th July 1846.

Dear Cary,

Do you still mean to come and see me before I leave N Y. I want either to see or hear from you, and should prefer the vision.

I go from here the 29th in aftn boat to Boston. From Boston 1st August Saty in the Cambria.

I go with a great pain in my heart, but that is nothing new, and nothing that I could hope to evade by staying.

I do not know where you are nor when you will get this letter. Perhaps it will come too late, or you will not come. If so, you must pass over to Rome this winter or else write to me. I do not yet know my address, but Richard or Mr Greeley will have it

Dear Cary, if it *is* farewell, (I hope not) know me more than ever yours in love

MARGARET

ALS (MH: bMS Am 1221 [250]). *Addressed:* To / Miss Caroline Sturgis / Care William Sturgis Esq / Boston / Mass. if Miss Sturgis / is absent, please / forward immedy. *Postmark:* Brooklyn NY July 21. *Endorsed:* July 1846.

629.   To Evert A. Duyckinck

Tuesday eveg
[21? July 1846]

Will Mr Duyckinck have the kindness to see whether the extract from Mr Mathews's poem "The Journalist," is correctly printed?[1] I had forgotten in sending home the book that this was still to come. I suppose the Appendix was found in the book. I desired it should be put there.

Mr Greeley is not willing to insert the letter on copyright.[2] It is long and the paper much crowded, beside he does not incline to publish what has appeared previously in[n] other journals. I am sorry, as the letter is good.

In my 2d number, the piece on Swedenborgianism follows that on Longfellow and that on the Wesleys concludes. You will find several mistakes marked[n] in them and I fear others that are not marked.

Your brother will hear from us in Rome at the *bureau* of Torlonia.[3]

In haste once more adieu,

S. M. FULLER.

Would you do me the favor to give this number of The Dial to Mr Simms and say that I am happy myself to find I have one to spare.[4] I take the liberty to trouble you in this hour of haste.

ALS (NN-M).

previously in] previously ⟨?⟩ in
mistakes marked] mistakes ⟨noted⟩ ↑ marked ↓

1. Cornelius Mathews's poem appeared in *Poems on Man, in His Various Aspects under the American Republic* (New York, 1843).

2. Fuller probably refers to Mathews's satiric letter, "John Smith, a Convicted Felon, upon the Copyright" (*Arcturus, a Journal of Books and Opinion* 3 [April 1842]: 369–70).

3. George Long Duyckinck (1823–63) graduated from New York University in 1843, studied law, and was admitted to the bar, but never practiced law. He was associated with his brother in several literary projects, including the *Literary World* and the *Cyclopaedia of American Literature* (New York, 1855) (*DAB*).

4. William Gilmore Simms (1806–70), a South Carolina novelist, had written to Fuller to ask for a back issue of the *Dial*: "My anxiety to complete my set of a work which I have learned to value, alone prompts me to intrude upon your attention, at a moment when I know your time is precious." He had written to James Munroe on 8 July in an attempt to find the issues (Mary C. Simms Oliphant, Alfred Taylor Odell, and T. C. Duncan Eaves, eds., *The Letters of William Gilmore Simms* [Columbia, S.C., 1953], 2:172–73). Fuller had given a very brief notice to Simms's *The Wigwam and the Cabin*: "These tales are told in a vigorous, graceful manner, and evince manly feelings with a happy eye for nature" (*New-York Tribune*, 11 October 1845). Simms was a friend of Evert Duyckinck.

630. To Samuel G. Ward

N. Y. 25th July
1846.

My dear friend,

I have been hoping to hear from you, and still am anxious to before I go away, as I have known nothing about you and Anna all summer and want the bulletin of health &c. You may not, as this is Saty, receive this note till Tuesday, in that case it would be too late to address me here, as I leave on the aftn of Wednesday 29th. Please write to me at Cambridge; to care of Mrs Farrar I shall be with my mother till Saty when we go.

I feared when prevented from coming to Lenox in May, that I should not at all. And, indeed, it has been impossible for me to go away I have lost so much time with headach this summer. I hope the voyage will do me good in that respect.

I thought, perhaps, you would give or get me some letters to people who could help me, but have not had time to write to you about it. I have a few good ones, among others one to Powers, though I shd have liked a line from Anna, too.[1]

As to money, I have nearly enough, and if an affair that I have left in the care of Mr Greeley turns out well, I shall not have to apply to any one else. If I did, it would be for a trifle, and not for some months. But I probably shall not need to at all.

If Caroline is in Lenox tell her I am [   ]

ALfr (MH: bMS Am 1465 [928]). *Endorsed:* 1846. / S.M. Fuller / July 25.

1. Hiram Powers (1805–73), the sculptor, moved to Italy in 1837. His *Greek Slave*, a nude female sculpture, was the first by an American to gain wide public notice. He and Fuller later became friends in Florence (*DAB*).

631. To Evert A. Duyckinck

Tuesday 28th, [July 1846]

To Mr Duyckinck,

I *should* like to have the account of Witchcraft at the end of the volume in smaller type and with a prefatory line, mentioning it as the work of a friend.

Would it not be possible to hurry them, so that I can see the last proof of my own writings[n] tomorrow at 2 p m. I go from here at 4. If this cannot be done, will you look at it. I have that from the M. S. I want a set of the sheets to take with me.

Mr Wiley mentioned your giving me a line to Mr Putnam, can you do so?[1]

In greatest haste a friendly farewell from

S. M. F.

ALS (NN-M). *Addressed:* To / Mr Duyckinck / 161 Broadway / please deliver this as soon / as possible.

own writings] own ⟨M.S.⟩ ↑ writings ↓

1. George Palmer Putnam (1814–72) moved from Boston to New York City in 1829. In 1833 he joined Wiley and Long, publishers, which became Wiley and Putnam in 1840. In 1841 he moved to England, where he opened a firm that sold American books. In 1847 Putnam was on the boat with Fuller from Marseilles to Genoa and later saw her often in Rome (*DAB*; George Haven Putnam, *George Palmer Putnam: A Memoir* [New York, 1912], pp. 15, 27, 88–89).

632.   To Richard F. Fuller

Tuesday 28th July [1846]

Dear Richard,

I shall be in Boston Thursday Morng, by *Norwich and Worcester rail-road*, comes in *very* early[n] and shall depend on finding you there at the Depot.

I have a great deal of baggage and need not carry all of[n] it out to Mothers, if there was any safe place in town where to deposit it.

Tired and harried to death. To bed at one, up at 5. No sleep or next to none between. Receive kindly your sister

M.

ALS (MH: fMS Am 1086 [9:134]); MsC (MH: fMS Am 1086 [Works, 1:139]). *Addressed:* To / R. F. Fuller / 6 State St. / Care Henry H. Fuller / Boston. *Postmark:* New York 28 July.

rail-road, comes in *very* early] *rail-road*, ↑ comes in *very* early ↓
carry all of] carry ↑ all of ↓

633.   To Margarett C. Fuller

Liverpool, 16 August 1846

My dear Mother: —

The last two days at sea passed well enough, as a number of agreeable persons were introduced to me, and there were several whom I knew before.[1] I enjoyed nothing on the sea; the excessively bracing air so affected me that I could not bear to look at it. The sight of land delighted me. The tall crags, with their breakers and circling sea-birds; then the green fields, how glad! We had a very fine day to come ashore, and made the shortest passage ever known. The stewardess said, "Any one who complained this time tempted the Almighty." I did not complain, but I could hardly have borne another day. I had no appetite; but am now making up for all deficiencies, and feel already a renovation beginning from the voyage; and, still more, from freedom and entire change of scene.

We came here Wednesday, at noon; next day we went to Manchester; the following day to Chester; returning here Saturday evening.

On Sunday we went to hear James Martineau; were introduced to him, and other leading persons.[2] The next day and evening I passed in the society of very pleasant people, who have made every exertion to give me the means of seeing and learning; but they have used up all my strength.

ELfr, from *Memoirs*, 2:171–72. Published in Van Doren, pp. 285–86.

1. Rebecca Spring remembered Lord and Lady Frankland of Halifax, Thomas Appleton of Boston, and Thomas Colley Grattan as fellow passengers (Spring, "Journal Abroad," p. 6).

2. James Martineau (1805–1900), Harriet's younger brother, was a Unitarian clergyman and theologian in Liverpool.

634.   To Alexander Ireland

Adelphi,
17th August, 1846.

Dear Sir,

I add to the books named last eveg, a sketch of travel in some of[n] our

Western States by myself, which you may never have seen. The books will reach me, if sent to the care of Thomas Delf, 16 Little Britain London; by the 20th September,

With much respect yours

S. M. FULLER.

PS.

I have marked in the index, with a pen three or four of Ellery Channing's poems that, I think, may please you. The pencil-marks are not mine.

S.M.F.

ALS (CU-B). *Addressed:* To / Mr Ireland.

Alexander Ireland (1810–94), a friend of Emerson and Carlyle, was publisher of the liberal *Manchester Examiner* (*DNB*).

in some of] in ↑ some of ↓

635.   To Thomas Delf

Edinburgh
1st Septr 1846

To Mr Delf.

Dear Sir,

I do not know whether you know that I am in the kingdom of Great Britain, or have time to be interested in the fact if you do know it. But as we have to assume much in this world I venture to assume this and write to you accordingly.

We expected to be in London by this time, but having been agreeably detained in the Lake region, and now so much so here that we do not like to[n] hasten away and are beside going what is called "The short tour" here in Scotland. I do not believe we shall get there till the middle, perhaps not till the last, of Septr We shall probably stay a fortnight and I hope you will be there at that time.

Is Mr Nathan now in London? He wrote to me that I[n] should find there either himself or a letter.[1] If he is there, perhaps he will come here as I am told he can in 24 hours by mail from London and go "The short tour" with us, thus giving me a good opportunity to see him. We shall be here (at[n] Mrs Cumming's, corner of Prince and Castle Sts) till next Monday.[n] If he cannot come, I hope he will not fail to wait for me in London. If he is not there and there is a letter to your care will you forward it to me here, Care Marcus Spring.

Will you write me a note giving your opinion as to where we had better go into lodgings. We want to take those that are comfortable and pleasant, though not extravagant in expense, and make ourselves at home, as we are here. Our friends have recommended Mrs Moore's Cheapside, Fitzroy Square, and a house in Cheapside. We do not know enough about London to judge[n] what place combines most advantages for us. Mrs Spring can only walk a few steps and we should like to be in the line of omnibuses. Perhaps we had better go to a hotel at first and choose lodgings from it; if so what hotel would you recommend?

Perhaps you may receive some books directed[n] to your care for me, before we come, if so, let them lie and I will send for them and pay, if anything is due when I come to London.[n] Pardon, dear Sir, the trouble I give. I would take as much for you and am much pleased at the thought of seeing you With regard

S. M. FULLER.

I believe there was some temporary misunderstanding about some books you sent me to N. Y. but before I recd your letter Mr McElrath assured me he had rectified it. I will explain it when we meet. I hope you will have some leisure hours to be with us when in London.

ALS (MSaE).
like to] like⟨ly⟩ to
that I] that ⟨he⟩ ↑ I ↓
here (at] here (⟨in⟩ at
next Monday.] next ⟨Saty or more probably⟩ Monday.
to judge] to ⟨know⟩ ↑ judge ↓
some books directed] some ↑ books directed ↓
London.] *At this point Fuller marked the letter with an x to direct attention to the postscript.*
1. So Nathan said to Fuller in his letter of 6 June 1846 (MH).

636. To Richard F. Fuller

Birmingham
27th Septr 1846.

Very dear Richard,

I am pausing here for a day or two on my way to London. After passing ten days very delightfully in Westmoreland and Cumberland, where, beside the enjoyment of that most beautiful scenery, I made several very agreeable[n] acquaintance and even friends, we went on to Edinburgh[1] There we passed a week on our way to the Highlands, and three days on return. We were fourteen days on[n] the Highland excursion, days of ever varying enjoyment. On the lofty Ben Lomond, I got lost, and passed the night out on a heathery Scotch mountain, alone, and only keeping my life, by exertions to ward off the effects of the cold and wet, to[n] which I should have feared my bodily strength and mental patience alike unequal, *if* I had not tried. I was rather ill for a few days[n] after it, and the Springs suffered much from anxiety and excitement, for they were up and had a crowd of shepherds out searching the mountain all the night, but, since I have got off without eventual injury, we are all glad of the experience for it was quite a deep one. You will find a sketch of the externals of the affair in the Tribune, but when I can have time, I shall try to write it in a form that will be more interesting to my intimates.[2]

On leaving Scotland, we passed by Melrose and Abbotsford to Newcastle There I descended into the coal mine, a somewhat rare feat for a lady. Thence to York and Sheffield and yesterday here, arriving about 2 this morn.

I find pleasure in every step of the way. There is every thing to see. My companions are most kind and we get on harmoniously. I find a surprizing number of persons who not only receive me warmly, but have a preconceived strong desire to know me. This is founded mostly on their knowledge of "Woman in the 19th &c" Among these a number of intellectual and cultivated men of whom I shall hereafter speak to you. I may add that from their habits of conversation so superior to those of Americans, I am able to come out a great deal more than I can at home, and they seem to be proportionately interested.

So much for self, such particulars[n] as I cannot write to others and know to be most interesting at home. This letter is necessarily a short one, as I write in the only hour of leisure I shall have before the steamer of 4th Octr I am very anxious to hear from you all again now and hope to find letters waiting in London. I want most to hear of dear Mother's arm, whether all is doing well; with her[n] Next to that of yourself. My feeling is rather a hope that you may not go to the [West?] yet am not sure but I am wrong about it. I am partly selfish, unwilling that you should go away. Of the two other alternatives, it does seem that, if you should must[n] be disappointed with Henry it *may* lead more to your happiness, as the country is so much more congenial to you than Boston. I do not, however, feel able, at this distance to have a decisive view, but leave all in confidence to destiny believing that *no way* will it turn out *ill* with one like you. Shall however be anxious to know the result.

Get *thin paper* when you write; letters are[n] paid for by weight and the next may have to follow me in my journies. My next will be to Mother. Love to Ellen Arthur and Lloyd. Heaven bless and keep yourself, dear Richard prays always your sister

M.

ALS (MH: fMS Am 1086 [9:136]); MsC (MH: fMS Am 1086 [Works, 1:141–45]). *Addressed:* To / Richard F. Fuller / Care H. H. Fuller / Boston / Mass. / U. S. A. by Liverpool / Steamer of 4th Octr.

several very agreeable] several ⟨delightful⟩ ↑ very agreeable ↓
days on] days ⟨i⟩ on
wet, to] wet, ⟨of⟩ ↑ to ↓
ill for a few days] ill ↑ for a few days ↓
self, such particulars] self, ↑ such particulars ↓
well; with her] well; ↑ with her ↓
should must] should ↑ must ↓
letters are] letters ⟨here⟩ are

1. According to Rebecca Spring, Matthew Arnold was one of the acquaintances (Spring, "Journal Abroad," p. 8).
2. She described the episode in the *Tribune* of 13 November.

637. To Richard F. Fuller

London 2d Octr [1846]

Dear Richard,

Arriving yesterday I was a good deal disappointed to find no letters here from any body. Pray write when you receive this. I shall be anxious to hear from you and also that Mother is well.

Will you have the kindness to look among my books for a copy of the First Part of Emerson's essays which I gave to Laura Hunt and which was returned to me at the time of her death and send it by some safe way to Mrs Manning. I promised it her and then forgot.

Will you also call on L. C. Bolles in Washington St. and ask if a remittance was made to Miss Martineau on her book "Life in the Sick Room."[1] He said it would go in the Steamer with us, but she had heard nothing of it when we last saw her. Will you tell me about this when you write.

We are pleasantly situated at Charing Cross, on Trafalgar Square, with two fine fountains playing opposite us, but are going into lodgings tonight or tomorrow in a little narrow street, as in this enormously expensive country people who are not very rich must be content, not merely with second but fourth or fifth best.

We have the promise however of plenteous consolation in picture galleries &c. Here I find my book and favorable notices of it in the London journals, one especially in the high-handed "Spectator" quite surprized me by its praise.[2]

Ever yours

M.

Address a[lw]ays to care Brown, Shipley and Co Yesterday was the anniversary of our Father's death I thought much of him. Thank Heaven we have still our dear Mother.

ALS (MH: fMS Am 1086 [9:250]); MsC (MH: fMS Am 1086 [Works, 1:145–47]).

1. Leonard Crocker Bowles (1796–1876), a Roxbury resident, had a bookstore at 111 Washington Street, Boston (*Boston Daily Advertiser*, 4 March 1876; Thomas M. Farquhar, *History of the Bowles Family* [Philadelphia, 1907], p. 199). Martineau published an account of her prolonged illness and subsequent mesmeric cure in *Life in the Sick-Room* (London, 1844). A Boston edition appeared the same year.

2. The *Spectator* for 26 September 1846 said of *Papers on Literature and Art*: "We have seen enough to assure us that Margaret Fuller is worthy to hold her place among the highest order of female writers of our day. . . . The present volumes present to us the thoughts of a full and discerning mind, delicately susceptible of all impressions of beauty; earnest, generous, and serene; expressing itself in language of varied compass, for the most part singularly graceful and appropriate" (pp. 930–31). The *Spectator* was established in 1828 by Robert Stephen Rintoul (1787–1858), who edited it until his death. Known for its "magisterial seriousness," the journal under Rintoul "was always a serious paper, inclined to regard writing as a useless, if pretty, accomplishment, unless devoted to the service of some moral or useful end." Not surprisingly, it praised Harriet Martineau and was severe with Dickens and Tennyson (*DNB*; William B. Thomas, *The Story of the Spectator, 1828–1928* [London, 1928], pp. 216–17, 220; Walter Graham, *English Literary Periodicals* [New York, 1930], p. 323).

638. To Thomas Delf

[2? October 1846]

To Mr Delf,

We have arrived at last, dear Sir, and are at Morley's as you advised. I should like to see you, so soon as you can make it convenient, but fear this is just the busy time with you, as the Steamer goes on Sunday. Until we do meet very truly yours

S. M. FULLER.

ALS (MSaE).

Dated from the assumption that Fuller wrote Delf immediately after her arrival in London on 1 October.

639.　To Alexander Ireland

London,
6th Octr 1846.

Dear Mr Ireland,

I found your note here several days since, and have been vainly try-ing to get a moment to answer it ever since. I am afraid now you may have sent the books before you were ready. If you have them still, pray keep them till the 20th of *this* month. We may not leave London till Novr. I wish you might come hither in the mean time. I am much pleased to hear your feeling of Margaret.[1] As you say, there are *such* beings in real life," yet I fancy the picture, like that of an antique Ve-nus, was painted from study of several models. The writer Sylvester Judd, (a name as truly American in its style, as that of one of his own in-vention *Beulah Ann Orff*) is a man approaching middle age who has heretofore only made himself remarked by one or two strokes of char-acter, of a kind noble and original. I have never seen him; but some years ago recd from him this message "that he wished me to know" I had one admirer in the State of Maine" a distinction of which I am not a little proud, now that I have read his book. He is a clergyman, but, it seems, has not for that forgot to be a Man. Time allows me now to say no more except that I am ever dear Sir in friendly heart and faith yours

S. M. FULLER.

Should you see Dr and Mrs Hodgson and Mrs Ames remember us to them with grateful regard.[2] I should be much interested at any time to know what any or all of you are doing for the good of others and your own, what feeling, what hoping. To the new fraternity I think we belong whose glory is service, whose motto *Excelsior*.

ALS (NjP); MsC (NNC). Published in part in Moncure Daniel Conway, *Autobiography Memories and Experiences* (Boston, 1904), 1:179.

such beings in real life,] *such,* ↑ beings in real life ↓
"that he wished me to know] "that ↑ he wished me to know ↓

1. Sylvester Judd (1813–53) published *Margaret: A Tale of the Real and Ideal*, the first of his novels, in 1845. The Unitarian minister at Augusta, Maine, Judd was a graduate of Yale and of the divinity school at Cambridge. He was a pacifist, temperance reformer, and antislavery advocate (*DAB*). When Fuller reviewed *Margaret* in the *Tribune*, 1 September 1845, she praised it for its "deep meanings, beautiful pictures, and real wit," and asked the author to "acquaint us with his name." Apparently Judd obliged.

2. William Ballantyne Hodgson (1815–80) was the principal of the Liverpool Institute. An educator, reformer, and political economist, he worked for the education of women. In her first letter from Europe, Fuller reported that Hodgson quoted from the *Dial* in an address to the Institute. In 1841 he married Jane Cox (d. 1860), a writer for the *People's Journal* (*DNB*; *New-York Daily Tribune*, 24 September 1846). Mrs. Ames is unidentified.

640.   To Mary Howitt

17 Warwick St
Octr 8th. [1846]

Dear Mrs Howitt,

As Mr and Mrs Spring are just going out for the day they wish me to write to you in their name as well as my own. If it is most convenient to you to call on us, we can be at home on Monday of next week from twelve till four p.m. The days up to that time are engaged. But we do not wish that you should call merely as a matter of etiquette we are aware that your time, as well as[n] that of Mr Howitt, is much occupied; our wish is to *see you*, and if you prefer and will appoint a time, we will come to you rather than you to us, for we, as strangers and sight-seers, are naturally on the move all the time.[1] So please arrange it, as best suits yourself, and so that we may see yourself and Mr Howitt when you are most at leisure, and believe us, dear Madam, yours with true respect, though I can only set to it the hand of

S. M. FULLER.

p.s. We shall remain here two weeks, if not longer.

ALS (PSt).
Mary Botham (1799–1888) married William Howitt (1792–1879) in 1821. Both of the Howitts were reformers and prolific writers. Mary Howitt published poetry, children's stories, translations of Hans Christian Andersen, and several biographies. William wrote travel books, works on spiritualism, and poetry (*DNB*).

time, as well as] time, ⟨and⟩ ↑ as well as ↓

1. Of her visits to the Howitts, Fuller said: "I saw them several times at their cheerful and elegant home. In Mary Howitt I found the same engaging traits of character we are led to expect from her books for children. Her husband is full of the same agreeable information communicated in the same lively yet precise manner we find in his books" (*New-York Daily Tribune*, 2 February 1847).

Mary Botham Howitt, by Margaret Gillies. By permission of The Huntington Library, San Marino, California.

641. To George Palmer Putnam

17 Warwick St
29th Octr [1846]

Dear Sir,

I shall with much pleasure come to Knickerbocker Cottage on Friday. With regards to Mrs Putnam yours truly[1]

S. M. FULLER.

ALS (Ia-HA).
1. In 1841 George Palmer Putnam married Victorine Haven (*DAB*).

642. To Evert A. Duyckinck

London
30th Octr 1846.

Dear Mr Duyckinck,

The letter which I intended to write you dwindles into a note, for many as were my interruptions in N.Y. they scarcely enabled me to form a notion of those inevitable to a London life. The only[n] way of escape is *to hide*; — this is what I tried to do today in order to writing some notes by Mr Welford, yet here it is three o clock before I can put pen to paper.[1]

Yet I like London, like England *very* much and have already formed so many interesting connections that I do not feel that I could be content to return to the U. S. without passing some time here again. Indeed I may come and pass some time here for the purpose of writing. Several fine openings have been made for me where I might have taken up important subjects and published my view in excellent places, but I cannot now possibly get time to write without sacrificing many valuable opportunities of learning. A year hence will not be too late.

I have been recd here with a warmth that surprized me; it is chiefly[n] to Women in the 19th &c that I am indebted for this; that little volume has been read and prized by many. It is a real misfortune to me that Mr Wiley took the course he did about my miscellanies; the vols have been kindly recd but every one mentions their being *thin*; the arrangement, too, that obliged me to leave out all I had written on Continental lite[rature] was very unfortunate for me. I have reason to feel daily how

234

much use it would have been to me if these essays and others of a radical stamp were now before the readers and that a false impression has been given here of the range and scope of my efforts. However it is of some use to have those that are printed with me now, though I have constantly to regret[n] the absence of some I intended to insert as now is just the time for them to make their mark here. I have seen some persons of celebrity and others that will attain it ere long. I wish I had time to write of this, but, as it is, must refer to the Tribune for such slight and public sketches as there is now time[n] to make. Mr Mathews made me promise to write to him of those to whom he gave me[n] letters, but I have seen none of them except Mr Horne and him only once, as he has been almost all the time in Ireland.[2] Miss Barrett has just *eloped* with Browning; she had to elope, Mr Horne says, from a severe hard father.[3] The influence of this father seems to have been crushing. I hope she may now be happy and well; perhaps I shall see them (i e her and Browning) in Italy. Mr Tupper I missed through an unlucky misunderstanding as to the time of his visit.[4] The others are, probably, out of town.

If you see Mr Godwin, please tell him that Hugh Doherty is here and that I see much of him and Dr Wilkinson of Swedenborgian celebrity and like them exceedingly.[5] In connection with the Howitts I see very pleasant persons and they, themselves, are very pleasant.

Now I must stop for lack of time, though much there is to say. Will you write to me at Paris. I shall be there in a week, your brother, if there, can hear of me at Galignani's.[6] I shall leave my address there, and shall stay a month or more. In Rome Torlonia is our banker. Will you be so kind as to send three sets of the "Papers on Literature and Art" to *Richard F. Fuller, 6 State St. Boston.* I will write him what to do with them. Please give my best regards to Mr Mathews. I should like much to hear from him, too, if he has time Letters are a true favor to me, now when *I* have no time to earn them.

Very truly yours

MARGARET FULLER.

Pray tell me a great deal if you write or rather let me say *when* you write

There are some copies of "Summer on the Lakes" still at Graham's Tribune Building could you not induce Mr Wiley to send some of them here on sale with my other book. I have given away two or three here and people seem interested in the book.

Tell me if there is anything special about which I might inquire for you or do any thing for you in *my* way.

Tell me if Mr Murdock is succeeding.[7] I see something of a young actress here who would be worth catching for America, if there were any Goethe to train her. She has great natural resources.

ALS (NN-M). Published in *Bulletin of the New York Public Library* 5 (December 1901): 455–56. *Addressed:* To / Evert A. Duyckinck Esq / New York. / U. S. A. Kindness of / Mr Welford.[n]

The only] The⟨y⟩ only
is chiefly] is ↑chiefly↓
now, though I have constantly to regret] now, ⟨but⟩ ↑though↓ I ↑have↓ constantly ⟨regretted⟩ ↑to regret↓
now time] now ⟨room⟩ ↑time↓
gave me] gave m⟨y⟩e

On the wrapper that bound the letter, Fuller wrote: I shall always receive letters, if sent to care of Brown Shipley and Co Liverpool.

1. Charles Welford (1815?–85) was an English book importer for the firm of Bartlett and Welford. In 1857 he joined with Charles Scribner to form Scribner and Welford, book importers (*New York Times*, 20 May 1885).

2. Richard Henry Horne (1803–84), a playwright and poet, had an erratic career: once a sailor in the Mexican navy, he began to write in 1828, carried on a correspondence with Elizabeth Barrett, and in 1852 emigrated to Australia. He was remembered as "a marvellous whistler" (*DNB*). Fuller reviewed his *A New Spirit of the Age* in the *Tribune*, 10 June 1846.

3. Elizabeth Barrett secretly married Robert Browning on 12 September 1846 and left for Italy on 19 September (Gardner B. Taplin, *The Life of Elizabeth Barrett Browning* [London, 1957], p. 178). Her father, Edward Barrett Moulton-Barrett (1785–1857), is one of the best-known parental tyrants in British literary history. "Papa," said Elizabeth, "will not bear some subjects, it is a thing *known*; his peculiarity takes that ground to the largest. Not one of his children will ever marry without a breach, which we all know, though he probably does not—deceiving himself in a setting up of *obstacles*, whereas the real obstacle is in his own mind" (Jeanette Marks, *The Family of the Barrett* [New York, 1938], p. 536; Frederic G. Kenyon, ed., *The Letters of Elizabeth Barrett Browning* [New York, 1897], 1:292). In 1851 she reported that her father sent back "all the letters I had written" with the seals unbroken (Kenyon, ed., *Letters*, 2:20). Fuller reviewed Barrett's *Drama of Exile and Other Poems* in the *Tribune*, 4 January 1845, and reprinted the essay in *Papers on Literature and Art*. A critic, said Fuller, could "rank her, in vigor and nobleness of conception, depth of spiritual experience, and command of classic allusions, above any female writer the world has yet known."

4. Martin Farquhar Tupper (1810–89) published the first volume of his very popular *Proverbial Philosophy* in 1838. Fuller reviewed his *Crock of Gold*, saying only that "this book, like others from the same hand is chiefly remarkable for the purity of moral feeling it evinces." He had become a correspondent of Mathews and Duyckinck (*DNB*; Derek Hudson, *Martin Tupper: His Rise and Fall* [London, 1945], p. 67; *New-York Daily Tribune*, 15 August 1845).

5. Hugh Doherty was a British writer and editor of the *London Phalanx*, a paper devoted to the socialism of Charles Fourier (*Dial* 3 [1842]: 239). A personal friend of Fourier, Doherty published some of the socialist's papers posthumously. James John Garth Wilkinson (1812–99) was a homoeopathic physician and a disciple of Swedenborg. He was a close friend of both Henry James, Sr. (who named a son after him), and Emerson. Emerson said that Wilkinson's writings on Swedenborg "throw all the contemporary philosophy of England into shade, and leave me nothing to say on their proper grounds" (*DNB*; *The Complete Works of Ralph Waldo Emerson*, ed. Edward Waldo Emerson [Boston, 1903–4], 4:111).

6. Giovanni Antonio Galignani (1752–1821) established a publishing firm in Paris, where he published *Galignani's Messenger*. In 1846 the firm was in the hands of his sons, John Anthony and William.

7. James Edward Murdoch (1811–93) was an actor and teacher. From 1845 to 1860 he was nationally known in both tragic and comic roles (*DAB*). He staged the New York production of Mathews's *Witchcraft*.

643. To Ralph Waldo Emerson

London
30th Octr 46.

My dear friend,

This note will be presented to you by Harro Harring of whom I have often spoken to you.[1] He can tell you of his Scandinavian *runes* in honor of toiling Gods and Heroes, while you on your side may breathe on him a calmness from your great doctrine of Compensation

Ever yours

S. M. FULLER.

ALS (MH: bMS Am 1280 [2379]). Published in Rusk, *Letters of RWE*, 3:381. *Addressed:* To / R. W. Emerson / Concord / Mass / U. S. A. *Endorsed:* Margaret Fuller / 1847.

1. Emerson received the letter and a copy of Harring's book from Eliza Cabot Follen in early March 1847. Though never enthusiastic about novels, Emerson took an interest in *Dolores*: "thought it much better than many novels I have seen, as it had certain real objects, which appeared, & interested me—mainly, the association of the friends of freedom in all countries,—& his theories of love & marriage" (Rusk, *Letters of RWE*, 3:381–82).

644. To Richard F. Fuller

London 3d Novr
1846.

My dear Richard

The accompanying letters you can put into the Post, except those to Mother, Arthur and Mrs F. I wish there was time to write one to you, but no! It is possible I shall find some in Paris, where I go next week to stay a month and then to Italy. Meantime I know it suffices you to feel sure^n that all is going well with me. My reception in England has been both pleasing and promising and all I need is *time* to make use of the advantages it opens.

Write to me of you and whether the Henry affair approaches a happy decision. I was very glad to hear of the "turn up bed in the office"; it is terrible to run into debt upon uncertainties.[1] I hope the Sundays still bring the good refreshment Mine have been so happy one at Hampton [Co]urt I shall tell you of sometime, at least of the outward beauty.

But when you write take *thin paper*. I have already had to pay near a dollar for your letters in consequence of your neglecting this.

I have written to N.Y. for Mr Wiley to send you three copies of my miscellanies One is for you, one for Arthur, one to [be] sent to Eugene.

I wish you wd let Mr Emerson know that I shall write to him as soon as I can get peace to tell all that has accumulated for him in a long full letter. The mail bag gapes for th[is and on]ly leaves me time for yrs ever

M.

Love to Ellen and Lloyd always

ALS (MH: fMS Am 1086 [9:137]); MsC (MH: fMS Am 1086 [Works, 1:147–49]). *Addressed:* To / Richard F. Fuller / Boston.

to feel sure] to ⟨know⟩ ↑ feel sure ↓

1. Richard was at this time working in the law office of his uncle Henry Holton Fuller. He described his economy in a letter to her of 27 September (MH): "I have now got a turn-up bedstead so as to room in the office, which will greatly retrench my expenses: & I shall attend the best music this winter."

645.   To Martin Farquhar Tupper

London
4th^n Novr 46

Dear Sir,

An unlucky fate has indeed presided over our acquaintance thus far, but I hope to defy it yet. You are very kind to pardon my carelessness, which, since I have found your note again, (not that it was lost, but only put aside for the autograph) seems to me almost *un*pardonable, you yourself had been so exact in the terms of the appointment. But I had no plan originally, of staying here more than a few days, so, reading in haste, I forgot you did not know my designs, and took the Wednesday following the receipt of the note, as the one appointed. Altogether it will come out that I am not so attentive always in these minor morals as I ought to be, but you will try, will you not? to have faith till we meet that I may have good qualities to atone for this. I hope now to return to England a year from this time,[n] and shall then surely let you know of my coming and read with the utmost care any documents with which you may favor me in return. We go to Paris early next week. Till we do meet and always believe me, dear Sir, With high respect yours

S. M. FULLER.

ALS (IU). Published in Derek Hudson, *Martin Tupper* (London, 1949), p. 68.
4th] (?) 4th
this time,] this ↑ time ↓ ,

646.   To John S. Dwight

London
10th Novr, 46.

Dear Mr Dwight,

   The bearer of this, Mr Delf, a citizen at once of England and America and a valued friend of mine, will tell you how you may do a great deal of good in your own best way. I know you will wish to if you can independent of request of mine, still any efforts in this cause would much oblige yours

S. M. FULLER.

ALS (MHi). *Addressed:* To / J. S. Dwight / West Roxbury / Mass.

647.   To Caroline Sturgis

[16? November 1846]

[   ] I find how true for me was the lure that always drew me towards Europe. It was no false instinct that said I might here find an atmosphere needed to develope me in ways *I* need. Had I only come ten years earlier; now my life must ever be a failure, so much strength has

239

been wasted on obstructions which only came because I was not in the soil most fitted to my nature, however, though a failure, it is less so than with most others and the matter not worth thinking about. Heaven has room enough and good chances enough in store, no doubt, and I can live a great deal in the years that remain.

As soon as I got to England, I found how right we were in supposing there was elsewhere a greater range of interesting character among the men, than with us. I do not find, indeed, any so valuable as three or four among the most marked we have known, no Waldo, none so beautiful as William when he is *the angel*, more like Charles on the Egyptian side, none so beauty-ful as S. was when he *was Raphael*, but so many that are strongly individual and have a fund of hidden life.[1]

In Westmoreland I knew and have since been seeing in London, a man such as would interest you a good deal; his name is Atkinson, some call him the "Prince of the English Mesmerizers" and he has the fine instinctive nature you may suppose from that.[2]

He is a man about thirty, in the fulness of his powers, body and mind. He is tall and firmly formed, his head of the Christ-like sort as seen by Leonardo, mild and composed, but powerful and sagacious. He does not think, but perceives and acts. He is intimate with the artists, having studied architecture himself as a profession, but has some fortune on which he lives, sometimes stationary and acting in the affairs of other men, sometimes wandering about the world and learning. He seems bound by no tie, yet looks as if he had children in every place.

I saw also a man, an artist, severe and antique in his spirit; he seemed burdened by the sorrows of aspiration, yet very calm, as secure in the justice of Fate. What he does is bad, but full of a great desire. His name is Scott.[3] I saw also another, a pupil of Dela Roche, very handsome, and full of a voluptuous enjoyment of Nature; him I liked a little in a different way.[4]

By far the most beauteous person I have seen is Joseph Mazzini.[5] If you ever see "Sanders People's Journal," you can read articles by him that will give you some notion of his mind, especially one on his friends the two Bandieras and Rufini, headed "Italian Martyrs.—[6] He is one in whom holiness has purified, but nowhere dwarfed the man. I shall make a little sketch of him in a public way for the Tribune. I do not like to say more of him here now. I can do it better when I have seen him more, which I shall do in the course of time.

I saw some girls in London that interested me. Anna Howitt,[n] daughter of W. and Mary Howitt about 22 has chosen the profession of an artist; she has an honorable ambition, talent, and is what is called a sweet pretty girl.[7] Margaret Gillies is older; she has given up many things highly valued by English women to devote herself to Art, and attained quite a high place in the profession; her pictures are full of grace, rather sentimental, but that she is trying to shake off.[8] For the rest she is an excellent, honest girl. But the one whom I like *very* much is Eliza Fox, only[n] daughter of the celebrated W. J.[9] She is about five and twenty; she also is an artist and has begun a noble independent[n] life. she seems very strong and simple, yet[n] delicate in the whole tissue of her. I could not find time to talk with her as I wanted but whenever I did she grew upon me. Whenever I did I thought of you and Jane and lamented that you did not embark on the wide stream of the world as artists, then all that has been so beautiful in your lives would have been embodied for others, too, who needed it so much. Eliza has a friend, also an English woman, now living at Rome of whom she spoke with such cordial esteem that I shall look for her when there.[n] they both[n] have had a great deal to contend with. They say men *will not* teach girls drawing with any care, and beside they find it so difficult to get chances to draw from living[n] models.

I saw another fine girl; she was not an artist, but has a great deal of life, and she is so tall, strong and beautiful, like the nymphs. But there is not room to tell you about *her* or much about any thing.

The three months in England were months of the most crowded life, especially the six weeks in London. I came here, resolved to rest, for I am almost sick. A strange place to rest, some would think, but till my letters are presented no one knows me, and I shall not send them for some days. We are *getting dressed* (I do not wonder as I look around me here at the devotion of a French woman to her *mise* it is truly *deliceuse* as they call it with that absurd twinkle of their pretty eyes.) Rachel is acting.[10] I have a letter to her and one to George Sand, but I do not want to see them, till I get to speaking French a little.[11] Today we have come to our private lodging a very cheerful elegant apartment in the Hotel Rougement, where I shall speak French[n] all the time, beside taking a master, and I hope to improve a good deal in a few days. Goodnight, as this must wait till next Steamer I shall add to it just before sending.

ALfr, collection of G. W. Haight. Published in part in *Memoirs*, 2:172–73, and Van Doren, pp. 286–89.

Anna Howitt,] Anna Howit⟨h⟩t
Fox, only] Fox, ↑ only ↓
noble independent] noble in⟨?⟩dependent
simple, yet] simple, ↑ yet ↓
look for her when there.] look ↑ for ↓ her ⟨up⟩ ↑ when there ↓ .
they both] ⟨s⟩they both
from living] from ↑ living ↓
speak French] speak ↑ French ↓

1. Emerson, William Henry Channing, Charles Newcomb, and Sam Ward.

2. Henry George Atkinson (1812–84), a phrenologist and mesmerist, was long an associate of Harriet Martineau. She wrote more than a thousand letters to him and willed him her head for research (Haight, *George Eliot Letters*, 9:372; Robert K. Webb, *Harriet Martineau: A Radical Victorian* [London, 1960], pp. 19–20).

3. David Scott (1806–49) was born in Edinburgh. Although accomplished, Scott was never popular, as Emerson noted after his visit in 1848: "He is a grave colossal painter, surrounded with huge pictures, in his hall of a studio, in a Michel Angelo style of size & of anatomical science. This man is a noble stoic sitting apart here among his rainbow allegories, very much respected by all superior persons, but far from popular as a painter" (*DNB*; Rusk, *Letters of RWE*, 4:20).

4. Hippolyte Paul Delaroche (1797–1856), a French painter, founded the Eclectic school. His favorite English pupil, the one Fuller probably met, was Edward Armitage (1817–96), who was later known as a fresco painter, butterfly collector, and yachtsman (*DNB*).

5. Giuseppe Mazzini (1805–72), the Italian revolutionary patriot, was exiled first to France and then to England. Fuller committed herself to his cause in her dispatches to the *Tribune* and then joined his revolution in Rome in 1848. In her report to the *Tribune*, Fuller said: "He is one of those same beings who, measuring all things by the ideal standard, have yet no time to mourn over failure or imperfection; there is too much to be done to obviate it" (*New-York Daily Tribune*, 19 February 1847).

6. John Saunders (1810–95), a novelist and dramatist, founded the *People's Journal* in 1846 and continued it for two years. He published Mazzini's essays as well as those of the Howitts, William J. Fox, and Harriet Martineau (*DNB*). In his introductory essay, Saunders said that he proposed to "make the *People's Journal* a zealous, and,—if it may be,— an efficient helpmate to the Working Man, by affording him full and timely information of what Philanthropists and Philanthropical Societies, of his own and every other class, have done, or are doing on his behalf" (*People's Journal* 1 [1846]: 1). "The Martyrs for Italian Liberty" was a two-part essay that Mazzini wrote for vol. 1 ("Attilio and Emilio Bandiera," pp. 121–23, and "Jacopo Ruffini [1833]," pp. 293–94).

7. Anna Mary Howitt (1824–84) was a writer, artist, and spiritualist. In 1859 she married Alaric Alfred Watts (Amice Lee, *Laurels and Rosemary: The Life of William and Mary Howitt* [London, 1955], pp. 74, 218; *DNB*).

8. Margaret Gillies (1803–87), daughter of a Scottish merchant, worked in water colors. She did portraits of Wordsworth and Dickens (*DNB*).

9. William Johnson Fox (1786–1864), a liberal Unitarian reformer and editor of the *Monthly Repository*. Prominent as an orator for the Anti-Corn Law League, Fox was a member of Parliament on several occasions (*DNB*).

10. Rachel (1820–58), born Élisa Félix, excelled in such tragic roles as Camille, Phèdre, and Lucrèce. The most celebrated actress of her time, she restored the Comédie-Française to prominence (*OCFL*). G. H. Lewes called her "a born empress." "Her grace," he said, "her *distinction*, her simple dignity, the ineffable majesty of her attitudes and gestures, crowned as they are by that small but singularly intellectual head, make her the most queenly woman now to be seen anywhere. *Where* has she learnt her dignity? It was given her by God!" (*Dramatic Essays*, ed. William Archer and Robert W. Lowe [London, 1896], p. 85).

11. George Sand, pseudonym of Aurore Dupin, baronne Dudevant (1804–76), had published many novels, several of which Fuller defended in her essays.

648. To Richard F. Fuller

[ca. 16 November 1846]

Dear Richard,

I recd your so pleasant and sweet letter here, and am sorry that I must avail myself of your affece permission *not to write* but here as in London I get scarce any leisure and the little I have am obliged to give to studying French. I work hard trying to learn to speak it, and every word I write in English is a drawback in my progress. I have an excellent master every day, but to improve at the rate I ought to make use of my sojurn here I ought to learn even *to think* in French. Could I only have given three months to prepartory study but 'tis of no use [to] fret, great advantages are open to me even now. Propositions are made to me for translating from my writing into the French journals and I hope to form some good connections here. But of all this more in my next.

This note will be brought you by a dear friend, Mr Delf, whom I saw every day in London. He can tell you all about me, what I did, whom I saw, more than I could in a dozen letters. If Mother is at C. P. and you can make a visit pleasant and comfortable for him, ask him to go out with you and see her, to stay all night, if he can.

I think your plans for [Mother][n] seem very judicious, if you can only get the right kind people into the house with [   ]

About my staying abroad another year I expect now to wish it, but cannot see clear before me till the summer of next year. I thank very much for what you say; as to what money I shall want cannot tell till I know better what we spend this year. London was very expensive and so is Paris, in the way we go on here and want to go on Mr S. is quite unwell, I feel anxious about him; something *may* occur that will cut all that prematurely. Sufficient for the day &c. The day however is entirely insufficient for what I want to so I must say goodbye dear Richard. God bless and keep you prays ever your sister

M.

You will find Mr Delf a man of equal modesty and worth very refined in his tastes and feel[ings] and able to give you much informat[ion about Europe][n]

ALS (MH: fMS Am 1086 [9:251]); MsC (MH: fMS Am 1086 [Works, 1:149–53]). *Addressed:* Richard.

Mother] *Added from the copy.*
Europe] *Added from the copy.*

649. To [?]

[ca. mid-November 1846]

Of Dr. Wilkinson I saw a good deal, and found him a substantial person,—a sane, strong, and well-exercised mind,—but in the last degree unpoetical in its structure. He is very simple, natural, and good; excellent to see, though one cannot go far with him; and he would be worth more in writing, if he could get time to write, than in personal intercourse. He may yet find time; — he is scarcely more than thirty. Dr. W. wished to introduce me to Mr. Clissold, but I had not time; shall find it, if in London again.[1] Tennyson was not in town.

Browning has just married Miss Barrett, and gone to Italy. I may meet them there. Bailey is helping his father with a newspaper![2] His wife and child (Philip Festus by name) came to see me. I am to make them a visit on my return. Marston I saw several times, and found him full of talent. That is all I want to say at present; — he is a delicate nature, that can only be known in its own way and time. I went to see his "Patrician's Daughter."[3] It is an admirable play for the stage. At the house of W. J. Fox, I saw first himself, an eloquent man, of great practical ability, then Cooper, (of the "Purgatory of Suicides,") and others.

My poor selection of miscellanies has been courteously greeted in the London journals. Openings were made for me to write, had I but leisure; it is for that I look to a second stay in London, since several topics came before me on which I wished to write and publish *there*. [   ]

I became acquainted with a gentleman who is intimate with all the English artists, especially Stanfield and Turner, but was only able to go to his house once, at this time.[4] Pictures I found but little time for, yet enough to feel what they are now to be to me. I was only at the Dulwich and National Galleries and Hampton Court. Also, have seen the Vandykes, at Warwick; but all the precious private collections I was obliged to leave untouched, except one of Turner's, to which I gave a day. For the British Museum, I had only one day, which I spent in the Greek and Egyptian Rooms, unable even to look at the vast collections of drawings, &c. But if I live there a few months, I shall go often. O, were life but longer, and my strength greater! Ever I am bewildered by the riches of existence, had I but more time to open the oysters, and get out the pearls. Yet some are mine, if only for a necklace or rosary.

ELfr, from *Memoirs*, 2:190–91.

The Memoirs *editors join this letter to a* Tribune *dispatch. The letter may be part of the one of 16 November to Emerson. The final paragraph of the letter may not belong to the rest.*

1. Augustus Clissold (1797?–1882) was a Church of England cleric who became an ardent Swedenborgian. He had just translated Swedenborg's *Principia rerum naturalium* and *Regni animalis* for the Swedenborg Association (*DNB*).

2. The poet's father, Thomas Bailey (1785–1856), was a Nottingham typographer and writer who was at this time the proprietor and editor of the *Nottingham Mercury*. The venture was short-lived, however, for his "opinions were too temperate to suit the taste of his readers" (*DNB*).

3. John Westland Marston's acclaimed drama *The Patrician's Daughter* was first published in 1841. Fuller reviewed it in the *Dial*. It failed as a tragedy, she said, "from an improbability in the plot, and a want of power to touch the secret springs of passion, yet has the merits of genteel comedy in the unstrained and flowing dialogue, and dignity in the conception of character. A piece like this pleases, if only by the atmosphere of intellect and refinement it breathes" (*Dial* 4 [1844]: 318). She was more enthusiastic when she saw it performed in London: "This play is one that, in its scope and meaning marks the new era in England" (*New-York Daily Tribune*, 3 March 1847).

4. Clarkson Stanfield (1793–1867) was known for his marine and landscape paintings. At his home in Hampstead he had a circle of literary and artistic friends that included Dickens, John Forster, and Thackeray (*DNB*). J. M. W. Turner (1775–1851), the most important English painter of the century, was no longer as active as he had been in earlier years (*DNB*).

650.   To Ralph Waldo Emerson

[I] Paris 16 Novr, 1846

I meant to write on my arrival in London, six weeks ago—But as it was not what is technically called "the season", I thought I had best send all my letters of introduction at once, that I might glean what few good people I could. But more than I expected were there; these introduced others, and in three days I got engaged in such a crowd of acquaintance that I had hardly time to dress and none to sleep during all the weeks I was in London.

I enjoyed this time extremely. I find myself much in my element in European Society. It does not indeed come up to my ideal; but so many of the encumbrances are cleared away that used to weary me in America, that I can enjoy a freer play of faculty, and feel, if not like a bird in the air, at least as easy as a fish in water.

On my very first arrival I encountered in Liverpool and Manchester, a set of devout readers of the Dial, still more of Emerson. Of the latter I found many wherever I went. In Westmoreland I found an English gentleman, one of the rich landowners, who live so charmingly that they scarce learn the need of thought, who yet had drawn from the Essays the impulse to a higher being, and knew them by heart, if not by head, so that he could have made a book of Excerpts in the style of Fanny

In Edinburgh I met Dr Brown.[1] He is still quite a young man, but with a high ambition, and I should think commensurate powers; but all is yet in the bud with him. He has a friend, David Scott, a painter full of imagination and very earnest in his views of Art. I had some pleasant hours with them; and the last night which they and I passed with De

Quincey a real Grand Conversatione, quite in the Landor style, which lasted in full harmony some hours.[2]

Of the Scotch People whom I saw you will find notices in the Tribune, as also of my Highland Tour and my hair-breadth escape with life on one of the peaks of Ben-Lomond— Of the people I saw in London you will wish me to speak first of the Carlyles.[3] Mr C came to see me at once, and appointed an evening to be passed at their house. That first time I was delighted with him. He was in a very sweet humor, full of wit and pathos, without being overbearing or oppressive. I was quite carried away with the rich flow of his discourse; and the hearty noble earnestness of his personal being brought back the charm which once was upon his writing, before I wearied of it. I admired his Scotch, his way of singing his great full sentences, so that each one was like the stanza of a narrative ballad. He let me talk a little now and then, enough to free my lungs, and change my position, so that I did not get tired.

That evening he talked of the present state of things in England, giving light witty sketches of the men of the day, fanatics and others— and some sweet homely stories he told of things he had known of the Scotch Peasantry. Of you he spoke worthily, as he seldom writes to you, and most unlike the tone of his prefaces, so that for the moment, I was quite reconciled to him.[4]

Especially he told with beautiful feeling a story of some poor farmer or artisan in the country, who on Sunday lays aside the cark and care of that dirty English world, and sits reading the Essays, and looking upon the Sea.

I left him that night, intending to go out very often to their house.— I assure you there never was any thing so witty as Carlyle's description of[n] [   ] it was enough to kill one with laughing. I on my side contributed the story of[n] [   ] to his fund of anecdote on this subject, and it was fully appreciated. Carlyle is worth a thousand of you for that, he is not ashamed to laugh when he is amused, but goes on in a cordial human fashion.

The second time Mr C had a dinner-party, at which was a witty french flippant sort of man[n] [   ], author of a History of Philosophy, and now writing a life of Goethe, a task for which he must be as unfit as irreligion and sparkling shallowness can make him.[5] But he told stories admirably, and was allowed sometimes to interrupt Carlyle, a little, of which one was glad, for that night he was in his more acrid mood, and, though much more brilliant than the former evening, became wearisome, at least to my mind which disclaimed and rejected almost everything he said

Thomas Carlyle. By permission of the Houghton Library, Harvard University.

For a couple of hours he was talking about poetry, and the whole harangue was one eloquent proclamation of the defects in his own mind. Tennyson wrote in verse because the schoolmasters had taught him that it was great to do so, and had thus unfortunately been turned from the true path for a man. Burns had in like manner been turned from his vocation, Shakespeare had not had the good sense to see that it would have been better to write straight on in prose, and such nonsense which though amusing eno' at first, he ran to death after a while. The most amusing part is always when he comes back to some refrain as in the French Revolution of the *Sea-Green*; in this instance it was Petrarch in *Laura*, the last word pronounced with his ineffable sarcasm of drawl. Although he said this over fifty times I could not ever help laughing when *Laura* would come, Carlyle running his chin out when he spoke it, and his eyes glancing till they looked like the eyes and beak of a bird of prey. Poor Laura! Lucky for her that her poet had already got her safely canonized beyond the reach of this Teufelsdrockh vulture.

The worst of hearing Carlyle is that you cannot interrupt him. I understand the habit and power of haranguing have increased very much upon him, so that you are a perfect prisoner when he has once got hold of you. To interrupt him is a physical impossibility; if you get a chance to remonstrate for a moment, he raises his voice and bears you down. True, he does you no injustice, and with his admirable penetration sees the disclaimer in your mind, so that you are not morally delinquent; but it is not pleasant to be unable to utter it. The latter part of the evening, however, he paid us for this by a series of sketches in his finest style of railing and raillery of modern French Literature, not [II] one of them, perhaps, perfectly just, but all drawn with the finest, boldest strokes, and, from his point of view, masterly. All were depreciating, except that of Béranger. Of him he spoke with perfect justice, because with hearty sympathy.

I had, afterward, some talk with Mrs. C., whom hitherto I had only *seen*, for who can speak while her husband is there?[6] I like her very much;—she is full of grace, sweetness, and talent. Her eyes are sad and charming. [   ]

After this, they went to stay at Lord Ashburton's, and I only saw them once more, when they came to pass an evening with us.[7] Unluckily, Mazzini was with us, whose society, when he was there alone, I enjoyed more than any. He is a beauteous and pure music; also, he is a dear friend of Mrs. C.; but his being there gave the conversation a turn to "progress" and ideal subjects, and C. was fluent in invectives on all our "rose-water imbecilities." We all felt distant from him, and Mazzini, after some vain efforts to remonstrate, became very sad. Mrs. C. said to me, "These are but opinions to Carlyle; but to Mazzini, who has given his all, and helped bring his friends to the scaffold, in pursuit of such subjects, it is a matter of life and death."

All Carlyle's talk, that evening, was a defence of mere force,—success the test of right;—if people would not behave well, put collars round their necks;—find a hero, and let them be his slaves, &c. It was very Titanic, and anti-celestial. I wish the last evening had been more melodious. However, I bid Carlyle farewell with feelings of the warmest friendship and admiration. We cannot feel otherwise to a great and noble nature, whether it harmonize with our own or not. I never appreciated the work he has done for his age till I saw England. I could not. You must stand in the shadow of that mountain of shams, to know how hard it is to cast light across it.

Honor to Carlyle! *Hoch!* Although in the wine with which we drink this health, I, for one, must mingle the despised "rose-water."

And now, having to your eye shown the defects of my own mind, in the sketch of another, I will pass on more lowly,—more willing to be imperfect,—since Fate permits such noble creatures, after all, to be only this or that. It is much if one is not only a crow or magpie;—Carlyle is only a lion. Some time we may, all in full, be intelligent and humanly fair.

I: MsCfr (MH: fMS Am 1086 [9:216–17]); II: *Memoirs*, 2:187–88; MsCfr (MH: fMS Am 1086 [Works, 1:209]). Published in part in *Memoirs*, 2:184–87; Higginson, *MFO*, p. 172; and Chevigny, p. 355.

description of] *The following word is blotted.*

story of] *The following word is blotted.*

of man] *The following word is blotted but undoubtedly is* Lewes.

1. John Brown (1810–82), a physician and son of a prominent Edinburgh divine, became best known for his books on doctors and medicine, published in the 1850s (*DNB*).

2. Thomas De Quincey (1785–1859), author of *Confessions of an English Opium-Eater*, impressed Fuller with his "urbanity, so opposite to the rapid, slang, Vivian-Greyish style current in the literary conversation of the day" (*New-York Daily Tribune*, 5 November 1846).

3. Fuller caught Carlyle at a bad time. Restless because he was not working on a book, he had quarreled with his wife over his friendship with the Barings, William Bingham (later second Baron Ashburton) and his wife, Lady Harriet Mary Montagu, with whom he had spent a portion of the summer. Jane Carlyle's jealousy and Carlyle's impatience wounded them both in the autumn of 1846. Carlyle wrote generously of Fuller to Emerson: "A high-soaring, clear, enthusiast soul; in whose speech there is much of all that one wants to find in speech"; but to his brother John he was acerbic: "A strange *lilting* lean old maid, not nearly such a bore as I expected" (James Anthony Froude, *Thomas Carlyle: A History of His Life in London, 1834–1881* [New York, 1884], 1:324–42; *Emerson–Carlyle Correspondence*, p. 410).

4. Carlyle was condescending in his preface to the 1841 English edition of Emerson's *Essays*. He called the volume an "unpretending little Book, composed probably, in good part, from mere Lectures which already lay written." Though he praised Emerson, Car-

lyle said that his friend was "perhaps far less notable for what he has spoken or done, than for the many things he has not spoken and has forborne to do." Fuller undoubtedly was stung by the description of the *Dial* as a "noteworthy though very unattractive work" (*Essays: By R. W. Emerson, of Concord, Massachusetts* [London, 1841], pp. vi, ix, x).

5. George Henry Lewes (1817–78) published his *Biographical History of Philosophy* (London, 1845–46) in four volumes and his life of Goethe in 1855. A friend of Thackeray, Carlyle, and Mill, Lewes wrote often on drama and German literature. From 1854 to his death he lived with Marian Evans (George Eliot) as her husband (*DNB*). Apparently he was impressed with Fuller's talk: "Lewes had few rivals as a conversationalist. But he told me he found one once. He was invited by W. J. Fox to meet, at his house, Margaret Fuller, afterwards Countess Ossoli. Carlyle was another guest that night. Fox, Carlyle, and Lewes were famous talkers; but when Margaret Fuller took her turn they were all silenced, and—their turn came no more" (George Jacob Holyoake, *Sixty Years of an Agitator's Life* [London, 1892], 1:244).

6. Jane Baillie Welsh (1801–66) married Carlyle in 1826. Each partner was brilliant and self-reliant but incapable of finding peace with the other. Yet, despite their stormy periods, Jane and Thomas Carlyle had an enduring marriage (*DNB*, under Thomas Carlyle).

7. Alexander Baring (1774–1848), first Baron Ashburton, was a financier, the son of Sir Francis Baring (1740–1810), who founded the banking firm of Baring Brothers. In 1798 Alexander Baring married Anne Louisa Bingham of Philadelphia. As a member of Parliament, Lord Ashburton was instrumental in easing tensions with the United States (*DNB*).

651. To Caroline Sturgis

28th Novr [1846]
eveg half past ten

dying of sleep and fatigued only time I can get to write to Carrie; it is a shame yes instead of resting I have not been able to help killing myself with fatigue and excitement I believe there is no rest for me in this world. When you come, you who have leisure to study, be sure you can speak French fluently first; else you must lose a great deal. I practice three hours in morng and every chance I can get, beside going to French play and opera every night except this, when I stay at home to write letters, yet I do not get on as fast as I hoped. My master says I shall speak really well in a month, meanwhile I speak badly the moment I become deeply interested because then I cannot help thinking in English I am engrossed in Rachel; she surpasses my hopes. I have not yet delivered my letter I want to see her in her greatest parts first; great as I already see her I perceive she will soar still higher. I have seen her in Mary Stuart, [*illegible*] and Phedre. There is nothing like her voice; she speaks the language of the Gods. to the noblest genius is joined the severest culture. She has a really bad reputation as woman. A liberal

Rachel as Phèdre. By permission of The Huntington Library, San Marino, California.

Frenchman says to me "Me *Sand* has committed what are called errors, but we doubt not the nobleness of her soul, but it is said that the private life of *Mlle Rachel* has nothing in common with the apparition of the Artist." Do not speak of this in America.

ALfr, collection of G. W. Haight.

652. To George Palmer Putnam

Paris, November 28, 1836 [1846]

Dear Sir:

[   ] Proposals have been made to me for translating some fragments of my writings into the French journals, and I think that, at least, the sketch of American literature and some part of "Woman in the Nineteenth Century" might be interesting here.[1] Will you have the kindness to send me five copies of the "Papers on Literature and Art," and to purchase for me as many of "Woman," etc., to send with them. I can give them away much to my advantage and pleasure to the persons with whom I am making acquaintance. As I have already given away the copies I brought with me, would you have the kindness to send the parcel as early as possible, and in some safe way, to my address here. [   ]

We are enjoying a great deal here; it is truly the city of pleasures.

Mademoiselle Rachel I have seen with the greatest delight. I go whenever she acts, and when I have seen the entire range of her parts, intend to write a detailed critique, which shall also comprehend comments on the high French tragedy. [   ]

With compliments,

MARGARET FULLER.

ELfr, from *Putnam's* n.s. 4 (October 1869): 473. Published in George Haven Putnam, *A Memoir of George Palmer Putnam* (New York, 1912), pp. 398–99.

1. "De la littérature américaine" appeared in *La Revue Indépendante* for 10 December 1846.

653. To Margarett C. Fuller

Paris, 26 December 1846

[I] In Paris, I have been obliged to give a great deal of time to French, in order to get the power of speaking, without which I might as well be in a well, as here. [II] That has prevented my doing nearly as much as I would. Could I remain six months in this great focus of civilized life, the time would be all too short for my desires and needs.

My Essay on American Literature has been translated into French, and published in "La Revue Indépendante," one of the leading journals of Paris;[1] only, with that delight at manufacturing names for which the French are proverbial, they put, instead of *Margaret, Elizabeth*. Write to —— ——, that aunt Elizabeth has appeared unexpectedly before the French public! She will not enjoy her honors long, as a future number, which is to contain a notice of "Woman in the Nineteenth Century," will rectify the mistake.

[III] I have been asked to remain in correspondence with "La Revue Independante," after my return to the U. S. which will be very pleasant and advantageous to me.

Madame Pauline Roland I find an interesting woman, an intimate friend of Beranger and of Pierre Leroux[2]

We occupy a charming suite of apartments *Hotel Rougement, Boulevard Poissonniére*, a new hotel, [IV] and has not the arched gateways and gloomy court-yard of the old mansions. My room, though small, is very pretty, with the thick, flowered carpet and marble slabs; the French clock, with Cupid, of course, over the fireplace, in which burns a bright little wood fire; the canopy bedstead, and inevitable large mirror; the curtains, too, are thick and rich, the closet, &c., excellent, the attendance good. But for all this, one pays dear. We do not find that one can live *pleasantly* at Paris for little money; and we prefer to economize by a briefer stay, if at all.

I: MsCfr (MH: bMS Am 1280 [111, p. 90]); II: ELfr, from *Memoirs*, 2:191–92; III: MsCfr (MH: bMS Am 1280 [111, p. 91]); IV: ELfr from *Memoirs*, 2:192–93. Published in part in *JMN*, 11:474–75.

1. In 1841 Pierre Leroux, George Sand, and Louis Viardot founded *La Revue indépendante*, a socialist and literary review. It ceased publication in 1847 (*OCFL*).

2. Pauline-Marie-Désirée Roland (1805–52) was a socialist and radical feminist who conducted a school at Leroux's commune at Boussac (Sand, *Correspondance*, 6:952–53; Edith Thomas, *Pauline Roland* [Paris, 1956]). Pierre-Jean de Béranger, whose poetry Fuller long admired, and Pierre Leroux were liberal politicians as well as men of letters.

Of the poet, Fuller wrote: "To me Béranger has been much; his wit, his pathos, his exquisite lyric grace, have made the most delicate strings vibrate" (*New-York Daily Tribune*, 3 March 1847).

654. To Félicité-Robert de Lamennais

Paris, 1847

Monsieur:—

As my visit to you was cut short before I was quite satisfied, it was my intention to seek you again immediately; although I felt some scruples at occupying your valuable time, when I express myself so imperfectly in your language.[1] But I have been almost constantly ill since, and now am not sure of finding time to pay you my respects before leaving Paris for Italy. In case this should be impossible, I take the liberty to write, and to present you two little volumes of mine. It is only as a tribute of respect. I regret that they do not contain some pieces of mine which might be more interesting to you, as illustrative of the state of affairs in our country. Some such will find their place in subsequent numbers. These, I hope, you will, if you do not read them, accept kindly as a salutation from our hemisphere. Many there delight to know you as a great apostle of the ideas which are to be our life, if Heaven intends us a great and permanent life. I count myself happy in having seen you, and in finding with you Béranger, the genuine poet, the genuine man of France. I have felt all the enchantment of the lyre of Béranger; have paid my warmest homage to the truth and wisdom adorned with such charms, such wit and pathos. It was a great pleasure to see himself. If your leisure permits, Monsieur, I will ask a few lines in reply. I should like to keep some words from your hand, in case I should not look upon you more here below; and am always, with gratitude for the light you have shed on so many darkened spirits,

Yours, most respectfully,

MARGARET FULLER.

EL, from *Memoirs*, 2:202–3.

Félicité-Robert de Lamennais (1782–1854) was an ultramontanist priest who became a Christian socialist with a following in both France and England.

1. Fuller was at first annoyed to find the priest with another visitor when she called on him, but she quickly changed her attitude when the man turned out to be Béranger. Of Lamennais she said: "I see well what he has been and is to Europe, and of what great force of nature and spirit. He seems suffering and pale, but in his eyes is the light of the future" (*New-York Daily Tribune*, 3 March 1847).

Félicité-Robert de Lamennais, by David d'Angers. Photo Musées de la Ville de Paris, copyright © 1986 by SPADEM.

655. To Elizabeth Hoar

Paris, 18 January 1847

You wished to hear of George Sand, or, as they say in Paris, "Madame Sand." I find that all we had heard of her was true in the outline; I had supposed it might be exaggerated.[1] She had every reason to leave her husband,—a stupid, brutal man, who insulted and neglected her. He afterwards gave up their child to her for a sum of money.[2] But the love for which she left him lasted not well, and she has had a series of lovers, and I am told has one now, with whom she lives on the footing of combined means, independent friendship![3] But she takes rank in society like a man, for the weight of her thoughts, and has just given her daughter in marriage.[4] Her son is a grown-up young man, an artist.[5] Many women visit her, and esteem it an honor. Even an American here, and with the feelings of our country on such subjects, Mrs.——, thinks of her with high esteem. She has broken with La Mennais, of whom she was once a disciple.[6]

I observed to Dr. François, who is an intimate of hers, and loves and admires her, that it did not seem a good sign that she breaks with her friends.[7] He said it was not so with her early friends; that she has chosen to buy a chateau in the region where she passed her childhood, and that the people there love and have always loved her dearly. She is now at the chateau, and, I begin to fear, will not come to town before I go.[8] Since I came, I have read two charming stories recently written by her. Another longer one she has just sold to *La Presse* for fifteen thousand francs.[9] She does not receive nearly as much for her writings as Balzac, Dumas, or Sue. She has a much greater influence than they, but a less circulation.

She stays at the chateau, because the poor people there were suffering so much, and she could help them. She has subscribed *twenty thousand francs* for their relief, in the scarcity of the winter.[10] It is a great deal to earn by one's pen: a novel of several volumes sold for only fifteen thousand francs, as I mentioned before.[11]

ELfr, from *Memoirs*, 2:193–94.

In the Memoirs, *this fragment is joined to an excerpt from Fuller's journal (MH). This latter portion was probably sent to Hoar by way of Emerson in a letter now lost (Rusk,* Letters of RWE, *3:394).*

1. Fuller was an early and vigorous defender of the French novelist George Sand, who was to Americans perhaps the most scandalous writer of the day. As she had done with Goethe, Fuller clearly attempted to turn her audience away from the life of the writer and toward the effects of the works. In both cases, Fuller called down the scorn of conservatives. Typical of her comments on Sand is Fuller's contention that "to her own

George Sand, by Charpentier. Photo Musées de la Ville de Paris, copyright © 1986 by SPADEM.

country Sand is a boon precious and prized, both as a warning and a leader, for which none there can be ungrateful. She has dared to probe its festering wounds, and if they be not past all surgery, she is one who, most of any, helps toward a cure" (*New-York Daily Tribune*, 1 February 1845).

2. On 17 September 1822 Aurore Dupin married François-Casmir Dudevant (1795–1871), the illegitimate son of François Dudevant, baron of the Empire. After an unhappy life together, the couple separated in 1830. In 1836 a bitter court battle led to a permanent separation (Curtis Cate, *George Sand* [Boston, 1975], pp. 91–92, 164–67, 398–99; Sand, *Correspondance*, 1:1004; *Dictionnaire de biographie française*).

3. Among Sand's lovers were Jules Sandeau, Stéphane Ajasson de Grandsagne, Alfred de Musset, Michel de Bourges, and (the one Fuller describes) Frédéric Chopin.

4. Solange Dudevant (whose father was probably Stéphane Ajasson de Grandsagne) was born in 1828. She had been engaged to Fernand de Preaulx but broke the engagement before the wedding, which had been set for April 1847. She married instead Auguste Clésinger, a sculptor, on 19 May 1847. Solange died in 1899 (Cate, *George Sand*, pp. 140, 549–56, 733).

5. Sand's son Maurice (1823–1889) took Sand as his surname. He was an accomplished artist and author (*Dictionnaire de biographie française*).

6. Beginning in 1835, Sand was powerfully influenced by Lamennais, but they went separate ways in 1841 when he published a pamphlet critical of women's intellectual abilities and she published her novel *Horace*, which upheld the rights of the masses (Cate, *George Sand*, pp. 363, 496–98).

7. Ferdinand François (1806–68), an author and physician, helped edit *La Revue indépendante*. A Saint-Simonian republican, François was jailed in 1849 and again in 1853 (Sand, *Correspondance*, 6:938).

8. Nohant, George Sand's estate, was in the province of Berry.

9. Fuller read *Teverino* (Brussells, 1845), which was published in Paris in 1846, and *La Mare au diable*, which had been published in the *Courrier français*, 6–15 February 1846. Sand had sold *Le Piccinino* to *La Presse*, which published the novel from 5 May to 17 July 1847 (Sand, *Correspondance*, 7:444).

10. First summer drought, then autumn floods had destroyed the harvest at Nohant. The suffering was extreme (Cate, *George Sand*, pp. 547–48).

11. Of the visit to Sand, Emerson wrote Fuller: "It was high time, dear friend, that you should run out of the coop of our bigoted societies full of fire damp & azote, and find some members of your own expansive fellowship" (Rusk, *Letters of RWE*, 3:394).

656. To Ralph Waldo Emerson

Paris, 18 January 1847

I can hardly tell you what a fever consumes me, from sense of the brevity of my time and opportunity. Here I cannot sleep at night, because I have been able to do so little in the day. Constantly I try to calm my mind into content with small achievements, but it is difficult. You will say, it is not so mightily worth knowing, after all, this picture and natural history of Europe. Very true; but I am so constituted that it pains me to come away, having touched only the glass over the picture.

I am assiduous daily at the Academy lectures, picture galleries, Chamber of Deputies,—last week, at the court and court ball. So far as my previous preparation enabled me, I get something from all these brilliant shows,—thoughts, images, fresh impulse. But I need, to initiate me into various little secrets of the place and time,—necessary for me to look at things to my satisfaction,—some friend, such as I do not find here. My steps have not been fortunate in Paris, as they were in England. No doubt, the person exists here, whose aid I want; indeed, I feel that it is so; but we do not meet, and the time draws near for me to depart.

French people I find slippery, as they do not know exactly what to make of me, the rather as I have not the command of their language. *I* see *them,* their brilliancy, grace, and variety, the thousand slight refinements of their speech and manner, but cannot meet them in their way.[1] My French teacher says, I speak and act like an Italian, and I hope, in Italy, I shall find myself more at home.

ELfr, from *Memoirs,* 2:201–2.

1. As he so often did, Emerson emphasized her conversational power in his response of 28 February: "It is too plain that you should conquer their speech first, which is to unlock such jewelled cabinets for you. They have translated modern civilization into conversation, and our queen of discourse cannot go by such a magazine until she has exhausted it" (Rusk, *Letters of RWE,* 3:376).

657.   To Richard F. Fuller

Paris 31st Jan 47.

My dear Richard,

I did not expect to write at all this steamer hoping to be off for Italy, by this time, but little Eddie has been[n] very ill and is only just now well enough to go, and out of this delay have grown up still further causes for delay. By the 10th or 15th I hope to be on the road, in that case you will have no letter by next steamer, after that they will begin to go once a fortnight and I to write when can.

I had a very good letter from Arthur by last steamer, thank him I shall write when I can. The arrangements that had been made for dear Mother seemed to me very good and Lloyd's continuity of place and apparent well being truly delightful. Much love to all. Homesick enough am I, very often, or rather as the people have laughed at my saying the other day, I should be homesick if I had a home. Much as there is to learn and be amused with there is something in this continual contact that makes the heart ache sometimes, makes one pine for the old familiar faces. Another thing is I am always unwell; the damp winter here disagrees with me more than our cold. But now spring begins to arrive; we have had a mild dry day and it did me good.

I have not time to write any particulars about myself; you must pick up what you can from the letters in the Tribune. I have been presented at Court and been to the Court ball (by the way I saw there your classmate Clarke who has also called and talked to me of you)[1] I have been in the Chamber of Peers. I have heard Arago lecture &c.[2] I study my French hard and begin to speak with some fluency. I steal some time to read books, but this hurts me as it is always by night. The results shall they not be written yet in a big[n] book for the persual of all who care for me. I saw your admission to the bar by chance in a Boston newspaper. I hope things are going on well with you. Do you visit Jane and try if you can be a friend to her at this time. What part has Anna Loring taken with regard to Jane and John.[3] What do you hear about it? I shall not write to you again for some time, but will try to one good letter from Italy.

AL (MH: fMS Am 1086 [9:252]); MsC (MH: fMS Am 1086 [Works, 2:803–9]). *Addressed:* To / Richard F. Fuller / 6 State St / Boston / Mass / U. S. A. *Postmark:* 3 Fe 1847. *Endorsed:* F. S. M. / S. Margarett Fuller / 31 Jan & 15 Septr 1847.

Eddie has been] Eddie ⟨is⟩ ↑ has been ↓
a big] a b⟨o⟩ig

1. James Gordon Clarke (1822–1906), who graduated from Harvard in 1844 and became a lawyer, served in the diplomatic corps at Brussells and Paris (Edward Wheelwright, *The Class of 1844, Harvard College, Fifty Years after Graduation* [Cambridge, 1896], pp. 52–53; Harvard archives).

2. François Arago (1786–1853) was a scientist, the director of the Paris Observatory. Fuller found his talk "clear, rapid, full and equal." The lecture was "worthy its celebrity," even after the four-hour wait to get a seat (*New-York Daily Tribune*, 3 March 1847).

3. Jane and John King had separated; the exact grounds are not clear (Margarett C. Fuller to Margaret Fuller, 7 February 1847, MH).

658.   To Benjamin P. Poore

23
Allie d'Antin
Wednesday 3d Feby [1847]

Dear Sir,

You have made me some kind offers of aid; perhaps you will know better than others how I can be helped on an occasion that interests me.

I wanted much to hear Dumas speak at his trial the other day but, after being assured that no such thing was necessary, I could not get in for want of the *billet* that the French eternally demand. Now the trial will finish I understand on Monday next.[1] Could you find some way to enable me to go in *Then*,[n] through your acquaintance with Paris; and without too much fatigue and vexation of spirit, it would much oblige me. Mr Spring begs the name of the engraver. Excuse our persecutions; they will not last long; we go soon into Italy. If you can go with me or find the way for me to go to hear Dumas; will you answer soon, that if you cannot I may seek elsewhere

Truly yours

S. M. FULLER.

ALS (PHC). *Addressed:* Major Benj. Perley Poore / No. 5 Rue Chanteilles / Faubourg St. Germain.

Benjamin Perley Poore (1820–87), a writer and editor, was working for the Massachusetts legislature to recover documents in the French archives that pertained to American history. He was the author of several biographies and histories *(DAB).*

in *Then,*] in ↑ *Then* ↓ ,

1. Fuller was unsuccessful in her attempt to hear the elder Dumas (*New-York Daily Tribune,* 3 March 1847). Dumas had left Paris for Spain and abandoned stories that he was publishing in five newspapers. What is more, he had broken generous contracts with *Le Constitutionnel* and *La Presse* to publish in the other papers. He was being sued by all seven papers to recover their damages. The trial quickly became a public event; Dumas "was witty and theatrical, and from start to finish he dominated the scene, provided entertainment of a most farcical kind and therefore won a good deal of sympathy." The court levied only a token fine (Edith Saunders, *The Prodigal Father* [London, 1951], pp. 188–90).

659. To Ralph Waldo Emerson

[I] Naples, 15 March 1847

Mickiewicz, the Polish poet, first introduced the Essays to acquaintance in Paris.[1] I did not meet him anywhere, and, as I heard a great deal of him which charmed me, I sent him your poems, and asked him to come and see me. He came, and I found in him the man I had long wished to see, with the intellect and passions in due proportion for a full and healthy human being, with a soul constantly inspiring. Unhappily, it was a very short time before I came away. How much time had I wasted on others which I might have given to this real and important relation. [II] In France, among the many persons that brought me some good thing, it was only with Mickiewicz, that I felt any deep-founded mental connection.

[III] After hearing music from Chopin and Neukomm,[2] I quitted Paris on the 25th February, and came, *via* Chalons, Lyons, Avignon, (where I waded through melting snow to Laura's tomb,) Arles, to Marseilles; thence, by steamer, to Genoa, Leghorn, and Pisa.[3] Seen through a cutting wind, the marble palaces, the gardens, the magnificent water-view of Genoa, failed to charm. Only at Naples have I found *my* Italy. Between Leghorn and Naples, our boat was run into by another, and we only just escaped being drowned.

I: ELfr, from *Memoirs*, 2:207; II: MsCfr (MH: bMS Am 1280 [111, p. 91]); III: ELfr, from *Memoirs*, 2:207–8. Published in part in *JMN*, 11:475.

The parts are joined on the supposition that Fuller described Mickiewicz to Emerson only once and that he omitted from the Memoirs *the portion he copied into his journal.*

1. Adam Mickiewicz (1798–1855) was a Polish poet and revolutionary then living in Paris. A friend of George Sand and others whom Fuller met, he exerted a powerful influence on her. They corresponded during her stay in Italy (her letters to him are now lost), and he was her son's godfather.

2. Fuller heard Chopin in the company of Jane Wilhelmina Stirling (1804–59), a pupil of Chopin to whom he dedicated several compositions (Fuller to Jane Stirling, 8 March 1848 [NBu]; Jane Stirling to Fuller, 6 December 1847 [MH]; Herbert Weinstock, *Chopin: The Man and His Music* [New York, 1949], p. 143). Of Chopin, whose affair with George Sand was coming to an end, Fuller wrote: "One must hear himself; only a person as exquisitely organized as he can adequately express these subtile secrets of the creative spirit." Sigismund von Neukomm (1778–1858), an Austrian pianist and composer, wrote *David*, a popular oratorio, in 1834. Fuller wrote of him: "Full, sustained, ardent, yet exact, the stream of his thought bears with it the attention of hearers of all characters, as his character, full of *bonhommie*, open, friendly, animated, and sagacious, would seem to have something to present for the affection and esteem of all kinds of men" (*New-York Daily Tribune*, 29 May 1847).

3. Laure de Noves of Avignon is the woman to whom Petrarch is thought to have addressed his poems. Although Fuller does not discuss the meeting in this letter fragment, in Genoa she visited Maria Mazzini, the patriot's mother (E. F. Richards, ed., *Mazzini's Letters to an English Family, 1844–1854* [London, 1920], p. 53).

660.   To Marcus and Rebecca Spring

Rome April 10th 1846 [1847]

I was by my nature destined to walk by the inner light alone. It has led, will lead me sometimes on a narrow plank across deep chasms, if I do not see clear, if I do not balance myself exactly I must then fall and bleed and die. For this intellectually I am always prepared. I wish to be free and absolutely true to my nature, and if I cannot live so I do not wish to live. I may shrink from pain, but I must not be really afraid of it.

From infancy I have foreseen that my path must be difficult, it has been less so than I expected. Still I feel in myself immense trials possible to me and can only hope to be inwardly ripened for them. If they do not come in this world they will in another, it is not for me to fix the time of their coming but only to avoid wasting my strength in frivolous excitements in factitious duties and try to keep the strings of action fresh and strong within me.

I have never sought love as a passion; it has always come to me as an angel bearing some good tidings I have wished to welcome the messenger noble, but never to detain it, or cling with a weak personality to a tie which had ceased to bind the soul, I believe I should always do the same, however I might suffer from loss or void in the intervals of love, if I did not I can only say I should act very unworthily and I hope I should be punished till I returned to my better self.

I do not know whether I have loved at all in the sense of oneness, but I have loved enough to feel the joys of presence the pangs of absence, the sweetness of hope, and the chill of disappointment. More than once my heart has bled, and my health has suffered from these things but mentally I have always found myself the gainer, always younger and more noble. I have no wish about my future course but that it should be like the past, only always more full and deeper.

You ask me if I love M.[1] I answer he affected me like music or the richest landscape, my heart beat with joy that he at once felt beauty in me also. When I was with him I was happy; and thus far the attraction is so strong that all the way from Paris I felt as if I had left my life behind, and if I followed my inclination I should return at this moment and leave Italy unseen

Still I do not know but I might love still better tomorrow; I have never yet loved any human being so well as the music of Beethoven yet at present I am indifferent to it. There has been a time when I thought of nothing but Michael Angelo, yet the other day I felt hardly inclined to look at the forms his living hand had traced on the ceiling of the Sistine. But when I loved either of these great Souls I abandoned myself wholly to it, I did not calculate, I shall do so in life if I love enough.[2]

MsCfr (CSmH: HM 46741); MsCfr (NjHi).

1. Adam Mickiewicz, who had often visited Fuller and the Springs in Paris.
2. At the end of the copy, Rebecca Spring wrote: "Margaret's letter was a long one of twentyfour pages. She had written it in the early morning in her room, and gave it to me at breakfast before she went to the Villa Borgesee where she saved our little boy from

Adam Mickiewicz in 1841, by Józef Kurowski. Muzeum Literatury im Adama
Mickiewicza, Warsaw. Photo by Anna Kowalska.

drowning in the great fountain. Sometimes Margaret could explain herself better by writing than by talking, as in this letter."

661.   To Richard F. Fuller

Rome,
15th April, 47.

My dear Richard

Two or three days ago came your good letter. When one comes it always makes even the most beautiful day seem better to me.

With regard to what you say of your position, I do not feel afraid of your letting go *the better part,* although the difficulties and temptations may be great. I feel as if you had taken it too seriously to heart ever to let it go and be content *settled* as others are into the *dregs* of an existence that once promised *wine.* But I feel anxious about your health and spirits. It does not seem as if you had pleasant and congenial things enough. But I do hope more may come. Seek the country, long country walks and drives. Go out sometimes with Jane; she is older, but is one of *our people,* and one of the noblest.

At this distance I cannot advise much about the Lorings; except I would not go there *much.* I am grieved Anna has acted so passively; no doubt she is quite ignorant of the true facts, but not a few would have divined them and acted otherwise on instinct. Mr Loring, too, has acted below what I expected, though I knew his views of marriage were not high. I am not at all surprised at what you say of Mrs Loring; she wants delicacy and even honor, though quite unconscious of these wants; still[n] she has in some ways very generous feelings. See her truly, keep a firm course, but say no rash words and do no harsh act towards her.

I hoped affairs at the office might look more promising, still I think that the opportunity you enjoy of making yourself known is *the* great thing. At five or six and twenty you may be known and not have to wait for all the joys and advantages of life till it is too late to make full use of them Then, if H. prove too slippery an eel you can separate from him.

With regard to what you think you could do for me, I certainly think money would avail me now as it never can again. And in staying abroad another year, I am very anxious to feel free from doubt and care. But I am afraid under present circumstances you are not really able to help me and dear Eugene is now married.[1] As to Mother[n] my first wish always was and is never to press on her.[2] I have told her I would now accept the hundred dollars, if she could add to it without any inconvenience to herself, then I should be glad, but you must be very guarded not to let her deprive herself of any thing for me, for she would be sure and wish to do so, if she thought I needed it.[n]

I shall not want this money till the autumn, perhaps not till the winter. But Write[n] me word as soon as you can after receiving this how much or how little I may depend on receiving from home that I may judge how much must be borrowed[n] if I remain.

I am very happy here in Rome; the weather is now beautiful and all around as magnificient as I expected. I have not yet formed any friendship of the mind, such as I had in London and Paris, but, perhaps I shall before going away. I should like a companion here just because it is so beautiful still the same makes it easy to do without one. Adeiu, dear Richard ever most affecy your friend and sister

M.

ALS (MH: fMS Am 1086 [9:251]); MsCfr (MH: fMS Am 1086 [Works, 2:799–803]). *Addressed:* To / Richard. *Endorsed:* F. S. M. / S. Margaret Fuller / 15. Jan. 1847.

wants; still] wants; ↑ still ↓
to Mother] to ⟨my⟩ ↑ Mother ↓
needed it.] needed ⟨re⟩ it.
But Write] ↑ But ↓ Write
be borrowed] be b⟨r⟩orrowed

1. In July 1846, Eugene married Eliza Rotta, a Philadelphia widow, in New Orleans.
2. In her letter of 7 February (MH), Mrs. Fuller offered her daughter $100 from a loan that Eugene had just repaid.

662.   To [?]

16 April 1847

a gift not a loan [   ] I want $1000 but can do very well with $500. If I hv. but $500 I shall hv. to renounce some things.

MsCfr (MB: Ms. Am. 1450 [18]). Copy in Higginson's hand.

663.   To Mary Howitt

Rome
18th April, 1847.

My dear Mrs Howitt

A letter received from you just before leaving Paris, ought to have been answered much earlier, but the truth is I have not known exactly how to answer. The biographical sketches you asked of me, it would be highly agreeable to me to make and had I recd the letter long enough before leaving Paris, I should have made the attempt. I did not know but there might again here be intervals whether of bad weather or from any other cause[n] which might give me the leisure and chance for concentrating my interest on these subjects. But such do[n] not come, and I begin to feel that they[n] will not till I am settled again next winter

I have such opportunities now of learning and seeing what may never be before me again that I cannot bear to lose them and I feel that I shall be so much better fitted to write after them that I am hardly willing to at present.

Especially as to the memoir of George Sand I have learned and thought so much about her position while in France and find the subject to involve so much and so difficult to be treated exactly to my mind that I cannot do it except just at the right moment and when circumstances favor my being undisturbed to fix my mind full and strong upon it. It is a thing I shall do, no doubt, but I may be too late for you, as you want it in connexion with these translations of Miss Hays.[1]

All this being so uncertain as to time, on my part, you will, probably, prefer to ask some other person. But, if you do not find one that suits you, and, of course, you will not want a sketch of a figure so important to our era unless you like it much, I can say that it is my present plan to return to Paris next winter and that then I shall probably be[n] willing to engage for sketches of George Sand, La Mennais, and, if you wish, them Beranger and Le Roux. I have some ideas which please me in relation to all four. But I do not care to express them unless I can do so to my mind, and in consecutive sketches.

In case you ask another, the best engraved[n] portrait of George Sand is from the picture by Charpentier but none[n] of them are good.[2] They all make her face too coarse or too tragic. She has really a noble face, and not tragic at all.

Of La Mennais David the Sculptor owns the best engraving.[3] I was told it is now needful to apply to him by writing, if you want a copy. This is hear say. I could not find in the shops[n] a good one for myself and had no time to write to M. David after receiving yr letter[n] before leaving Paris.

At the same time that you wrote to me first about your Journal, Mazzini wrote to me about the Peoples[4] I thought at first it was the same request as his name was on your list of contributors and answered in the affirmative. I suppose it makes no difference to you as the two journals have, of course, different sets of readers. If I find any thing to write about Italy that might seem of value to Mazzini, I will send it to him, if any thing more likely to interest you, it shall be yours. But I hardly hope to write any thing, the impressions are too numerous and important. I may not be able to write of them at all till I am elsewhere.

Remember me to Mr Howitt and to Anna Mary. I hope happy hours in Rome are in store for her. Please tell Miss Fox I have seen Miss Raincock, but not yet her pictures.[5] Mr and Mrs S. and Eddie send much love, all are very well now We always think in connection with you of others of your friendly circle, of Dr Smith, the Misses Gillies, of Gertrude.[6] Will you write a line to let me know how you all are and whether you shall ask another to write the sketch of Me Sand and, if so, who it shall be. I am anxious England should have one in the true feeling I should be proud and pleased if it were for me to give it. Me Sand personally inspired me with warm admiration and esteem; she would have done so, if I had read no word of hers. Adieu yours with friendliest faith and good will

MARGARET FULLER

I gave Mr Nicauel a French gentleman an introduction to you. If he delivers it you will find him possessed of valuable and accurate information as to the Parisian world.

Could you ascertain for me, whereabouts Mrs Browning, Elizh Barrett, is in Italy If I go near I am anxious to see her. Address me here Care Torlonia and Co.

ALS (MeHi).

other cause] other c⟨ourse⟩ause
But such do] But ⟨it does⟩ ↑ such do ↓
that they] that ⟨it⟩ ↑ they ↓
probably be] probably ↑ be ↓
best engraved] best ↑ engraved ↓
Charpentier but none] Charpentier ⟨for th⟩ ↑ but none ↓
find in the shops] find ↑ in the shops ↓
David after receiving yr letter] David ↑ after receiving yr letter ↓

1. Matilda Hays's translation of Sand's *The Last Aldini* was favorably reviewed in the *People's Journal* 3 (1847): 65–66.

2. Auguste Charpentier (1813–80) was a painter who was known for his paintings of writers and actors: Dumas, Sand, Rachel, and Scott *(Dictionnaire de biographie française)*.

3. Pierre-Jean David d'Angers (1788–1856) was a sculptor who was known for his busts of Bentham, Goethe, and Victor Hugo and for his medallions of many contemporary writers.

4. Despite his contractual obligation to write for the *People's Journal*, William Howitt was planning the first volume of his own magazine, *Howitt's Journal of Literature and Popular Progress*. It ran from January 1847 through June 1848 (Carl Ray Woodring, *Victorian Samplers: William and Mary Howitt* [Lawrence, Kan., 1952], pp. 127–28).

5. Sophia Raincock lived in Rome and painted figurative subjects there from 1847 to 1873 (Christopher Newall Wood, *Dictionary of Victorian Paintings* [Woodbridge, England, 1978], p. 385).

6. Thomas Southwood Smith (1788–1861) was an Edinburgh minister, doctor, philanthropist, and reformer. An authority on fever and infectious diseases, he was an early advocate of dissection. Jeremy Bentham left his body to Smith, who kept the fully dressed skeleton in his office *(DNB)*. The Misses Gillies are Margaret and her sister, Mary Leman Gillies (1800?–1870), a writer of tales for the *People's Journal (DNB;* Haight, *George Eliot Letters,* 5:113). Gertrude Hill (1837–1923) was Smith's granddaughter. In 1865 she married Charles Lewes, George Henry Lewes's son (Gordon S. Haight, *George Eliot: A Biography* [New York, 1968], pp. 381, 593).

664.   To Thomas Hicks

Rome
23d April
47.

Dear Youth

You do not come to see me, so I can think of no way but this which is so awkward to pay the little debt of the other day. I do not know what you paid, if more than this money, you must tell me.

I do not understand why you do not seek me more. You said you were too hard at work and had not time. I tried to believe you, because you seem to me one[n] who always wishes to speak the truth exactly, but I could not. I can always find time to see any one I wish to; it seems to me it is the same with every one.[1]

You are the only one whom I have seen here in whose eye I recognized one of my own kindred. I want to know and to love you and to have you love me; you said you had no friendliness of nature but that is not true; you are precisely one to need the music, the recognition of kindred minds. How can you let me pass you by, without full and free communication. I do not understand it, unless you are occupied by some other strong feeling. Very soon I must go from here, do not let me go without giving me some of your life. I wish this for both our sakes, for mine, because I have so lately been severed from congenial companionship, that I am suffering for want of it, for yours because I feel as if I had something precious to leave in your charge.

When we are together it does not seem to me, as if you were insensible to all this? Am I mistaken yet, after I had been with you, I could not meet you the next day as I wanted to, at the Palazzo Borghese I mean. I wanted to speak to you with frank affection, and I could not. Something prevents what is it? Answer

AL (MH: fMS Am 1086 [9:130]); MsC (MH: fMS Am 1086 [Works, 1:211–13]). Published in *Signs* 2 (1976): 457, and Chevigny, p. 425.

Thomas Hicks. National Portrait Gallery, Smithsonian Institution, Washington, D.C.; gift of Dr. and Mrs. Jacob Terney.

Thomas Hicks (1823–90), a Pennsylvania-born artist, was living in Rome. In 1849 he returned to the United States and became a distinguished portrait painter *(DAB)*. Fuller described his work rather coolly: "His pictures are full of life, and give the promise of some real achievements in Art" *(New-York Daily Tribune,* 5 August 1847).

Chevigny first identified the recipient (pp. 423–24, and in "The Long Arm of Censorship: Myth-making in Margaret Fuller's Time and Our Own," Signs 2 [1976]: 450–60).
me one] me ⟨like⟩ one
1. In his reply of 4 May (MH), Hicks said: "I would like to tell you all about myself, you would then see that there is but little fire in the hut and that could you enter you would find but a few embers on the hearth of a lonely ambitious man. . . . You speak of my youth; is it by years then that *life* is measured? Do you not perceive that my heart has grown grey?"

665.   To William H. Channing

Rome, 7 May 1847

I write not to you about these countries, of the famous people I see, of magnificent shows and places. All these things are only to me an illuminated margin on the text of my inward life. Earlier, they would have been more. Art is not important to me now. I like only what little I find that is transcendentally good, and even with that feel very familiar and calm. I take interest in the state of the people, their manners, the state of the race in them. I see the future dawning; it is in important aspects Fourier's future. But I like no Fourierites; they are terribly wearisome here in Europe; the tide of things does not wash through them as violently as with us, and they have time to run in the tread-mill of system. Still, they serve this great future which I shall not live to see. I must be born again.

ELfr, from *Memoirs,* 2:209. Published in Chevigny, p. 427.

666.   To Evert A. Duyckinck

Rome
23d May 1847.

Dear Mr Duyckinck,
I thought I should receive a note from you or Mr Mathews, but no! I am obliged to be content with reading your news in the Literary World,

of which some numbers have reached Rome. I regret only that signatures are not attached to the pieces there. I recognize the authors of some, but of many not.

Tell Mr Mathews that thus far I vainly seek Mr and Mrs Browning here in Italy; nobody seems to know where they are, and I console myself for not seeing them by the hope that they are in some solitude of Italian beauty and Italian leisure, enjoying themselves as none can who keep upon the beaten track of travel.

Admirable as Browning's sketches of Italian scenery and character seemed before, they seem far finer now that I am close to the objects. The best representation of the spirit of Italy which our day affords.

It is difficult to speak with any truth of Italy: it requires *genius, talent,* which is made to serve most purposes now, entirely fails here.

I crowded your brother with many messages, but there is one subject of which I spoke that I ought to mention to yourself. It is whether you would like Mr Wheaton, son of Mr W. formerly U. S. ambassador at Berlin, as a correspondent to your journal.[1] He will send you some essay as specimen. I saw nothing of his writing, but he seems a young man of refined aspiring mind, and has great opportunities for observation. For the rest you will judge from what he sends. I merely present his name and wish to be received in some good journal on good terms, and having thus presented him must curtsey my adieu as having already written more than time permits.

Truly yours

S. M. Fuller.

I have just seen in the "Literary World" a notice of Mr Griswold's attack on my judgment of "Witchcraft."[2] Did your brother mention how much interest the extracts excited in Paris? My essay was translated for "La[n] Revue Independante" but without any of the quotations in verse, as the translators did not feel able to render them adequately. Those who read them were French, who read English!

ALS (NN-M). *Addressed:* To / Evert A Duyckinck Esq / City of New York, / U. S. A.

for "La] for ⟨the Independ⟩ "La

1. Henry Wheaton (1785–1848) of Providence graduated from Brown and embarked on a distinguished career as a lawyer, diplomat, and writer. Minister to Prussia beginning in 1837, Wheaton negotiated several tariff treaties. He was a noted authority on international law *(DAB)*. Robert Wheaton (1828–51) was his only surviving son (Clarence E. Peirce, "Genealogical Notes on the Wheaton Family," Rhode Island Historical Society, p. 71).

2. In his *Prose Writers of America* (Philadelphia, 1847 [1846]), Rufus Griswold continued a quarrel with Mathews by sneering at Fuller and the excerpt from "a wretched drama, called *Witchcraft,*" which she had published in *Papers on Literature and Art.* Fuller,

Griswold said, "commends or censures every thing with about an equal degree of earnestness" (p. 538). A writer for the *Literary World* of 27 March 1847 (possibly Duyckinck) defended both the play and Fuller, calling her "a species of antagonist of whom a man of moderate abilities should be particularly careful, in the contests of the pen" (p. 183).

667. To Mary Rotch

Rome
23d May 1847.

Dear Aunt Mary,

it is very long since I have written, but very often that I think of you. This is such a rich book, this of Europe, I know not how to spare time from studying it to write to my friends at home. Yet I hope their love and thoughts follow me. I know yours do. Beside your two letters, I have heard of you through W. Channing, Mother and others; very sweet to me was your little intercourse with Mother; it gave her a great deal of pleasure; do see her again if you go to Boston.

The only thing wanting in your letters has been that you should speak more particularly of your health. Although I know it must be better or you could not do the things I hear of your doing, I want to know particularly about it. Will you not write to me of that and our other topics of mutual interest and direct to care of *Greene and Co* Paris. I think now I shall remain abroad another year. I cannot content myself without;— a single year is so entirely inadequate to see all which I wish to see.

All winter in Paris, although my life was rich in novelties of value, I was not well; the climate was too damp for me, and then I had too much intellectual excitement of the same kind as at home. I need a respite, a long leisure of enjoyment, a kind of springtime to renovate my faculties. But Paris is the very focus of the intellectual activity of Europe, there I found every topic intensified, clarified, reduced to portable dimensions: there is the cream of all the milk, but I am not strong enough to live on cream, at present. I learned much, I suffered to leave Paris, but I find myself better here, where the climate is so enchanting, the people so indolently joyous, and the objects of contemplation so numerous and admirable, that one cannot pass the time better than by quietly *looking* one's fill. It is entirely the [   ] of the Past. The tendency of the present Pope to Reform gives an interest by drawing out the feelings of the people, but it is not sufficient to affect importantly the state of things in Italy which presents the most striking contrast to

The Letters of Margaret Fuller

that of our country, and, *as* a contrast, is for the time desirable especially for me who find invitation to a trance of repose here.[1] Its influence is so good that I have had the headach only twice during a two months' abode in Rome and I am really strong now.

How I wish, dear Aunt Mary, that you could come to Europe with Mary and, if it was not for the voyage, the rest would not be difficult. When Mary does come, let is be with very sure friends. My travelling companions are extremely amiable, else should I suffer, for the friction of travelling is very great upon the temper.

Of the gorgeous pageant of the Roman church, I have now seen enough to be thoroughly sated It is imposing often, but oftener frivolous, and must I think be very oppressive to the present Pope, who seems truly a thoughtful noble minded man. I shall tell one or two good anecdotes of him in my next letter to the Tribune.[2]

And now adieu, dear Aunt Mary, and Mary. I had but a quarter of an hour today to write this letter just to say dont forget to think affectionately of yours in the distance

MARGARET.

ALS (MH: fMS Am 1086 [9:131]); MsCfr (MH: fMS Am 1086 [Works, 1:57–59]); MsCfr (MH: bMS Am 1280 [111, p. 90]). Published in part in *JMN*, 11:474. *Addressed:* To / Miss Mary Rotch / New Bedford / Mass / U. S. A.

1. Giovanni Maria Mastai-Ferretti (1792–1878) became Pope Pius IX in 1846. He immediately raised hopes for liberal reforms when he freed political prisoners. By May 1847 he was the focus for the rapidly developing Italian nationalist movement. Fuller reflected the faith of many progressives in the *Tribune*: "He is a man of noble and good aspect, who, it is easy to see, has set his heart upon doing something solid for the benefit of Man" (*New-York Daily Tribune*, 5 August 1847). These expectations intensified her revulsion when the pope failed to pursue his reforms and became the instrument of reaction.

2. In the same issue of the *Tribune*, Fuller described an illuminated procession that wound from the Piazza del Popolo up the Quirinal Hill to thank the pope for allowing the formation of a representative council.

668. To Maria Rotch

Rome,
23d May 47

My dear Maria,

Some months have passed since I received a letter from you; it gave me true pleasure, yet I have not been able to find time to answer it, nor can I now do more than say I thank you, dear Maria and wish you would write again. You so late returned may easily see how difficult it is to write, a difficulty heightened in my case, by the miserly feeling which I have about my time, desiring to spend every moment of it on the objects before me. I feel, too, that as to the mere outside of my experience, those who are interested in me find it in the Tribune letters; further experiences I shall probably write out in another form, and my friends will have their full share yet in what belongs to me.

But I want to hear from you again, for you are to me an object of permanent interest. Direct to Care of Greene and Co. Paris. I expect to remain abroad another year.

You asked about the Walshes.[1] I found them very pleasant and kind, but they had no habit of assembling people at their house when I was in Paris. Mr W. was ill and I always found them at home, but much alone.

I had some very agreeable connections in Paris, but chiefly among foreigners. I do not cultivate much the society of Amerns; they generally lose the benefit of being abroad, by herding too much together. Here I often see Mr Terry, who has lived here so long that he knows Italy like an Italn.[2] He remembers you and Frank with much pleasure.

I am enchanted with Italy. England and Scotland and France were more attractive than I expected. Italy fulfils my hopes; it could not^n do more, it has been the dream of my life.

Adieu, dear Maria. If we ever meet again, I will tell you many things, but at present have only time for Your friend as ever

S. M. FULLER.

ALS (MH: fMS Am 1086 [9:112]). *Addressed:* Miss Maria Rotch / Butternuts / N. Y.

could not] could ↑ not ↓

1. Robert Walsh (1784–1859) was an editor, teacher, and writer who became consul general to France in 1844. His wife was Elizabeth Clark Stocker (1797–1865), whom he married in 1834 (*DAB*; *Columbian Centinel*, 12 November 1834; John Clark, *Records of the Descendants of Hugh Clark of Watertown, Mass., 1640–1866* [Boston, 1866], p. 86).

2. Luther Terry (1813–69) of Enfield, Connecticut, settled in Italy in 1837 and pursued a career in painting. In 1861 he married Louisa Ward Crawford, Julia Ward Howe's sister, the widow of Thomas Crawford (George C. Groce and David H. Wallace, *The New-York Historical Society's Dictionary of Artists in America, 1564–1860* [New Haven, 1957]).

669. To Ralph Waldo Emerson

[I] Florence, 20 June 1847

I have just come hither from Rome. Every minute, day and night, there is something to be seen or done at Rome, which we cannot bear to lose.

We lived on the Corso, and all night long, after the weather became fine, there was conversation or music before my window. I never seemed really to sleep while there, and now, at Florence, where there is less to excite, and I live in a more quiet quarter, I feel as if I needed to sleep all the time, and cannot rest as I ought, there is so much to do.

I now speak French fluently, though not correctly, yet well enough to make my thoughts avail in the cultivated society here, where it is much spoken. But to know the common people, and to feel truly in Italy, I ought to speak and understand the spoken Italian well, and I am now cultivating this sedulously. If I remain, I shall have, for many reasons, advantages for observation and enjoyment, such as are seldom permitted to a foreigner.

I forgot to mention one little thing rather interesting. At the *Miserere* of the Sistine chapel, I sat beside Goethe's favorite daughter-in-law, Ottilia, to whom I was introduced by Mrs. Jameson.[1] [   ] [II] I am glad to hear of the new journal which will answer to a deep want, though I doubt by the list of names you send me, the danger there will not be a sufficient range and diversity of power to make it a fair journal.[2] Yet how precious was the old Dial, with all its faults. I felt this indeed after being in England. It had been manna in the wilderness to people there.

I: ELfr, from *Memoirs*, 2:210; II: MsCfr (MH: bMS Am 1280 [111, p. 124]). Published in part in Van Doren, pp. 289–90, and *JMN*, 11:480.

These fragments are joined on the supposition that Fuller would have written but one letter to Emerson in the last week of June. The notebook fragment is dated merely "Florence June 1847."

1. Ottilie von Pogwisch married Goethe's son, Julius August, in 1817. Anna Brownell Jameson was the author of several books on literature and art.

2. In April Emerson had told Fuller of the plans for a new journal, *The Massachusetts Quarterly Review*. Among the dozen men at the meeting were Bronson Alcott, William Henry Channing, Charles Sumner, and Theodore Parker (who became the force behind the magazine when it was launched in 1847) (Rusk, *Letters of RWE*, 3:394).

670.   To Richard F. Fuller

Casa Greca
via Sa Apollonia
Florence,
1st July 1847

My dear Richard,

I cannot remember when I wrote last, but it must have been some weeks ago; the two months passed at Rome seemed but a moment; the five weeks since have been equally crowded; my utmost strength and spirits suffice only to sieze a very small portion of what each day presents; the riches of Italy seem immeasurable and I cannot endure to go away without my fair share.

I have here recd and answered a letter from Arthur giving the family news. By some mistake our letters by the last steamerⁿ have not been sent here. I hope to find them at Venice where I shall arrive the 10th or 11th of this month, taking Ravenna, Bolognaⁿ and Ferrara by the way. I hope much there will be one from you and one from Mother. I begin at moments to feel a yearning for the loved familiar faces, but I shall not yield to it.

My first object in this letter being business, I will write about that first as it is very important to me now and there is no knowing how many interruptions may occur to prevent my finishing the letter as I would.

Mr and Mrs Spring think now they shall go into Germany for only a few weeks. I do not wish to go in that hurried way, am equally unsatisfied to fly through Italyⁿ and shall therefore leave them in Switzerland take aⁿ servant to accompany me, and return hither and hence to Rome, for the autumn, perhaps the winter. I should always suffer the pain of Tantalus thinking of Rome, if I could not see it more thoroughly than I have as yet even begun to, for it was all *outside* the two months, just finding out where objects were. I had only just begun to live with their life when I was obliged to leave.[1]

This prospect presents many charms, but it leaves me alone in the midst of a strange land. While with Mr S. he managed all my little affairs and, if my own money had failed, I could not have been at a loss. But now any failure in that way would place me in a desolate condition and I want to be *"forehanded"* and quite tranquil, at least on that side, for there is no one in Italy to whom I should feel entitled to go for aid. Arthur has written me that the death of Uncle Abraham makes it possible to raise some money for me soon if I want it.[2] If you can now get five hundred dollars for me, either advanced by Mother or otherwise, I want it remitted direct to *Greene and Co Bankers, Paris.* I say if you *can,* but truly I depend upon it, and I believe dear Mother will let me have it, if there is no better way. You will receive this letter early in August. I want you to remit by the steamer of 15th August [the] money to Greene and Co and have a credit sent to me hereⁿ at Florence to care of J. Mozier Esq. Sculptor.^{n,3} I shall come to his house when I return here in Septr. And write to me yourself, dear R. at the same time.

I say no more but rely on your affection and business habits that I shall not suffer anxiety and annoyance here alone amid strangers A credit from Greene and Co is the same as money. There are other ways, but I want the most simple taken, as I have not much head for these things.

I find myself happily situated here in many respects. The Marchioness *Arconati Visconti*,[4] to whom I brought a letter from a friend of hers in France has been good to me as a sister and introduced me to many interesting acquaintance. But this Me Arconati is herself the most interesting[n] The sculptors Greenough and Powers I have seen much and well,[5] other acquaintance I possess less known to fame, but not less attractive.[n] Florence is not like Rome; at first I could not bear the change, yet for the study of the fine arts, it is a still richer place. Worlds of thought have risen in my mind, some time you will have light from all these stars. Meanwhile I must pause it is almost dark. I have no more time. Write now on single sheets like this and without envelope; they charge in Italy enormous postage and not by weight but on each piece of paper. Adeiu my beloved brother; all the family be specially remembered if I have not room to say Love. Forgive all omissions now in my letters; they are inevitable My next will be to Mother.

Ever yours

MARGARET

ALS (MH: fMS Am 1086 [9:138]); MsC (MH: fMS Am 1086 [Works, 2:809–17]). Published in part in *Memoirs*, 2:210–11. *Addressed:* Mr Richard F. Fuller / 6 State St Boston / Massachusetts / U. S. of America. *Postmarks:* 10 Juil / Ponte [   ] / Firenzi 3 Lug 1847; New York Ship Aug 24. *Endorsed:* F. Margaret Fuller / 1. July 1847.

letters by the last steamer] letters ↑ by the last steamer ↓

Ravenna, Bologna] Ravenna, ⟨Ra⟩ Bologna

way, am equally unsatisfied to fly through Italy] way, ↑ am equally unsatisfied to fly through Italy ↓

Switzerland take a] Switzerland ⟨and⟩ ↑ take a ↓

me here] me ↑ here ↓

Esq. Sculptor.] Esq. ↑ Sculptor. ↓

But this Me Arconati is herself the most interesting] ↑ But this Me Arconati is herself the most interesting ↓

less attractive.] less ⟨interesting⟩. ↑ attractive ↓

1. According to Emelyn Story, Ossoli had proposed to Fuller during her first stay in Rome. Her desire to return thus was strengthened by her affection for him (*Memoirs*, 2:283).

2. At his death on 6 April, Abraham Williams Fuller left an estate valued at $61,337 in addition to $20,805 in real estate. After leaving bequests of $1,000 to several relatives and friends, he left a "ninth share" of the remainder to be divided among Timothy Fuller's children. On 11 August 1847 Margaret received her share: $214.28 (Suffolk Probate, no. 35086).

3. Joseph Mozier (1813–70) was a Vermont businessman who became a sculptor. He permanently settled in Italy in 1845 (Banks, *Genealogical Notes*, pp. 34–39). Hawthorne's report of Mozier's hostile comments on Fuller and Ossoli created a controversy in the 1880s when Julian Hawthorne published them in his biography (Julian Hawthorne, *Nathaniel Hawthorne and His Wife* [Boston, 1884], 1:259–62).

4. Costanza Trotti Bentivoglio (1800–1871) married a cousin, the marchese Giuseppe Arconati-Visconti (1797–1873), in 1818. She was for many years a worker for Italian independence. Fuller considered her her most trusted European friend (Alessandro Luzio, *Profili biografici e bozzetti storici* [Milan, 1927], pp. 1–60).

5. Horatio Greenough (1805–52), whom Fuller had known in Cambridge, had settled in Florence *(DAB)*. She commented favorably on both Greenough and Hiram Powers in the *Tribune:* "Greenough has in clay a David which promises high beauty and nobleness. . . . In busts Powers seems to me unrivalled; still, he ought not to spend his best years on an employment which cannot satisfy his ambition nor develop his powers" *(New-York Daily Tribune,* 11 September 1847).

671. To George Curtis

July 2 1847

My dear George,

I thought you would come and bid good bye, but perhaps you forgot we were going. For Cranch's letter thanks, please give my love to them. I shall write when I can If Cranch's guitar does not get to him any other way I shall try to take it when I go back to Rome.[1] Come to Venice soon and then we shall see you before parting. With regards to Burril, and Mr Hunzelt yours

MARGARET F.

ALS (Universiteits-Bibliotheek, Amsterdam, Holland).

1. George Curtis (who in 1856 married Anna Shaw) had come to Europe with his brother Burrill and Christopher and Elizabeth Cranch. After a tour of southern Italy early in 1847, Curtis spent the summer in Venice (Milne, *George William Curtis,* pp. 38–39).

672. To Marcus and Rebecca Spring

Venice 10 July 1847

My dear friends,

Dominico brought me just now this letter. It looked so short and came so quick that I feared some sudden ill news from your little Jeanie and I ventured to break the seal. I hope you will excuse this, as I looked at it in such a way as to be sure I could do no harm. I only read the first line as that showed me it was a common letter, I mean not one that announced a misfortune.

George Curtis by Samuel Laurence. Staten Island Institute of Arts and Sciences. Photo by Geoffrey Clements.

Anna Shaw Curtis, by Samuel Laurence. Staten Island Institute of Arts
and Sciences. Photo by Geoffrey Clements.

Natural tears I shed at parting,[1] but tried to dry them with the thought we had certainly done what was best under the circumstances. The excessive beauty of last night and my visit to the Madonna del Orto have made me regret for you that you did not stay longer, but you will find fine things where you are and I much hope better health for dear Marcus.[2] For me, All seems to arrange itself pleasantly. On returning to the house I asked the polite clerk to show me the cheaper room. I did not like it and said I shall keep the one I have at present but I think you[n] ask too much— He replies "pay what you please I certainly do not wish to disturb you for such a trifle as a franc or two a day!! and accordingly they had the two rooms put in fine order so that one is like a little vestibule. How much *iced water* is to be charged on for[n] all this gallantry I do not yet know. I went to St Marks to pay the three zwanzigers. Mr Sparks joined me and we sat at Florian's together. Cecco is the pearl of devotion. He has got his black top for me thinking I shall so have a more retired ladylike[n] air now I am alone, and I acquiesed and find it cool enough. He has taken me to your fruit man at the Rialto— stands guard behind me while I buy and carries it to the boat when bought. Addio dear friends— good Spirits attend your steps I know— Accept love for yourselves and two kisses for Eddie from

M.

Cecco really mourns for Eddie. He wanted to know last night where I thought *the piccolo* was *then*— and if he would never come back. He was afraid not— "as he had heard him say "e l'ultima Canal Grande!"

MsC (MH: fMS Am 1086 [9:218]); MsC (MH: fMS Am 1086 [Works, 1:213–15]).
The Works copy varies from the text in the following ways:
but I think you] but think you
charged on for] charged for
retired ladylike] retired and lady like
    1. A version of Milton's description of Adam and Eve leaving Eden: "Some natural tears they dropped, but wiped them soon" (John Milton, *Complete Poems and Major Prose*, ed. Merritt Y. Hughes [New York, 1957], p. 468).
    2. The church of the Madonna dell'Orto in Venice was the parish church of the painter Tintoretto, three of whose paintings hang there (*Grant Allen's Historical Guides: Venice* [London, 1898], p. 260).

673. To Richard F. Fuller

[Late July 1847]

My dear Richard,
    I received your letter at Venice, and shed many tears on first reading

of your engagement.[1] Not that I know any thing against it, except that you yourself say it is hasty, and in the present arrangements of society a choice of a companion for life acts as a Fate on the whole of life

I know nothing of Anna De Rose, except that I have heard she was a lovely girl, but of you I know that you have acted chiefly from the need of love. It does not at all follow that you are mistaken in the choice of its object; but I feel far less security, than I did in the case of Eugene for instance. I felt sure with him that his companion would possess some, if not all, of the qualities requisite for his happiness and good.

With you, I could[n] wish that this engagement might rest private for awhile, and that you both might fairly try how deep the affinity is, before rivetting the bond. Tell your Anna that I say this if it is not too late. For the woman, even more than for the man, it is important that the foundation for this structure of domestic life be deep placed and impervious to flood or other undermining cause. Beyond this I could have nothing to say. Should you indeed have found *the* friend you need I should greatly rejoice, for I feel the entire justice of what you say of your needing the tie, and that there ought to be an atmosphere for the flowers of your nature and a source of inspiration before it is too late. God grant it may be so. In your cause there is much to gain and much to lose; you can do and be much, if you are wise and do not draw upon yourself adverse influences.

For myself I should have been glad if fate had united you and[n] for your own happiness with that other Anna whom I loved. I think that might have been if you had not been *hasty*. But I have long ceased, if ever I began, to be su[re] that I know what is best for another in such cases. For you, I shall abide by your view; if you are sure all is well for you, I shall repose upon that surety.

You have desired I should write sincerely and I have done so. You have also asked me not to write coldly, and I think it cannot so affect you. I feel such sincere warm tenderness, such a warm hope for your happiness and such a conviction of the need in every human heart for love. Be sure you take it as meant, my dear brother, and let no word of mine disturb, needlessly, happy days. If I were with you, I am sure it could not, but letters are awkward things especially written in such haste and with so many interruptions as mine have to be.

Here, Riva di Trento, for some brief hours in sight of the Tyrol, I have taken a quiet room, thinking in a place where I was unknown, and where there was nothing, except the mountains to distract my attention, I could write a number of letters. But here comes just as I was in the middle of this and was thinking of you an Irish gentleman who is staying here and hearing from the Captain of the *Benace* that an English lady came up the lake alone thought it would be a good plan to call.

For the rest, he made a pleasant talk, and brought with him his daughter a pretty sweet girl.

To other counts of your letter I will answer at Milan. I hope to find letters there and wish to hear again, if might be before closing up the parcel for America. Commend me with affect good will to your Anna and hold me always your faithful sister

M.

I have marked with the pen the window of my room at Venice. The first week there I was ill, but the last eight or nine days were glorious. In the gondola at that window or in the galleries and churches to see the great works of Venitian art I passed happier and more thoughtful hours than at all before in Europe.

ALS (MH: fMS Am 1086 [9:129]). *Addressed:* Richard F. Fuller / 6 State St. Boston / State of Massachusetts / U. S. A.

I could] I ⟨?⟩ could
you and] you ↑ and ↓
1. His fiancée was Anna de Rose, a nineteen-year-old teacher in Canton, Massachusetts. The engagement ended abruptly in 1848 when she ran away from home "with a female friend" (Fuller, *Recollections*, p. 87; Richard F. Fuller to Margaret Fuller, 20 February 1848, MH).

674. To Margarett C. Fuller

Lago di Garda 1 August 1847

Do not let what I have written disturb you as to my health. I have rested now, and am as well as usual. This advantage I derive from being alone, that, if I feel the need of it, I can stop.

I left Venice four days ago; have seen well Vicenza, Verona, Mantua, and am reposing, for two nights and a day, in this tranquil room which overlooks the beautiful Lake of Garda. The air is sweet and pure, and I hear no noise except the waves breaking on the shore.

I think of you a great deal, especially when there are flowers. Florence was all flowers. I have many magnolias and jasmines. I always wish you could see them. The other day, on the island of San Lazaro, at the Armenian Convent, where Lord Byron used to go, I thought of you, seeing the garden full of immense oleanders in full bloom.[1] One sees them everywhere at Venice.

ELfr, from *Memoirs*, 2:212; MsCfr (MH: bMS Am 1280 [111, p. 33]). Published in part in *JMN*, 11:465.

1. The Armenian Mekhitarist convent was founded in 1717 on the island of San Lazzaro, "near the Lido about two miles from the Piazza San Marco." Byron wrote Thomas Moore that he was "studying daily, at an Armenian monastery, the Armenian language" (Leslie A. Marchand, *Byron* [New York, 1957], p. 671; Leslie A. Marchand, ed., "*So Late into the Night*": *Byron's Letters and Journals* [Cambridge, Mass., 1976], 5:130).

675.   To Marcus Spring

Milan 9th Aug. 1847

My dear Marcus,

I arrived here late the night of the 4th and sending to the banker's found your letter. It was a great comfort to know that every thing was going so well with you and especially that the air was doing you so much good. But I was disappointed to find no indications of your plans after leaving Vienna because it was was on my arrival become impossible to write to you so that you could receive it there[n] and thus I cannot hope to see you again in Switzerland, nor do I know how to send this letter unless[n] through Greene and Co which will make it a long time in reaching you.

I am glad Rebecca and Eddie shed some tears for me. I assure you they were not uncalled for though I had made up my mind to part with you all I had hoped to do so under different circumstances when the greater part of my journey was[n] performed and I had only to return to Florence, when I felt in better health than I did in Venice and when I had heard from home to know[n] that I should be sure of[n] a remittance in money.

Altho' I have been much alone in our own country, yet it was never as it is here where there is no one on whom I can call for aid in any case. Now I can only hope it will not be too much needed.

I remained at Venice near a week after your departure, got pretty well and tranquil again, and saw all the pictures if not enough yet pretty well. My journey here was very profitable to the mind. Vicenza, Verona, Mantua, Lago di Guarda, I saw really[n] well, and much, much there is to see,[n] but at Brescia I was taken ill with fever and affection of the stomach. I cannot tell you how much I suffered in my mind, especially when it seemed to me it was affecting my head. I had no medicine, nothing I could do except entirely to abstain from food and drink cold water. The second day I had a bed made in a carriage and came on here so[n] I am now pretty well only very weak.

I am disappointed as to counsel from Madame Arconati. Her nephew is just dead She came on here post, to go to the family I saw her a few minutes; she was in distress and overwhelmed with fatigue, but did what she could for me, leaving me in charge of a friend who is most polite, but to whom I cannot speak frankly as I could to her. I shall see her again bye and bye but too late for my plans. I find myself obliged to retain Dominico and I cannot trust him in the least as to money. He is in other respects a Miani, but I have not time to speak on that now for the clock strikes for the mail and I have nearly killed myself finishing a letter for the Tribune. Suffice it to say that he has made it so expensive for me that I find myself obliged to curtail my journey and give up many things on which I had most set my heart for fear I shall not have money to get back to Florence. This is cruel to me. I shall I know regret it always. But what I most wish of you, my dear Marcus, is to write to Mr. Mozier at Florence and ask him to let me have money there, if I do not receive my remittances, until I do. Write without delay for under these circumstances I may be back early in September, and it would pain me much to ask him myself. I have received no letter here for either of us. I do not know where any thing is. You know I felt entirely uncertain about money from Mr. Manning— I have written to my brother but if any accident should occur[n] to my first letter it will be very long before I can receive any thing— [   ]

My only reliance is on your kindness ever prompt and as sure as any thing can be that rests on a letter and a letter you may not even receive before my arrival in Florence. Adieu[n] dear friends. Of other things I will write when in a happier frame of mind— Yours affectionately ever

MARGARET

MsCfr (MH: fMS Am 1086 [9:218]); MsCfr (MH: fMS Am 1086 [Works, 1:217–21]). Published in part in *Memoirs*, 2:212–13.
The Works copy varies from the text in the following ways:
it there] my letter then
unless] except
journey was] journey should have been
to know] to be sure
should be sure of] should have
saw really] saw very
to see,] to be seen
here so.] here
should occur] should happen
Adieu] Addio

676.   To Ralph Waldo Emerson

Milan, 10 August 1847

Since writing you from Florence, I have passed the mountains; two full, rich days at Bologna; one at Ravenna; more than a fortnight at Venice, intoxicated with the place, and with Venetian art, only to be really felt and known in its birth-place. I have passed some hours at Vicenza, seeing mainly the Palladian structures; a day at Verona,—a week had been better; seen Mantua, with great delight; several days in Lago di Garda,—truly happy days there; then to Brescia, where I saw the Titians, the exquisite Raphael, the Scavi, and the Brescian Hills.[1] I could charm you by pictures, had I time.

To-day, for the first time, I have seen Manzoni.[2] Manzoni has spiritual efficacy in his looks; his eyes glow still with delicate tenderness, as when he first saw Lucia, or felt them fill at the image of Father Cristoforo. His manners are very engaging, frank, expansive; every word betokens the habitual elevation of his thoughts; and (what you care for so much) he says distinct, good things; but you must not expect me to note them down. He lives in the house of his fathers, in the simplest manner. He has taken the liberty to marry a new wife for his own pleasure and companionship, and the people around him do not like it, because she does not, to their fancy, make a good pendant to him.[3] But I liked her very well, and saw why he married her. They asked me to return often, if I pleased, and I mean to go once or twice, for Manzoni seems to like to talk with me.

ELfr, from *Memoirs*, 2:213–14.

1. The Palladian structures are the architectural works of Andrea Palladio (1508–80), who was raised in Vicenza. Reacting against baroque ideas, Palladio recased the basilica in Vicenza and built a number of villas, palaces, and the Teatro Olimpico (*OCA*). Brescia, which sits at the foot of imposing hills, is the home of a polyptych that Titian painted in 1522. It is mounted over the high altar of the eighteenth-century church of Saints Nazaro and Celso (Edward Hutton, *The Cities of Lombardy* [New York, 1912], pp. 192–93). The Raphael is *Christ Blessing*, a small wooden panel painted between 1502 and 1505. Fuller saw it in the collection of Count Paolo Tosio (Luitpold Dussler, *Raphael: A Critical Catalogue of His Pictures, Wall-Paintings, and Tapestries*, trans. Sebastian Cruft [London, 1971], p. 17). The "Scavi" are excavations of Roman Brescia. In 1820 the remains of a temple of Hercules, said to have been erected by Vespasian in A.D. 72, had been uncovered (Augustus J. C. Hare, *Cities of Northern Italy* [New York, 1883], 1:244–45).

2. Alessandro Manzoni (1785–1873), a poet and novelist, was best known for his *I promessi sposi*. He was active in the uprising in Milan in 1848.

3. Teresa Borri (1799–1861) was the widow of count Stefano Decio Stampa. In 1836 Manzoni married her, his first wife having died in 1833. The public was hostile, for they

associated Manzoni with an uncompromising fidelity to his first wife, thanks to his novel. Even such friends as Costanza Arconati were disappointed (Natalia Ginzburg, *La famiglia Manzoni* [Turin, 1983], pp. 157, 312–13; Archibald Colquhoun, *Manzoni and His Times* [London, 1954], pp. 234–41).

677. To [?]

Bellagio, Lake of Como, [22?] August 1847

You do not deceive yourself surely about religion, in so far as that there is a deep meaning in those pangs of our fate which, if we live by faith, will become our most precious possession. "Live for thy faith and thou shalt yet behold it living,"[1] is with me, as it hath been, a maxim.

Wherever I turn, I see still the same dark clouds, with occasional gleams of light. In this Europe how much suffocated life!—a sort of woe much less seen with us. I know many of the noble exiles, pining for their natural sphere; many of them seek in Jesus the guide and friend, as you do. For me, it is my nature to wish to go straight to the Creative Spirit, and I can fully appreciate what you say of the need of our happiness depending on no human being. Can you really have attained such wisdom? Your letter seemed to me very modest and pure, and I trust in Heaven all may be solid.

I am everywhere well received, and high and low take pleasure in smoothing my path. I love much the Italians. The lower classes have the vices induced by long subjection to tyranny; but also a winning sweetness, a ready and discriminating love for the beautiful, and a delicacy in the sympathies, the absence of which always made me sick in our own country. Here, at least, one does not suffer from obtuseness or indifference. They take pleasure, too, in acts of kindness; they are bountiful, but it is useless to hope the least honor in affairs of business. I cannot persuade those who serve me, however attached, that they should not deceive me, and plunder me. They think that is part of their duty towards a foreigner. This is troublesome no less than disagreeable; it is absolutely necessary to be always on the watch against being cheated.

ELfr, from *At Home and Abroad*, ed. Arthur B. Fuller (Boston, 1856), pp. 425–26.

1. In a *Tribune* essay, Fuller attributes this otherwise unidentified saying to Schiller (*New-York Daily Tribune*, 19 February 1847).

Bellagio, Lake Como. By permission of The Huntington Library, San Marino, California.

289

678.   To Jane Tuckerman King

Bellagio, Lake of Como, [22?] August 1847.
The Springs have gone into Germany on their return, and I am alone
here, alone with glorious Italy. Glorious and beautiful she is, as ever my
hopes conceived. How much I shall have to tell you when we meet, —
but now there is no time. Imagine if I do not enjoy being here, in
"Bellagio's woods". From my window I see that which Taylor must have
chosen as Elena's, it belongs to the Villa Serbellini. — [1]

MsCfr (MH: fMS Am 1086 [Works, 1:109]).
The copyist combined this letter with another.

1. Henry Taylor (1800–1886) wrote *Philip Van Artevelde*, a dramatic romance in two
parts (*DNB*). "The Lay of Elena" is a poem-prologue that opens part 2. In it Elena describes her home in "Bellagio's Woods," on the banks of Lake Como.

679.   To Caroline Sturgis

Bellagio,
Lake of Como, 22d August 47.
Dearest Carrie,
I am sorry you never write. I often wish to hear from you and then I
am afraid you will get out of the habit of telling me any thing. It may be
so long before we meet again.
I remember I wrote to you from Rome in the first weeks, when I was
suffering terrible regrets and could not yet find myself at home in
Italy. I do not know whether you ever received that letter, but if not, I
could not go back upon those things.
Rome was much poisoned for me so, but, after a time; its genius tri-
umphed and I became absorbed in its peculiar life. Again I suffered
from parting, and have since resolved to return there and pass at least
a part of the winter
People may write and prate as much as they like about Rome, they
cannot convey thus a portion of its spirit. It must be inhaled wholly,
with the yielding of the whole heart. It is really something transcendant, both spirit and body.
Those last glorious nights in which I wandered about amid the old
walls and columns or sat by the fountains in the Piazza del Popolo, or by
the river, seem worth an age of pain both after and before only one
hates pain in Italy.

Tuscany I did not like so well; it is a great place to study thoughts, the history of character and art. Indeed there I did really begin to study as well as gaze and feel. But I did not like it. Florence is more in its spirit like Boston, than like an Italian city. I knew a good many Italians, but they were busy and intellectual, not like those I had known before. But Florence is full of really good, really great pictures. There first I really saw some of the great masters. Andrea del Sarto, in particular, one sees only there, and he is worth much. His wife, whom he always paints, and for whom he was so infatuated, reminds me of Mrs Greeley; she has just the same bad qualities, and in what is good the same wild nature, the same of what is called deviltry.[1]

Bologna charmed me. This is really an *Italian* city, one in which I should like to live, full of hidden things and also the wonders of art are very great there. The Caracci and their friends had vast force, not much depth, but enough force to occupy for a good while, and Dominichino, when great at all, is very great.[2]

At Bologna I saw a man who seems to me the type of some of George Sand's characters   he knows her well.

Venice was a dream of enchantment! *there* was no disappointment, art and life are one, there is one glow of joy, one deep shade of passionate melancholy. Giorgione, as a man, I care more for now than any of the artists though he had no ideas.[3]

At Venice, the Springs left me, and it was high time, for I had become qui[te] insupportable I was always out of the body, and they, good friends, were *in*. I felt at times a wicked irritation against them for being the persons who took me away from France, which was no fault of theirs. Since I have been alone I ha[ve] grown reasonable again; indee[d] in [the] first week floating about in [a] go[nd]ola, I seemed to find myself again

I was not always alone in Venice, but have come through the fertile plains of Lombardy and counted its treasures seen the Lakes Garda and Maggiore, and a part of Switzerland alone, except for occasional episodes of companionship sometimes romantic enough. Especially [   ] takes me to heart in Europe, and more than ever in Italy.

In Milan I staid awhile and knew some radicals,[n] young and interested in ideas. Here, on[n] the lake, I have fallen into contact with some of the high society, duchesses, marquises and the like. My friend here is a marchioness who bears the name of *Visconti*, by my side I have formed connection with a fair and brilliant Polish lady, born princess *Radzivill*, it is rather pleasant to come a little on the traces of these famous histories, also both these ladies take pleasure in telling me of spheres so unlike mine and do it well. The life here on the lake is precisely what we once at Newbury imagined as being so pleasant; these people have charming villas and gardens on the lake, adorned with fine works of art; they go to see one another in boats; you can be all the time in a boat, if you like. If you want more excitement or wild flowers you climb the mountains. I have been here sometime and shall stay a week longer. I have found soft repose here. Then I return to Rome seeing many things on the way. Do write to me *Care of Greene and Co Paris.* I want a letter from you and am ever yours in love

MARGARET.

I shall go back to Paris by and by, but do not yet know precisely when. If you write soon after receiving this I shall get the letter in R[ome].

ALS (MH: bMS Am 1221 [252]). Published in part in *Memoirs*, 2:216–18, and Chevigny, pp. 428–30. *Addressed:* To / Miss Caroline Sturgis / Care William Sturgis Esq / Boston, Mass / U. S. A.

some radicals,] some radica⟨s⟩ls,
Here, on] Here, ⟨I⟩ on

1. Fuller had long admired the work of Andrea del Sarto (1486–1531). About 1517, Sarto married Lucrezia del Fede (1490?–1570), a widow (John Shearman, *Andrea del Sarto* [Oxford, 1965], pp. 3, 6, 9). Thanks to the comments of Giorgio Vasari, who had briefly been apprenticed to Sarto, Lucrezia had a terrible reputation. She was, said Vasari, a poor daughter of a vicious father, a manipulating, grasping woman who alienated Sarto's friends. These tales are now thought to have been motivated by spite. Fuller was quite familiar with Vasari's *Lives* (*Lives of Seventy of the Most Eminent Painters, Sculptors, and Architects*, ed. E. H. Blashfield et al., trans. Mrs. Jonathan Foster [New York, 1926], 3:251–52).

2. The Carracci were a family of Bolognese painters: Agostino (1557–1602), his brother Annibale (1560–1609), and their cousin Ludovico (1555–1619). They founded the Accademia degli Incamminati at Bologna, the school of "eclectics" that included Il Domenichino, Guido Reni, and Guercino (*OCA*).

3. Il Giorgione (Giorgio Barbarelli) (ca. 1478–1511) was a Venetian painter who influenced Titian.

680.   To J. Westland Marston

Milan, Italy
6th Septr 1847.

My dear Sir,
The other day in an Italian circle of high culture, when the conversation turned on the drama, I spoke of "The Patrician's Daughter" in the terms it merits, and a warm wish was expressed by those present to read it. Although I might gratify this wish by sending to a London bookseller for it, I have thought it might not be unpleasing to yourself

to be placed in relation[n] with these persons, the rather as I heard in London you were writing another play and perhaps, if that is now published, you would like to have that also come into the Italian sunshine.[1]

If this suggestion be agreeable to you, it will be a favor to me also, if you will send to care of Sigr *Enrico Mayer Leghorn*,[n] a copy of "The Patrician's Daughter" for the Marchioness *Arconati Visconti* and of the other play for Sigr *Berchet*. The former has of the visconti serpent the wisdom only without the wrong, the latter is the well known patriot poet of Italy.[2]

I should be very glad if you will acknowledge the receipt of this by a few lines addressed to me, at *Rome, Posta Restante*

I pass the winter at Rome. A few words about the world of books and men in England would be most welcome. I hear so little since leaving France. With respects to Mrs Marston,[3] dear Sir, yours

S. MARGARET FULLER.

ALS (NNHi). *Addressed:* To / J. Westland Marston Esq / London / England.
in relation] in ⟨repe⟩ relation
Mayer Leghorn,] *Mayer* ⟨Florence⟩ ↑ *Leghorn*, ↓
　1. Unlike his *Patrician's Daughter*, Marston's *The Heart and the World* (London, 1847) was a failure on the stage. He sent the books, for Costanza Arconati wrote Fuller on 30 December that she and Berchet had received them (MH).
　2. Enrico Mayer (1802–77) was an educator who was born and educated in Livorno. A supporter of Mazzini (through whom Fuller met him), Mayer took part in the revolution of 1848 (*Enciclopedia Italiana*). Giovanni Berchet (1783–1851) was a Milanese poet who had been living in exile. His *Lettera semiseria* was a manifesto of Italian romanticism. Fuller refers to the Visconti coat of arms, a seven-fold serpent devouring a child.
　3. In 1840 Marston married Eleanor Jane Potts (*DNB*).

681.　To Elizabeth Hoar

Florence Septr 1847

My dear Lizzie,

Last steamer brought a letter from you. I cannot think why you always distrust the value of these letters they are just what I want, only continue to write me such an one once in two months.

I cannot even begin to speak of the magnificent scenes of nature nor the works of art that have raised and filled my mind since I wrote from Naples. Now I begin to be in Italy. But I wish to drink deep of this cup before I speak my enamored words. Enough, to say Italy receives me as a long lost child and I feel myself at home here, and if I ever tell [　　] anything about it you will hear something real and domestic. —

As to persons it would be easier to speak, if I had time, and there are several; Americans and English of whom I wish to when I can. Among artists, Hicks at Rome, Powers here I prize, Greenough is also very agreeable, Lizzie Cranch was beautiful with her little George Curtis, though very suffering; she did not know strangers.[1] I want most to speak to you of a friend I have made in Italy, the Marchioness Arconati Visconti; she is a Milanese, but I knew her first at Rome, she is now here. She is a specimen of the really highbred lady, such as I have not known, without any physical beauty, the grace and harmony of her manners produce all the impression of beauty. She has also, a mind strong clear, precise and much cultivated by intercourse both with books and men. She has a modest nobleness that you would dearly love. She is intimate with many of the first men; she seems to love me much and to wish I should have whatever is hers. I take great pleasure in her friendship. I wish I had more time to write about these things, but there is alas, no time, I have stolen this from the gardens which I have not yet seen and where are the nightingales which I have not yet heard and now there is only room and time for dear Lizzie.—

Yours ever,

MARGARET.

Give my love to Anne Whiting, I wish I could show you some of the letters she wrote me about those things. And to Almira too, and ask Mrs. Ripley not to forget me.[2]

MsC (MH: fMS Am 1086 [Works, 2:823–29]); MsCfr (MH: bMS Am 1280 [111, pp. 43–45]). Published in part in *Memoirs*, 2:219–20, and *JMN*, 11:466–67.

1. George William Cranch (1847–67), son of Christopher Pearse and Elizabeth Cranch, was born in March and named for George William Curtis (Milne, *George William Curtis*, p. 37; Leonora Cranch Scott, *The Life and Letters of Christopher Pearse Cranch* [Boston, 1917], p. 258).

2. Ann Whiting was a Concord resident, daughter of William Whiting, a carriage maker and abolitionist. Almira Penniman Barlow, a friend from Fuller's childhood, was separated from her husband, David Barlow. After a stay at Brook Farm, Almira was living in Concord. Mrs. Ripley is Sarah Bradford Ripley, wife of the Reverend Samuel Ripley of Waltham, Massachusetts.

682. To Richard F. Fuller

Florence
25th Septr 1847.

My dear brother

I received a day or two since your letter direct to me at Florence, and

today the credit from Greene and Co. I warmly thank you and Mother
With regard to further remittances, I hope not to want one for a long
time. I shall not, if I can settle myself at Rome so as to avoid spoliation.
That is very difficult in this country. Mr Spring suffered from it, so
have I since I parted with him. The haste, the fatigue, my frequent illness in travelling, have been against me. At Rome I shall settle myself
for five months and make arrangements to the best of my judgement
and with counsel of experienced friends, and have some hope of economy while there, but am not sure as a constant vigilance against the
treachery of servants, and the cunning of landlords is needed, equally
uncongenial with my character and my pursuits.

I am not surprized you are disappointed by my letter from Rome.
But I did not feel equal then to speaking of the things of Rome and
shall not, till more familiar acquaintance has steadied my mind about
them. It is a matter of conscience with me not to make use of crude impressions and what they call here "coffee-house intellegence," as travellers in general do. I prefer skimming over the surface of things till I
feel solidly ready to write.

You will have recd before this two private letters from me, both, I
think, mailed at Milan. I left that city with great regret and hope to return. I knew there a circle of the aspiring youth, such as I have not in
any other[n] city. I formed many friendships and learned a great deal.
One of the young men Guerrieri by name (and of the famous Gonzaga
family, being by title Guerrieri Gonzaga) I really love.[1] He has a noble
soul, the quickest sensibility, and a brilliant and ardent, though not a
great, mind. He is eight and twenty, after studying medicine, for the
culture, he has taken law as his profession. His mind and that of Hicks,
an artist of our country a little younger[n] now here are two that would
interest you greatly. Guerrieri speaks no English. I correspond with
him in French. I speak French now as fluently as our tongue, but incor-
rectly. I ought to have learned earlier to make use of it.

Arriving here, Mr Mozier, an American, who from a prosperous
merchant has turned sculptor, came here to live, and promises much
excellence in his profession, urged me so much to his house that I
came. At first I was ill from fatigue, and staid several days in bed, but
his wife took tender care of me and the quiet of their house and regular simple diet have done me much good.[2] Now I feel well, and as soon
as I can arrange matters here and see some few things once more, I
shall go to Rome.

On my way I stopped at Parma, saw the works of Correggio and
Parmigiano.[3] I have now seen what Italy contains most important of
the great past. I begin to hope for her also a great future. The signs
have improved so much since I came. I am most fortunate to be here at

this time. I feel most deeply interested, but of these things I shall write in a Tribune letter.[4]

Interrupted as always. How happy I should be, if my abode at Rome would allow some chance for tranquil and continuous effort, but I dare not hope much from the difficulty of making any domestic arrangements that can be relied on. The fruit of the moment is so precious that I must not complain. I learn much, but to do any thing with what I learn under such circumstances, impossible. Beside I feel deeply at present the need of repose. I am almost inert from fatigue of body and spirit. To return to you or rather come to you, I am most tenderly sensible to the resolves you express in my behalf. I shall try not to abuse your feelings or strain hard on your young life. I wish you happy and to have a free and noble life and it will be so much longer than mine now that it is as to happiness, more important. Yet I shall avail myself of your kindness so far as I can without hurting you, for there is still time enough for me to be [   ] and do something, but my physical energies are so exhausted, that I need aid and favoring circumstances.

Perhaps it will prove a blessing to you if this or any other cause should induce you to defer your marriage. I do not wish to see you married before six or seven and twenty; it is early enough for a man, and I do not believe that you will be clear and sure of yourself before I rejoice to find that you and your Anna take this as you do, as experience. Such close contact between characters is most precious, if it does not compromise fatally for life. I have dreaded for you that life-long repentance of a momentary dream, that slow penance of years wasted in unfit relations, which I have seen endured by other men, and which not only inflicts much unhappiness, but blights the first germs of character.[5] But, if you are both sincerely desirous of doing only what shall seem best after full trial, if some time is to be past in the test of absence and presence there is no danger.

As to her being sometime with me, if you finally choose her, I should naturally wish to do all I could for her. The future awaits us.

I am sorry the Henry arrangement brings so much trouble. But is not Mr Stone dead? and will not that make him rich? How is Aunt Sally. I think with real sympathy now of that poor hard-hearted old woman.[6] I am very glad dear Mother is gone to Cincini. Ever affecy yours

M.

Mr. Spring has the power of Attory to take back to you. I have written about this before

ALS (MH: fMS Am 1086 [9:139]); MsC (MH: fMS Am 1086 [Works, 2:829–39]). Published in part in *Memoirs*, 2:218–19.

any other] any ↑ other ↓
country a little younger] country ↑ a little younger ↓

1. Anselmo Guerrieri Gonzaga (1819–79) studied at Padua and then became active in Milan politics after 1840. He was a prominent Republican, as was his brother Carlo (1827–1913), who was then studying at Innsbruck (*Enciclopedia italiana*).

2. Mozier married Isabella Hogg (1818–89) in 1835 (Banks, *Genealogical Notes*, pp. 34, 39).

3. Correggio (Antonio Allegri da Correggio) (1494–1534) founded a school of painting at Parma. He was a strong influence on Il Parmigianino (Girolamo Franscesco Maria Mazzuoli) (1503–40), who was born at Parma.

4. Fuller's next two *Tribune* letters, the first dated 18 October, the second undated, discussed Italian political affairs in detail. While unsure of the resolution of the struggle, she was sure of its meaning: "Still Europe toils and struggles with her idea, and, at this moment, all things bode and declare a new outbreak of the fire, to destroy old palaces of crime!" (*New-York Daily Tribune*, 25 December 1847 and 1 January 1848).

5. Many of Fuller's friends had unhappy marriages. Almira and David Barlow, Jane and John King, Belinda and Alfred Cumming, Ellen and Robert Hooper, Horace and Mary Greeley, Julia and Samuel Gridley Howe, Elizabeth and Jospeh Angier all had troubled marriages, as had Ellen and Ellery Channing.

6. Mr. Stone was an in-law of Henry Holton Fuller, Margaret's uncle. Aunt Sally is Sarah Fuller, Timothy Fuller's oldest sister.

683. To William James Linton

Rome, October, 1847

Some English journal may be glad to print a few lines written in Italy at this interesting period.[1] Obeying the proverb, 'that in Rome it is well to do as the Romans do,' I venture to present some verses, which are without interest except from allusions explained in the notes. True, it is a poor text that needs so much gloss; but those who are not really rich, must be allowed to hide the wall with drapery as they can. The simplest form were best: but only that is inexcusable through which no meaning is conveyed.

ELfr, from *People's Journal* 4 (1847): 327.

William James Linton (1812–98) was an engraver and political reformer who was associated with W. J. Fox and Richard Horne. A friend of Mazzini, Linton took part in the creation of the "International League" of patriots who worked for political freedom in Europe. He then joined the "Friends of Italy" movement (*DNB*).

1. The poem, which the *People's Journal* published on the same page as the excerpt from Fuller's letter, was "To a Daughter of Italy":

> To guard the glories of the Roman reign,
> Statesmen and warriors had toil'd in vain;
> If vestal hands had fail'd to tend the fire,
> That sacred emblem of pure strong desire.

If higher honors wait the Italian name—
If the fire strive to rise again to flame—
Vestals anew are call'd that glow to fan,
And rouse to fervent force the soul of man.

Amid the prayers I hourly breathe for thee,
Most beautiful, most injured Italy!
None has a deeper root within the heart,
Than to see woman duly play her part:
To the advancing hours of this great day
A morning Star be she, to point the way;
The Virgin Mother of a blessed birth,
The Isis of a fair regenerate earth,
And, where its sons achieve their noblest fame,
Still, Beatrice be the woman's name.

684.   To Marcus Spring

[I] Rome, October 1847

I arrived in Rome again nearly a fortnight ago, and all mean things were forgotten in the joy that rushed over me like a flood. Now I saw the true Rome. I came with no false expectations, and I came to live in tranquil companionship, not in the restless impertinence of sight-seeing, so much more painful here than anywhere else.

I had made a good visit to Vicenza; a truly Italian town, with much to see and study. But all other places faded away, now that I again saw St. Peter's, and heard the music of the fountains.

The Italian [II] autumn not so beautiful as expected neither in the vintage of Tuscany, (the best of the vintage was really to eat the grapes,) nor here. [III] The country is really sere and brown; but the weather is fine, and these October feasts are charming. Two days I have been at the Villa Borghese. There are races, balloons, and, above all, the private gardens open, and good music on the little lake.

I: ELfr, from *Memoirs*, 2:221–22; II: MsCfr (MH: bMS Am 1280 [111, p. 33]); III: ELfr, from *Memoirs*, 2:222. Published in part in *JMN*, 11:465.

685. To Richard F. Fuller

[16? October 1847]

My dear Richard,

An unexpected opportunity of a "bearer of despatches" offering to night, I send off this letter to Mother having no time to add any thing. You will learn by reading it of my arrangements here. Find out now when the Havre Steam Packets go and write sometimes by them, it is cheaper for me than the Cunard Line. Direct to me. *Care Maquay Pakenham & Co—Rome.* Mention Eugene particularly, I am anxious, hearing so much of yellow fever in N. O.— tell all other things. I hear little from U. S. Your ever affectionate Sister,

M.

Mr. Spring sailed 1st Octr from Havre and brings you the power of Attorney.—

MsC (MH: fMS Am 1086 [Works, 2:797]).

The date on the copy, "Dec. 1. 1846," is wrong, for the contents show Fuller in Rome for the second time, and she refers to her letter of 16 October to her mother.

686. To Margarett C. Fuller

Rome, 514 Corso.
2d etage.
16th Octr 1847.

Dearest Mother,

Here I am, fairly installed in a home that promises to be permanent for six months. You cannot guess how rejoiced I am! During the three months I travelled in the north of Italy, was upon the lakes and in Switzerland— my enjoyments were great and many, my privileges extraordinary, but my sufferings were commensurate. On the bright side the weather was beautiful and the heat less than is usual in an Italian summer. I made many and ardent friends, of all ranks, from the very highest to the lowest; the Italians sympathize with my character and understand my organization, as no other people ever did; they admire the ready eloquence of my nature, and highly prize my intelligent sympathy (such as they do not find often in foreigners) with their sufferings in the past and hopes for the future. It will take me weeks when I return to give you sketches of the persons and stories I learnt at that time. I also learnt a vast deal of the history and art of Italy. I found myself far better situated to be travelling alone, as now I was thrown constantly with foreigners who would tell me what I wanted to know, and with whom I made progress in the language. My mind made a vast stride in these three months, and my perception of beauty was all the keener for the sickly nervous state I was in. Yet that sickliness was the darkest shade on the other side. I had continually attacks of cholera which prostrated my strength as nothing ever did before. I could find no medicine, no food that suited me. When I rose up if I took any thing to sustain me, it caused fever. One time I was so ill that I was afraid I should die on the road, and nobody know it but my courrier, a brutal wretch who robbed and injured me all he could under the mask of obsequiousness. He wasted a good deal of money for me, before I could learn how to prevent it. At present I understand well, all that is needed for Italian travel and can never be so situated again. When I leave here I shall take precautions of which once I did not dream.

I felt often very anxious about money. Grateful as I am for Uncle A's bequest, and for its coming just when needed to save[n] me from a check in all my plans which would have been so bitter, it was not enough. If he had left me ten or even five thousand dollars I should have been so happy, for money now is all[n] I want, firm health I see I cannot have; it is too late. I have been sometimes much encouraged, but am sure now that my health will never stand against shocks and difficulties. But more money would, in a great measure, free me from them. Let me thank you here for your prompt attention to my wishes about money. You are always the same. I received the five hundred dollars in Florence   There I was detained for[n] a time by illness, the sequel of all I had in the north. But I was with good friends who nursed me with refined care and tenderness, and when I began to revive, saw that I had repose, proper nourishment and gentle exercise, and did for me those little things needed before I could come away. The name of these friends is Mozier   they were originally from Ohio. Mr M. is a man of fortune, who has taken to sculpture from love, and shows promise of much excellence; his wife a very good and sweet woman.

I arrived here some days ago, having seen the Tuscan vintage, which disappointed me; it is delightful to eat the grapes fresh from the vines, and the mild-eyed Tuscan peasants seem very pleasant and joyous but the Italian landscape in autumn is so sere and brown, so different from ours or even that of England, I longed for the accustomed shows of earth, beneath these serene heavens, in this lovely light. I saw also Sienna, one of those true Italian towns, where the old charm is unbroken. I came here some days ago, and after a good deal of search, have taken charming rooms. They are on the Corso, so that I see all that goes on in Rome, near the Pincian Mount, Piazza del Popolo, and Villa Borghese, so that I have for every day the pleasantest walks of Rome. The rooms are elegantly furnished, everything in the house so neat, more like England than Italy, service excellent, every thing arranged with a reasonable economy, and at fixed prices for all the six months. I have my books, my flowers, every thing leads me to hope the six months of quiet occupation I want, here is glorious Rome, where all the pleasures I most value, so rich and exalting, are within my reach. The only drawback is a little danger from the character and position of my hostess. She was formerly the mistress of a man of quality who loved her so much that she made him marry her before his death, so that she is a Marchioness, but not received into society. The bankers who chose my apartments with me thought this no objection, nor will it be, if she lets me alone enough, but she is a most insinuating creature and disposed to pet me too much. I am a little afraid of her going too far, so that if I should be obliged to decline any overture from her, she will be angry and hate me. But if we can get along I like her much; she has black eyes and red hair like Aunt Martha,[1] a pretty color and fine skin, very graceful manners, and speaks Italian beautifully, which is a good practice for me. She has introduced to me her present lover. He is a distinguished[n] Italn artist, who has been devoted to her for some years. He is an officer of note in the newly organized Civic guard, and will bring all the news to the house, he is also very agreeable.[2] Of course I seem to ignore all these circumstances; he appears here merely as a friend and visitor, and if she observes strict good sense and propriety in her relations with me, all will go on well, but the ground is a little delicate   I hope however all will go well; every thing else promises so sweetly. I am now very well, and the air of Rome seems to agree with me, as it did before. I shall not write to my family oftener than once a month, as I must apply all my strength now to gather the fruit of my travels, but hope you will not put too great an interval between your letters. I am very glad you are at Cincini and hope from you some detailed acct of Wm and Fanny and their little ones. Remember me most affecy to them and feel me ever with warmest love your daughter

M.

P.S.

I ought to observe to give you a clearer idea of my position with the Marchioness, that the custom of Rome is to take your apartment, and live entirely separate from the family to whom the house belongs. The house is divided into suites; they occupy one, each tenant, or family of tenants another. I did not expect even[n] to see [her] except when I paid my bills. But it is her pleasure to come in and arrange my flowers, and serve me at table, which she does standing! and yesterday when I had the headach to attend me. I think she will do this less, when I cease to be a new toy, and she sees how seriously I am occupied, and then matters will arrange themselves.

A flood of joy came over me when I was able at last to see Rome again.[n] To live here, alone and independent, to really draw in the spirit of Rome, Oh! what joy! I know so well how to prize it that I think Heaven will not allow anything to disturb me! My protecting ang[els] have been very tender of late and led me carefully out of every difficulty.

Do not fail when you write to tell me how your arm is. I have not heard this great while

ALS (MH: fMS Am 1086 [9:140]); MsC (MH: fMS Am 1086 [Works, 1:223–31]). *Addressed:* To / Mrs Margaret Fuller. / Care Mr. William H. Fuller / merchant / Cincinnati / Ohio. *Postmark:* Boston 3 Dec.

to save] to sa⟨l⟩ve
now is all] now ↑ is all ↓
detained for] detained ↑ for ↓
a distinguished] a⟨n⟩ distinguished
expect even] expect eve⟨ry⟩n
Rome again.] Rome ↑ again ↓ .

1. Martha Fuller Whittier, whom Fuller often visited in her childhood.
2. The creation of a civic guard was important to Italian nationalists as a requirement for self-rule. The pope had granted a guard for Bologna in December 1846 and for Rome on 5 July 1847, actions that were among the most important of his reforms (G. F. H. Berkeley and J. Berkeley, *Italy in the Making, June 1846 to 1 January 1848* [Cambridge, 1936 (1968)], pp. 91, 98).

687. To Richard H. and Mary Weeks Manning

Rome
18th Octr 1847

Dear Mr Manning,

The remittance reached me in Florence just at the right moment. Many thanks and also for dividing it; that was exceedingly well judged as what you do is sure to be. I have another remittance[n] from another quarter and may not want the second half for a long time. I will write about it towards the Spring. Meanwhile I am anxious to know how all goes with you in these times of English failure.[1]

Please write to me, care of *Maquay, Pakenham & Co Rome, by Havre.*

I have taken charming apartments here and hope for a peaceful winter after six months of constant travel, mixed with a good deal of illness. But I have only just got into them and have not begun to rest yet. From two letters sent to "The Tribune" you will know something of what I have seen and thought in these later days.

Dear Mrs Manning

I wish you could see Harro, and assure him of my continued interest in his welfare. I am afraid he thinks I am cruel also, as I do not have time and strength to write I want too, to know how he is.

I have not Esther's letter, but hear of the birth of a daughter. With my love, say I am very glad.

You will soon see the Springs among you; they sailed 1st Octr and will have much to tell.

I write these few lines in haste by Mr Baker of N. York, to send the heart and cross to Ade. Tell her there is no danger of my head with the Pope: he is so kind he would not willingly hurt a fly. Hope other things have come safe ivory pin by Miss Fay of Boston, cameo and mosaic by Mr Fairman of N. Y.[2] In great haste but ever with much friendship

AL (PSt).

another remittance] another ↑ remittance ↓

1. First the potato famine of 1845 and then the harvest failure of 1846 disrupted markets and commerce in Great Britain. In 1847 wheat prices fell and corn firms failed, followed soon by East India merchants, bankers, iron firms and cotton brokers. In October 1847 the Bank Act was suspended to alleviate the shortage of money by authorizing the Bank of England to issue money beyond its securities (A.W. Ward et al., eds., *Cambridge Modern History* [New York, 1909], 11:14).

2. Probably Maria Denny Fay (1820–90), daughter of Samuel Prescott Phillips Fay of Cambridge. Fuller knew the Fay family quite well in her childhood (MVR 411:70). Mr. Baker and Mr. Fairman are unidentified.

688. To Mary Rotch

Rome
22d Octr 1847.

Dear Aunt Mary,

I wrote to you last Spring from Rome and have been hoping for some time to receive some lines addressed in that clear firm hand which always used to come to me in my embroiled fatiguing life like a benediction from some distant shore looking calm and bright in the radiance of sunset. Not that your sun is set, but it rests now upon the mountains, and all things about you have that look of breadth and calmness.

I am sure my letter was ill worth the answering, as has been the case with all letters of mine written from Europe, but you always are to me so considerate and so much better than I can claim that it makes me afraid you are ill to get no letter. Do, on receipt of this, if you are not able, or if Mary's eyes do not permit her to write, get some of the healthy nephews and nieces to pen some lines just to tell me how you are, where you have passed the summer &c. It may be long before we meet again, but I depend on your thinking of and loving me. You may, perhaps, have heard that an uncle, who would certainly have never wished that objects of mine should be promoted through him, dying unexpectedly, by legal division of his property, a little porti[on] came to me, only a few hundreds, but it came just as I was at my money's end, has enabled me to remain here, and will, I hope, last, while I earn more to carry out my plans. If I can, I shall stay away, yet two years more, pass one winter in Paris, and see Germany well, as I have seen Italy. For I am really seeing Italy, differently from what mere travellers do, and when we meet again shall have things to tell that will, I am sure, interest my dear Aunt Mary.

My companions have gone home; they left me in July. I have travelled and returned here alone, and am now most pleasantly settled for the winter. My health has suffered from the heat of the Italian summer, but the pleasure was worth it. I wanted to see the country in its glow. The mere outline of my life you see in Tribune; more I do not feel free to give at present. Adieu. My love to Mary. Do have a letter written to me care of Maquay Pakenham and Co, Rome. Ever your affectionate

MARGARET.

ALS (MH: fMS Am 1086 [9:141]); MsCfr (MH: fMS Am 1086 [Works, 1:61–63]). *Addressed:* To / Miss Mary Rotch / New Bedford / Mass. / U. S. A. *Postmark:* Boston 17 Mar.

689. To Emelyn Story

2d piano
514ⁿ Corso
Friday eveg
[ca. 25 October 1847]

Dear Mrs Story

This afternoon just as I was going to the reading-room of San Carlo,

I heard you were here[n] and looking for apartments, so I told Mr De Angelis, who keeps the reading–room, to send you his card, for he has a good apartment I thought you might like to look at, as it is one of the very best places in Rome for the time of Carnival.

When you are settled I shall take the liberty to come and see you and ask some news of mutual friends— especially of Mr and[n] Mrs Loring and Anna. I have long heard no news. Perhaps you and Mr Story, if not better engaged, would come in to see me on Sunday eveg; it is then I am always at home, and Mr and Mrs Cranch and others whom you may know will probably be here. With best regards to Mr Story yours

S. M. FULLER.

The mistress of this house has also an apartment to let [in the] via Laurina, she keeps the key here. That apartment also has windows on the Corso and she is an excellent housekeeper. Excuse the liberty of my offering these directions unasked.[1]

ALS (TxU). *Addressed:* To / Mrs Story / Europa.

Emelyn Eldridge (1820–94) married William Wetmore Story in 1843. In 1847 they moved to Italy, where he became a sculptor (Gertrude Reese Hudson, ed., *Browning to His American Friends* [London, 1965], p. 363).

5 14] 5 1⟨7⟩4
were here] were ↑ here ↓
of Mr and] of ↑ Mr and ↓

1. Thus began a warm friendship between the Storys and Fuller, who had mistrusted them during their youth in Boston and Cambridge. Emelyn was struck with the change she saw in Fuller: "To me she seemed so unlike what I had thought her to be in America. . . . It was true, that I had not known her much personally, when in Boston; but through her friends, who were mine also, I had learned to think of her as a person on intellectual stilts, with a large share of arrogance, and little sweetness of temper. How unlike to this was she now!" (*Memoirs*, 2:281–82).

690. To Sarah Shaw

Rome.

25th Octr 1847.

My dear Sarah,

You wrote in May, I answer in October, but that is quick interchange for a life so crowded as mine has been of late. Within this six months, I have seen almost every important place in Italy and begin to know as well as to feel about this country, dream of my heart and realization of my mind. I cannot write about it in a little letter, a book would be too short. In writing to my friends I aim only to let them see I am thinking of them, and to lure them to tell me of the events of their own lives. With you I am anxious to know if your eyes continue in good condition, and whether any thing has happened to you, and how you feel. Tell me too of Anna, of Sarah Russell and of Elizabeth, also where Carrie is, for she does not write and nobody writes of her.

You regret not being in Italy at the same time with your[n] sister and me, but when you get here you will feel nothing of that sort.[1] Italy alone will suffice you. Come with all your children and live quietly here! to any one who can feel, who is not very shallow, it must be torture merely to *travel* to Italy and give a passing stare at[n] the beautiful body without ever having time or peace to come in contact with its soul.

I have returned to Rome to stay six months; do not know exactly where I shall go after that; you will see in the Tribune. For the present I drop all thought of the future seeking to take my share of what lies before me.

It is a most beautiful day, so warm and bright, but I have been very busy; my head begins to ache; I must go to my walk, go to the villa Borghese. A troop of the Trasteverini in those costumes we admire in Pinelli have just passed, colours flying, drums beating, five minutes earlier, a procession of Monks chanting a requiem.[2]

I live on the Corso and every day yields some fair show. Tonight I expect to hear Rubini sing; he is on a visit here, but I do not hear much good music in Italy.[3] Germany or even France are far better for[n] that.

Adieu, dear Sarah, love me, I pray and write sometimes to your friend.

M. F.

ALS (MH: bMS Am 1417 [184]). Published in Wade, p. 578.

with your] with ⟨?⟩ your
stare at] stare ⟨to⟩ ↑ at ↓
better for] better ⟨than⟩ ↑ for ↓

1. Susan Parkman Sturgis (1810–69) married her cousin John Parkman (d. 1883) in 1835. Fuller often saw them in Rome (*Sturgis of Yarmouth*, p. 52).

2. The Trasteverini were the inhabitants of the west bank of the Tiber, an area with its own dialect and customs. Fuller took part in the October festivals, when Rome celebrated each Monday and Thursday in the month (William Wetmore Story, *Roba di Roma* [Boston, 1899], p. 337). Bartolomeo Pinelli (1781–1835) published several books of drawings of Roman costumes, such as *Raccolta di costumi pittoreschi* (Rome, 1809) (*Enciclopedia italiana*).

3. Giovanni Battista Rubini (1795–1854) was an Italian tenor who sang often in the major European cities.

691.   To Francis G. Shaw

Rome
25th Octr 1847.

Dear Frank,

I write two little notes just like what you and Sarah sent to me. I do not wish to write at all; my mind is too crowded and I get myself too tired only I want to hear from you, and see, too, if I can not get your sympathy as to some objects you being a practical man. In first place I want to know how has succeeded in America "Le Compagnon &c"[1] it is a book in which only those who are in earnest and willing to think will take an interest I fancy. Then of the remnant of the Brook Farmites and if you are likely to carry out the thought of which you spoke of an Associate Home near New York.

I want also to lure you into sympathy with some of my objects of interest. First there is a painter here, a young American, one of the "right kind of stuff" for our land, who has raised himself up from the difficult circumstances of his childhood by sheer force of talent and will to a high position in life and mind, which he is still obliged to maintain by continual struggles and privations. His name is Hicks; he has rich relations in America but rich relations seldom aid or sympathize till the hour of effectual aid is passed, that precious moment when men can really help one another, which a few, like Mr Carey in our country and Burke in England, have had the soul to seize and become the protecting angels of young lives.[2] This man will interest you as being perhaps the only artist yet, deeply penetrated by the idea of social reform, and especially by the hopes of the Associationists. If he lives, he will illustrate those ideas, in his own way. Your brotherly love for Page makes me think of you as friend also to this friend of mine.[3] He has in his mind pictures which would really express his thoughts, if he could find time and freedom to paint them in order to [do] this it is very desirable for him to sell some that he has sent to N.Y. to the Art Union.[4] These do not present a sample of his thoughts, but they do of his practical talent. What I want of you is to look at them, and, if they please you, turn the attention of others to them, with a view to their being sold.

Be so good, too, as to write me a little of Mrs Child. I hear nothing of her for so long. Now, I have asked much of you, but it is blessed to give, and I continue to by letters to *care Ma[qu]ay Pakenham and Co Rome*, ever yours

S. M. FULLER.

Reading over my letter I see I have forgot one of my requests. It is that, in reading a letter I have sent to the Tribune about an American expression of sympathy for Italy at this moment, you will seriously consider whether it suits *you* to stir at all in such a matter.[5] If two or three on the spot take an interest, it could be done so easily, and me it would please much, if the Guard, that earnest of National Institutions to Italy should have something in their possession called the Columbo.

ALS (MH: bMS Am 1417 [183]). Published in Wade, pp. 576–77. *Addressed:* To / Francis G. Shaw Esq / 683 Broadway / New York.

1. George Sand, *Le Compagnon du tour de France* (Brussels, 1841).
2. Fuller refers to Matthew Carey (1760–1839), the Irish writer who became a publisher in Philadelphia, and to Edmund Burke (1729–97), the statesman. Several obituaries took note of Carey's generosity to the young: "There was one feature in his life which was of inestimable value to the young; and it cannot be too much commended to other gentlemen of leisure and fortune. It was the disposition to extend the hand of kindness to young men, whom he observed of promising talents. . . . His home, his counsel, his library, his heart, all were open to the young and deserving" (*American Almanac* 12 [1841]: 276). Burke, too, was generous to many men, though Fuller undoubtedly refers to his friendship with George Crabbe (1754–1832). In 1781 the destitute, unknown poet wrote to Burke in an attempt to avoid debtors' prison. Burke agreed to help, "and for ever, changed the nature of [Crabbe's] worldly fortunes. He was, in the common phrase, 'a made man' from that hour." The incident is described in *Poetical Works of the Rev. George Crabbe* (London, 1834), pp. 89–94, which Fuller reviewed (*Western Messenger* 1 [June 1835]: 20–29).
3. William Page (1811–85) studied painting with S. F. B. Morse and consciously imitated Titian. He was a good friend of James Russell Lowell and painted the portraits of many prominent New England writers and politicians (*DAB*).
4. The American Art-Union was founded in 1838 as the Apollo Association for the Promotion of the Fine Arts in the United States. The Union purchased works by American artists and distributed them to its members through an annual lottery (Charles E. Baker, "The American Art-Union," in *American Academy of Fine Arts and American Art-Union*, ed. Mary Bartlett Cowdrey [New York, 1953], 1:98–108).
5. Fuller made this appeal: "I earnestly hope for some expression of sympathy from my country toward Italy. Take a good chance and do something; you have shown much good feeling toward the Old World in its physical difficulties—you ought to do so still more in its spiritual endeavor" (*New-York Tribune*, 27 November 1847). Two days after this essay was published, a meeting attended by several thousand people was held at the Broadway Tabernacle to support the pope. Horace Greeley was chairman of the committee that drew up an address to his holiness. Other demonstrations occurred in Philadelphia and New Orleans (*New-York Daily Tribune*, 30 November 1847; Howard R. Marraro, *American Opinion on the Unification of Italy, 1846–1861* [New York, 1932], pp. 5–12).

692.   To Ralph Waldo Emerson

Rome, 28 October 1847

I am happily settled for the winter, quite by myself, in a neat, tranquil apartment in the Corso, where I see all the motions of Rome,—in a house of loving Italians, who treat me well, and do not interrupt me, except for service. I live alone, eat alone, walk alone, and enjoy unspeakably the stillness, after all the rush and excitement of the past year.

I shall make no acquaintance from whom I do not hope a good deal, as my time will be like pure gold to me this winter; and, just for happiness, Rome itself is sufficient.

To-day is the last of the October feasts of the Trasteverini. I have been, this afternoon, to see them dancing. This morning I was out, with half Rome, to see the Civic Guard manoeuvring in that great field near the tomb of Cecilia Metella, which is full of ruins.[1] The effect was noble, as the band played the Bolognese march, and six thousand Romans passed in battle array amid these fragments of the great time.

ELfr, from *Memoirs*, 2:220–21.

1. The tomb of Cecilia Metella, daughter of Metellus Creticus, is about a mile outside of the Porta San Sebastiano. In the thirteenth century the Caetani family built a fortress that turned the tomb into a battlement. The castle was razed by Sixtus V, creating the ruins that Fuller mentions (Karl Baedeker, *Central Italy and Rome* [Leipzig, 1909], p. 444).

693.   To Elizabeth Hoar

Rome
29th Octr 1847.

My dear Lizzie

I have but a moment and write this line only to say I want one of your letters in the course of the winter. If you write when you receive this (which will be about 1st Jan) I shall get your letter in Rome, for I have taken rooms here till first April. I feel happy in the prospect of some tranquil time here, very happy. I hope I shall be well. I have been getting better every hour since I came back to Rome. Tell me of your summer, tell me of yourself dear Lizzie I am sure you are very glad Waldo is gone to England, but will it not leave yr winter very dark.[1] Where is Belinda?[2] Direct Care Maquay, Pakenham and Co, Rome.

MARGARET.

ALS (MHarF); MsCfr (MH: bMS Am 1280 [111, p. 47]). Published in part in *JMN*, 11:467.

1. On 5 October Emerson sailed on the *Washington Irving* for England (Rusk, *Letters of RWE*, 3:419).

2. Belinda Randall Cumming.

694. To Richard F. Fuller

Rome,
29th Octr 1847.

My dear Richard

A private oppoy offering to send letters to America, I have prepared some notes for my friends, but as the gentleman goes first to Naples and Paris, he will not sail till 4th Decr and it is not worth-while to write to you as the news of me will then be old. A single letter I can send by post. I am trying all I can to economize in these little things, anxious to keep the Roman expenses for six months within the limits of four hundred dollars. Rome is not as cheap a place as Florence, but then I would not give a pin to live in Florence. We have just had glorious times with the October feasts when all the Roman people were out. I am now truly happy here, really *in* Rome, so quiet and familiar no longer, like the mob, a staring, sight-seeing stranger riding about finely dressed in a coach to see the Muses and the Sibyls. I see these things now in the natural manner and am happy. Yes I *am* happy here. Goodbye, dear Richard, heaven bless you and show you how to act. Keep free of false ties they are the curse of life. I find myself so happy here alone and free.

MARGARET.

ALS (MH: fMS Am 1086 [9:142]); MsC (MH: fMS Am 1086 [Works, 2:841−43]). Published in part in *Memoirs*, 2:221; Van Doren, pp. 290−91; and Chevigny, p. 434. *Addressed:* To / Mr R. F. Fuller / 6 State St. Boston / Massachusetts / U. S. A. *Postmark:* New York 16 Mar. *Endorsed:* F. S. M. / S. Margaret Fuller / 29. Oct. 1847.

695. To [?]

Rome, 17 November 1847
It seems great folly to send the enclosed letter. I have written it in my nightly fever. All day I dissipate my thoughts on outward beauty. I have many thoughts, happiest moments, but as yet I do not have even this part in a congenial way. I go about in a coach with several people; but English and Americans are not at home here. Since I have experienced the different atmosphere of the European mind, and been allied with it, nay, mingled in the bonds of love, I suffer more than ever from that which is peculiarly American or English. I should like to cease

from hearing the language for a time. Perhaps I should return to it; but at present I am in a state of unnatural divorce from what I was most allied to.

There is a Polish countess here, who likes me much. She has been very handsome, still is, in the style of the full-blown rose. She is a widow, very rich, one of the emancipated women, naturally vivacious, and with talent. This woman *envies me*; she says, "How happy you are; so free, so serene, so attractive, so self-possessed!" I say not a word, but I do not look on myself as particularly enviable. A little money would have made me much more so; a little money would have enabled me to come here long ago, and find those that belong to me, or at least try my experiments; then my health would never have sunk, nor the best years of my life been wasted in useless friction. Had I money now,—could I only remain, take a faithful servant, and live alone, and still see those I love when it is best, that would suit me. It seems to me, very soon I shall be calmed, and begin to enjoy.

ELfr, from *Memoirs*, 2:222–23.

696.   To Marcus and Rebecca Spring

Rome—Dec. 9, 1847

Dear Marcus and Rebecca:

A letter received this morning from Mr. Manning brings the most welcome intelligence of your safe arrival in our country, and that you were all well. You must have had a long voyage, wearisome, I fear to Rebecca, though not to you Marcus and to Eddie who don't suffer as we do. But of the voyage and all particulars of arriving at home I trust you will both write me fully as soon as you can for to no other will the narrative be so interesting as to me.

We may never pass much time together again, but with me remains a precious memory of that act of real valid friendship which enabled me to satisfy that long abandoned but secretly fervent desire to see Europe, especially Italy. This act was followed by many others breathing the same sweet life of affectionate generous character, and while my consciousness exists, the sense of these things, and friendship for you both so firmly based, will never die out of my heart.

Many acts and words of dear Eddie also are embalmed in my memory, and his temporal honor, and his immortal advancement will ever be dear to me as if he were my own child or brother. [   ]

I see your forms as I pass in the streets where we used to go together. On the road from Bologna here I seemed to see Eddie running lightly before me with his stick always! and also in the Villa Borghese running with Theodore.[1] I have been to the fountain where he fell in.[2] It is covered with dead leaves now, and there are no flowers to make garlands of. [   ]

TCfr (NjHi).

1. Theodore Parkman (1837–62), oldest of the seven children of Susan and John Parkman, died in battle in the Civil War (*Sturgis of Yarmouth*, pp. 52, 57).

2. Rebecca described the scene: "Eddie ran after [Margaret]. I called him back, but when he promised not to disturb her, she let him go with her. At first he played about, keeping near her. He gathered wild flowers and made garlands of them, and wishing to sail them in a great fountain, he wandered away. As Margaret sat thinking, she heard a splash and a cry. She rushed to the fountain and saw Eddie sink and rise. Other ladies came, and they held out their parasols, but they could not reach him. He was sinking the third time, and Margaret in her desperation was about to plunge in when the child remembered his stick. He held it out; they caught it and drew him out of the fountain" (Spring, "Journal Abroad").

697. To Margarett C. Fuller

[I] Rome, 16 Dec. 1847.

My life at Rome is thus far all I hoped. I have not been so well since I was a child, nor so happy ever as during the last six weeks.

I wrote you about my home; it continues good, perfectly clean; food wholesome; service exact.— I pay but not immoderately. The sum total of my expenses here for 6 months will not exceed 400, or, at most, $450.

The air of Rome agrees with me as it did before and Rome is so dear I do not know how I can ever be willing to live anywhere else.

[II] My *marchesa*, of whom I rent my rooms, is the greatest liar I ever knew, and the most interested, heartless creature. But she thinks it for her interest to please me, as she sees I have a good many persons who value me; and I have been able, without offending her, to make it understood that I do not wish her society. Thus I remain undisturbed.

Every Monday evening, I receive my acquaintance. I give no refreshment, but only light the saloon, and decorate it with fresh flowers, of which I have plenty still. How I wish *you* could see them!

Among the frequent guests are known to you Mr. and Mrs. Cranch, Mr. and Mrs. Story. Mr. S. has finally given up law, for the artist's life. His plans are not matured, but he passes the winter at Rome.

On other evenings, I do not receive company, unless by appointment. I spend them chiefly in writing or study. I have now around me the books I need to know Italy and Rome. I study with delight, now that I can verify everything. The days are invariably fine, and each day I am out from eleven till five, exploring some new object of interest, often at a great distance.

I: MsCfr (MH: bMS Am 1280 [111, pp. 129–30]); II: ELfr, from *Memoirs*, 2:223–24. Published in part in Van Doren, pp. 291–92, and *JMN*, 11:480–81, 491.

698. To Richard H. and Mary Weeks Manning

Rome
16th Decr 1847.

To Mr and Mrs Manning
dear friends,

A few days since I was gladdened by the reception of a letter from you. I assure you both yours have brought me great pleasure, giving an account of many things I wanted to know, and the grateful assurance of your own continued interest. However much the "outward-bound" may be enjoying, there is at times a sense of exile and loneliness, a sense that if you die, or fall sick or sad, the smiles of all those new acquaintance may be withdrawn like a mask, and a painful cold indifference be[n] left staring you into stupefaction or if all be over, your dust will be blown aside so carelessly without a tear to hallow it. At moments when such feelings come up, and I think they must sometimes in the most pleasant life away from tender ties, and the associations of home, an unexpected remembrance from some friend comes soothingly and does a good beyond what the sender dreamt of.

I thank you much, dear Mr Manning, for sending the money. I recd by the next post, after that which brought yr letter[n] advice of its[n] reception from Greene and Co. I may as well here formally acknowledge the reception from you of a credit on Greene in two drafts for 1300 francs each, as, in case of my death, this acknowledgement gives you a claim on any property of mine remaining in care of my family. I hope however to live to pay you in person some pleasant day of reunion.

I had said in a letter which you will receive before this, (I find it was delayed on its way by some accident) that I would write when I wanted the money, but it is just as well that you have sent it. I shall want it ere long.

It is a time in my life whe[n] the possession of a few thousand would make me very happy; but I do not mean to feel care from the want of money.[n] I trust Heaven which has guided me thus far, will show me ways and means for the future.

I am very glad you were pleased with the ornaments. I believe from[n] your letter, I have sent Ade the heart and cross twice, if so, perhaps she will give one to Henry, if he is not too much of "a boy" to like them. I mean to bring him some little pictures of costumes here, when I come so as to tell him about them myself. If you wished and[n] could send me *twenty dollars* I could choose for you some three or four beautiful engravings enough to furnish one room.— I should like to do it for you, if you felt reliance on my taste, and for Mr Hicks, if he wished; he has given me so many beautiful flowers I think I could please him. My regards and best wishes to him and his wife.

Yes, dear Mrs Manning, I am very glad to hear you are not so "*anxious*" as before. I looked on your too conscientious anxiety as the only real drawback in your happiness.

AL (ViU). *Addressed:* R. H. Manning Esq / Pine St New York. / U.S.A. *Postmark:* New York Jan 19. *Endorsed:* Margaret Fuller.

indifference be] indifference ↑ be ↓
post, after that which brought yr letter] post, ↑ after that which brought yr letter ↓
of its] of ⟨that⟩ ↑ its ↓
of money.] of ⟨it⟩ ↑ money. ↓
believe from] believe ⟨by⟩ ↑ from ↓
you wished and] you ↑ wished and ↓

699. To Ralph Waldo Emerson

Rome, 20 December 1847

Nothing less than two or three years, free from care and forced labor, would heal all my hurts, and renew my life-blood at its source. Since Destiny will not grant me that, I hope she will not leave me long in the world, for I am tired of keeping myself up in the water without corks, and without strength to swim. I should like to go to sleep, and be born again into a state where my young life should not be prematurely taxed.

Italy has been glorious to me, and there have been hours in which I received the full benefit of the vision. In Rome, I have known some blessed, quiet days, when I could yield myself to be soothed and instructed by the great thoughts and memories of the place. But those days are swiftly passing. Soon I must begin to exert myself, for there is this incubus of the future, and none to help me, if I am not prudent to face it. So ridiculous, too, this mortal coil,—such small things!

I find how true was the lure that always drew me towards Europe. It was no false instinct that said I might here find an atmosphere to develop me in ways I need. Had I only come ten years earlier! Now my life must be a failure, so much strength has been wasted on abstractions, which only came because I grew not in the right soil. However, it is a less failure than with most others, and not worth thinking twice about. Heaven has room enough, and good chances in store, and I can live a great deal in the years that remain. [   ]

I don't know whether you take an interest in the present state of things in Italy, but you would if you were here. It is a fine time to see the people. As to the Pope, it is as difficult here as elsewhere to put new wine into old bottles, and there is something false as well as ludicrous in the spectacle of the people first driving their princes to do a little justice, and then *evviva*-ing them at such a rate. This does not apply to the Pope; he is a real great heart, a generous man. The love for him is genuine, and I like to be within its influence. It was his heart that gave the impulse, and this people has shown, to the shame of English and other prejudice, how unspoiled they were at the core, how open, nay, how wondrous swift to answer a generous appeal!

They are also gaining some education by the present freedom of the press and of discussion. I should like to write a letter for England, giving my view of the present position of things here.

ELfr, from *Memoirs*, 2:224–25. Published in part in Van Doren, pp. 292–93; Miller, pp. 277–78; and Chevigny, p. 435.

The *Memoirs* *editors published this letter in two parts, but probably there was but one original.*

INDEX

Library of Congress Cataloging-in-Publication Data
(Revised for volume 4)

Fuller, Margaret, 1810–1850.
The letters of Margaret Fuller.

Includes bibliographies and indexes.
Contents: v. 1. 1817–38—v. 2. 1839–41—[etc.]—
v. 4. 1845–47.
1. Fuller, Margaret, 1810–1850—Correspondence.
2. Authors, American—19th century—Correspondence.
I. Hudspeth, Robert N.   II. Title.
PS2506.A4   1983   181'.309   82-22098
ISBN 0–8014–1386–9   (v. 1)